JANE AUSTEN AND THE ENLIGHTENMENT

Jane Austen was received by her contemporaries as a new voice, but her late twentieth-century reputation as a nostalgic reactionary still lingers on. In his radical revision of her engagement with the culture and politics of her age, Peter Knox-Shaw argues that Austen was a writer steeped in the Enlightenment, and that her allegiance to a sceptical tradition within it, shaped by figures such as Adam Smith and David Hume, lasted throughout her career. Knox-Shaw draws on archival and other neglected sources to reconstruct the intellectual atmosphere of the Steventon Rectory where Austen wrote her juvenilia, and follows the course of her work through the 1790s and onwards, showing how minutely responsive it was to the many shifting movements of those turbulent years. *Jane Austen and the Enlightenment* is an important contribution to the study both of Jane Austen and of intellectual history at the turn of the nineteenth century.

PETER KNOX-SHAW is a Research Associate at the University of Cape Town. He is author of *The Explorer in English Fiction* (1987) and has published widely on eighteenth-century and Romantic literature. He is a contributor to the new Cambridge edition of the works of Jane Austen

JANE AUSTEN AND THE ENLIGHTENMENT

PETER KNOX-SHAW

CAMBRIDGE
UNIVERSITY PRESS

CAMBRIDGE UNIVERSITY PRESS
Cambridge, New York, Melbourne, Madrid, Cape Town, Singapore, São Paulo, Delhi

Cambridge University Press
The Edinburgh Building, Cambridge CB2 8RU, UK

Published in the United States of America by Cambridge University Press, New York

www.cambridge.org
Information on this title: www.cambridge.org/9780521759977

First published 2004
Third printing 2006
First paperback edition 2009

Printed in the United Kingdom at the University Press, Cambridge

A catalogue record for this publication is available from the British Library

Library of Congress cataloguing in publication data
Knox-Shaw, Peter, 1944–
Jane Austen and the Enlightenment / Peter Knox-Shaw.
p.   cm.
Includes bibliographical references and index.
ISBN 0 521 84346 4 (hardback)
1. Austen, Jane, 1775 1817 – Philosophy.   2. Literature and society – Great Britain – History – 19th
century.   3. Austen, Jane, 1775–1817 – Political and social views.   4. Great Britain – Intellectual
life – 18th century.   5. Enlightenment – Great Britain.   6. Skepticism in literature   I. Title.
PR4038.P5K68   2004
823′.7 – dc22   2004049658

ISBN 978-0-521-84346-1 hardback
ISBN 978-0-521-75997-7 paperback

For Barbara

Contents

Acknowledgements

This book grew slowly, and thanks are due to Oxford University Press for permitting me to rework material that first appeared in their journals. Chapter 3 is based on '*Northanger Abbey*, and the Liberal Historians' in *Essays in Criticism*, 49 (1999). Chapters 8 and 6 draw at times on ideas from two articles in the *Review of English Studies* – '*Persuasion*, Byron, and the Turkish Tale', 44 (1993), and 'Fanny Price Refuses to Kowtow', 47 (1996). Elsewhere I repeat information from two pieces in *Notes and Queries* – '"Liberal" Earlier than in OED', 47 (2000), and '*Persuasion*, James Austen, and James Thomson', 247 (2002). Chapter 4 developed from an essay in the *Cambridge Quarterly*, '*Sense and Sensibility*, Godwin, and the Empiricists', 27 (1998) from which it now differs in scope, form, and emphasis.

My thanks are also due to the librarians and staff of the institutions where I did my research: the British Library, the Cambridge University Library, the Hampshire Record Office, the India Office, the Jane Austen Memorial Trust, the Kent Archives, the National Maritime Museum, the Oppenheimer Library, the Public Record Office, and the South African Library. I am especially thankful to Tom Carpenter for his help at Chawton, and to Tanya Barben for her readiness to seek out items from the Special Collections at the University of Cape Town.

No encouragement is required by those who choose to study a writer as endlessly rewarding as Jane Austen, but I am grateful to the many friends and colleagues who gave advice, discussed ideas, defended the opposite view, kindly took me aside to explain the error of my ways, or allowed me the luxury of forgetting my work altogether. I should like particularly to thank the following for their stimulus and support: John Baatjies, John Coulton, Janette Deacon, Niel and Ina Du Plessis, Rodney Edgecombe, Geoff and Tish Hughes, Lucy Iago, Robert and Caroline Jackson, Lesley Marx, Ermien van Pletzen, Frank and Ida Raimondo, Francis and Anne Thackeray, Constance Walker, and Stephen Watson. I am greatly indebted to the two anonymous readers of the manuscript without whose insightful criticism and comments the book would be very much the worse; and grateful to Linda Bree for her patience and good counsel at every stage in guiding it through the press, as also to Maureen Leach for her skilful and sensitive editing. To Barbara, whose love of the novels remains undiminished, I owe as always the most.

Note on chronology

Of the six novels by Jane Austen published between 1811 and 1817, three were first drafted before 1800, and two of these unsuccessfully offered to publishers. 'First Impressions', drafted in 1796–7 and rejected unseen by Cadell in 1797, later became *Pride and Prejudice* (1813). 'Susan', drafted in 1798–9 and accepted by Crosby in 1803, was left untouched by them until bought back in 1816 to be published posthumously as *Northanger Abbey* (1817). How much these novels changed between their first submission and their final state is a matter of conjecture, but it is clear that they were revised rather than reconceived. In the case of 'First Impressions', Cassandra Austen noted 'alterations & contractions', and Jane wrote of having 'lopt & cropt' the manuscript. In a brief preface to *Northanger Abbey* she stressed that the novel had been 'finished' thirteen years back and was in parts 'comparatively obsolete'. *Sense and Sensibility* which began life in 1795 as 'Elinor and Marianne', and was redrafted in 1797, became the earliest of her published works in 1811.

To draw out the contexts of the novels I have taken them in the sequence that they were first prepared for publication rather than in the order in which they finally appeared. Provided due weight is given to the original period of composition, this format seems to be the one best suited to a historical approach.

PART ONE

The eighteenth-century legacy

CHAPTER I

Auspices

Historical approaches to Jane Austen have often had the paradoxical effect of sidelining her from history altogether. With an irony she herself would have enjoyed, the old and long-standing icon of a writer untouched by events has been broken up only to make way for the portrait of a misty-eyed reactionary. Over the last decades the idea that Austen was bent on reviling the French Revolution and all its works has stuck, and since the position has never been systematically challenged, even her fervent defenders have been saddled with the sense that she is a figure out of key with her time, while for others she appears as the arch party-pooper, darting withering looks at each fresh trend and cult. Though dissent on the part of her contemporaries is commonly taken as a mark of constructive engagement, in her case it is rarely seen as anything other than defensive, the product of denial, or even of ignorance. The military tactics promisingly assigned to her subject by Marilyn Butler in *Jane Austen and the War of Ideas* turn out, in the end, to be those of siege rather than battle. Far from being granted the dignity of a resourceful campaigner, Austen the Anti-Jacobin comes over as a lodger in the keep, time-warped for once and all by her early exposure to 'old-fashioned' sermons and conduct-books.[1] When, in the new preface to her seminal study, Butler returns to the question of Austen's failure to respond to her age, the harsh verdict of the re-trial is well summed up by the Rowlandson cartoon on the cover. 'Disturbers of Domestic Happiness' shows three cockaded men raiding a living-room, where the representatives of domestic life, slumped on a sofa, sleep on undisturbed.[2]

Though Butler's work appeared at the start of a period that saw the rise of women's criticism and of a new historicism, it has kept its currency. It owes this hardiness partly to its thoroughgoing historical approach. Butler

---

[1] Marilyn Butler makes this point explicitly in *Romantics, Rebels and Reactionaries* (Oxford, 1981): 'Her reading, in sermons and conduct-books, must have given her old-fashioned notions of social cohesion and obligation', p. 102.

[2] Marilyn Butler, *Jane Austen and the War of Ideas* (Oxford, 1987), ix–xlvi.

sets out to construct the meaning that the novels had in their original context, and pursues her findings regardless of whether or not they are attractive to contemporary readers, as when she warns that Austen's morality is 'preconceived and inflexible', and 'of a type that may be antipathetic to the modern layman'.[3] This is not usually the case with gender-centred studies of Austen, which tend to concentrate on the significance that the novels have for the present.[4] And while many writers in this tradition have managed to combine relevance with sophisticated historical insight, such readings – being of an essentially different order – almost invariably sidestep rather than interlock with Butler's, so that battle over the war of ideas has seldom been joined.[5] In consequence the Anti-Jacobin Austen is still very much at large, not only among those who have built on Butler's work but also among those who, writing from a different perspective, have tried to integrate her thesis within a postmodernist account, one recent critic deferring to the 'Tory feminism', and 'counter-revolutionary' plotting of *Mansfield Park* while describing the novel itself as 'an evangelical sermon'.[6] A further reason for Butler's prevalence is that her work is rooted in a tradition that was fully conversant with formalism and with textual analysis. Subsequent attempts to question the view of Jane Austen as a Tory reactionary have often had to draw on a more limited – and less demonstrative – range of critical methods.[7] While it is true that the most vivid and finely focused of recent accounts of Jane Austen have implicitly opposed the Butlerian thesis, they have done so without providing a rebuttal. The time is ripe, then, for a

[3] Ibid., pp. 298, 296. I am indebted here to Alistair M. Duckworth's thought-provoking essay, 'Jane Austen and the Conflict of Interpretations' in Janet Todd's anthology, *Jane Austen: New Perspectives* (1983), pp. 39–52. For a valuable review of feminist critics of the eighties see the opening pages of Janet Todd's 'Jane Austen, Politics and Sensibility', in Susan Sellers, ed., *Feminist Criticism: Theory and Practice* (Hemel Hempstead, 1991), pp. 71–87.

[4] Highly influential in this category is Mary Poovey's *The Proper Lady and the Woman Writer* (Chicago, 1984). Particularly sensitive to textual nuance and period concerns is Margaret Kirkham's *Jane Austen: Feminism and Fiction* (1983, rev. edn 1996).

[5] The most important exceptions here are Claudia L. Johnson's two pioneering books, *Jane Austen: Women, Politics, and the Novel* (Chicago, 1988) and *Equivocal Beings* (Chicago, 1995), and Mary Waldron's *Jane Austen and the Fiction of her Time* (Cambridge, 1999), but this last excellent study touches only incidentally on Austen's thought and politics.

[6] Clara Tuite, 'Domestic Retrenchment and Imperial Expansion: the Proper Plots of *Mansfield Park*', in You-me Park and Rajeswari Sunder Rajan, eds., *The Postcolonial Jane Austen* (2000), pp. 96, 99, 102. The same line is adopted in her *Romantic Austen* (Cambridge, 2002), despite the retrieval of sensibility there.

[7] Nancy Armstrong in her study of early eighteenth-century fiction compellingly argues, in passing, that Austen, rather than being seen as a Tory or as a member of the landed gentry, should be approached as a linguistic identity that voices 'a middle class aristocracy'. See *Desire and Domestic Fiction* (Oxford, 1987), pp. 159–60. Butler's thesis is implicitly opposed by Roger Gard in a series of commonsensical and subtle readings in *Jane Austen's Novels: The Art of Clarity* (1992).

study that confronts Butler's more squarely, and more on its own terms – a rash undertaking were it not for the many critical contributions of the last decades that yield some higher ground.

My brief in this book is that Jane Austen is a writer of centrist views who derives in large measure from the Enlightenment, more particularly from that sceptical tradition within it that flourished in England and Scotland during the second half of the eighteenth century. This tradition stands at some remove from the popular conception of the movement as a whole. While celebrating reason, scientific method, and social reform, the Anglo-Scottish school dwelt on the irrationality of human nature, tempered the optimism of the *philosophes* with an emphasis on the limits of individual heroism, and instilled a distrust of dirigism and of the doctrinaire. Less militant than its French counterpart, the sceptical Enlightenment nurtured a particular dislike of civil faction and of the bigotry that went with it, and this relaxed spirit of partisanship made it accessible to many institutions and intellectual cults of the age. We shall see how deeply the ideas of writers like David Hume and Adam Smith penetrated movements as diverse in tone and mode as the picturesque and the Evangelical revival. But of particular significance here, is the openness of the contemporary Anglican church to the Enlightenment, for it is precisely the assumption of its imperviousness that has so often been invoked to underline Jane Austen's mental seclusion.

Exponents of the reactionary Austen have regularly stressed her religious beliefs, even though she has often been found deficient in this quarter – even 'supremely irreligious' in one instance – by the devout.[8] Readings of this kind tend to place Austen as an Evangelical (which she was not) or as an 'orthodox' Christian rather than as the Anglican Erasmian that she was,[9] the better to insist on the fixity of her views, or – in the case of materialist approaches – on their archaic character as the product of an outmoded infrastructure. If her religion is unusually secularized, as Butler implies, that is what was immediately demanded to buttress the status quo, and to shield it from the eroding forces of change.[10] This approach relies, all too clearly, on the old and long-entrenched view that Christianity and the Enlightenment were as chalk and cheese, as far removed from each other as reason and *l'infâme*.

---

[8] G. K. Chesterton, 'The Evolution of *Emma*', collected in Ian Littlewood, ed., *Jane Austen: Critical Assessments*, 4 vols. (Mountfield, 1998), I, 444. See also Cardinal Newman's remarks to Anne Mozley, *Letters and Correspondence of Newman*, ed. Anne Mozley (1891), II, 223.

[9] For discussion of the tolerance and rationalism of the Erasmian tradition see Hugh Trevor-Roper, *Catholics, Anglicans, and Puritans* (1988), particularly ch. 2.

[10] Butler, *War of Ideas*, pp. 1–2, 93–9.

From writers who have focused on Jane Austen's religion there emerges a different picture, however, and one that joins up convincingly not only with the accounts of church historians but with recent studies of the neglected course of the Enlightenment in Britain itself after the earlier part of the century.[11] For European historians like Venturi, drawing principally from the continent in the mid-century, the true *riformatore* leads a life independent of public office, and certainly free of the least whiff of the ecclesiastical; but across the channel, the philosopher and theologian had long existed on better terms, owing in part to the enduring influence of Locke's *The Reasonableness of Christianity* (1695). But thanks for this are also due to the character of Anglicanism itself, a rambling edifice raised on very different kinds of foundation, better able to cope with additions and alteration than other creeds of more imposing design. Erastian in original conception ('by law established'), Catholic by descent, and invigorated by Calvinism, it was an institution particularly ill-suited to preserving any fixed body of belief. Indeed, to some chroniclers, surveying its protean history, this ability to adapt appears as something of a fatal flaw. E. R. Norman in his *Church and Society in England 1770–1970* remarks on the eagerness of the church, in almost every generation, to appropriate 'the most progressive ideas available', often at the cost of weakening morale.[12]

Though the Enlightenment undoubtedly sparked division as well as debate in the Anglican church, its traces are as far-reaching as its impact was forceful. Attempts to address the corpus of doctrinal writing in this period as a thing *sui generis* swiftly reveal just how integral philosophical traditions were to its development. It takes a work of comprehensive scope like Leslie Stephen's *English Thought in the Eighteenth Century* (1876) to bring any sense of relation to bear on the many divines treated by Abbey and Overton in their strictly in-house *English Church in the Eighteenth Century* (1878). In a telling phrase Stephen describes the continual concessions made by Joseph Butler and other mainstream theologians to empiricist thought as 'bowing the knee in the house of Rimmon' – a breach of taboo that was no sin when made in the service of Jehovah.[13] It could equally be said, however, that philosophers went out of their way to attach their systems

---

11 For Austen and religion see, principally, Irene Collins, *Jane Austen and the Clergy* (1994), and *Jane Austen: The Parson's Daughter* (1998); Christopher Brooke, *Jane Austen: Illusion and Reality* (Cambridge, 1999); William Jarvis, *Jane Austen and Religion* (Stonefield, 1996); Oliver MacDonagh, *Jane Austen: Real and Imagined Worlds* (1991), ch. 1; and George Tucker, *Jane Austen: The Woman* (1994), ch. 10.

12 E. R. Norman, *Church and Society in England, 1770–1970* (Oxford, 1976), p. 42.

13 II Kings, 5: 18. Leslie Stephen, *History of English Thought in the Eighteenth Century* (1962 edn), II, 42.

to doctrine; Joseph Priestley, for example, speculating on the composition of the resurrected body, or David Hartley exploring the effects of hellfire on vibratiuncles. In most controversies, it is not unusual to find philosophers and divines siding together against earlier positions – positions held, invariably, by both philosophers and divines.

This complexity is often missed by critics who are after a clear-cut 'background' to Jane Austen. Writing on education in the novels, D. D. Devlin, for one, reduces the empirical tradition to Shaftesbury and Hutcheson, forgetting that writers like Hume and Smith reacted against the idea of an innate moral sense and the related premium on intentionality every bit as vigorously as did Butler or Reid.[14] Indeed, a Christian apologist in the later part of the century would have been hard put to find better arguments against Deism or 'natural religion' than those advanced by Hume, whose dramatic and scrupulously balanced *Dialogues* (1779) were generally taken to be of a theistic tendency throughout the nineteenth century, and even beyond.[15] During Jane Austen's lifetime both Hume's *History* and *Essays* were widely recommended for educational reading by writers of a didactic turn,[16] and the same holds true for Adam Smith's *Theory of Moral Sentiments*, echoes of which are to be found in both *Pride and Prejudice* and *Sense and Sensibility*.[17]

Adam Smith supplies a good instance of how a classic of the Enlightenment could lend itself to – or even seem to invite – endorsement by the devout, for at strategic points in his moral treatise he tags a Christian gloss to his arguments and vocabulary. Nor were such bridging tactics by any means purely retrospective, for a passage on the subject of conscience that closely follows Joseph Butler probably formed part of the original lecture series from which the book grew.[18] Though Smith drew heavily on both empiricist and Stoic traditions for his ethics – dwelling on the power of self-love

[14] See D. D. Devlin (who believes that Butler's idea of conscience is distinct), *Jane Austen and Education* (1975), pp. 68–75.

[15] A list of such readers would include Dugald Stewart and James Hastings of encyclopaedia fame; see *Hume's Dialogues Concerning Natural Religion*, ed. Norman Kemp Smith (Oxford, 1935), pp. 74–6.

[16] For the *History* see 'Appendix 1: Books for Young Ladies' in Frank W. Bradbrook, *Jane Austen and her Predecessors* (Cambridge, 1966), pp. 141–2; and for the *Essays* see *Letters Written by the Earl of Chesterfield to his Son* (1775), IV, 88–9. The four-volume collection made by Hume under the title *Essays and Treatises on Several Subjects* was a popular vehicle for his writing, and included practically all the essays as well as both *Enquiries*.

[17] Maria Edgeworth's Belinda keeps a copy of the *Theory* on her dressing table see *Belinda*, ed. Kathryn J. Kirkpatrick (Oxford, 1994), p. 228; and see Kenneth Moler, 'The Bennet Girls and Adam Smith on Vanity and Pride', *Philological Quarterly*, 46 (1967), 567–9.

[18] See Adam Smith, *The Theory of Moral Sentiments*, ed. D. D. Raphael and A. L. Macfie (Oxford, 1979), III.5.5, 164–5, and see footnote. Hereafter *TMS*.

and the need for self-command – he repeatedly calls attention to the way in which his theory yields a precise understanding of the commandment. 'Love your neighbour as yourself'.[19] And just as he gives psychological substance to Butler's entirely intuitive sense of the term 'conscience', he supplies a material basis for this commandment too, describing an internal process through which self-interest is mediated by the desire for social approval, and by our ability to imagine the feelings of others. Discourse of this kind gave a new and exhilarating dimension to religious authority. It pointed to the way things actually worked in the ordinary world, grounding the dictates of Scripture on all-too-human needs and natures. It had the virtue, in sum, of translating the fiat of faith or of reason into a descriptive language that gave full value to the force of earthly desires.

In the second of her two rewarding studies of Jane Austen's relationship to the Anglican church, Irene Collins evokes the mental atmosphere at Steventon rectory during the years of the novelist's adolescence. She argues, with the aid of fresh research, that Jane's father was latitudinarian by inclination and that he was, like many other parsons of his generation, 'a true son of the Enlightenment': an avid and omnivorous reader, a keen classicist, a dabbler in science, and a warm-hearted upholder of the Stoic maxim that individuals be recommended to their own care.[20] It is certainly not necessary to posit any formal belief on George Austen's part in 'natural religion' to appreciate that he was of the sect that delighted in the many new – and still opening – fields of inquiry that were giving greater definition to the created world. No doubt there were parsons' daughters whose horizons terminated in evening prayers and needlework, but as a teenager Jane Austen was, even by the admission of a brother, remarkably sharp-eyed about the outside world.[21] And while the exact nature of her political opinions and religious faith are likely to remain open to dispute and reinterpretation, there is little room for disagreement about her responsiveness to her times. In his recent study *Jane Austen and the Navy* (2000), Brian Southam has shown just how minutely sensitive novels like *Mansfield Park*, *Emma*, and *Persuasion* are to the home-front history of the respective years in which they are set. But the other major novels, each of which first took shape in the 1790s, are as firmly rooted in observation as the later group, and tell as much about the vicissitudes of the social and cultural climate on which they drew. When viewed contextually they

---

[19] *TMS*, I.i.5.5; and III.I.I.   [20] Collins, *Clergy*, xix, p. 19. See *TMS*, VI.ii.I.I, 219.
[21] In the course of a brief memoir of his sister, Francis Austen remarks as 'a matter of surprise' on how extraordinarily observant she was 'at a very early age'. See M. A. D. Howe, 'A Jane Austen Letter', *Yale Review*, 15 (1925–6), 321.

show just how receptive Jane Austen was, and how keenly she engaged with contemporary ideas.

This engagement was no less acute for being on the whole more exploratory than dogmatic. Austen seems, like other enlightened writers before her, deliberately to have steered clear of allegiance to Party; and she may well have sustained this stance even in private, for her niece Caroline could recall no obvious political 'bias' from her conversation, nor – however she racked her brains – any sign of partisan views on the French Revolution or other upheavals of the age.[22] Consistent with this report is a passage from a letter written to Cassandra in 1808 that shows Jane adroitly deflecting to her brother Edward an appeal made to her own 'interest' on behalf of the Hampshire Tory candidate, Thomas Heathcote.[23]

As far as religion goes, it is clear that Jane Austen died a believer, but she ranks among the least proselytizing of Christian novelists, and may, without ever having ceased to believe in the utility of belief, have been something of a private sceptic in the first part of her career. References to her faith throughout this period are both few and light in tone, and Irene Collins has noted, from the same years, the 'remarkably stereotyped terms' used by her in letters to bereaved relations.[24] It is significant, perhaps, that of the two versions of the letter she wrote to her brother Francis telling him of their father's death, only the first contains any mention of an afterlife, and a non-committal one at that. Instead of referring to her father's 'constant preparation for another world', she dwells in the second on her family's 'preparation' for the shocking event.[25] In all probability, her novelistic reticence towards the supernatural had to do with the strong preference she shows as a writer for sticking to the observable; but the resulting solidity of her fiction calls inference into play. Though questions of politics and religion are continually raised in the reading of the novels, and will occupy a good part of this study, I shall start on more neutral ground by examining some of the ways in which Jane Austen reveals herself habitually, even unconsciously, as a person fully alive to her age.

---

[22] See Caroline Austen, 'My Aunt Jane Austen: A Memoir', in Littlewood, ed., *Critical Assessments*, I, 48.

[23] See *Jane Austen's Letters*, ed. Deirdre Le Faye (Oxford, 1995) (hereafter *Letters*), p. 154. Jane Austen's poem 'On Sir Home Popham's Sentence – April 1807' opens with a scathing attack on the recently dissolved Ministry of Talents, but even Sheridan lampooned this ministry in its last months of office, and championship of Popham transcended Party interests – the City awarding him a sword of honour shortly after his official reprimand. See p. 165 below for Coleridge's remarks on this ministry.

[24] Collins, *Parson's Daughter*, p. 181.   [25] 21 and 22 Jan. 1805, *Letters*, pp. 96–7.

SCIENCE, THE SELF, AND A CHANGING WORLD

'Man is perpetually changing every particle of his body; and every thought of his mind is in continual flux and succession.'[26] So Adam Smith wrote in an essay first published in 1795, and his linkage of organic and mental process, and his stress on the fluid nature of each, is typical of the sceptical Enlightenment as a whole. Earlier in the century, Newton's 'mechanical philosophy' – remarkable for its mathematical expression of physical forces – had inspired a confidence in the general applicability of 'laws sublimely simple' as the poet Thomson put it. And though the occasional note of caution was sounded, as by Alexander Pope – 'Could he, whose rules the rapid Comet bind, / Describe or fix one movement of his Mind?', the answer to this question was often taken to be in principle 'yes'.[27] As the century wore on, however, faith in the possibility of a rationally deduced ethics receded,[28] and other doubts were fed by the spread of associationism in psychology, and by major advances in the life sciences. In so far as Jane Austen is allowed a context in the history of ideas today, it is usually as an Augustan aftercomer, clinging to the certainties of a fast-vanishing era. In the nineteenth century, however, she was renowned as a chief innovator of the 'modern' novel, the originality of which was tied to its insight into inner complexities.[29] A Victorian critic spoke for many readers when he declared that Austen's characters unfolded 'a living history', noting that morality in the novels had to do with disposition and process rather than with subscription to an inflexible code: 'She contemplates virtues, not as fixed quantities, or as definable qualities, but as continuous struggles and conquests, as progressive states of mind, advancing by repulsing their contraries, or losing ground by being overcome.'[30]

One of the quotations that has served to back up Austen's image as an apostle of fixity is a half-sentence lifted from the biographical note written by her brother Henry for the first edition of *Northanger Abbey* and

---

[26] Adam Smith, 'History of the Ancient Logics and Metaphysics', *Essays on Philosophical Subjects*, ed. W. P. D. Wightman and J. C. Bryce (Oxford, 1980), p. 121.

[27] See James Thomson, *Summer*, line 1562, see *The Seasons* and *The Castle of Indolence*, ed. James Sambrook (Oxford, 1972), p. 80; and see Alexander Pope, *An Essay on Man*, ii, lines 35–6.

[28] Among the 'rationalists' who believed that morals could be derived in a quasi-mathematical fashion were Ralph Cudworth (1617–88), Samuel Clarke (1675–1729), and John Balguy (1686–1748).

[29] Walter Scott, 'Unsigned Review: *Emma*', *Quarterly Review*, 14 (Mar. 1816), collected in Littlewood, ed., *Critical Assessments*; see particularly i, 288, 291.

[30] Richard Simpson, 'Jane Austen', *North British Review*, Apr. 1870; in B. C. Southam, ed., *Jane Austen: the Critical Heritage*, [i]:1812–1870 (1968), pp. 249–50.

Persuasion: 'she seldom changed her opinions either on books or men'.[31] In context this lapidary inscription was meant to accentuate Jane's reported enthusiasm for Gilpin and the picturesque, an aesthetic movement of liberal character that warred against clean-cut lines and unswerving views. Within the family it was especially James who shared this interest (among many others) with his younger sister, but the role of public elegist fell finally to Henry who, in the absence of his already sickening eldest brother, arranged the Winchester funeral. The 'Biographical Notice' with its Evangelical insistence on the God-fearing piety of Jane set the tone for later memorials, laying the first stone in that edifice that so well suited the book of those late twentieth-century critics who favoured a prim portrayal of their subject. Austen's own last written words – her lines on the Venta with their glance at an altogether worldly immortality – are characteristically spry and irreverent. Too irreverent, by half, to be admitted into the mausoleum benevolently assembled by the family, for as Caroline Austen put it, 'the joke about the dead Saint, & the Winchester races, all jumbled up together, would read badly as amongst the few details given, of the closing scene'.[32]

As might be suspected of a novelist who wrote so compellingly about mistaken first impressions, Jane Austen did indeed change her opinions of women and men – and of books too, if Henry's word on her disapproval of Fielding is to be trusted.[33] The certainty that readers like Marilyn Butler take to be the key feature of her world is indeed a characteristic of the way she writes,[34] but not of the realities she represents, and here, again, she is typical of the sceptical Enlightenment. Doubts, muddles, delusions,

---

[31] See *The Novels of Jane Austen*, ed. R. W. Chapman, 3rd edn (Oxford, 1933), v, 7. All future references to the novels will be to this text unless otherwise stated. In the definitively extended *Family Record* we read, for example: 'in her teens she was staunchly anti-Whig and anti-Republican . . . she probably always retained these early views, for "she seldom changed her opinions either on books or men"'; see Deirdre Le Faye, *Jane Austen: A Family Record* (1989), p. 55. This invaluable work began as a revision of Willliam and Richard Arthur Austen-Leigh's *Jane Austen: Her Life and Letters, a Family Record* (1913).

[32] For further discussion of this particular suppression see Margaret Doody's introduction to the finely annotated edition of the juvenilia by herself and Douglas Murray, *Catharine and Other Writings* (Oxford, 1993), xxi–xxiii; and for Caroline's letter see Deirdre le Faye, 'Jane Austen's Verses and Lord Stanhope's Disappointment', *Book Collector*, 37 (1988), 86–91. Margaret Kirkham seems to have been the first critic to call attention to the way Jane Austen's image was shaped by familial intervention; see the opening chapters of *Feminism and Fiction*.

[33] As is clear from her first surviving letter, Jane Austen once delighted in *Tom Jones*. See To Cassandra, 9–10 Jan. 1796, *Letters*, p. 2. An instance, perhaps, of what she noted in *Pride and Prejudice*: 'the feelings of the person who wrote, and the person who received it, are now so widely different' (368).

[34] See Butler, *War of Ideas*, pp. 1–3, and *passim*.

mixed motives and feelings are the stuff of the experience she handles, but her famous comment in *Emma* on the elusiveness of truth is no less forceful for being expressed in a clear and measured way – 'Seldom, very seldom, does complete truth belong to any human disclosure; seldom can it happen that something is not a little disguised or a little mistaken' (431). A determination to get at the truth made her all the quicker to seize on signs of self-deceit and inconsistency, and to recognize distortion as part of the texture of life, her own included.

A glimpse into Jane Austen's understanding of the self is given by a letter written from Bath during the spring of 1805, when the thought of how much change she has felt causes her to compare mental and bodily processes in a striking way. After noting, with her usual accuracy about dates, that seven years and four months have passed since she last visited the same Ridinghouse in town – then to see Miss Lefroy perform, now to watch 'Miss Chamberlayne look hot on horseback', she exclaims:

> What a different set are we now moving in! But seven years I suppose are enough to change every pore of one's skin, & every feeling of one's mind.[35]

The period had brought great alteration to her life – the deaths, within the last four months, of both her father and her beloved Anne Lefroy (mother of Lucy, the first rider), and, within as many years, the huge upheaval caused by the family's move from country to town. But a shift in manners is also at stake, as is brought home in her next letter, when she compares a woman who reminds her of Lucy Lefroy with a group who talk nonsense and go in for 'a monstrous deal of stupid quizzing'.[36] That she is caught up in her new set, however, is fully apparent. She chatters on about the success of the visit to the Chamberlaynes, and revels in the buzz of activity that was one portion of the legacy of Bath. But the switch from social engagement to a detachment nourished by memory and principle is quintessential, answering in part to her own (shorthand) weighing off of Johnson's 'full tide of human existence at Charing Cross' against Cowper's reflective country verse,[37] as also, indeed, to the continual to and fro, in her novels, between the first-person other of character and the third-person self of narration. No matter how cool her gaze, Austen not only recognized the constitutive power of the society around her, but went so far as to relate a change in its set-up to physical change in herself.

---

[35] To Cassandra, 8–11 Apr. 1805, *Letters*, p. 99.   [36] To Cassandra, 21–3 Apr. 1805, *Letters*, pp. 103–4.
[37] To Cassandra, 3 Nov. 1813, *Letters*, p. 250.

Porousness is the key to Jane Austen's sense of self-making, and to appreciate how forward-looking she was on this point, it is necessary only to glance at her brother Henry's biographical note with its massive emphasis on her preparation for death, which he reads as a conflict between 'decaying nature' and an immortal spirit. Orthodox notions of the soul did much to encourage the image of the essential self as something self-contained, properly aloof, 'scarce touching' – to quote Marvell in his exploratory analogy in 'On a Drop of Dew'; and in Christian fiction of the eighteenth century this dissociation often finds a correlative in plots that revolve around a heroine's defence of her chastity. Significantly, the last clause of Jane's dictum on the way time changes every feeling of the mind has a philosophical ring to it. Though more restrained than Hume's provocatively worded passage from the *Treatise* on the self as a 'bundle of perceptions', it tallies well with some later observations from his *Dialogues* (1779):

What is the soul of man? A composition of various faculties, passions, sentiments, ideas; united, indeed, into one self or person, but still distinct from each other . . . New opinions, new passions, new affections, new feelings arise, which continually diversify the mental scene, and produce in it the greatest variety, and most rapid succession imaginable.[38]

Hume makes provision for the bonding effects of memory and habit, and concedes the potentially tight organization of separate episodes – to which he allows the coherence of 'discourse'. But the inability of the same individual to 'think exactly alike at any two different periods of time' explains the inexhaustible freshness of the imaginative life,[39] and it is the material base of the mind's contents that enables the exercise of sympathy, for the stuff of thought, carrying no proprietary stamp, is easily shared. A process of chameleon-like adaptation is vividly described by one of the dialogue's speakers:

When I read a volume, I enter into the mind and intention of the author: I become him, in a manner, for the instant; and have an immediate feeling and conception of those ideas, which revolved in his imagination.[40]

With some recall of this passage perhaps, T. S. Eliot was to write, 'you are the music, / While the music lasts';[41] and the parallel is not entirely fortuitous, for it was the empiricist critique of identity that prepared the way for what was to become a commanding model of the imagination throughout the post-Romantic period.

---

[38] See *Hume's Dialogues*, p. 196. [39] Ibid., p. 199.
[40] Ibid., p. 193. [41] T. S. Eliot, 'The Dry Salvages', v, *The Four Quartets* (1956), p. 33.

Jane Austen's great popularity today, strikingly at odds with the construction of her as a dour Anti-Jacobin, certainly owes something to the vigorous roots she put down in the foundations of the modern world. To link her to James Joyce may seem perverse, but the great technical innovation she introduced to *style indirect libre*, her scarcely perceptible and sometimes deceptive erasure of the line between narrator and character,[42] does point forward to the avant-garde writer who steered the dramatic novel to its logical (and readerly) conclusion. Pertinent, too, is the passage from *Ulysses* which puts forward the most far-reaching of the book's metaphors for artistic creation:

As we, or mother Dana, weave and unweave our bodies, Stephen said, from day to day, their molecules shuttled to and fro, so does the artist weave and unweave his image . . . In the intense instant of the imagination, when the mind, Shelley says, is a fading coal, that which I was is that which I am and that which in possibility I may come to be.[43]

Stephen's seminal idea that writers are shape-shifters by virtue of the changeableness of their being, is made good by Joyce who gives all the characters of *Ulysses* the potential of artists, crossing into each other's experience continually, but still, as he puts it, walking through themselves.[44] As the reference to Shelley's fading coal shows, the philosophical basis for such conjecture goes back a long way. One of the fullest expositions comes from Godwin, and would certainly have been known to the author of the *Defence of Poetry*,[45] and quite possibly to the Austen family too:

First, ideas are to the mind nearly what atoms are to the body. The whole mass is in a perpetual flux; nothing is stable and permanent; after the lapse of a given period not a single particle probably remains the same. Who knows not that in the course of a human life the character of the individual frequently undergoes two or three revolutions of its fundamental stamina?[46]

Godwin uses this picture of a totally renewing self to support his contention in *Political Justice* that there is no such thing as 'an irremediable error'. Of that line of argument Jane Austen would certainly have disapproved, for she never overcame a heartfelt distrust of 'Regeneration & Conversion'.[47]

---

42 See Graham Hough on what he terms 'coloured narrative' in his pioneering article 'Narrative and Dialogue in Jane Austen' (1970), collected in his *Selected Essays* (Cambridge, 1978), pp. 46–82.

43 James Joyce, *Ulysses* (1960), p. 249.   44 Ibid., p. 213.

45 *Peacock's Four Ages of Poetry, Shelley's Defence of Poetry*, ed. H. F. B. Brett-Smith (1923), p. 55.

46 William Godwin, *Enquiry Concerning Political Justice*, ed. F. E. L. Priestley (Toronto, 1946), I, 35–6.

47 See her remarks on the sermons of her Evangelical cousin, the Reverend Edward Cooper: To Cassandra, 8–9 Sept. 1806, *Letters*, p. 322.

But Godwin also uses the idea to underline the powerful effects of social conditioning on the individual, and in *St Leon* traces the radical impact of different kinds of social structure on the character of his hero. And notwithstanding her distaste for the 'perfectibilian' ethos, and her inclination to dwell tactically on alterations that are for the worse, Austen does seem deliberately to have engaged with Godwin's second novel in *Sense and Sensibility*, where she explores the re-ordering effects of what would now be called group psychology. Despite their great differences, it is a mistake to suppose that Austen designed her novels as a negation of all that Godwin stood for; she should rather be seen as working from some similar empirical premises in a distinct and constructive way.

But what was the material origin of the idea that the human subject undergoes periodical 'revolutions in its fundamental stamina' as Godwin so dramatically put it? Just as in our own day scientists disputing over whether brain cells can be renewed through neurogenesis (it seems that some are) have informally invoked claims about the stability of human personality,[48] so too did thinkers of the late eighteenth century, to whom the idea was relatively new. In *Disquisitions* (1777) Joseph Priestley had raised altogether hypothetically – as something very hard to square with belief in identity – the extreme case of a body and brain every particle of which changed in the course of a year.[49] Erasmus Darwin, less than two decades later, speaks of such a 'mysterious process of generation' – without exempting the brain – as an established fact: the body, until it begins to die, continuously replenishes what is 'abraded by the actions of the system [through] digestion and sanguification'.[50] A possible source for Jane Austen's remark on changing every pore of the skin would be John Hunter's treatise on gunshot wounds (all but required reading for her two brothers in the navy), for in this pioneering work Hunter had treated the regeneration of skin and other kinds of tissue as an extension of the normal mechanisms of renewal.[51] It was while working on teeth that he had arrived at the idea that 'absorbents' dissolved and carried away material in the

[48] See Michael Specter, 'Rethinking the Brain', in Matt Ridley, ed., *The Best American Science Writing 2002* (New York, 2002), pp. 151–70; especially pp. 157–8. Opposed to the idea of replenishment, the neurologist Pasko Rakic suggests that it would be like 'trying to rip out two floors of the Empire State Building and replace them brick by brick without affecting the rest of the building': even if something equivalent to this was possible, the price would be 'that you – as a unique person with a unique group of memories – would no longer exist' (p. 158).

[49] Joseph Priestley, *Disquisitions Relating to Matter and Spirit* (1777), p. 158.

[50] Erasmus Darwin, *Zoonomia* (1794–6; 3rd edn, 1801), II, 176–7. See section xxxvii, 'Of Digestion, Secretion, Nutrition'.

[51] John Hunter, *A Treatise on the Blood, Inflammation, and Gun-Shot Wounds* (1812), see especially 'Of Skinning', II, 362–72.

system which the supply of nutrients would then replace,[52] and in the eighties he conducted and wrote up a series of experiments on bone growth in which the assimilation of dyes showed that areas of increase kept pace with those of waste, 'so as to give to the new the proper form'.[53]

Another of Hunter's ideas from this period contributed to a scientific theory with which the Austen family certainly were familiar. In a letter from Steventon dated November 1800, Jane records a party at Ashe where her brother James and a female friend alternately read from, and no doubt discussed, 'Dr Jenner's pamphlet on the cow-pox'.[54] Crucial to Jenner's explanation of why a cowpox vaccination was effective against smallpox was his belief that the more serious disease was a strain of the mild one, 'accidental circumstances' having worked 'new changes upon it'. He speculates further that diseases as apparently different as 'ulcerous throat', measles, and scarlet fever 'have all sprung from the same source, assuming some variety in their forms according to the nature of their new combinations'.[55] This was to be a fertile theory, for it stressed differentiation, showing that variety and uniqueness were a modality of organic existence, while hinting also at the generative role played by chance. As a model for his idea of variation through descent, Jenner cites an essay by Hunter on the relation between the wolf, jackal, and dog. There, from the evidence of comparative anatomy, his old teacher had argued, in a remarkable anticipation of Darwin, that the three species derived from a common ancestor through a process of continuous evolutionary change. Jenner neatly introduces his readers to this thought at the start of his cowpox pamphlet, remarking that

the Wolf, disarmed of ferocity, is now pillowed in the lady's lap. The Cat, the little Tyger of our island, whose natural home is the forest, is equally domesticated and caressed.[56]

Similar relationships, he goes on to say, hold true for the multifarious forms of infectious disease, which seem, however, to be all the more volatile, some gaining in virulence over a period of months, some – disobligingly in the case of docile forms – vanishing altogether.

When Jane Austen writes amusingly about changes in the style and behaviour of young girls coming out into society, she draws out a metaphor that plainly owes something to Jenner:

[52] See John Abernethy, *Physiological Lectures* (1817), p. 196.
[53] See 'On the Growth of Bones', John Hunter, *Observations on Certain Parts of the Animal Œconomy* (1786), ed. Richard Owen (1835 edn), p. 318.
[54] To Cassandra Austen, 20–2 Nov. 1800, *Letters*, p. 62.
[55] See Edward Jenner, *An Inquiry into the Causes and Effects of the Cow Pox* (1800), p. 48.
[56] Ibid., p. 1 and fn.

What is become of all the Shyness in the World? – Moral as well as Natural Diseases disappear in the progress of time, & new ones take their place. – Shyness & the Sweating Sickness have given way to Confidence & Paralytic complaints.[57]

Jocular though it may be, the comparison is full of implication. If fads come and go like epidemics, they are also, by inference, catching. And if the method of their transmission is understood to be a sort of sympathetic copycatting of the kind commented on by Hume, there is a pre-echo, here, of the present-day theory of the 'meme' – Richard Dawkins's comparison of the way ideas spread to the replication of a successful gene.[58] The reading of Jenner's paper in 1800 certainly had an unexpected outcome in the Austen family when the 'great discoverer' befriended James at Cheltenham, and insisted on revaccinating his daughter Caroline himself.[59]

Science re-orders the ordinary in many unforeseen ways. Its findings reach into seemingly unrelated areas, sometimes through direct application, sometimes for no better reason than that they offer an arresting paradigm. Leslie Stephen may have overstated the case when he claimed that Darwin's observations on the breeds of pigeons 'had a reaction upon the structure of European society', but artificial speciation was indeed a powerful idea, and he was surely right to argue that new ideas can 'suddenly start into reality, and pass from the sphere of remote speculation to that of immediate practice', and to suggest that this was particularly true of the eighteenth century.[60] Jane Austen did not have to focus on scientific matters with any rigour to experience the impact of explanations that had penetrated her world. Yet her public reception reveals, as we shall see, that she was perhaps of all great creative English writers of her generation the one most easily associated with an empirical habit of mind. There is much to suggest that she was exposed from an early age to an attitude towards contemporary science that was unusually wholehearted even for the time, and it is worth taking stock of her adolescence from this point of view.

One early landmark in Jane's reading was the present from her elder brother Edward (no doubt when he had outgrown it) of Thomas Percival's *Tales, Fables and Reflections* (1775), a manual on science and liberal opinion disguised as a conduct-book.[61] Percival introduced his young readers

---

[57] To Cassandra Austen, 8–9 Feb. 1807, *Letters*, p. 119.
[58] First expounded by Richard Dawkins in *The Selfish Gene* (Oxford, 1976), but enlarged on in his later books, and by other writers such as Daniel Dennett, see his *Darwin's Dangerous Idea* (Harmondsworth, 1995), pp. 341–70.
[59] *Reminiscences of Caroline Austen*, introd. Deirdre Le Faye (Overton, Hants., 1986), p. 31.
[60] Leslie Stephen, *English Thought*, I, 10–11.
[61] See Sir Zachary Cope, 'Dr Thomas Percival and Jane Austen', *British Medical Journal*, I (1969), 55–6; and Collins, *Parson's Daughter*, pp. 27–8.

to Shaftesbury, Voltaire, Robertson, and Smith; took them through an impressive range of famous experiments; taught them to abhor slavery, and to regard a merchant as a more valuable member of society than a court toady. But he urged them, above all, to be vigilant. Aiming to excite a 'spirit of inquiry', the tales associate empiricism with youthful wonder – so a boy is scolded for making fun of a grave old man absorbed in bubble-blowing:

> you now behold the greatest Philosopher of the age, Sir Isaac Newton, investigating the nature of light and colours by a series of experiments, no less curious than useful, though you deem them childish and insignificant.[62]

Whether it is Archimedes in the bath, Newton under the apple tree, Harvey at the dissecting table, or Franklin noticing the effects of oil on the wake of a ship, what marks the pioneer is the combination of a sharp eye and open mind.[63] Time and again, science is tied in with a celebration of the ordinary, a microscope revealing a housefly to be 'ornamented with plumes and decorations, which surpass all the luxuries of dress, in the courts of the greatest of princes'.[64] For this reason perhaps, Percival sprang to mind when Jane Austen imagined the education of her benign anti-heroine Catherine Morland who struggles to learn the 'Beggar's Petition' by heart, the longest poem from the *Tales*, but cannot forget the lines inserted in the first essay on cruelty:

> The poor beetle, which we tread upon,
> In corporal sufferance feels a pang as great
> As when a giant dies.[65]

Either Jane Austen copied these lines direct from the *Tales* or, like Catherine, had them by heart, for she preserves both of Percival's deviations from Shakespeare.[66] Later in life she met a Dr Percival who turned out to be the son of the 'famous Dr Percival of Manchester',[67] from which it looks as if she probably knew something of the work done by this noted humanitarian in his adoptive city, work which included research on mortality rates and the establishment of sanitation schemes. She may also have had word of him as a luminary of the Manchester Literary and Philosophical Society, known for his links with the *philosophes*, and for his lasting friendships with William Robertson and David Hume. Histories by the latter writers formed

---

62 Thomas Percival, *A Father's Instructions: Tales, Fables, and Reflections* (1776), p. 41.
63 See particularly 'Vigilant Observation', *Tales*, pp. 180–2.
64 Ibid., p. 67.   65 *Northanger Abbey*, p. 16; *Tales*, p. 30.
66 *Measure for Measure*, III.i.79–81. Percival gives *which* for *that*, *feels* for *finds*.
67 To Cassandra Austen, 7–9 Oct. 1808, *Letters*, p. 145. Austen refers to Percival's 'Moral Tales', which suggest she may have used the much expanded fourth edition, so subtitled (1779).

an important part of Jane Austen's early reading, and though these grown-up books belong to the milieu of Eleanor Tilney rather than Catherine Morland,[68] they uphold in a full-bodied way the principles enunciated by Percival in his preface when he declares that 'a strict attention has been paid to truth and nature . . . the narrations are conformable to the usual course of things, or derived from the records of history'. If it took some time for the writer of the juvenilia to come round to this view, similar ideals of probability and accuracy – classical in origin but much buttressed by the empirical tradition – were certainly to govern the work of her maturity. And, though hardly evident in her writing, a continuing interest in natural history is suggested by her ownership of the eight volumes of Goldsmith's *History of the Earth and Animated Nature*, an encyclopaedic work in the French style that harps tirelessly on the theme of cosmic benevolence.

At the start of 1789, shortly after Jane had turned thirteen, James with the help of Henry began producing a periodical paper, *The Loiterer*, which was to run for over a year. James is reported by his son – who wrote the first life of Jane Austen – to have had 'a large share in directing her reading and forming her taste', and though it would not do to underestimate the independence of Jane's opinions,[69] the arrival of the weekly number from Oxford was bound to have left a deep impression on an author well-advanced by then in *Volume the First*.[70] Family theatricals had already brought the Austen offspring together as a group, and must have done much (to judge from the provocative choice and prologuing of the plays) to kindle a sense of youthful complicity among them. We can be sure that Jane felt herself to be part of an irreverent cult that had found a public voice when the periodical started to appear.

Science is among *The Loiterer*'s strongest suits. In its fourth issue James not only mocked the *a priori* theologizing of Soame Jenyns – for proving that 'there was no such thing as time' – but gave a puff to some lectures currently being given in Oxford by the first Radcliffe Observer, Dr Hornsby, an observational astronomer of exceptional finesse.[71] This 'remarkably entertaining'

---

[68] See *Northanger Abbey*, pp. 109–10.

[69] See *Memoir of Jane Austen* by her nephew James Edward Austen-Leigh, ed. R. W. Chapman (Oxford, 1963), p. 12. The attribution to Jane of the letter from 'Sophia Sentiment' (*The Loiterer*, 9, 28 Mar. 1789) is attractive but questionable, for it is not easily read as a consistent burlesque (see Park Honan, *Jane Austen: Her Life*, 1987, pp. 60–1), and its contents – which include a request for 'some nice, affecting stories' – run clean contrary to the stance taken towards sentimental fiction and marvellous tales in the juvenilia. Claire Tomalin convincingly makes it over to 'a transvestite Henry or James' looking for a pretext for an editorial change of tack (see her *Jane Austen: A Life*, 1997, p. 63).

[70] See Le Faye, *A Family Record*, p. 63.

[71] His results were thought worth publishing by a later Radcliffe Observer; see Harold Knox-Shaw, *The Observations of the Reverend Thomas Hornsby* (1932), particularly pp. 1–2.

series which loiterers are urged on no account to miss, would have been the popular course on 'experimental philosophy' that Thomas Hornsby delivered as Sedleian professor. It is possible that James managed to press the star-gazer into contributing to the periodical, for a couple of numbers with a scientific slant are identified not by initials, as is the way elsewhere, but by a row of stars. More probably it was a member of Hornsby's audience who obliged; in any case, the satiric defence of experimental method is amusingly (if at times ponderously) sustained by someone well versed in contemporary discoveries. Mention is made not only of the most famous – Lavoisier, Priestley, Cavendish, and Harrison – but of lesser luminaries like Joseph Black, Richard Kirwan, Adair Crawford, and a Hartington whose theories seem to have sunk without trace. What reads as flatly as a roll-call today was then the record of ground-breaking work in a variety of rapidly expanding fields, ranging from the quantification of chemical reactions to the isolation of elements. It was work, moreover, that saw off such quaint conceptual survivors as phlogiston and transmutation,[72] ideas that seemed with hindsight to be 'more ingenious than solid' to apply the phrase that James used of Soame Jenyns's metaphysics.

One piece by the starred contributor concerns a fantastic machine that turns heads transparent, a variant on Addison's spectatorial device that causes emotions to be as visible in the breast as bees in a dioptric hive. In the conventional way, a number of hypocritical subjects are exposed by being wired up, but the essay comes to life when a crusty old naturalist is given his turn. The ventricles of his brain are found to swarm with 'thousands of little animated masses creeping, and striking in every direction', and the scene seems to be set for a Swiftian spree on the materiality of thinking matter, but the animalcules turn out to be fleas which the naturalist is convinced are a species of lobster; indeed an assistant brings him the news that out of the fifteen thousand he has had boiled, only ten have gone red:

But instead of reply, the Philosopher cast a look of contempt upon the Experimentalist, which convinced me, that ten arguments in favour of a preconceived hypothesis, will at any time outweigh as many thousand to the contrary.[73]

The essay ends with the reflection that the moral study of human nature should inspire the 'same zeal, which induced our Botanists and Astronomers to transverse the remotest regions of the southern hemisphere, or the French

[72] See Charles Singer, *A Short History of Scientific Ideas* (Oxford, 1982), p. 339.
[73] *The Loiterer*, 35, 26 Sept. 1789, pp. 10–11.

Academicians to ascend the summits of the highest mountains'. In that last clause, the ideal of a transparent head is finally associated with the attempt by De la Caille and his forbears to establish a precise shape for the earth, an enterprise that seemed then to show how experiment had the power to disrupt paradigms, for Caille's measurement of the distance corresponding to one degree of latitude down south had had the effect of displacing Newton's symmetrical model of the globe with a pear-shape. Only many decades later did it become clear that Caille's result was a red boiled flea.

It was invariably the boast of Enlightenment studies in the humanities that their foundations were scientific. David Hume began his *Treatise* by declaring his allegiance to a new science of human nature, arising from 'the application of experimental philosophy to moral subjects'.[74] Such claims were to some extent mere manifesto talk, and Hume himself insisted in the second *Enquiry* that the field of morals, at least, was not susceptible to the same sort of certainty that was possible in the survey of the earth, of the tides, or of stars.[75] Nor would Hume have been put out to hear that the *Treatise* was every bit as 'unmathematical as Ovid's Metamorphoses'.[76] Even so far as it is inductive, Hume's argument proceeds not by any redaction of statistics, but by an appeal to consensus, or by evocative reminders of what experience is like. Rather than behavioural 'laws', the reader encounters 'examples' which command imaginative assent. If the *Treatise* is less a scientific study of mankind than a philosophy of science with an attached discourse on humanity that is consistent in principle with it, the same sort of consistency could be claimed for other discourses, including fictional ones.

As far as Jane Austen's reception by her contemporaries goes, it is surprising to find how often her work is approached in idiom borrowed from the sciences. Nor is this approach confined to critics and intellectuals. Among the 'Opinions of Mansfield Park' recorded by Austen herself, the praise of Mrs Pole turns on the way the novels are written by someone intimately or 'experimentally' acquainted with what she describes.[77] And the term 'experimental' does indeed take on substance when the kind of advice that Austen gave her niece Anna for revising a manuscript novel is brought to

---

[74] See David Hume's Introduction to *A Treatise of Human Nature*, ed. L. A. Selby-Bigge (Oxford, 1968), xx. Hereafter *THN*.
[75] David Hume, *An Enquiry Concerning the Principles of Morals*, ed. Tom L. Beauchamp (Oxford, 1998), p. 152. Hereafter *EPM*.
[76] James Noxon, *Hume's Philosophical Development* (Oxford, 1973), p. 112.
[77] *Minor Works*, p. 435.

mind. One principle continually invoked is that fictive actions should tally with repeated observations from real life:

I have scratched out Sir Tho: from walking with the other Men to the Stables &c the very day after his breaking his arm – for though I find your Papa *did* walk out immediately after *his* arm was set, I think it can be so little usual as to *appear* unnatural in a book – & it does not seem to be material that Sir Tho: should go with them.[78]

Linked to this principle of avoiding the abnormal is another that declares war on the unnecessary, the joint import of the two being that when deviation occurs it does so to some effect. A further requirement is that anything relating to the public world should be represented with scrupulous fidelity. So Jane Austen takes pains to check that hedgerows grow in Northamptonshire, or that Gibraltar has a Government House; and expects her niece to do the same:

Lyme will not do. Lyme is towards 40 miles distance from Dawlish & would not be talked of there . . . They must be *two* days going from Dawlish to Bath; They are nearly 100 miles apart.[79]

The corollary to this passion for accuracy is an extreme caution about venturing into territory that is not known at first hand:

Let the Portmans go to Ireland, but as you know nothing of the Manners there, you had better not go with them. You will be in danger of giving false representations. Stick to Bath & the Foresters. There you will be quite at home.[80]

Austen took this rule of sticking to the observed so far that she notoriously altogether avoided scenes in which men confer together in the absence of women. Her limitations of range have been ascribed with good reason to the constraints under which middle-class women laboured in her period, but they are also a condition of the 'experimental' discourse to which she was pledged. Later critics approaching her work from the perspective of the full-blown sociological novel of the nineteenth century have put a construction on these limits that negates their special implications. Raymond Williams, in a pithy phrase, remarked adversely of the novels that where there is only one class there is no class at all; but he was cannily forestalled on this issue by G. K. Chesterton who preludes some shrewd commentary on the exposure of Emma's class-bound attitudes with the following:

---

[78] To Anna Austen, 10–18 Aug. 1812, *Letters*, p. 268.
[79] Ibid., pp. 268–9, and see To Cassandra, 24 and 29 Jan. 1813, *Letters*, pp. 198, 202.
[80] Ibid., p. 269.

It is true that Jane Austen did not attempt to teach any history or politics; but it is not true that we cannot learn any history or politics from Jane Austen. Any work so piercingly intelligent of its own kind, and especially any work of so wise and humane a kind, is sure to tell us much more than shallower studies covering a larger surface.[81]

By analogy with other kinds of discourse that are empirically grounded, the 'experimental' novel does not need to offer a general theory in order to have real significance.

Among the handful of reviews that Austen received in her lifetime a piece on *Emma* makes much of the reader's pleasurable shock at recognizing 'modes of thinking and feeling which experience every day presents in real life'. Whereas human nature seems almost uniform when conveyed by 'a more sweeping observer', the reviewer continues, Austen's characters come to life as individuals because of the way they are 'surveyed in this microscopic detail'.[82] Nature study in one form or another became a regular source of metaphor for critics drawing attention to the variety of Austen's creations throughout the nineteenth century. Perhaps one reason for this is that the novels seem to have had a special appeal for readers with a scientific background. Ardent Janeites of the early decades of the century included polymaths like William Whewell, an authority on inductive method, and Archbishop Richard Whately, a founding father of statistical sociology and an editor of Francis Bacon. Whately's justly famous essay on the novels takes off from Walter Scott's notion of Austen as the founding figure of an entirely new class of fiction distinguished by its fastidious 'copying from nature', and its attention to 'the current of ordinary life'.[83] A chief point made by Whately – later to be developed by Macaulay as the basis of his comparison of Austen to Shakespeare – is that the minor characters of the novels are as finely differentiated as the central ones. Such alertness to diversity immediately puts him in mind of the expert in taxonomy: 'to the eye of a skilful naturalist the insects on a leaf present as wide differences as exist between the elephant and the lion'. Later, this metaphor is extended when John Thorpe, 'the Bang-up Oxonian' from *Northanger Abbey*, is classified

---

[81] See G. K. Chesterton, 'The Evolution of *Emma*', collected in Littlewood, ed., *Critical Assessments*, I, 443.

[82] See 'Anonymous Review of *Emma*', *The Champion*, 31 Mar. 1816, in Littlewood, ed., *Critical Assessments*, I, 297–8, 300.

[83] See Walter Scott, 'Unsigned Review: *Emma*', *Quarterly Review*, 14 (Mar. 1816), collected in Littlewood, ed., *Critical Assessments*, I, 287–8. Whately's opening pages contain several echoes of Scott's phrasing, plus the idea of 'a new school of fiction'; see 'Unsigned Review: *Northanger Abbey* and *Persuasion*', *Quarterly Review*, 24 (Jan. 1821), collected in Littlewood, ed. *Critical Assessments*, see I, 318–19.

as 'the best portrait of a species, which, though almost extinct cannot yet be quite classed among the Palæotheria'.[84] Such hand-rubbing glee in the pinning down of a type (more accurately identified in this case as the Loiterer's 'Rattle')[85] seems unattractive to modern sensibilities, but allowance needs to be made for the novelty of encountering social observation so acute that it distinguished not only unremarked (and often fleeting) role models, but the play also of individuality within them. Ever since Theophrastus extended botanical taxonomy to human character, natural history has typified this sort of fine discrimination, and the rationale of such linkage is perhaps most memorably articulated by Pope reflecting on the diversity of the 'ruling passion':

> There's some Peculiar in each leaf and grain,
> Some unmark'd fibre, or some varying vein:
> Shall only Man be taken in the gross?
> Grant but as many sorts of Mind as Moss.[86]

A fascination with 'Shyness & the Sweating Sickness' and other passing vogues or social symptoms is one aspect of an intelligence riveted on the interface between the generic and the peculiar.

Austen's contemporary popularity in Whig circles does not make her a Whig, and the same could be argued of the naturalist overtones that are typical of her critical reception. But nature study appears, as it happens, to have been a hobby of the Austen family for over a generation. Not only did George Austen have a microscope as well as a 'small astronomical instrument' in his possession (no doubt frequently put to use by the children),[87] but the poetry that James continued to write throughout his life abounds in such reference. The bearing on Jane's novels of this only very recently published body of work has never been examined,[88] even though there are, for example, conspicuous parallels between the famous autumnal walk in *Persuasion* and the poem 'Autumn' (1815) in which James prescribes exertion for those who are drawn to identify with the 'pale declining year'.[89] James

---

[84] Ibid., I, 327, 330.

[85] For some discussion of Jane Austen's use of the Oxford types satirized in *The Loiterer*, see my article 'What Jane Austen Meant by "Raffish"', *Persuasions*, 22 (2000), 105–8. See also Li-Ping Geng's introduction to the facsimile edition (2000), pp. 14–15.

[86] *Epistle to Cobham*, lines 15–18.

[87] 'The Sale at Steventon Parsonage', *Jane Austen Society Report* 1993, pp. 14–15.

[88] *The Complete Poems of James Austen*, edited and introduced by David Selwyn (Chawton, 2003), appeared at the close of 2003 after the completion of this study.

[89] Compare from *Persuasion* the 'counteracting' energies of the farmer (85). James clearly belongs among the many poets 'worthy of being read' (84) who have been spurred into poetry by the

puts inverted commas round the last phrase which comes from *The Seasons* and it is echoed in Anne Elliot's rumination on the poets' 'apt analogy of the declining year', along with another phrase of Thomson's, 'the last smiles of Autumn'.[90] James also gives his true nature-lover 'philosophic eyes' – Thomson's shorthand for the ideal poet who, shunning superstition, combines wonder with empirical curiosity, 'inquisitive to know / The causes and materials, yet unfixed / Of this appearance beautiful and new'.[91] A later poem, 'Lines written in the Autumn of 1817 after a recovery from sickness', includes a whole paragraph in praise of scientific pursuits; delight being the reward of those who seek

> To analyse, transmute, and reproduce
> With chemic science the component parts
> Of Earth, Air, Water, and to ascertain
> By fresh experiments the latent powers
> Of the metallic produce of the mine.

The passage ends by picturing a figure botanizing in a narrow country lane, 'pleased to cull'

> Its green and various harvest; and arrange
> With skill Linnaean every plant distinct
> In its due class and order.[92]

There is no reason to suppose that the figure is Jane's, but there exists in her hand a nine-verse poem, 'Kalendar of Flora', which, as David Selwyn dryly remarks, only botanical interest could have induced her to copy.[93]

---

season. For James Austen's 'Autumn' see the Austen-Leigh Archive in the Hampshire Record Office, 23M93/60/3/1 (unnumbered folio). For a fuller discussion of the parallels see my '*Persuasion*, James Austen, and James Thomson', *Notes and Queries*, 247 (Dec. 2002), 451–3.

[90] James, in fact, conflates two phrases from Thomson's 'Autumn': 'the cool declining year', line 707 and 'The pale descending year', line 988. Compare Thomson's 'the last smiles / Of Autumn beaming o'er the yellow woods' (lines 1052–3) with 'the last smiles of the year upon the tawny leaves' (*Persuasion*, p. 84). Wentworth's loaded apostrophe to the 'beautiful glossy nut' (88) may well owe something to the set-piece on nutting with its personification of the burnished hazels: 'A glossy shower and of an ardent brown / As are the ringlets of Melinda's hair – / Melinda! formed with every grace complete, / Yet these neglecting, above beauty wise, / And far transcending such a vulgar praise' (lines 620–4). See *The Seasons*, ed. Sambrook, pp. 105, 108, 116, 117. Jane Austen's copy of Thomson's *Works* survived to be owned by Virginia Woolf.

[91] James writes: 'Still the "pale declining year" / Marked by philosophic eyes, / Teaches us to moralize'. See 'Autumn', lines 1133–7. The immediate subject here is the mystery of the aurora borealis. For a discussion of the passage see Alan Dugald McKillop, *The Background of Thomson's Seasons* (1942), pp. 63–6, and more generally chapter 2, 'Description and Science'.

[92] See the Chawton copy of 'Collected Verses: James Austen', p. 163.

[93] *Collected Poems and Verse of the Austen Family*, ed. David Selwyn (1996), appendix, p. 106.

It is telling, too, that Linnaeus should spring to mind when she writes to her brother Francis, then sailing in the Baltic: 'Gustavus-Vasa, & Charles 12th, & Christiana, & Linneus – do their Ghosts rise up before You?'[94] Revealingly, the scientist is placed in the exalted company of other patron saints and prodigies of the Enlightenment. The family copy of Voltaire's *Charles XII* survives, and would have been one source of Jane's familiarity not only with Gustavus Vasa – the King who delivered his country from both Danes and Bishops ('the real tyrants of the state'), but with Queen Christina, who provoked Protestant slander by giving up her throne to follow the arts.[95] It seems likely that Jane was widely read in Voltaire; for she drew from *Louis XIV*, and the *Essai sur les mœurs* as well as from *Charles XII*, and appears to allude to *Candide* in *Persuasion*.[96]

In the next sentence of her letter, however, Austen lauds Sweden for its Protestantism, and this twofold allegiance to religion and to reason was to generate many new directions in the novels that were begun at Chawton. Dualities of the same kind mark the writings of her brother James once settled as rector of nearby Steventon, and it seems likely that Jane kept closely abreast of his interests when they were not already her own. James read his work at family gatherings, and on one occasion Jane records, from London, her annoyance at having left behind his most recent poem.[97] His visits to Chawton were regular and often two or three days in length, which meant that he was, on the whole, the brother of whom Jane saw most.[98] If too little has been made of their relationship, it is partly because there are no surviving letters (and in view of their proximity probably few in the first place), and partly because Jane and James's second wife, Mary, failed to get on. This posed no lasting threat to the intimacy between brother

94 3–6 July 1813, *Letters*, p. 214.
95 See David Gilson, *A Bibliography of Jane Austen* (Winchester, 1997), p. 434; and see the first chapter of *The History of Charles XII* for substantial accounts of both Gustavus Vasa and Queen Christina. Both figures recur in the popular *Ancient and Modern History*, where Voltaire praises Gustavus Vasa as 'one of the foremost to exterminate a religion which had been made the means of committing such execrable crimes', and describes Queen Christina's story as 'the greatest example we have of the real superiority of the arts, of politeness, and of social perfection, over mere nominal greatness'. See *Works of M. de Voltaire* (1761), x, 69–72, 70; iv, 68–9; vi, 68.
96 See To Anne Sharp, 22 May 1817, *Letters*, p. 341; and *Mansfield Park*, p. 189. Chapman's suggestion that Chesterfield may have been the source of the information on Galigai de Concini does not hold up to scrutiny, for the form of the name is different there – 'Galigai Maréchale d'Ancre' (*Letters*, III, 269). For *Candide* see Bradbrook, *Predecessors*, p. 122.
97 James ends his poem 'Lines written in the Autumn of 1817' with a description of such an occasion; and see Jane's letter to Cassandra, 18–20 Apr. 1811, *Letters*, p. 181.
98 Caroline remarks that her father 'went frequently to Chawton for one or two nights', and that even after the onset of his illness: 'Not many months ever passed without his riding over to Chawton, and he gave up this habit very unwillingly'; see *Reminiscences of Caroline Austen*, pp. 47, 51.

and sister, however, and even when things between them were at a low ebb Jane described James as 'so good & so clever a Man'.[99]

Though the life of a country parson might be thought more than enough to extinguish the rationalism that is so much to the fore in *The Loiterer*, James stood by many of the liberal tenets of his youth. In his poetry he continued to champion liberty and the English constitution, to write vividly about rural and urban poverty, and to uphold the reading of the Latin classics, and of historians like David Hume. But he did grow into more of a conformist, and his choice of Linnaeus as the exemplary scientist is perhaps symptomatic of this, for few heroes of the Enlightenment were more easily accommodated by traditional belief. Where through Jenner's eyes the organic realm was rife with shifts and mutations, to Linnaeus it presented a hierarchy of species fixed by the Creator for once and all. The real hero of that most comforting of nature studies, Gilbert White's *Selborne* (1789), is Linnaeus; and if James Austen had a hero it was Gilbert White. Some two dozen lines of eulogy are made over to him in the poem 'Selbourne Hanger' (1812), and James's unfinished and most ambitious work 'The Œconomy of Rural Life' builds on White's sense of the benign interplay between the natural and human orders. If White's interest in nature stops just short of the point at which observation turns inductive, he was at least in touch with a range of serious naturalists such as Joseph Banks and Thomas Pennant, and he certainly supplied a living example of how Anglicanism and empiricism could flourish under the same roof. Steventon vicarage, however, at the time Jane Austen was about to enter her teens and James had already come of age, bore witness to a much more challenging version of the Enlightenment, and it is to this period of dramatic foment that we now turn.

STAGING THE ENLIGHTENMENT

Theatricals in the Austen household go back at least as far as 1782 when James, at the age of seventeen, wrote a prologue and epilogue for a performance of Thomas Francklin's *Matilda*, a bombastic work of just the sort that Jane would later take a delight in burlesquing. It was during Christmas 1787, however, and through the early months of the following year, that these entertainments took on a particular, even programmatic character. Seminal to the enterprise was the European tour from which James had returned that autumn. He had stayed at Nerac with the French family of

---

[99] To Cassandra Austen, 8–9 Feb. 1807, *Letters*, p. 121.

his vivacious cousin Eliza, the Comtesse de Feuillide, who was now to be a leading light on the Steventon stage, and he was impatient for an occasion to show off his new-found intellectual confidence and savoir-faire.

The winter season at the rectory opened with Susanna Centlivre's *The Wonder: A Woman Keeps a Secret* (1714), a robust Restoration-like comedy in which cousin Eliza took the part of the feminist heroine Violante. The play focuses on a confrontation between the old absolutist order and the modernizing forces of a commercial society, and upholds individual liberty as its touchstone, particularly the freedom of women. With the help of his curtain-verses, James turned the occasion into what amounted to a bold Enlightenment manifesto, complete with appropriate historiography. Next in the series came *The Chances*, a play which in Garrick's version is very much as the Duke of Buckingham left it: Don Juan – far from being sent to Hell as he is by Molière – gets off scot-free, and is even rewarded, albeit with marriage. With this exceptionally risqué piece James may have felt that he had gone too far, for his prologue topples into nervous irony – through which he poses some searching questions that challenge his earlier credo. These were of a kind framed by many latter-day Enlightenment thinkers and were to prove central, in the years ahead, to the more serious of his deliberations in *The Loiterer* (1789–90), a periodical that was to remain liberal in tenor. With *Tom Thumb*, Fielding's devastating burlesque of heroic tragedy, the season ended,[100] and in his prologue to this play James returned to an unqualified celebration of hedonism.

While James was writing his speeches, possibly also some plays, and transforming himself into the editor of a professional weekly, Jane was at work on juvenilia that are perhaps even more conspicuously the product of genius than the early pieces of Mozart. Though difficult to place, this writing is marked by her masterful abstraction of a wide range of literary conventions, and reveals a number of allusions to the family theatre, and a debt, beyond that, to a genre that seems to have been particularly popular at Steventon – burlesque of the heroic. Fielding and Sheridan are as likely parents for the many pieces that were to fill up the three volumes as any that can be found. And in addition to *Tom Thumb* – which seems to have passed on a whole clutch of genes to the minor works, Jane was certainly familiar at this stage both with *The Rivals* (she may have been part of the Steventon production of 1784),[101] and with *The Critic*. A line from the last is echoed in 'Love and Freindship' (1790), and the satirized historian of 'The

[100] This is to exclude an evening of unnamed pieces, and the later *High Life Below Stairs* and *The Sultan* from the start of 1790.
[101] See Le Faye, *A Family Record*, p. 46.

History of England' (1791) is dotty enough to use the critic Puff's absurd play on the Spanish Armada as a primary source for the reign of Elizabeth. The absence of Sheridan from the family repertoire in 1787 and 1788 may have been in deference to the presence of their glamorous cousin, for in those years the playwright was to the fore in the impeachment of Warren Hastings, Eliza's generous patron.[102]

The brilliance of Austen's early work was quite lost on her nineteenth-century descendants who regarded its humour as puerile, but James Austen-Leigh chose well when he published – as a sample of the juvenilia in his *Memoir* – the two-page playlet, *The Mystery*.[103] It is tempting to believe that this superb and highly finished piece was among the offerings of the 'private Theatrical Exhibition' at Steventon in 1788, for it cries out for performance.[104] Its three very brief scenes revolve around interrupted speeches and the whispering of a secret that the audience never learns. Behind this governing device it is possible to detect the parodies directed at absurd stage effects by Fielding and Sheridan.[105]

Austen's intention in *The Mystery*, however, is distinct from her forerunners'. She is less concerned with the parody of a specific trait than with exposing a general principle that is latent in all comedy; and she exposes this principle by turning it upside-down. With an economy unusual in a young writer, she sticks to two ideas: first, that the audience is never to be let into the mystery, second, that the mystery will be shared finally by the entire cast. The play opens with Corydon (in the absence of his Daphne) making his exit on the line, 'But Hush! I am interrupted'; and it ends with a Colonel Elliott confiding the secret (which seems to have something to do with Corydon and Daphne) to a Sir Edward Spangle fast asleep on a sofa:

Shall I tell him the secret? . . . No, he'll certainly blab it . . . But he is asleep and won't hear me . . . So I'll e'en venture. (*Goes up to* Sir Edward, *whispers him, & Exit*)[106]

Inverting all conventional *éclaircissement*, the play ends, in effect, with its head in the sand. It is the exception that proves the rule that plots have to do not only with the making of mystery but with the undoing of it too. In refusing to let anyone into the picture, it calls attention both to the

[102] Deirdre Le Faye has put paid to claims that Eliza was Hastings' illegitimate daughter, see her recent biography, *Jane Austen's 'Outlandish Cousin': The Life and Letters of Eliza de Feuillide* (2002), pp. 19–21.
[103] Austen-Leigh, *Memoir*, pp. 44–7.   [104] See Le Faye, *A Family Record*, p. 63.
[105] See particularly *Tom Thumb*, II. ii; and *The Critic*, III. i.
[106] *Minor Works*, p. 57. All further references to the juvenilia are to this edition.

privileged vantage-point which is normally the audience's due and to the blinkering which is the habitual lot of the comic character. This is indeed the revenge of those hapless players on the eighteenth-century stage who had to turn a deaf ear to asides, and a blind eye to figures bulging from behind curtains or from laughter-shaken screens. But metafictional intrigue apart, the piece is given broad appeal by the fact that it was obviously intended to be acted by children for an audience of grown-ups. On stage, Old Humbug instructs Young Humbug to behave as he has been told, but the secret rouses an excitement that plays havoc with authority:

DAPHNE: I'll tell you. (*whispers* Fanny)
MRS HUMBUG: And is he to? . . .
DAPHNE: I'll tell you all I know of the matter.
                                      (*whispers* Mrs Humbug & Fanny) (p. 56)

In performance before the adults (and the play was dedicated by Jane to her father), all the transitive whispering specified by the stage directions would have allowed for no end of face-pulling and innuendo.

Praise of mirth is the theme of the prologue that James wrote for *The Wonder*, the play that launched the newly fitted-out tithe barn, and opened the season of all seasons at Steventon. The first performance fell on Boxing Day 1787, prompting James to take as his subject the celebration of Christmas in England through the ages, and he treats the feast in an altogether secular way. High spirits give birth, he argues, to a whole gamut of 'social joys', and the great value of the occasion lies in the way it brings a genial glow even to 'the coldest breath'. All that is hostile to this zest is epitomized in a sketch of Commonwealth England where bigotry and self-righteousness fray the bonds of social trust, destroying 'sense and peace' along with merriment. Mischief, too, is part of the feast, and James appears at times as a Lord of Misrule, ushering in 'the gambols of this night', and giving vent to brain-storming views.[107] For *The Chances*, a week later, he wrote a dramatic monologue in which the speaker urges the audience to join forces with a new liberating order and have done with the old:

To throw at once their Gothic fabric down,
And on their system's ruins, build our own,
Hail happy times! hail halcyon days of mirth
When pleasure courts us from our very birth.[108]

---

107 With this phrase James ends his prologue to *The Wonder*. Quotations from the prologues and epilogues are, throughout, from the manuscript in the Hampshire Record Office (hereafter HRO), 23M93/60/3/2, unless otherwise stated.
108 Prologue to *The Chances*.

James proceeds to paint a lurid picture of what follows on the loosening of 'rank & station' – 'the important little and the vulgar great, / Young men of threescore, and old men of one', but the topsy-turvydom is conveyed with a jubilance that the dramatic irony of the speech scarcely succeeds in dampening.[109] Indeed, by the end of the prologue the gamester has become a college man whose identity begins to merge into James's ('we alas! ourselves are gamester here'). Like the character of the Lounger in *The Loiterer*, who shares the editor's passion for card games, and neglects his studies to read Hoyle on whist, the gamester neglects his books to read Hoyle, but also Thomas Paine.[110]

As an upholder of 'mixed' government with its separation and balance of powers, it is not surprising that James disapproved of the 'democratic republicanism' first sketched by Paine in *Common Sense*, but in this he joined company with many liberal spirits including Charles James Fox who was to attack *The Rights of Man* as a libel upon the constitution.[111] In France the Glorious Revolution had been hailed by the *philosophes* throughout the eighteenth century as a landmark in the gradual but steady secularization of Europe, and it is precisely such a 'grand narrative' that James endorses without trace of equivocation in his epilogue to *The Wonder*, which opens:

> In barbarous Times, e'er learning's sacred light
> Rose to disperse the shades of Gothic night
> And bade fair science wide her beams display
> Creation's fairest part neglected lay.

The imagery is classic stuff, and runs through James's whole series which unfolds, by degrees, an Enlightenment credo, the chief article of which is that freedom, prosperity, and happiness are inextricably linked – so much so that James seems to have been in some doubt as to which to place first. In one version of his prologue to *Tom Thumb*, the commercial economy is given pride of place:

---

[109] Compare, for example, with the 'old men of one', the picture of rejuvenated age from the prologue to *The Wonder*: 'To festive joys each festive mind prepares / And age almost forgets his pains and cares / And whilst their sports his vigour half restores / He courts the gambols of his youth once more.'

[110] The Lounger, a character slightly more far gone than the Loiterer, reads Hoyle in bed until ten, and confines composition to begging letters to his father, 'the *Bore*'. The Gamester from the prologue to *The Chances*, 'Throws Lilly's grammar by, and learns the chances. / O'er Hoyle and Paine all day intent he pores, / And cheats his father's fortune at all fours.' See *The Loiterer*, 4 (21 Feb. 1789), pp. 10–16. The prologue may have been touched up at some point after the performance on 7 Jan. 1788.

[111] Gregory Claeys, *Thomas Paine: Social and Political Thought* (Boston, 1989), pp. 45, 127, 140.

But chief in this, our Heaven protected land,
Where wealth & liberty walk hand in hand
Through all our cultivated fields or rocky coasts,
A numerous train of votaries pleasure boasts.
On all her varied gifts the Goddess flings,
And each new day a new enjoyment brings.[112]

But elsewhere the second line appears as 'Where Liberty & Wealth walk hand in hand', a form all the stronger for admitting something of Proudhon's, 'Liberty is the mother not the daughter of order.'[113] Peace is identified as a further ground-condition, and associated with good sense in the prologue to *The Wonder* where warring logomachies put it to flight, along with pleasure. These themes were to be, as we shall see, central preoccupations of *The Loiterer*, but the atmosphere of festive daredevilry at Steventon would have made their first airing all the more exhilarating.

Theatricals over that Christmas season were certainly of a kind to have given Fanny Price a tremor. Sets no less elaborate than those in *Mansfield Park* were ordered to give the barn the look of a theatre, and costumes were no doubt of a matching sophistication. The young Austens had every opportunity for losing themselves in their roles, and their situation was arguably as delicate as the Bertrams', for Eliza was present without her husband, and both Henry and James seem to have been hell-bent on flirting with her. Even a didactic writer as well-disposed to amateur theatricals as Madame de Genlis (much quoted in this period by the Austens) drew the line at Restoration comedy, and would certainly have ruled out *The Chances*. Nor would it have been easy to find a play more richly inscribed with Enlightenment precepts than Susanna Centlivre's *The Wonder*, a comedy as tough-minded as any by Wycherley or Etherege, but undertaken from a standpoint that was both Whig and feminist.

True to the 'barbarous Times' of the epilogue, *The Wonder* (1714) is set in a notionally sixteenth-century Lisbon, though its real setting is the transition between the feudal and modern worlds. Don Lopez, a nobleman of ancient lineage, arranges dynastic matches for his son and daughter; but both Felix and Isabella show themselves determined to control their own lives. Conventionally enough, free choice in courtship supplies the crux of the comic plot, but this choice becomes symbolic of the openness that makes for a desirable society – a truly wonder-working ploy, for what can offer a more glowing advertisement for human rights than a love match? 'Every

---

[112] HRO version; second the Chawton text.
[113] Quoted by Norman P. Barry in *On Classical Liberalism and Libertarianism* (New York, 1987), p. 14.

Man's Happiness consists in chusing for himself', Felix declares after he and his lover Violante have been reconciled, and the principle is politicized by the play's internationalism which telescopes a stadial history, Britain being credited with rather more freedom than she could boast even after 1688.[114] 'Liberty is the Idol of the *English*, under whose Banner all the Nation Lists', remarks an enlightened Portuguese merchant, frustrated in love by the odium attaching in his society to trade.[115] But no index is more sensitive to social freedom than the life of women. Faced with imprisonment, suicide, or the veil after refusing her father's favoured suitor, Isabella reflects on how different her lot is from that of her English maid:

> The Custom of our Country inslaves us from our very Cradles, first to our Parents, next to our Husbands; and when Heaven is so kind to rid us of both these, our Brothers still usurp Authority.[116]

It is while escaping from parental tyranny that Isabella is rescued by the colourful hero, Colonel Britton, a randy Scot (sex-starved by the kirk) who treats her with the decency due to his name, delivering her to the protection of Violante. Isabella's fear of betrayal by her brother Felix gives rise to the resulting plot. Violante has to keep Isabella's presence a secret from Felix, her own lover, knowing that he will believe it his duty to report it to his father; and she has also, for the sake of her own affair, to camouflage the presence of the Colonel, who hangs around for Isabella. There follow the usual narrow escapes and closet collisions so typical of Restoration comedy, but with one striking difference. The role of the stage-managing rake, who disposes his visitors behind assorted screens and improvises cover-stories until he emerges unscathed, falls to a woman. And what is more, Violante adds a new dimension of heroism to the panache of Wycherley's Horner, for she risks losing her own lover for the sake of standing up for her sex. All the secrets of the play are in her keeping, and the implications of this pointed inversion of gender, this restoration of secrecy to those whom it is was ordinarily denied, would not have been lost on the young author of 'The Mystery' whose idea it was to push secret-keeping on the stage as far as it could be taken.

No doubt in calling her play *The Wonder: A Woman Keeps a Secret*, Susanna Centlivre threw a sop to sneering male wits, but from the perspective of stage history, the title was, in another sense, not far from the truth. 'Secrecy denied' is taken up by James as a feature of sexual oppression

---

[114] Susanna Centlivre, *The Wonder: a Woman Keeps a Secret* (1736 edn), v. i, p. 77.
[115] Ibid., I. i, p. 2.   [116] Ibid., I. i, p. 8.

in his epilogue where he finds a memorable phrase to underline the part played by masculine writing in the creation of social roles that favour men:

> Such was poor woman's lot – whilst tyrant men
> At once possessors of the sword and pen
> All female claim, with stern pedantic pride,
> To prudence, truth & secrecy denied,
> Covered their tyranny with specious words
> And called themselves 'Creation's mighty Lords'.

These words ('Spoken by a Lady in the Character of Violante') seem to haunt the great scene in the rewritten ending to *Persuasion* where Anne argues that comparison between the sexes cannot be settled by an appeal to books, because 'men have had every advantage of us in telling their own story . . . the pen has been in their hands' (234).[117] There the idea of possessing the pen is further underlined, when Captain Wentworth audibly drops his ('his pen had fallen down . . . the pen had only fallen') in an effort to catch, or rather overhear, what Anne has to say about the constancy of women (233). Centlivre's liberally minded play was probably the first feminist work that Jane Austen encountered, and the impression it left – mediated by her brother James's acute commentary – seems to have been a lasting one. Wollstonecraft, whose presence in *Persuasion* is unmistakable, belongs to the same tradition, but came into Jane Austen's life later, first introduced perhaps by her reading of Robert Bage's 'liberal' novel *Hermsprong* (1796) which includes a substantial summary of the *Vindication*.[118]

Feminism is seen in *The Wonder* as conditional upon a secularized society where the operation of individual choice has broken down the constraints of feudalism. James attaches to the play a historical narrative that is part chronicle and part allegory, since liberty is bracketed with the present and embodied in the central figure of an expressive woman who epitomizes Enlightenment. That 'women hold a second place no more' is owing to the dispersal of a social ethos that enshrined only the manly:

> In vain the form where grace and ease combined
> In vain the bright eye spoke th' enlightened mind.

---

[117] This parallel has been noted independently by Paula Byrne in her excellent recent study, *Jane Austen and the Theatre* (2002), p. 11.

[118] Robert Bage, *Hermsprong; or, Man as He is Not* (1982 facs. edn, original pagination, II, 168–77). The novel uses 'liberal' in its modern political sense, see my '"Liberal" Earlier than in OED', *Notes and Queries*, 47 (2000), 218. Jane Austen's copy of the novel survives, see Gilson, *Bibliography*, pp. 437–8; and see p. 102 below.

Vain the sweet smiles which secret love reveal
Vain every charm, for there were none to feel.
From tender childhood trained to rough alarms,
Loving no music but the clang of arms;
Enthusiasts only in the listed field,
Our youth then knew to fight, but not to yield
Nor higher deemed of beauty's utmost power,
Than the light play thing of their idler hour.[119]

But the spread of 'learning's sacred light' is reversible, and in his pageant-like prologue, James parades Cromwellian England in the guise of a further dark ages, reserving for last an image of victimized womanhood:

Then came a set of men with formal faces,
Canting quotations wild, with strange grimaces,
To smirk then was a sign of reprobation,
To smile was sinful, but to laugh, damnation,
They could high treason in plum porridge spy
And smelled plain Popery in a Christmas pie,
For ten long years the nation groaned and sighed,
And the men canted while the women cried.[120]

With its shunning of theatre and Christmas festivity, the Commonwealth provided James with a perfect cultural *bête noire*, and in this respect, too, his outlook is true to the liberalism of the period. Adam Smith, for example, in his discussion of religious institutions in the *Wealth of Nations* (1776) enlarges on his assertion that 'science is the great antidote to the poison of enthusiasm and superstition' by dwelling on the salutary effects of the arts, particularly those of a festive character:

The state, by encouraging, that is by giving entire liberty to all those who for their own interest would attempt, without scandal or indecency, to amuse and divert the people by painting, poetry, musick, dancing; by all sorts of dramatic representations and exhibitions, would easily dissipate, in the greater part of them, that melancholy and gloomy humour which is almost always the nurse of popular superstition and enthusiasm.[121]

Such entertainments are the 'objects of dread and hatred' to those fanatics who recognize that gaiety and humour are inconsistent with 'that temper

---

[119] I have adopted the Chawton text for line 5 which seems stronger than the HRO version: 'Enthusiastically in the listed field'.

[120] Prologue to *The Wonder* (28 Dec. 1787).

[121] Adam Smith, *An Inquiry into the Nature and Causes of the Wealth of Nations*, ed. R. H. Campbell and A. S. Skinner (Oxford, 1976), v.i.g.15, 796. Hereafter *WN*.

of mind, which was fittest for their purpose, or which they could best work upon'.[122] Perhaps Smith is open here to the charge of calling for bread and circuses, but it is easy to underestimate the strength of enlightened reaction to the aggressive sectarianism of Puritan England, or its formative influence on the Age of Reason. Bigotry still spelt bloodshed, and a climate of scepticism had led to it being associated, too, with the evasion of the simple truths that really mattered. The last point is well made by Thomas Percival in a piece entitled 'The Bigot and Visionary' from the conduct-book that Jane so vividly remembered:

The speculative doctrines of religion, as they have no influence on the moral conduct of mankind, are comparatively of little importance. They cannot be understood by the generality even of Christians; and the wise, the learned, and the good have in all ages differed, and will ever continue to differ about them. An intemperate zeal therefore, for such points of faith, betrays a weak understanding and contracted heart: And that zeal may justly be deemed intemperate which exceeds the value of its object; and which abates our benevolence towards those who do not adopt the same opinions as ourselves . . . our Saviour describes himself as demanding of the trembling sinner, not of what church are you a member? or what creeds have you acknowledged? But have you fed the hungry? have you clothed the naked? have you visited the sick?[123]

A stress on the social, practical and moral aspects of religion entailed a soft-pedalling of doctrine, and this encouraged an easygoing ecumenicalism, reflected in the Austen household by the choice of a conduct-book written by a Unitarian.[124]

In an early *Loiterer* piece on the benefits of studying history, James ventured his own pronouncement on the sort of compromise necessary for a stable society. After warning against the dangers of absolute monarchy like any *philosophe*, he praises the constitution that wards off tyranny by guarding the representation of rival interests. Such security, however, has as much to do with a spirit of toleration and compromise as with the letter of law:

Thus each party, by mutually receding from the rigid inflexibility of their favourite opinions, and partially relinquishing their separate rights, prevent the collision of jarring principles, and secure the general happiness of the whole on a firm foundation.[125]

[122] Ibid., 797.   [123] Thomas Percival, *Tales*, pp. 117–19.

[124] Though the inscription of her name is not in her own hand, Jane Austen may also have owned *The Works of the Marchioness de Lambert* (1749); see Gilson, *Bibliography*, pp. 443–4. Anne Thérèse Lambert, a Catholic writer of enlightened views, was a champion of intellectual education for women.

[125] 'Use and Advantages of Studying History', *The Loiterer*, 7, 14 Mar. 1789, p. 8.

The essay is typical of the earlier issues of the periodical in its preservation of a copperplate propriety of tone. Later James was to develop a quasi-comical mode that enabled him to be more adventurous, without abandoning his air of open-mindedness. In irony, in particular, he found a useful two-edged weapon that allowed him to be satiric at the expense of more than one party, or to undercut what he expressed without quite withdrawing from it. Irony with its subversive mimicry was a means, too, to an adroit evacuation of received ideas. In this respect, *The Loiterer* can be seen as the precursor to Jane Austen who was to specialize in shot-silk mixtures of tone, and in elliptical utterances that often elude paraphrase. Storytelling, too, allowed for the play of conflicting perspectives; and in a piece on the 'Pleasures of a Complainer' James returned to the theme of doctrinal intransigence, tracing back the habitual, self-induced misery of a young man to the perverse mindset of his father, an implacable Non-Juror.[126] Roy Porter remarked that it was not so much Methodism as the Enlightenment that 'inoculated the English against the French, indeed against all subsequent revolutions', but the immunity can be traced back further.[127] It seems that the old fester of the Jacobite could still be used, at a pinch, as a serum against the Jacobin.

Idealism, and the distrust of it pulled against each other to weave the fabric of enlightenment thinking during the second part of the eighteenth century, and in England the thread of distrust was of a particularly strong ply. In a fascinating account of the Erastian tendencies of Anglicanism through this period, Pocock proposes a reason for this:

both Anglican reaction and English Enlightenment displayed a revulsion against 'enthusiasm', in the precise sense of that term, more vivid in its historical memories than is found in the other Enlightenments which shared it.[128]

Civil war had exposed a gaping faultline in English society, and the fear of it gave force to a range of remedial imperatives. Imposing edifices of *a priori* construction were to be abandoned for something simpler and closer to the ground, and to the liberal historian there fell the critical task of charting the danger zone. David Hume began the writing of his great history with the accession of the Stuarts in order to straighten out, from the start, the 'misrepresentations of faction'.[129] It is as revealing, perhaps, of Jane

---

[126] *The Loiterer*, 31, 29 Aug. 1789.
[127] Roy Porter, *Enlightenment: Britain and the Creation of the Modern World* (2000), p. 483.
[128] J. G. A. Pocock, *Barbarism and Religion* (Cambridge, 1999), I, 296.
[129] See David Hume, 'My Own Life', included in *The History of England* (Indianapolis, 1983 edn), I, xi, and xxx.

Austen's own 'History of England' that it ends with the Civil War, for this comic send-up of the old-fashioned dogmatic chronicle was not equipped to enter waters as deep as those that transformed the state under 'the Gang' (148).

James Austen's hatred of 'canting' and of sanctimony naturally disposed him towards the literature that developed at the Restoration in reaction to the interregnum and its repressive creeds. Virtually all the plays put on at Steventon have their roots in Restoration comedy, and if James is to be credited with *The School for Jealousy* and *The Travelled Man*, 'those celebrated Comedies' applauded by his sister, he himself chose to write in that vein, for the titles unmistakably echo Sheridan and Goldsmith.[130] The Restoration saw the foundation of the Royal Society, and the forging of scientific method by men who in Hume's words 'trod, with cautious, and therefore the more secure steps, the only road, which leads to true philosophy'.[131] Though the comedy of this age was to receive a mixed press from the Enlightenment, it did convey a bold materialism that was in keeping with it. Pecking orders cutting across social hierarchy, money as a determinant of courtship and the married life, perplexities and perversities of group membership – all were exposed with a cheerful heartlessness. All the more refreshing after the romantic comedies of the late Jacobean period was the new explicitness about sex.

Even before entering her teens Jane Austen was quite used to seeing women on the stage make a clean breast of their desires. In *The Wonder* Isabella chooses her male at first sight, and her friend Violante on hearing that she wishes to marry him offers to arrange the rest. In *The Chances*, Don Juan's advances are cut short by Constance who tells him 'I have at this present very great need of you', and is told, on refusing to lift her veil, 'If thou art young, it's no great matter what thy face is.' Later the rake exclaims of another character named Constance, in a passage that calls for stage business, 'What points she at? My legs, I warrant; or / My well-knit body. Sit fast, Don Frederick.'[132] Not to be outdone, young Jane also pushes at the limits of candour, and turns the polite stereotypes of courtship inside out, making a speciality in the juvenilia of flinty, narcissistic, affectless

---

[130] See *Minor Works*, p. 49, and see *Catharine and Other Writings*, ed. Margaret Anne Doody and Douglas Murray (Oxford, 1993), for its note, p. 305. Goldsmith's *Good-Natur'd Man* (1768) was a satire on the ideal of universal benevolence.

[131] Hume, *The History of England*, VI, 541.

[132] George Villiers, Duke of Buckingham, *The Chances; A Comedy with Alterations*, altered by David Garrick (1773), IV. ii, p. 51; and I. iii, p. 26. The original text was by John Fletcher, see n. 209 below.

men, and of women half-crazed with desire. In 'Jack and Alice', a spoof on Richardson's supposedly irresistible Sir Charles Grandison, poor Alice is driven to drink in her desperation, a condition which leaves her still plainer and all the more inflamed. Lucy, the Welsh lover, adopts the course of accosting Charles Adams by letter, and lets it be known after her third that she is taking 'Silence for Consent', but is stopped on her approach when caught by the leg in 'one of the steel traps so common in gentlemen's grounds' (22).[133]

The Steventon comedies would also have initiated Jane into the practice of stating the exact financial value, per annum, of competing suitors. From *The Wonder* she may have remembered that the rich 'fool' to whom Isabella is to be married is thought no fool because of his income of 20,000 crowns: £12,000 does not save Mr Rushworth, in *Mansfield Park*, from being thought stupid (40).[134] Though Jane Austen's attitudes certainly did change with the years, there is no hint of her looking back at the 'gambols' in the vicarage barn with either remorse or regret. Shortly after finishing *Mansfield Park*, she took two nieces, aged twelve and thirteen, to an evening performance that included a version of Shadwell's *Don Juan* 'whom we left in Hell at 1/2 past 11'. She was pleased with the response of the girls who 'were very much delighted' especially by Don Juan – '& I must say that I have seen nobody on the stage who has been a more interesting Character than that compound of Cruelty & Lust'.[135]

No classical maxim was more popular among enlightenment writers than Horace's *sapere aude* – dare to know, but if the quest for knowledge was regarded as almost sacramental, knowledge itself might turn out to be a poisoned chalice. In his early *Loiterer* essay on history, James Austen stumbled on a paradox that would return to haunt his later writing.[136] If consciousness of the past was the mark of 'an enlightened age and a polished nation', it had inevitably to include 'an enumeration of the madness, folly, and crimes of mankind'.[137] What if history should repeat the worst as well as the best, and conscious imitation turn out to be a force for the bad,

---

[133] Lucy is clearly intended as a send-up of Richardson's Clementina della Porretta. For a valuable gloss on such traps see *Catharine and Other Writings*, pp. 294–5.

[134] *The Wonder*, I. i, p. 3.   [135] To Cassandra, 15–16 Sept. 1813, *Letters*, p. 221.

[136] See the discussion on pp. 63–7 below of Adam Ferguson's influence on later essays in *The Loiterer*. In a digression on monasteries in his wartime poem 'Selbourne Hanger' (1812), James praises quietism and infers from feudal schism a state of 'endless' conflict from which 'Some gentle minds, unfit to mix / In the World's hustling politics / Or join in War's destructive rage' are lucky to be able to retreat.

[137] *The Loiterer*, 7, 14 Mar. 1789, p. 4.

corrupting – as it evidently could – even a figure as exemplary as Frederick the Great?

> Thus an heroic frenzy seems to have descended (in a kind of entail) from Achilles to Alexander, from Alexander to Lewis the Fourteenth, and from Lewis to the late King of Prussia; each of whom was particularly careful to imitate the other, in the very worst parts of his character.[138]

For a moment James seems poised on the brink of a Faustian reading of personal and imperial ambitions, but the dark thought is confined to a marginal eddy, and he goes on to expound the grand narrative of liberal historiography which supplies an undertow to the first volume of his periodical. It is worth pausing to piece together this doctrine, which was undoubtedly the medium of Jane Austen's early mental growth, though one against which she would react to some significant degree later.

In the most confident of his expositions, James places his own nation and era at the most advanced point of a historical progress which is seen as potentially universal, stadial in being tied to changing economic conditions, and dependent on the rise of learning or 'science' – a word which though broad in denotation carries strongly empirical overtones. The true historian is an 'accurate investigator of human nature', but what is on offer is as gratifying as any myth, and cause for the patriotic reader to gloat:

> chiefly will he be pleased to observe the various and progressive steps, by which science has gained her present exalted height, and mark the rapidity with which she is hourly extending the influence of her reign, and the happiness of mankind, over enlightening savages, and regions just emerged from barbarity. He will view her with pleasure, rising after a long night of Gothic darkness, and dispersing by degrees the clouds of ignorance, and the mists of superstition; and he will boast, with a pardonable partiality, that if she has chosen Europe for her temple, she has also selected England for her shrine.[139]

The coming global dawn finds its reverse image in the dark ages that spread over Europe 'from the tenth to the fifteenth century', a period characterized politically by 'feudal chieftains', and culturally by ignorance, or by the 'corruption' of historical studies at the hands of monks. Crucial to England's recovery from its relatively recent reversion to civil anarchy is the Constitution (implicitly the Revolution Settlement of 1689) which is viewed as a guarantee against despotism. James was to return to this Whiggish theme in a poem written at the end of his life, where he praises

---

[138] Ibid., pp. 5–6.   [139] Ibid., pp. 10–11.

The well enlightened Spirit of our Sires
Who framed Britannia's fair impartial laws.
    Who reads the page of Clarendon or Hume
And is not thankful that he lives in days
When Britain's well praised constitution gives
Security to all?[140]

But *The Loiterer* leans heavily, too, on the premiss, deriving from the Scottish Enlightenment, that the establishment of a commercial or manufacturing economy – one of those 'progressive steps' mentioned by James – has an important bearing not only on prosperity but on social freedom also. The belief that production and exchange stimulate individualism, and that human rights were first articulated in town guilds and charters is frequently implicit in *The Loiterer*. It lurks behind phrases such as 'the BENEVOLENCE of commerce', and sustains the ranking of European nations in terms that make cultural and economic development pointedly coincide.[141] In a piece entitled 'Contempt of Trade absurd, and illiberal', commerce is identified as 'our distinguishing Characteristic, a Characteristic that has raised us to an enviable height of Power, that has made us the most flourishing People, of the most flourishing Quarter of the Globe'.[142] But in the same piece a discord is struck when the writer urges that the time is ripe to put an end to one thriving branch of trade:

I cannot neglect this opportunity, the only one which may perhaps offer, of congratulating my Countrymen on the probable approach of that period, when the only blot that disgraces the annals of Trade shall at length be erased . . . when the Rights of Humanity rise superior to the Dictates of Interest; when Parties, in other respects the most opposite, become the joint Advocates of Misery; when the Liberty we ourselves feel shall be diffused to the most remote Parts of the World, and the Religion which we ourselves enjoy, shall spread its refining Influence over Nations at present immers'd in Barbarity.[143]

Though this clarion call might have put devout readers in mind of the Bible on the equality of freeman, bondsman and slave, the Loiterer's plea for the abolition of slavery is made through the language of human rights and free exchange, and would not have seemed at all out of place, in its day, for coming at the close of a eulogy to commerce. Adam Smith had contributed an armoury of strong economic arguments to the cause, and

---

[140] 'The Œconomy of Rural Life'. One result of the legislation of 1689 was to put the army at the command of Parliament and to disallow standing armies.
[141] The phrase is from *The Loiterer*, 24, 11 July 1789, p. 11; but for the theme elsewhere, see particularly nos. 10, 47, and 48.
[142] *The Loiterer*, 24, p. 7.   [143] Ibid., p. 11.

there is a veiled reference, earlier in the essay, to Pitt's reliance on his counsel. In fact, the united forces of the Tory and Whig leadership had failed in 1788 to raise a majority in favour of abolition from the House. But debate had reopened after Clarkson's report to the Privy Council and Wilberforce's stirring parliamentary speech of 12 May 1789, and in the last issue of that June, James had already drawn attention to the promising new Bill.[144]

The number that defends commerce and calls for universal emancipation came out on 11 July, three days before the storming of the Bastille, and could be said to represent the height of the Loiterer's confidence in progress and the fulfilment of the 'Rights of Humans' – a phrase that would have pleased Mary Wollstonecraft. Yet there is no obvious abatement of euphoric tone on political matters until the 'Agrestis' essay and the 'Memoirs of a Highland Chieftain' which follow, respectively, on the first efflux of French nobles and the confiscation of Church property, later in the year. A warning is sounded in these pieces (the second of which is richly complex) on the dangers of violently disrupting the social fabric, but a reformist message emerges all the same. In her study of Jane's Christian upbringing, Irene Collins speculates that the Austen family probably 'joined the majority of England's literate population in approving France's attempt to secure greater freedom and justice'.[145] This is a refreshing rejoinder to the hindsight that throws the entire family into a rabidly Anti-Jacobin posture from the first, sometimes on the sole grounds that Eliza de Feuillide's husband was guillotined in the last stages of the Terror. While there is every reason to believe that the family became disillusioned and disgusted by the course of events across the channel, there is ample evidence also of their distaste for the *ancien régime*. What is wrong with the Anti-Jacobin account of Jane Austen is that it does both too little and too much. It foreshortens the rapidly changing politics of the period, concealing the fact that virtually all writers of the late nineties were opposed to Jacobinism albeit in significantly differing ways, and puts out of sight the larger structure of belief to which the younger generation of Austens adhered. What can be assembled of their feelings towards France before reports of massacre and of the Terror became legion, chimes in well with the views of other enlightened observers.

Two Austen brothers took a tour through France shortly before the Revolution – Edward and James; two Austen brothers wrote short European

---

[144] See Hugh Thomas, *The Slave Trade* (1997), pp. 505, 511–12. James makes honourable mention of the 'Supporters of the Bill for the Abolition of the Slave Trade' in the course of a piece on advertisements a fortnight before, see *The Loiterer*, 22, 27 June 1789, p. 9.

[145] Collins, *Parson's Daughter*, p. 104.

travelogues – James and Henry.[146] Henry's tour is no less interesting for never having taken place, since its literary affinities are all the more transparent. Though Henry alludes to *A Sentimental Journey* in his two travel pieces, his real model is its jaundiced anti-type, Smollett's *Travels*: 'Smelfungus' was Sterne's satiric stand-in for Smollett, along with Samuel Sharp, his brother in grime.[147] In defiance of romantic attitudinizing, Henry follows Smollett in underlining the superiority of the more commercial and Protestant of European nations over their backward Catholic neighbours. Of Italy, he declares that 'the whole nation exhibited one melancholy proof of that intimate connection which subsists between political and mental vigour', adding Smelfungianly, 'If I entered [the country] with inconsiderate rapture, I left it with settled contempt.'[148] His anatomy of Germany is the classical liberal one of the period;[149] there he sees

Peasants oppressed by partial taxes, and Society contracted by the Pride of Individuals, or countroled by the suspicion of a Despot. The policy of Government was inimical alike to the affluence, the freedom and the security of the subject. – A number of petty Principalities checked each others growth, and blasted the general prosperity.[150]

Whether Smollett's Smelfungianism was integral to his overall outlook (as fungus is to mycelium) is open to doubt, but it became the vogue, and in other respects his perceptions were as influential as they were acute. Many writers hinted at future upheavals in France, but few were more deft in exposing the rift between the apparatus of an absolutist state and a rapidly growing secularism:

In proportion to the progress of reason and philosophy, which have made great advances in this kingdom, superstition loses ground; antient prejudices give way; a spirit of freedom takes the ascendant. All the learned laity of France detest the hierarchy as a plan of despotism, founded on imposture and usurpation.[151]

The state edifice that he repeatedly singles out for censure is taxation, and particularly the organization known as the *fermiers généraux*, a privileged

---

[146] Henry in two numbers of *The Loiterer* (47, 48), and James in his prologue to *Tom Thumb*. Henry's plan to visit Nerac with Eliza fell through in 1788. Edward kept a journal of the Swiss part of the Grand Tour he took in 1786, which Jon Spence comments on appreciatively in *Becoming Jane Austen* (2003), pp. 35–6.

[147] Sharp was read by both Austen sisters, see below p. 108.

[148] *The Loiterer*, 48, 26 Dec. 1789, pp. 4–5.

[149] Compare the commentary on Germany in Ann Radcliffe's *A Journey made in the Summer of 1794* (1795), pp. 85–153, especially pp. 151–2; and for some discussion of this travelogue, see below p. 113.

[150] *The Loiterer*, 48, 26 Dec. 1789, p. 5.

[151] See Tobias Smollett, *Travels through France and Italy*, ed. Frank Felsenstein (Oxford, 1981), p. 299.

and autonomous élite of tax collectors who engrossed, he claims, one third of all the revenues they 'farmed'. The scrapping of this institution which is envisaged as a malignancy in the tissue of government should be 'the first act of reformation'.[152]

James opens the spirited prologue-cum-travelogue which he wrote for *Tom Thumb* with his usual Enlightenment motif, and plays off one nation against the other in setting the European scene:

> In every clime where science spreads her reign
> In ever lively France, or sluggish Spain,
> Midst generous Britains, or ungenerous Dutch,
> Midst those who save too little or too much . . .[153]

What unites these enlightened climes is the assumption that 'Pleasure, of all exists the common aim', a phrase part hedonist part utilitarian, but when James proceeds to sketch the sporting activities of each nation in turn, the merrymaking of the French turns into a frenzied tarantella:

> Through all the wide extent of laughing France,
> How madly gay the many Beggars dance!
> Thrice happy race! your mirth's exhaustless store
> Much I admire, but praise your patience more
> Who, while each various ill your country threats,
> Of private poverty & public debts,
> Whilst Britain's fleet o'erhangs your humbler shore,
> Whilst Farmers General torment you more
> Wisely in scenes of mirth your hours employ
> Practice new steps, & halloo Vive le Roi!
> Ne'er can your woes be of resource bereft
> Whilst you have one yard of catgut left.

His sketch abounds in suggestive detail,[154] but the special indictment reserved for the Farmers-General clearly spells out the liberal tendency of the whole critique, for here was an institution that represented the *ancien régime* not simply at its most brutal but at its most antiquated. Part of

---

[152] Ibid., pp. 36–7, 296–9, 299.

[153] 'Prologue to the Tragedy of Tom Thumb, acted to a small circle of friends and spoken by the Author.'

[154] By juxtaposing public debt and a stand-off at sea, James points to the huge expansion of the French navy in the eighties, itself a major cause of the financial crisis that was to lead to the calling of the Estates-General. He praises the resilience of a poverty-stricken peasantry, but seems to mock the crowds who protested against programmes for deregulation in the name of loyalty to the old order ('halloo Vive le Roi!'). See 'Oceans of Debt' in ch. 2 of Simon Schama, *Citizens: A Chronicle of the French Revolution* (1989), and also pp. 61, 80, 84–5, 124, 324. For Adam Smith's awareness of these loyalist attitudes, see Ian Simpson Ross, *The Life of Adam Smith* (Oxford, 1995), p. 387.

the farmers' domain was the notorious salt tax which not only fixed prices (both for producer and consumer) but also fixed, by law, a minimum annual amount each household had to buy. Not surprisingly, the Farmers-General had come in for particular attention in Adam Smith's *Wealth of Nations*, where they elicit the acid remark, 'Those who consider the blood of the people as nothing in comparison with the revenue of the prince, may perhaps approve of this method of levying taxes.'[155] Smith partly ascribed the relative prosperity of the British economy to its removal of internal customs barriers, and in Paris his suggestions for tax reforms (which included the return of 'the exorbitant profits of the farmers general' to the state)[156] were lost neither on progressively minded ministers like Turgot or, later, on constitutionalists like Sieyès. After serving as a focus for revolutionary rhetoric for decades, the Farmers-General passed eventually into history, their great customs wall in Paris torn down in the same month as the storming of the Bastille, and their headquarters turned into a prison. Thomas Paine – before he himself joined the ranks of the imprisoned – found an effective way of worsting Burke when, aligning himself with Adam Smith on this issue, he pointed out that a championship of seigneurial traditions was inconsistent with respect for even the most elementary of freedoms.[157]

However much their attitude towards the Revolution in France altered with the years, the Austens seem never to have held the *ancien régime* in any kind of retrospective affection. Jane Austen changed the title of one of her songs, originally called 'The Lamentation of Queen Marie-Antoinette on the Morning of her Execution', to 'Queen Mary's Lamentation', and went on playing the 'Marseillaise'.[158] To her father, in 1798, she read Francis Lathom's *The Midnight Bell*, a novel that dwells on the oppression of pre-revolutionary France as epitomized by life in the Bastille.[159] This well-worn topic recurs in *The Loiterer*, and it is in one of the last numbers that the reader is asked to picture the joy of a man 'lately escaped from the horrors' of the old feudal pile.[160] A similar liberation (touched with some mischief) inspires the closing sentence to the piece from *Volume the First* that Jane Austen entitled 'Henry and Eliza'. With that pairing of names in view, no one in her circle could have failed to relate her sprightly heroine to Eliza de Feuillide. Sure enough, it is to France that Eliza flies – after stealing £50 from the couple who adopt her as a haystack-orphan, and

[155] *WN*, v.ii.k.75, 904; and see v.ii.k.73–8.   [156] Ibid., pp. 904–5.
[157] Thomas Paine, *Rights of Man, Common Sense, and Other Political Writings*, ed. Mark Philp (Oxford, 1995), p. 126.
[158] See Honan, *Her Life*, p. 98.   [159] To Cassandra, 24 Oct. 1798, *Letters*, p. 15.
[160] *The Loiterer*, 54, 6 Feb. 1790, p. 6.

after making off, too, with the fiancé intended for her daughter by the Duchess who takes their place. Her story comes to its end when she finds a way of avenging her seigneurial-like imprisonment on a scale worthy of her formidable patroness: 'she raised an Army, with which she entirely demolished the Dutchess's Newgate, snug as it was, and by that act, gained the Blessings of thousands, & the Applause of her own Heart' (39). 'Snug' fits the opportunism of the Eliza character well, and restores a sense of proportion to the habitual gothicizing of confinement, reflecting too, as it happens, the rather tame latter-day history of the Bastille. But the opening of the story deviates from expectation in a way that touches a raw nerve, for it portrays oppression as a deeply ingrained, everyday occurrence, jolting the reader into recognition with a joke. Where readers of *Udolpho* would unblinkingly absorb a lesson in serene patronage from St Aubert who doles out the weekly wage with a handshake, 'listening patiently to the complaints of some, redressing the grievances of others, and softening the discontents of all, by the look of sympathy and the smile of benevolence',[161] truculent Jane refuses to play along with this type of cliché:

Sir George and Lady Harcourt were superintending the Labours of their Hay-makers, rewarding the industry of some by smiles of approbation, & punishing the idleness of others, by a cudgel . . . (33)

It is plain that Austen, from the very start of her career, was neither by nature or inclination at all disposed to trim herself into a partisan figure. The Enlightenment scene so deftly evoked by James in the Steventon barn was to shift, in the course of her adolescence, to the world stage, and to be put to the test in a theatre that seemed, in the throes of revolutionary change, to have cut loose of all scripts and conventions. Not for this reason alone would Jane's examination of received ideas lead her in the direction of new kinds of writing.

UNHEROIC SENTIMENTS

The Anti-Jacobin reading of Jane Austen begins in earnest with 'Love and Freindship', the hilarious satire on the novel of sensibility that was finished by 13 June 1790, not long after the expiry of *The Loiterer*. Marilyn Butler takes this piece to be the opening gambit in Austen's concerted defence against revolutionary ideologies, 'the first chapter of a consistent story' which unfolds two career-sustaining themes: first, that the

---

[161] Ann Radcliffe, *The Mysteries of Udolpho* (1794), ed. Frederick Garber (Oxford, 1991), p. 15.

'sentimental system' is selfish, and second, that 'realization of the self' is destructive and delusory.[162] Austen's dedication of her piece to Eliza de Feuillide has given a useful grappling-hook to other critics bent on providing political interpretations of a related kind. Eliza's Count was guillotined, however, only in 1794, and may well earlier have shared the anti-despotic fervour of the Eliza of *Volume the First*.[163] His massive project for draining the Marais belongs to the modernizing face of the *ancien régime*, and has precedents among reforming spirits like the famous Simon Linguet who, in addition to his hair-raising *Memoirs of the Bastille* (favourably noticed in *The Loiterer*),[164] had published plans in 1764 for cutting a canal through Picardy and dredging the entire Somme.[165] The affected but tough heroine of 'Love and Freindship' bears some resemblance to the Eliza of 'Henry and Eliza', and the dedication to Madame La Comtesse De Feuillide is far from a seal of reactionary intent.[166]

'Love and Freindship' not only pre-dates that determined undermining of sensibility that became a stock-in-trade of Anti-Jacobin satire later in the nineties, but has other origins and breathes an altogether different air. Claudia Johnson is surely right to argue that far from indicting fellow-feeling and evincing a distrust of emotion, Austen's brilliant squib is concerned primarily with literary parody, with exploding stereotypes and conventions that had yet to become 'conspicuously freighted with political urgency'.[167] Freighted they nonetheless were, and much of the misreading of Jane Austen's satire of sensibility – right from these beginnings in 'Love and Freindship' through to *Sense and Sensibility* – turns on a misconstruction of intellectual history in the period. Many Austen critics have worked on the premiss that the Enlightenment effectively ran out in England before the mid-century, the baton then passing to the continent and chiefly to the *philosophes*.[168] Sensibility, on this argument, is associated with belief in an innate moral sense, and the satire of sensibility is assigned to an orthodox Christian assault upon natural benevolence and other Pelagian

---

[162] Butler, *War of Ideas*, pp. 169–70.

[163] Claire Tomalin has suggested that Eliza's acquaintance with the Comte d'Antraigues may go back to pre-revolutionary days, for like de Feuillide he 'was a Gascon, and a favourite young officer at Versailles' (*A Life*, p. 224). This would be a revealing connection, for the Count was a famous disciple of Rousseau, who made himself deeply unpopular among fellow nobles in the National Assembly by upholding the principle that the state exists for the people. For a discussion of his politics, see Alfred Cobban, *Rousseau and the Modern State* (1964), pp. 123–5, 172–7.

[164] *The Loiterer*, 21, 20 June 1789, p. 12.

[165] For an account of de Feuillide's draining of the Marais, see Tomalin, *A Life*, pp. 50–2; and for Linguet see Schama, *Citizens*, p. 196.

[166] De Feuillide's title was in fact self-conferred.   [167] Claudia L. Johnson, *Women*, pp. 29–31.

[168] See the remarks on D. D. Devlin above, p. 7.

tendencies included in the legacy of Deism. This, however, is to ignore the fact that writers like David Hume, Adam Smith, and Adam Ferguson were tougher-minded than their antecedents, and that they, too, reacted against the intuitive morality of the Shaftesbury school, playing off utility against intentionality, and insisting, above all, on the limitations of human nature. Hobbes and Mandeville, though spurned by Rousseau and his followers, were an important presence in this latter-day phase of the British Enlightenment, which was, in effect, an inspired synthesis of the old empirically derived philosophies of self-interest with the social ethics of sympathy that succeeded them. It was chiefly under the influence of this powerful summation that the creed of sensibility was reappraised in the last decades of the century. In any case, the satire of sensibility in this period needs to be read against a more inclusive aim, the debunking, from the same quarters, of that form of moral heroism known as 'enthusiasm'. What underlay this critique was precisely the suspicion of overstrained behaviour so central to the ethics of Hume. Not only was ordinariness to be taken as a necessary premiss in any realistic estimate of human affairs, but the generating principle of social virtue – the innate endowment of sympathy – owed its strength to the very fact that it was ordinary.

At the start of his *Treatise*, Hume pictures himself as a 'leaking weather-beaten vessel' which, having only just escaped shipwreck in a small firth, is about to make for the open sea. This sense of frailty follows on his jettisoning of rationalism as a guide to moral precepts – his refusal to follow Locke in believing that clear-cut ethical rules can be deduced *a priori*. But the real source of his diffidence lies in the conviction that human conduct is initiated by feelings – by passions which are self-centred even if at times sympathetic, which never add up to a guarantee of beneficence, and are complexly shaped by 'natural beliefs'. Because feelings do not provide a reliable base for moral action (so far from being guided by an intuitive moral sense, we might satisfy an itch rather than save the world),[169] the natural expressions of social responsibility which flow from fellow-feeling have to be supplemented by 'artificial virtues', a body of codes and practices that any society receives as a legacy and renews creatively. Though the moral subject learns to apply reason in an attempt to compensate for instinctive self-bias – much as a knowledge of distance goes into our reading of visual data – a respect for external law remains imperative.[170] A spontaneous

---

169 *THN*, II.iii.iii, 416.
170 Ibid., III.iii.i, 580–4; and *EPM*, 5.41, 115. The perspectival metaphor was later taken up by Adam Smith, see *TMS*, III.3.3–4, 135–7.

expression of outgoing feeling, combined with a readiness to control the *selfishness* 'inherent in our frame and constitution',[171] holds out the best prospect for a moral being. And it is the vision of a happy balance struck between these two propensities – the one natural and the other acquired – that sustains Hume's seminal essay 'Of Superstition and Enthusiasm' which opens with the maxim, 'the corruption of the best things produces the worst', a maxim given proof in this instance 'by the pernicious effects of *superstition* and *enthusiasm*, the corruptions of true religion'.[172]

Enthusiasm and superstition, those excessive forms of self-reliance and self-oblation, are associated by Hume with the Civil War and particularly with the turbulent political schisms that were its cause and aftermath. Such fanaticism, or 'false religion',[173] has its psychological origin in acts of imagination untempered by scepticism. In the essay 'Of the Dignity or Meanness of Human Nature', Hume counters the view that virtue is a disguised form of egotism, arguing that belief in human grandeur or abjection is allied to the adoption of perspective, and that these perspectives can become habitual. So Superstition which leads to elaborate theological systems (such as Scholasticism) is rooted in the attempt to propitiate an external order that inspires awe. It has its emotional matrix in 'fear, sorrow, and a depression of spirits', and expresses itself in the worship of established forms. Enthusiasm, on the other hand, stems from a mood of self-confidence, and in its milder reaches flowers into a benign spirit of independence that makes for freedom and healthy social renewal. Taken to an extreme, however, it is uniquely antisocial in its effects, for the fanatic of this brand 'bestows on his own person a sacred character' together with a proportionate 'contempt for the common rules of reason, morality, and prudence'.[174]

If enthusiasm of this unbounded kind is responsible for the 'most cruel disorders in human society',[175] there is the comfort, at least, that it tends to be fitful and short, not simply because it encourages a careless disregard for the institutions necessary for preserving it, but because it goes against the grain of natural inclination. Hume's point here, enlarged on in the *Dialogues*, is that 'nature is always too strong for principle', and that any attempt to override the limitations of human nature will lead in the long run to hypocrisy (the occupational hazard of priestly castes), and produce results that are likely to be counteractive.[176] Attention riveted upon

---

[171] *THN*, III, iii.i, 583.
[172] David Hume, *Essays Moral, Political, and Literary*, ed. T. H. Green and T. H. Grose (1898), I, 144.
[173] Ibid., I, 145.   [174] Ibid., I, 146, 148–9.   [175] Ibid., I, 149.
[176] See David Hume, *An Enquiry Concerning Human Understanding*, ed. Tom L. Beauchamp (Oxford, 1999), XII. ii, p. 207.

eternal salvation, for example, may well 'beget a narrow, contracted selfish-ness'.[177] Hume finds a vivid analogy to illustrate his contention that 'the smallest grain of natural honesty and benevolence' has a stronger effect on human conduct than the 'most pompous views suggested by theo-logical theories and systems': man's natural inclinations may be slight but they operate continuously just as 'the smallest gravity will, in the end, prevail above a great impulse; because no strikes or blows can be repeated with such constancy as attraction and gravitation'.[178] And what holds true of religious fervour applies also, in Hume's view, to other forms of self-abnegating behaviour. In the *History of England*, for example, he repeatedly displays a prejudice against heroism, even when the motives of those concerned are not in doubt. Of the Earl of Strafford's magnificent letter to Charles I, pleading with him not to stop his execution, he notes that the Earl's 'noble effort of disinterestedness' turned out to be 'as per-nicious to his master, as it was immediately fatal to himself'.[179] Com-mon decencies, and small unremembered acts count for more in Hume's scheme of things than large-mannered gestures, or the contortions of enthusiasm.

Hume's case against heroic pretension is eloquently rehearsed by Edgar Wind in his pioneering study *Hume and the Heroic Portrait*, which explores the richly significant background to the contemporary quarrel between the upholders of the grand style and of naturalism in the pictorial arts, and to the rivalry between Reynolds and Gainsborough in particular. Wind's argument, in sum, is that Hume was an important presence in the reaction against a stilted academicism that revelled in the elevating devices of clas-sical allusion, figural transposition, and other kinds of 'literary' metaphor. Wind points out, indeed, that Hume is to be glimpsed skulking among the nasty allegorical figures in the portrait of his arch-opponent James Beattie that Reynolds submitted to the Academy under the title *The Triumph of Truth*.[180] His thesis is of course replete with implication for other kinds of representation during this period, including the novel, but it is worth notice in passing that all the surviving indications of Jane Austen's taste in the visual arts place her firmly on the side of the naturalists. That she failed to find a convincing Elizabeth Bennet at the Reynolds exhibition which she attended in 1813 has often been mentioned, but the interesting thing about her comment is that it was made before she ever went:

177 *Hume's Dialogues*, p. 275.   178 Ibid., p. 273.
179 Hume, *The History of England*, V, 324.
180 Edgar Wind, *Hume and the Heroic Portrait: Studies in Eighteenth-Century Imagery*, ed. Jaynie Anderson (1986), pp. 28–31.

perhaps however, I may find her in the Great Exhibition which we shall go to, if we have time; – I have no chance of her in the collection of Sir Joshua Reynolds's Paintings which is now shewing in Pall Mall, & which we are also to visit.[181]

The painter she most warmly praised was Benjamin West, and his dispute with Reynolds over the propriety of using contemporary dress in history painting, sparked off by his 'Death of General Wolfe', was widely publicized. West, who was proud of his American roots, renowned for his democratic pronouncements, and fêted as an innovator on his visit to Paris in 1802, was hailed in England (none too accurately) as the painter who had discovered how 'to exhibit heroes in coats, breeches and cock'd hats'.[182] Jane Austen declared that his portrayal of Christ in the 'Rejection by the Elders' was the first that ever contented her.[183] And the painting provides a good illustration of what Wind describes as West's gift for transforming the tragic hero 'from an imaginary to a familiar figure',[184] for although historical costume is meticulously preserved, the figure of his unmuscular Christ is given universality – even domesticity – by the simple sheet that covers his nakedness, and the naturalness of his silent and gentle rapport with his followers is thrown into relief by the histrionic and elaborately costumed Caiaphas.

Jane Austen herself displays a love of ease and simple elegance in writing that gives her a conspicuous place among the proponents of the natural style. No other novelist of the period developed a language quite as free of ornament and overt metaphor as hers.[185] As a narrator she seems to have debarred on principle not only the biblical and classical allusions that were so much a staple of her peers, but all kinds of obtrusive rhetorical figure. Though her narration is more carefully cadenced and often more formal than her letters, it subscribes to the same ideal of directness that she pins down while scribbling to Cassandra: 'the true art of letter writing [is] to express on paper exactly what one would say to the same person by word of mouth'.[186] Her conscious avoidance of self-consciousness provides the

---

[181] To Cassandra, 24 May 1813, *Letters*, p. 212.

[182] John Galt quoted by Edgar Wind, *Hume and the Heroic Portrait*, p. 100.

[183] See To Martha Lloyd, 2 Sept. 1814, *Letters*, p. 273. Rather than selling this huge picture West exhibited it to the public at 125 Pall Mall, charging one shilling for admission; see Helmut von Erffa and Allen Staley, *The Paintings of Benjamin West* (1986), pp. 358–9. Reproduced in MacDonagh, *Real and Imagined Worlds*, see p. 6, and plate 6.

[184] Wind, *Hume and the Heroic Portrait*, p. 91.

[185] Maria Edgeworth agreed with this policy of plain speaking in principle, though not always in practice. In *Belinda* she dissects a flowery metaphor with the remark, 'the heart has nothing in common with a rosebud . . . we should reason ill, and conduct ourselves worse, if we were to trust implicitly to poetical analogies', p. 239.

[186] 3 Jan. 1801, *Letters*, p. 68.

material for a joke when responding to her niece's reported praise of her style:

I wish the knowledge of my being exposed to her discerning Criticism, may not hurt my stile, by inducing too great a solicitude. I begin already to weigh my words & sentences more than I did, & am looking about for a sentiment, an illustration or a metaphor in every corner of the room. Could my Ideas flow as fast as the rain in the Storecloset, it would be charming.[187]

By keeping her narrative voice relatively unadorned Austen throws the language of her characters into bolder relief, whether spoken, reported, or implied. Through their speech she gives at times a symbolic dimension to her scenes, as when, for example, Elizabeth Bennet improvises an analogy from her piano-playing for Darcy's benefit (175), or Maria Bertram pointedly inquires whether the smiling prospect before her at Sotherton is to be taken 'literally or figuratively' (99). A transparency of medium confers all the greater significance on what is *there*.

While this plainness of practice has frequently been pointed up by quotations from the letters that reveal a distaste for obtrusive diction (most famously for 'novel slang'), ostentation, and for studied and strained effects of all kinds,[188] there has been notably little speculation on what cultural premisses lie behind these counsels of restraint. The obvious point of departure for such an inquiry is the juvenilia, the 'pure, simple English' of which was noted by the writer of the *Memoir* who found such freedom from 'the over-ornamental style' a defining characteristic of their author.[189] But of value here also are two essays on language from *The Loiterer*, the last and more satiric of which Walton Litz once hailed for offering not only a compendium of the stylistic affectations burlesqued in the minor works, but a guide to the principles governing Austen's later writing.[190]

Both *Loiterer* essays uphold the virtues of directness, and take issue with what is perceived to be a fashionable regard for polish at the expense of substance. James, after outlining the periodical's original prospectus in its first number – as a review, interestingly, of 'the best modern Classics, both in History and Poetry', opens the second with a typically modernist appeal for simplicity of expression:

---

[187] To Cassandra, 24 Jan. 1809, *Letters*, p. 169.
[188] See, for example, To Cassandra, 30 Jan. 1809, and To Anna Austen, 28 Sept. 1814; *Letters*, pp. 172, 277.
[189] Austen-Leigh, *Memoir*, p. 44.
[190] A. Walton Litz, '*The Loiterer*: A Reflection of Jane Austen's Early Environment', *Review of English Studies*, 12 (1961), 260–1.

Language has been commonly defined by Grammarians to be the Art of expressing our Ideas. Nor was the definition a bad one, during those times when our rude ancestors were sufficiently uninformed in the *Ars Rhetorica*, to speak always what they really thought.[191]

Henry returned to this theme in the second last number, sending up, with his friend Benjamin Portal, the 'occult principles' of writing *à la mode*. These mock-rules include the incorporation of 'mythological allusions' (the more cliché-ridden the better), the favouring of words with Greek or Latin roots over their native equivalents, of euphony over sense, and the cultivation of 'swoln, and sublime' diction – more especially when the subject is slight. The general aim is a 'radiance of ornamental expression [that] diffuses itself over every void', and opacity is always in demand since 'to thicken the foliage' will conceal 'scarcity of fruit'.[192] A clue to the cultural direction from which the Loiterer's squib is fired comes with the aside: 'The Critical Essayist therefore I allow freely to quote Aristotle, Longinus, and the Halicarnassian, but positively forbid him to drop a syllable of Blair.'[193]

Hugh Blair, no less a member of the Scottish Enlightenment for being in orders, was a Moderater of the Kirk who as Professor of Rhetoric at Edinburgh approached his subject in a spirit of modern scientific inquiry, and defended, in the most sophisticated way, the tradition of plain expression that goes back to Thomas Sprat, historian of the Royal Society. A lifelong friend of David Hume and William Robertson, he also had the good fortune to be befriended by Samuel Johnson, and it is in the company of these three luminaries that his most celebrated work, *Lectures on Rhetoric* (said to have been inspired by some notes of Adam Smith's), is brought to the attention of Catherine Morland in *Northanger Abbey*.[194] It is clear, however, that Jane Austen was already familiar with the lectures when she wrote 'Love and Freindship', for one of its funniest scenes revolves around Blair's caveat against the opportunistic insertion of 'moral reflections' into tragedies. These, Blair contends, are likely to appear pedantic (especially when 'unseasonably crowded') unless they seem spontaneous; and, as an example of a well-managed reflection, he cites the soliloquy in which Shakespeare's Cardinal Wolsey reflects on his fall and 'bids a long farewell to his greatness'.[195] The Cardinal accordingly takes his place in Austen's burlesque

---

[191] *The Loiterer*, 1, 31 Jan. 1789, p. 7; and *The Loiterer*, 2, 7 Feb. 1789, p. 3.
[192] *The Loiterer*, 59, 13 Mar. 1790, pp. 4, 6.   [193] Ibid., p. 10.
[194] For Blair's debts to Smith, acknowledged and unacknowledged, see Ian Simpson Ross, *Adam Smith*, pp. 95–6; and see *Northanger Abbey*, pp. 108–9.
[195] 'On Tragedy', *Lectures on Rhetoric and Belles Lettres* (1806), III, 313–14.

of studied speech, when the melancholy reveries of her two heroines are broken by the crash of an overturned carriage:

We instantly quitted our seats & ran to the rescue of those who but a few moments before had been in so elevated a situation as a fashionably high Phaeton, but who were now laid low and sprawling in the Dust –. 'What an ample subject for reflection on the uncertain Enjoyments of this World, would not that Phaeton & the Life of Cardinal Wolsey afford a thinking Mind!' said I to Sophia as we were hastening to the field of Action. (99)

Laura's verbal jacking up of the phaeton ('in so elevated a situation as') sets the scene for bathos, but the diction, once Laura's voice subsides, is otherwise scrupulously neutral and plain. There were evidently spectacular comic dividends to be had from following Blair's tip of avoiding at all costs 'the affected and frivolous use of ornament'.[196]

To say that 'Love and Freindship' is principally a work of literary burlesque, concerned with the deflation of high-flown and self-aggrandizing language, is not to say, of course, that it is without extra-literary reference. But though the novel of sensibility is one of its chief targets, what it mocks is not the virtue of sympathy, but the hypocritical assumption of it. When Sophia refuses to visit her lover in Newgate after his unexpected arrest, giving as her reason 'my feelings are sufficiently shocked by the *recital*, of his Distress, but to behold it will overpower my Sensibility' (89), it is certainly not compassion that is under fire. The novella's four proponents of fine-feeling are obsessed with style, believing that if they get their self-presentation right they can get away with murder, which they do. Violence for them is typically a sin of omission – parents are left to dwindle or die after their savings are stolen, but the money is taken with the proper éclat – 'gracefully purloined', in the case of Augustus, 'from his Unworthy father's Escritoire' (88). Even sex for the two charmed couples (whose relationships seem unimpaired by the imprisonment of one hero and the unaccounted disappearance of the other) turns out to be a matter of words. Just as distress is a question of *recital*, so friendship is a matter of *protestations*, and love of *vows*:

In the Society of my Edward & this Amiable Pair, I passed the happiest moments of my Life: Our time was most delightfully spent, in mutual Protestations of Freindship, and in vows of unalterable Love, in which we were secure from being interrupted, by intruding & disagreable Visitors. (87)

---

[196] Ibid., ii, 28; Lecture xviii.

This golden period in the lives of the lovers has been compared, in one Anti-Jacobin reading of the juvenilia, to the sort of retreats enjoyed by libertine covens in the works of Sade, but this is to credit Austen's supine foursome with an energy to which only Laura, the survivor, can lay claim.[197] She is led to decry, at last, the swooning and other induced symptoms of physical delicacy essential to her cult, urging readers to learn from the dying words of Sophia: 'Run mad as often as you chuse; but do not faint –' (102).

Though 'Love and Freindship' cocks a snook across the channel at Goethe's *Werther*, and perhaps, by implication, at the works of Rousseau (though none leaves a mark), its satire belongs to a tradition that is liberal in character. Burlesque drama of the Steventon brand remains the presiding influence, and Austen has her sights on literary extravagance of any sort – even Burney's *Evelina* is mocked in the hilarious recognition scene that galvanizes an entire carriage.[198] To theatre, again, Austen owes her strategic and tidy plotting – a relief after that of her sister novelist. 'Love and Freindship' opens on the idea that lovers of sensibility can make no claim to moral heroism unless they marry in a way that outrages their parents. Cursed with a lover whom his family like, Edward Lindsay changes his name to Talbot, and randomly chooses Laura; later the couple will persuade a Scottish youth to elope with a stranger in order to avoid the stigma they themselves have escaped – marriage to the parentally approved. This recurring motif was drawn from Sheridan's *The Rivals* (1775) where the heroine Lydia Languish, much addicted to novel-reading, causes her well-born and parentally sanctioned suitor to disguise himself as a half-pay Lieutenant, and take another name.[199]

A further presence behind the wings in 'Love and Freindship' is *The Critic* (1781), the farce in which Sheridan debunks the sentimental and the heroic side by side as the action shifts from low-life comedy, set in the stage-manager's parlour, to the play-within-the-play, a bombastic piece by

---

[197] See R. F. Brissenden, *Virtue in Distress: Studies in the Novel of Sentiment from Richardson to Sade* (1974), p. 281.

[198] The first of Fanny Burney's grand recognition scenes takes place in a carriage. See *Evelina*, ed. Edward and Lillian Bloom (1990), pp. 51–3, 321–23, and 'Love and Freindship', pp. 103–4, 91–2; for a further point of connection see note to *Catharine and Other Writings*, pp. 317–18.

[199] The play includes yet another comic perspective on sensibility in its portrait of a perverse lover who titillates himself with jealous agonies of his own making; and it ends on an anti-heroic note by ridiculing the '*honour*' involved in duelling. *The Rivals* had been performed at Steventon in 1784, and Deirdre Le Faye has suggested that the part of Lucy might have been taken by Jane, then eight (see *A Family Record*, p. 46). For the duel see IV. i, 17–31, *The Dramatic Works of Richard Brinsley Sheridan*, ed. Cecil Price, 2 vols. (Oxford, 1973), I, 118.

Puff.[200] In 'Love and Freindship' Austen finds the occasion for a deft take-off of the madness-speech dear to writers of heroic tragedy (who seem to have revelled in the spectacle of female disorder), when Laura is distracted by pangs of grief – and perhaps of hunger too:

> 'Talk to me not of Phaetons' (said I, raving in a frantic, incoherent manner) – 'Give me a violin –. I'll play to him and sooth him in his melancholy Hours – Beware ye gentle Nymphs of Cupid's Thunderbolts, avoid the piercing Shafts of Jupiter – Look at that Grove of Firs – I see a Leg of Mutton – They told me Edward was not Dead; but they deceived me – they took him for a Cucumber' (100)

Her model here is the memorable parody from *The Critic* aimed principally at Belvidera's mad speeches from Otway's *Venice Preserved*: '– The wind whistles – the moon rises – . . . Is this a grasshopper!' etc.[201] Coleridge was fond of using Belvidera's 'seas of milk, and ships of amber' as an illustration of the associative basis of fancy, and in 'Love and Freindship' Laura's speech provides the satiric climax to a series of far-fetched associations. Through Thomas Percival, if no one else, Jane knew of Hartley's theory that associations have an ameliorative effect (because experience, overall, is good rather than bad): in the *Tales* she had read of how 'the affections of a generous heart are extended by the early associations of ideas, to almost every surrounding object',[202] but she poses a countercase. What happens to the uplifting process if the subject is in a sour mood?

> – 'Do not again wound my Sensibility by Observations on those elms. They remind me of Augustus –. He was like them, tall, magestic – he possessed that noble grandeur which you admire in them' . . .
> 'What a beautifull Sky!' (said I) 'How charmingly is the azure varied by those delicate streaks of white!'
> 'Oh! my Laura (replied she hastily withdrawing her Eyes from a momentary glance at the sky) do not thus distress me by calling my Attention to an object which so cruelly reminds me of my Augustus's blue sattin Waistcoat striped with white!' (98)

With the help of Hartley, sentimental novelists had turned association into a device for moral ennoblement, but the empirically minded Jane demonstrates that its mechanisms can equally well be put into reverse. She was fascinated, too, by that inversion of a vaunted intensity of feeling

---

[200] The sentimental taste in drama comes under steady fire in the opening scene of *The Critic*; see particularly *Dramatic Works*, II, 501–2.

[201] Compare *Venice Preserved* v. 483, 'The Winds! hark how they whistle!' (*The Works of Thomas Otway*, ed. J. C. Ghosh, 1932, II, 286); and see note in *Catharine and Other Writings*, p. 120. Sheridan's reference to Belvidera's speech seems to have escaped notice, see note 1 in *Dramatic Works*, II, 548.

[202] Percival, *Tales*, p. 82.

presented by the swoon. No doubt Sheridan was at the back of her mind when she mischievously animated the conventional tableau with which Laura closes a scene: 'We fainted Alternately on a Sofa' (86). No fewer than three of Puff's players are required to faint '*alternately in each other's arms*'.[203]

Puff apologizes in *The Critic* for having been obliged in his first scene to be 'plain and intelligible', promising to make up thereafter with 'trope, figure and metaphor, as plenty as noun-substantives'.[204] But inflated language is only one aspect of the heroic style that playwrights like Sheridan set out to puncture, for its register extended to gesture, and, beyond that, to the striking of statuesque attitudes. In the eighteenth century the theatre was a principal source of these. Reynolds borrowed copiously from the stage, and prints from his portraits contributed, in their turn, to spreading the grammar of visual heroics. The 'great style' was, in Reynolds's view, 'artificial in the highest degree', which meant that it required continuous cultivation, so his pupils were urged to 'feign a relish, till we find the relish come; and feel, that what began in fiction, terminates in reality'.[205] Fashion plates showing models impersonating figures copied off classical or Etruscan vases were another stand-by, and the many different strains of mannerism were no doubt mutually reinforcing.[206]

Opposed to the whole tendency of this movement was the dramatic tradition that first enabled Jane Austen to find a voice. Her debt was to a satiric drama that offered, however formalized itself, a manifesto for a theatre that was closer to everyday experience, plainer in its representation, and altogether more naturalistic. She owed a particular debt, within this school, to a tradition of literary parody that took apart popular conventions while asserting – through an appeal to a greater realism – an independence from them. The metafictional qualities of Sheridan's *The Critic* and Fielding's *Tom Thumb* carry over into the juvenilia, and to Fielding's piece there can also be traced Austen's early delight in grotesquerie and knockabout farce. The great original of these complex dramatic travesties was *The Rehearsal*, the play in which Buckingham, with the help of Thomas Sprat, made merciless fun of the heroic drama whose exponents 'scorn to imitate nature, but are given altogether to elevate and surprise'.[207] It seems likely from internal

---

[203] *The Critic*, III. i; see *Dramatic Works*, II, 541. [204] Ibid., II. ii; see II, 525.
[205] See Joshua Reynolds, *Discourses on Art*, ed. Robert R. Wark (Huntingdon, 1959), xv, p. 277. Reynolds is quoting at this point from James Harris's 'Rules Defended'; and see Edgar Wind, *Hume and the Heroic Portrait*, p. 21.
[206] Ibid., p. 47; and see K. G. Holmstrom, *Monodrama, Attitudes, Tableau Vivant, 1770–1815* (Stockholm, 1967).
[207] George Villiers, Duke of Buckingham, *The Rehearsal*, ed. D. E. L. Crane (Durham, 1976), I. i; p. 4.

evidence that Buckingham's masterpiece was known to Jane Austen as well
as his *Chances*,[208] but in the latter play alone – which effectively adds a
low-life plot to Fletcher's original Don Juan story, thereby upstaging it –
she had a further model of a legend cut down to life size.[209] It is revealing that David Hume who denied the title 'Augustan' to literature of the
Restoration on the grounds that its tragedies were absurd, had only praise
for Buckingham whose good sense he associates with the beginnings of
scientific discourse in the period.[210]

'Love and Freindship' bears a number of birthmarks that reveal its genesis
in the satire of grand style. Laura and Sophia are twice said to be inspired
by 'Heroic Fortitude' (the last word appears in the *Loiterer's* collection of
pompous Latinisms); and Augusta, the real heroine, is given out to be – in
a phrase that becomes motival – 'of the middle size'.[211] Though Augusta
is a fount of good sense she is by no means exempt from the sallies of
her creator's wit which seems to have played fast and loose with moral
boundaries from the very first. Comic penalties attach to Augusta's good
nature: when her family discovers, on a picturesque tour of Scotland, that
her penniless brother-in-law has set himself up as a coach-driver between
Edinburgh and Sterling, their sightseeing is charitably curtailed to trips,
back and forth, along his route – an endless round in a stuffy carriage that
throws the drama of Laura's dynamic career into sharp relief. The funniest
of the many jokes in 'Love and Freindship' – and one long remembered by
Jane herself[212] – is effectively at the author's expense.

Burlesque is the dominant genre in the juvenilia, and a wide range of
pretensions are submitted to its play. *Volume the First* opens by dismantling, in turn, two prevailing paradigms of female and male perfection. In
'Frederic and Elfrida' the romantic lovers, as finely affined as their names,
are so absorbed in questions of punctilio and purity of motive that they
never find the right moment to become engaged, though their friend Charlotte twice accepts proposals out of sheer delicacy, before drowning herself to protect everyone from embarrassment. In 'Jack and Alice', where
sexual difference seems to be profound, Charles Adams is surrounded
by a circle of despairing women, repeating the situation of Sir Charles

---

208 See note on 'The Mystery' in *Catharine and Other Writings*, p. 307. Bayes's play opens with protracted
      whispering, leading Smith, the common-sense commentator, to exclaim, 'Begin the Play, and end
      it, without ever opening the Plot at all?' *The Rehearsal*, II. iii; p. 22.
209 For an account of Buckingham's radical alterations to Fletcher's play see A. C. Sprague, *Beaumont
      and Fletcher on the Restoration Stage* (1926), pp. 221–7.
210 Hume, *History of England*, VI, 540–5.
211 See *Minor Works*, pp. 85, 87; and pp. 80, 82, 85. *The Loiterer*, 59, 13 Mar. 1789, p. 5.
212 See To Cassandra, 23–4 Aug. 1814, *Letters*, p. 270.

Grandison, whom he is clearly intended to reflect. With a dazzle of solar and kingly metaphors drawn, as Margaret Doody has noted,[213] from Richardson's influential novel, the superhero makes his entrance in the manner of a heroine at a masquerade, but

the Beams that darted from his Eyes were like that of that glorious Luminary tho' infinitely superior. So strong were they that no one dared venture within half a mile of them; he had therefore the best part of the Room to himself. (13)

Belinda, Pope's coquette from *The Rape of the Lock*, has eyes that outdo the sun, and like Belinda, again, Austen's Charles is 'polite to all, but partial to none' (15). What has been taken for his mask by the half-blinded assembly turns out to be his blemishless face, but before long that, too, is exposed as the front of a person as cold, and sickeningly vain as any imitator of Richardson's superman might well have proved to be.[214] Though no such satiric zest is apparent in the separate item 'Sir Charles Grandison', Austen's part in the composition of this limp playlet may scarcely have gone beyond that of amanuensis to Anna, her niece.[215]

It is ironic that a novelist who was to inspire generations of romance writers should have begun her career by offering an unusually abrasive view of courtship, but marriage, too, is a favourite target in these tiny comedies of diminishment. From them the reader learns of a chaplain who returns from the sea and fails to recognize his wife seated opposite him in a carriage, of a baronet who cancels his wedding because it conflicts with a hunt, of sisters who marry to spite each other or in the hope of acquiring a chaise, of couples who become engaged by force of circumstance – a sleepless night in beds that are too short being followed by unaccustomed proximity at the dinner table where there are too few chairs.[216] Through such light-hearted

---

[213] See *Catharine and Other Writings*, xxvii–xxxiii, and p. 292.

[214] For an account of Austen's very real debts to Richardson see Jocelyn Harris, *Jane Austen's Art of Memory* (Cambridge, 1989), pp. 130–68; and Appendix 2, 'Sir Charles Grandison in the Juvenilia', pp. 228–38.

[215] Fanny Lefroy (Anna's daughter) claimed that the play was dictated by Anna to her aunt, but Southam rules out Anna's authorship on the grounds that she was too young (at most seven) at the time of the play's completion. Deirdre Le Faye has suggested, however, that 'Sir Charles Grandison' dates to the summer of 1805 when Austen was at Godmersham with the twelve-year-old Anna, who is known to have taken part in theatricals on this visit (*A Family Record*, pp. 133–4). Since watermarks give little to go by – the first two quires of *Sanditon* bear the date 1812 – an even later date is possible. The first pages are written in an immature hand, and Southam may be right in saying they are the young Jane's, but it is worth considering whether they are not actually in Anna's writing. Though some sort of collaboration is likely, no phrase in the entire play carries Austen's stamp. See *Jane Austen's 'Sir Charles Grandison'*, ed. Brian Southam (Oxford, 1980).

[216] All from *Volume the First*: 'The Adventures of Mr Harley', 'Sir William Mountague', 'The Three Sisters', 'The Visit'.

rites of exorcism Jane Austen freed herself from the more idealistic reaches of her novelistic inheritance. Richardson was to prove a major influence on her career, but when it came to characterization she probably had more to learn from the sprightly Anna Howe and Charlotte Grandison – and from Lovelace – than from Clarissa, Clementina, or Sir Charles. *Pride and Prejudice* is perhaps the first novel to invert the Richardsonian formula of a paragon of female virtue being attended by a more sprightly companion – the sparkling Elizabeth Bennet taking precedence over her elder, more sober and conventionally beautiful sister Jane. But just as Austen's parodies of Richardson allowed her to put the more didactic and exemplar-stuffed features of his fiction behind her, so her other juvenile burlesques cleared the stage for those works of outstanding naturalism which were (in first draft at least) soon to follow.

When the brief on heroism was reopened by Austen in the novels begun after the onset of the Napoleonic wars, the mode of representation continues to have a modifying effect. It was at the end of her career, after all, that she remarked to a niece, 'pictures of perfection as you know make me sick & wicked'.[217] Even when Austen upholds the notion of the heroic wholeheartedly, there is a shift of expected emphasis. In *Mansfield Park* it is soft-touch Fanny who proves as intransigent as Macartney in China. In *Emma* Harriet is bowled over not by Frank Churchill's fully-blown romantic rescue of her from the gypsies but by Knightley's small but imaginative act of kindness to her at a ball, while Emma herself learns the importance of shunning 'heroism of sentiment' (431). And in *Persuasion* Sir Walter's jealous custodianship of Elliot knight-errantry throws the matter-of-fact bravery of Captain Wentworth into attractive relief, though the ultimate palm is reserved for less obtrusive kinds of strength.

CIVILITY AND THE PASSIONS

Although Austen's satires of sensibility bear some resemblance to those (mainly by Canning) that were later to appear in the *Anti-Jacobin* (1797–8), they belong, in fact, to a tradition established earlier by Sheridan who, as an opponent of Burke and a diehard supporter of France, was hardly backward-looking. If the juvenilia are to be placed culturally, there is no better gloss to them than those passages in *The Loiterer*, where James singles out *affectation* as the pre-eminent 'fault of modern manners'. His analysis here takes off from David Hume's contention in 'Of the Rise and Progress of

---

[217] To Fanny Knight, 23–5 Mar. 1817, *Letters*, p. 335.

the Arts and Sciences' that contemporary society had gained in refinement over the self-assertive manners of old, but at the cost of 'running often into affectation and foppery'.[218] This is the gist also of Hume's essay on style where 'excess of refinement' is identified as the symptom of a sophisticated age, and rated as the vice 'now more to be guarded against than ever'.[219]

James Austen takes the diagnosis a step further, however, when he comes up with an explanation for the origins of this excess that has its roots in the sociology of the Scottish Enlightenment. He argues that 'affectation' is an unfortunate side-effect of those very processes that have strengthened civility, remarking that an important condition for these is a weakening of social hierarchy, since it is 'the mixt intercourse of ranks [that] has promoted the refinement of our manners, and improved the Charms of Society'.[220] James sketches the last stages of a stadial history in which the rise of a commercial culture has led, as we would say, to shame being replaced by guilt, and status by personality:

In the last century nothing so effectively secured our Reputation against the attacks of Slander, as a strict regard to propriety in our conversation, our behaviour, even our dress: Provided these external appearances were preserved, few concerned themselves about our good temper, liberality or candour . . . At present we seem to profess a very different system of Ethics; certainly not too observant of the Form, we flatter ourselves we are more attentive to the substance of Virtue; and while we modestly give up all claim to a nice propriety of conduct and behaviour, we pride ourselves on our superior proficiency in those qualities which conduce most to the happiness of Society.[221]

In a society that allows fuller expression to individuality there will be greater competition for social approbation, and all the more cause to affect those qualities judged likely to win esteem. To illustrate this urge 'to make ourselves conspicuous by appearing to possess qualities in a superior degree to the generality of those around us', the *Loiterer* assembles a gallery of character types, ranging from the Oxford student who tries to appear even more idle and ignorant than he really is, to the youth who affects always to be 'unaffected'. Such is the gamut of 'over-strained behaviour' to which the rage for personal distinction gives rise.[222]

Prominently placed in this gallery of characters is a portrait of 'the Feeling Woman', and Henry was later to vary this theme in a piece that lays the blame for an 'excess of sentiment and susceptibility' on a tradition of

---

[218] *Essays Moral, Political, and Literary*, I, 191.
[219] Ibid., 'Of Simplicity and Refinement in Writing', I, 243.
[220] '*Affectation*, the Fault of Modern Manners', *The Loiterer*, 33, 12 Sept. 1789, p. 5.
[221] *The Loiterer*, 50, 9 Jan. 1790, pp. 3–4.   [222] *The Loiterer*, 33, 12 Sept. 1789, pp. 5, 12.

novel-writing introduced by the 'great Rousseau'.[223] The last epithet might seem sarcastic were it not for the earlier number in which Henry vigorously defends all the outdoors muscle-building of *Émile*, ridiculing the snobbery of those who claim that it will turn gentlemen into 'Carters and Bargemen'.[224] When it comes to female education, however, Henry sides firmly with Madame de Genlis's attack on Rousseau's reactionary views, remarking caustically that in her eagerness to teach her daughter literature, music, and dancing, the educationalist has forgotten 'the more important duties of wrenching her neck in a collar, and her feet in the *Stocks*'.[225] It is against the background of these emancipatory views on gender and class that Henry accuses Rousseau and his followers of using sentiment as a mask to conceal 'the grossest allurements of sense, and the most daring attacks of Deism'.[226]

This last quotation from *The Loiterer* together with two pieces written by the Warren cousins, criticizing hedonism, have given a purchase to Anti-Jacobin readings of the journal *tout court*. The first of the Warren essays, entitled with irony 'Modern Times Vindicated from the Charge of Degeneracy', points to the ease with which social responsibilities are neglected in a society where the pursuit of individual happiness is perceived as a proper goal. A similar line is taken by James in his Prologue to *The Chances* where the slogan of a gamester raises the vision of a social fabric torn by predatory instinct:

> Consider every man thou meet'st thy foe.
> 'Pay where you must, & cheat wher'ere you can,
> The proper plunder of mankind is man.'[227]

Such anxieties had, however, been a burning issue for many enlightened thinkers long before the upheavals in France. In Britain, as we have seen, a dread of social schism haunted the later course of the Enlightenment, muting the celebrations of natural sympathy coming from writers like Hume and Smith, who steered well clear of the Pelagian tendencies of Shaftesbury or of the English Deists. The economic and political systems of these two giants took shape under the long shadows cast by Hobbes, and were fully alive to the need for social stability as a condition for effective reform. Pocock, in his compelling reconstruction of Gibbon's intellectual environment, distinguishes between rival traditions of liberal thought in the period,

---

[223] *The Loiterer*, 47, 19 Dec. 1789, p. 4.   [224] *The Loiterer*, 27, 1 Aug. 1789, p. 5.
[225] Ibid., p. 6.   [226] *The Loiterer*, 47, 19 Dec. 1789, p. 4.
[227] 'Prologue to *The Chances*' (7 Jan. 1788).

reclaiming a central place for the sceptics, since 'in them, the Enlightenment which tried to set limits to the human mind confronted an Enlightenment which made the mind the object of its own self-worship'.[228] Part of the stress on human limitation, by writers like Hume, involved a pragmatic respect for institutions and social codes, for these were understood to be an essential expression of the individual's need for social forms, and seemed all the more wholesome for being 'artificial' and hence tractable. But as the century drew to a close, a less optimistic strain became audible in liberal discourse as doubts were increasingly voiced about the natural beneficence of the commercial era. In successive revisions to the *Theory of the Moral Sentiments* (1759–90), Adam Smith worried more openly over the thought that the pursuit of wealth and fame cuts across the path that leads to wisdom and virtue, and that the best possible world may be far from a good one. The same dilemma had already inspired Adam Ferguson to write the darkest classic of the Scottish Enlightenment, *An Essay on the History of Civil Society* (1767), a work with which James and his circle seem clearly to have been familiar.

No narrative piece in *The Loiterer* captures the mood of its period more fully than the 'Memoirs of a Highland Chieftain', the work of John-Willing Warren, the young Oxford don to whom Jane Austen was to take a liking seven years later, notwithstanding the competition of Tom Lefroy.[229] The piece appeared on 7 November 1789, five days after the laws for the confiscation of Church property were passed in France; and it deserves to be better known for the insight it gives into the psychological effects of rapid social change – it makes an intriguing comparison with Wordsworth's portrait of the idealistic Beaupuy.[230] Though the piece warns against the dangers of sudden social disruption, it is sympathetic to modernization, and reveals a subtlety that transcends partisanship. Told in the first person, the story pivots on the Highland Chieftain's early disillusion with the feudal outlook and role that are his inheritance. Fighting as a volunteer in a Highland regiment in North America, he becomes a convert to the new, democratic order:

There it was I first learnt to doubt the propriety of those ideas that had hitherto regulated all my actions. In the Americans I saw a people illustrious without rank, united without subordination; and who in the equal claims of citizens sunk all the pride of distinction, while they exercised the virtues I believed inherent in it.

---

[228] Pocock, *Barbarism and Religion*, I, 68–9.
[229] See To Cassandra, 9–10 Jan. 1796, *Letters*, pp. 1–2.
[230] William Wordsworth, *The Prelude* (1805–6), IX, lines 126–554.

In those of the English with whom I associated, I beheld birth degraded by every depravity of which nature is capable; and if they ever seemed alive to their rank, it was merely to assert it with the most disgusting petulance, and an arrogance offensive to the human feelings over the wretched victims whom fortune had humbled to their caprice.[231]

However much he comes to regret the implications of this judgement, the Chieftain never goes back on it (referring later to the 'delusions' on which feudalism is based),[232] and he proceeds to act on his change of heart. Abandoning the regiment, he cuts ties with his Highland family on his return to Scotland, opting for what he sees as a more authentic kind of existence as a parliamentarian in London where he marries, becomes wealthy and famous, only to be faced with a feeling of total futility, worsened by a nagging sense of loss at the life he has thrown away. Warren uses the two modalities of his Chieftain's career to provide a comparison of what might now be called *Gemeinschaft* and *Gesellschaft*: his Highlander exchanges the tight loyalties of the clan for an urban life in which he feels indifferent to the society around him. His final judgement on this newer form of community matches Ferguson's portrayal of a malaise peculiar to 'polished' society in a commercial age: 'I see myself looked up to, caressed and admired by them – but unattached and unattaching, in the midst of flattering crouds feel a real solitude of soul, whenever for a moment I turn my eyes inward.'[233] Ferguson had noted that only in modern society was man 'sometimes found a detached and a solitary being', and James takes up the same theme in a piece on a shy youth who, valuing his freedom above everything else, comes before long to yearn for death since he has found 'nothing attaching in public life'.[234] Stimulated perhaps by Hume's account of the hollowness of Epicurean pleasure-seeking, Ferguson – after invoking the extraordinary spirit of kinship in 'rude' societies – writes eloquently of the consequences for those who consider 'life as a scene for the gratification of mere vanity, avarice, and ambition; never as furnishing the best opportunity for a just and a happy engagement of the mind and the heart':

They pine in the midst of apparent enjoyments; or, by the variety and caprice of their different pursuits and amusements, exhibit a state of agitation, which, like the disquiet of sickness, is not a proof of enjoyment or pleasure, but of suffering and pain.[235]

---

[231] *The Loiterer*, 41, 7 Nov. 1789, p. 6.   [232] Ibid., p. 9.   [233] Ibid., p. 13.
[234] Adam Ferguson, *An Essay on the History of Civil Society* (1767), ed. Duncan Forbes (1966), p. 19; and see *The Loiterer*, 46, 12 Dec. 1789, p. 9.
[235] See David Hume, 'The Epicurean', *in Essays Moral, Political and Literary*, I, 197–203; and Ferguson's *Essay*, pp. 258, 260.

Pressing home his argument that every age has its particular misery and hardships, Ferguson (once Chaplain to the Black Watch) recalls that Celtic warriors, no longer fit for battle, would beg death from their friends rather than suffer the 'langours of a listless and inactive life'.[236]

If 'Memoirs of a Highland Chieftain' is, on one plane, a defence of an ancient form of social dispensation that, though seemingly outmoded, was still thriving on the British Isles,[237] it is also, and more broadly, an inquiry into what place there is for heroism in the modern world. The Chieftain's decision to break away from his inheritance is a notable instance of modern bravery, rationalistic in kind, and bred of the new order, but it leaves him an emotionally broken man. Hume, who so shrewdly insisted on the slender limits of self-denial, would have appreciated the Chieftain's explanation of how he lost the 'best energies of life' in asserting 'a philosophical superiority to the impressions of habit'.[238] A further act of moral idealism brings ruin to the Highland district he represents in the Commons, when he is swayed by the 'philanthropic zeal' of his opponents to put their agenda above the interests of the needy constituents he has sworn to serve. Throughout the story, self-effacement is shown to be a less effective source of social welfare than the pursuit of interest, moderated by common decency. All is over for Warren's Highlander when he grows used to 'exulting in the discernment' that cuts him off from his roots and from a community distinguished by the exceptional intensity of its sympathies.

If opportunities for heroism in the moral sphere are limited under the new dispensation, what becomes of the physical daring that men like the Highland Chieftain had expressed in battle? Ferguson in his *Essay* provides an unusually tough-minded account of the part played by conflict not only in the history of societal development – where war has a creative as well as destructive role, but also in the economy of the individual life, which he compares to a meteor that shines only by expending its energy in resistance, for 'the moments of rest and of obscurity are the same'.[239] If commerce and manufactures had brought more freedom and greater security with the rule of law, the prosperity that came in their train was laden with enervating consequences. As Ferguson saw it, Duncan Forbes quips,

---

[236] Ibid., p. 106.

[237] Governmental respect for the variety of existing social structures was an important issue for the Scottish Enlightenment as Nicholas Phillipson has shown; see his remarks on 'the regional integrity of the different communities of the kingdom' in his essay, 'The Scottish Enlightenment', in Roy Porter and Mikuláš Teich, eds., *The Enlightenment in National Context* (Cambridge, 1981), pp. 19–42, 31.

[238] *The Loiterer*, 41, p. 5.   [239] *An Essay*, p. 210.

the real danger of the age was the absence of danger.[240] This held true for the upper echelons of society especially, since one result of the commercial age was that 'inequalities of fortune' were greatly increased, leading to the existence of an entire class whose expectations of life were raised on the treacherous foundation of leisure.[241] Unexpressed energies were troublesome, but could be sublimated through a variety of cultural activities, and in the *Essay* Ferguson makes a point of tracing – sometimes wryly – the socially covenanted outlets for what he describes as man's 'natural talents and forces'. He remarks, for example, that 'sports are frequently an image of war', adding that man's 'love of amusement has opened a path that leads to the grave'.[242]

It seems likely that these pages had a strong impact on James Austen, for we find him in his piece on 'Gaming' citing the same passage from Tacitus as Ferguson, and applying it to the same end – to show that the passion for gambling flares up as strongly in the drawing room as it did among the Germanii of old.[243] Ferguson seems to be a presence, too, behind the catalogue of national diversions that James cobbled together for his prologue to *Tom Thumb*. His card game there is fraught with deep compulsions ('you of all pastimes most, / Over each sex a power resistless boast'); and his players, who 'Attack with vigour' to the accompaniment of violent thumps, look forward to the Loiterer's remark that it is only over backgammon that the modern British prove that the blood of tribal warriors runs in their veins. His further lines on a hunt answer to Ferguson's aphorism, 'The most animating occasions of human life, are calls to danger and hardship':[244]

> With manly hearts our sufferings we deride
> And freeze and shiver by the Coverts' side –
> Cheered by the rattling crash, & screaming halloo
> O'er clayey vales, or flinty hills we follow.
> Pent o'er the common fields low level plains,
> Strain up steep banks, & plunge thro' boggy lanes:
> Each animated heart the scenes enjoys.
> And finds true bliss in danger, dirt, & noise.[245]

This polite containment of fierce, ancient passions is finally symbolically compressed (with a glance at Pope's 'little moderns' from *The Rape of the Lock*) in tiny Tom, the subject of the evening's play: 'Though small indeed

---

[240] Duncan Forbes's Introduction to Ferguson's *Essay*, p. xxxvi.
[241] *An Essay*, pp. 217, 248.   [242] Ibid., p. 24.
[243] Ibid., ii. ii, pp. 93–4; and *The Loiterer*, 56, 20 Feb. 1790, pp. 5–6.   [244] Ibid., p. 45.
[245] 'Prologue to the Tragedy of Tom Thumb' (22 Mar. 1788). Chawton copy, p. 22.

the Hero of tonight / He can live like other Heroes, love and fight.' In this context, James's debts to Pope are not surprising, for recidivism always was the mainspring of mock-heroic.

It is a mark of Jane Austen's creative vigour that her work is less superficially revealing of literary influence than is the case with her brother James. Ferguson may or may not have been among the many historians whom she had read; but well read in history she was – and this biographical feature is among the few that she was to pass on directly to a character. We are told that the heroine of her *Catharine, or the Bower* has done her reading in modern history – and the dedication to that unfinished piece is dated August 1792.[246] In *Catharine*, Austen made her first attempt at a realistic portrait of a young man, and he is first in a long line of listless heroes who answer well to Ferguson's picture of the modern malaise in having plenty of energy, but nothing to do. Most complex of these figures is Henry Crawford who, as Roger Sales has shown, cavalierly conducts his courtship of Fanny Price as though it were a campaign, against the sombre background of the real thing, the Napoleonic war.[247] In *Catharine* a similar aura of theatricality hovers over the life of the sprightly Edward Stanley, who (without the excuse of the *ci-devant* Comte de Feuillide) flits from the South of France to England and back again, with no expense spared, to dramatize the calamity of losing his best mare. His diversions continue, however, on another plane when he meets Catharine, who is impressionable enough to be forgiving even when she learns that the kiss Edward has planted on her cheek, in the seclusion of the Bower, was intended merely to shock her approaching guardian aunt, the obsessively protective Mrs Percival. Catharine's wavering recognition that Edward has taken to flirtation as 'his principal Sport', carries with it a momentary insight into his total absence of feeling (234). Where Richardson's Lovelace attunes his strategies to seduction, Edward Stanley's light-hearted, boyish gamesmanship is an end in itself. But the certainty with which he selects Catharine as an object of play, is given a particular resonance by Austen's insight into the way attitudes are shaped by money and class, an insight carried through with a sureness of touch no less epoch-making for being the work of a sixteen-year-old.

The force of necessity is the theme round which the opening narrative of the novella evolves. Catharine, who has lost both parents when very young, finds herself in the hands of an anxious maiden aunt. She has also lost her

---

[246] 'She was well read in Modern history herself' etc., *Minor Works*, p. 198. Compare Henry's testimony in the 'Biographical Notice' originally prefacing *Northanger Abbey* and *Persuasion* (v, 7).
[247] Roger Sales, *Jane Austen and Representations of Regency England* (1994), pp. 90–1, 106–16.

closest friends, the young Wynnes, who have been thrown on the mercies of the world by their father's death. In the Bower, which she still associates with them, Catharine reflects on the fate of these old and true friends: the elder daughter dispatched ignominiously to India to find a husband (a story that closely follows the biography of Jane's paternal aunt); the younger forced to become a paid companion to a proud relation; and the sons, one sent into the army, the other to sea, despite his wish of entering the Church. Against this chronicle of dispersal and decline, there is set an account of the new family who have replaced the Wynnes at the vicarage: Mr Dudley, a tithe-grabbing rector, scorns the profession that has been brought on him by lack of funds; while his wife 'an ill-educated, untaught Woman of ancient family' hopes to win back status and wealth through her daughter. When the empty-headed Camilla Stanley joins the scene, trailing the trappings of her rich London set, merit and position appear to be as disjunct as they ever did to Warren's Highland Chieftain. Snobbery in this provincial setting not only gives licence to the worst, but feeds on contempt of the best. If the Dudleys dismiss the Percivals 'as people of mean family' while secretly envying them as people of means, the Stanleys are rich enough to despise them openly as the beneficiaries of *trade* (196, 224).

Attempts to claim *Catharine* as an Anti-Jacobin text invariably involve the promotion of the punctilious Mrs Percival into a moral standard-bearer. The fact that she is inclined to make a refrain of her favourite jeremiad ('all order [is] destroyed over the face of the World') has not stopped it from being taken as seriously as her absurd grouse that the smallest lapse in propriety on the part of young girls will bring disaster to the nation (200, 212, 232). Even Mrs Percival's belief that Catharine's bower is malign and long overdue for demolition has been felt to carry the stamp of authorial approval. Such readings are maintained, however, only by turning a blind eye to Jane's skittish invention and frequently mischievous tone. Take, for example, the moment that Catharine hits on a ploy to be left to herself in the bower, reminding her aunt of how colds are brought on by damp:

'I begin to feel very chill already' [said Mrs Percival]. 'Let me see; This is July; the cold weather will soon be coming in – August – September – October – November – December – January – February – March – April – Very likely I may not be tolerable again before May. I must and will have that arbour pulled down.' (233)

The entire triangular relationship between Catharine, Edward, and Mrs Percival amounts to a triumph of comic contrivance, raised on a set of ingeniously interlocking character traits. In the first place, the relation between aunt and ward revolves around a coupling very familiar to contemporary readers, the duo of superstition and enthusiasm. Catharine is twice described as an Enthusiast (193, 231), but she has the humour only in the mild form that Hume judged to be a fault on the right side. Quite unlike that of the earlier 'Freinds', her sensibility is expressed in a quickness to feel what others feel, and is free of the affectations of cult. Mrs Percival, on the other hand, is superstitious to a much less qualified degree. Her life is dominated by fears that can only be kept at bay by prostration to etiquette and rule, and the warm glow of Catharine's good nature is fuel to her deepest suspicions. In combination, the two spark each other off, and the result is comic sure-fire. As far as experience goes, Catharine might have been better off with Mrs Norris, for with the best intentions her aunt redoubles every effort to keep her out of harm's way, turning down balls attended by officers, and frowning on every kind of excursion. Starved of company, Catharine is only too ready to turn Edward Stanley into a Prince when he bursts, unannounced, into her aunt's house in her absence. And when Mrs Percival gets her own back after the Cinderella-like ball at which the young couple make a surprise entry, it is to arrange for the instant departure of Edward, who is then provoked into making his kiss. In retrospect it is clear that the very precautions Mrs Percival takes to prevent Catharine from falling in love with the wrong man, have sped on the event.

Edward's premature return to Lyon has the untoward effect of giving freer rein to Catharine's imagination, enabling her to delude herself into believing, after all, that Edward cares for her deeply – a belief quite impossible to sustain in his presence. The processes by which Catharine, dryly percipient as a rule, falls victim to self-deceit only begin to come under scrutiny where the text peters out and would no doubt have held centre-stage until, perhaps, the younger Wynne reappeared on the scene and lived up to his name. Austen may have felt that the shift to a lonely heroine, with the promise of a more inward interest, involved using a key too remote from the broad comedy that had gone before, or she may simply have underestimated Mrs Percival's power as a narrative suppressant. In any case, Austen ends her first experiment in the realist novel in full command, as Mary Waldron has noted, of the *style indirect libre* which was to play such a crucial role in her mature work.[248] She ends it, too, on what was to be a major theme:

---

[248] Mary Waldron demonstrates the importance of such interior representation in *Fiction of her Time*; see especially pp. 20–1, 165, 181 fn. 12.

the unregarded difficulties experienced by the self in putting together and maintaining a realistic view of the world. Something of the complexity of this daily process is hinted at in the image of the picturesquely inclined heroine of 'A Tour through Wales' whose drawings are not as exact as might be wished, 'from their being taken as she ran along' (176).

There has been a tendency in critical writing to link Austen's concern with the theme of self-recognition to a political conservatism, a tendency that seems all the more curious when it emanates, as so often, from the left. Sometimes the argument has taken the form that it is out of a commitment to Christian dogma that a succession of her heroes and heroines are submitted to an ordeal of abasement in which they learn that they are empty vessels of 'no innate worth'.[249] Various kinds of misreading are implicated in this approach; and the type of Christianity invoked is demonstrably distinct from the faith that Jane Austen was brought up in. Nor indeed is a concern with self-knowledge in any way distinctively Christian. Stress on the vital role played by reason in the self's construction of a proper relation to the world is a perennial theme of the Enlightenment ethics that writers like David Hume and Adam Smith popularized for the late eighteenth century. Even at prayer with her family, Austen remains within this ethos, when – at just the point in the surviving manuscript that she took over the pen – she asks to be inclined

> to be severe only in the examination of our own conduct, to consider our fellow-creatures with kindness, and to judge of all they say and do with that charity which we would desire from them ourselves.[250]

The allowance made for partiality towards the self, combined with a sense of the subject/object reciprocity involved in all moral judgements, chimes in well with Hume's caveats on the extreme difficulty of establishing an external view of the self,[251] or with Smith's notion of the 'impartial spectator' from his *Theory of Moral Sentiments*, a work which leaves its imprint both on *Pride and Prejudice*, as Kenneth Moler has shown, and on *Sense and Sensibility*.[252] It would be difficult to find a better comment on the sort of moral struggle and clarification typified by *Emma* than Smith's famous dictum:

---

[249] Butler, *War of Ideas*, p. 206.
[250] *Minor Works*, p. 456; and for an account of the MS see Bruce Stovel's valuable essay, '"The Sentient Target of Death": Jane Austen's Prayers', in Juliet McMaster and Bruce Stovel, eds., *Jane Austen's Business* (1996), especially pp. 193–4.
[251] See *THN*, III.iii.i; 580–4.   [252] Moler, 'Bennet Girls', pp. 567–9.

This self-deceit, this fatal weakness of mankind, is the source of half the disorders of human life. If we saw ourselves in the light in which others see us, or in which they would see us if they knew all, a reformation would generally be unavoidable.[253]

Smith tellingly describes the 'veil of delusion' that covers the self's voracity as 'mysterious', a pointer to his own grappling with the unexamined processes by which the individual develops 'conscience' through a myriad compensations for 'the natural misrepresentations of self-love'.[254] Far from being innate, moral sense is acquired accordingly by 'habit and experience' and, while being dependent on modalities of relation, it is entirely separable from the *vox populi*, or the internalization of a social code.[255] It less resembles the transcendent 'small voice of calm' acclaimed by tradition than the dead reckoning carried out by a small boat on a rough sea. This is a position that corresponds very fully with Austen's. The novels reveal a similar fascination with the actual workings of morality, with the instinctual forces engaged in it, and with the way a capacity for judgement is learnt almost imperceptibly, and by degrees, like a skill.

Smith was at pains to show that his theory of the 'impartial spectator' was consistent with Christian doctrine, but he departed from orthodoxy in one important respect. In an account of his ethics, Athol Fitzgibbons describes Smith as taking the low road:

He recommended the natural road to social improvement, rather than the high and esoteric road that Graeco-Christianity had tried to ascend. Smith's new system was meant to harness lower and stronger motives than the Christian idealism that had thrilled the saints but confirmed the ignorance and poverty of Europe.[256]

Chief among these lower and stronger motives was the passion of pride which – because it found satisfaction in winning the approval of others – comprised an essential goad to civility. Here Smith was in line with Hume who carefully distinguished between pride that was good and bad in its effects, and who told Boswell that it was in his annexation of pride and vanity that he principally differed from Christian moralists, obliged, as they were, to view pride as the cardinal sin.[257] In the last quarter of the eighteenth century this heterodoxy became a mantra among the enlightened who tended to believe that pride was as integral to morality as the appetite

---

[253] *TMS*, III.4.6, 158–9. [254] *TMS*, III.3.3–5, 158, 137.
[255] *TMS*, III.2.32; III.3.1–3; VII.ii.1.49. For an outstanding discussion of these issues see D. D. Raphael's 'The Impartial Spectator', in Andrew S. Skinner and Thomas Wilson, eds., *Essays on Adam Smith* (Oxford, 1975).
[256] Athol Fitzgibbons, *Adam Smith's System of Liberty, Wealth, and Virtue* (Oxford, 1995), p. 37.
[257] See 'An Account of my Last Interview with David Hume, Esq.', in *Hume's Dialogues*, p. 97.

for gain was to a healthy economy. Taken together, the desire for a good self-image (for praiseworthiness rather than simply for praise), and the all-important disposition to feel for others were the raw materials of sociability. On this crucial issue Jane Austen undoubtedly sided with the philosophers. Pride in the novels – as has frequently been pointed out (most trenchantly by Isobel Armstrong)[258] – is both good and bad, and Adam Smith's account of the potentially virtuous vice is clearly echoed in *Pride and Prejudice*. We shall see, too, that the triad of sympathy, approbation, and self-esteem, so central to this ethics, is constantly called into play in the later fiction.

To strip away what Smith had termed the 'vices of affectation',[259] and unveil the rag-and-bone-shop of the human heart sounds like a grim undertaking for a comic novelist. But Jane Austen had no compunction about taking the low road, and the form of comedy she devised abounds in the energies of self-love.

[258] See Isobel Armstrong's excellent Introduction to the World's Classics edition of *Pride and Prejudice*, ed. James Kinsley (Oxford, 1990), vii–xxx, particularly xi–xx.

[259] *TMS*, III.2.4, 115.

CHAPTER 2

Pride and Prejudice, *a politics of the picturesque*

'What are men to rocks and mountains?', Elizabeth Bennet exclaims with a touch of sarcasm at the prospect of a scenic tour that will end not as planned at the Lakes, but in Derbyshire, and in the company of Darcy. But if the picturesque initially holds the promise of satire (154, 53), this expectation soon ranks high among the novel's misleading first impressions. Elizabeth may glance mischievously at Gilpin's veto on groups of four, but the itinerary of her progress north follows one of his most famous travelogues to the letter. And the Pemberley estate that works so powerful a sea change on her attitude to Darcy turns out to be modelled on the best Gilpinesque principles, chat about which fills an awkward gap in the long-awaited scene of their re-encounter. If the picturesque proves to be as deeply founded in the novel as are Elizabeth and Darcy's feelings for each other, it is because Jane Austen extends it to embrace not merely rocks and mountains but men and women also.[1]

The aesthetics of the movement were reapplied in this extensive way by several authors during the 1790s, and we shall see how closely many of Austen's conceptions tally, in particular, with those of Uvedale Price. Yet it is clear from the juvenilia that Jane in her teens was already making her own intuitive extrapolations from the original visual theory, some of which pre-date the formulations of the treatise-writers. A witness to this teenage passion was her brother Henry, who recalled how 'at a very early age she

---

[1] Though my approach in this chapter is distinct in direction, and draws for the most part on fresh material, I owe numerous debts to previous work in the field; see particularly A. Walton Litz, 'The Picturesque in *Pride and Prejudice*', *Persuasions* 1 (1979), 13–15, 20–4; Jill Heydt, 'The Place of the Picturesque in *Pride and Prejudice*', *Studies in the Humanities*, 12 (1985), 115–24; Isobel Armstrong's Introduction to *Pride and Prejudice*, vi–xxx; Frank Bradbrook, *Jane Austen and her Predecessors* (Cambridge, 1966), ch. 3: 'The Picturesque', pp. 50–68; Nigel Everett, *The Tory View of Landscape* (New Haven, 1994), ch. 6: 'The View of Donwell Abbey', pp. 183–203; William Galperin, 'The Picturesque, the Real, and the Consumption of Jane Austen', *Wordsworth Circle*, 28 (1997), 19–27.

was enamoured of Gilpin on the Picturesque', but the whole family seem to have shared the craze.[2]

The Austens' enthusiasm for natural scenery can be gauged from the fact that, over the years, no fewer than four of them took scenic tours through Britain. Spurred on perhaps by the recently published *Pride and Prejudice*, Henry journeyed over the border via Matlock, and – though cheated of the Highlands by ill-health – met, as Jane observes, with 'Scenes of higher Beauty in Roxburghshire than I had supposed the South of Scotland possessed'.[3] Cassandra and Charles plumped for the Wye valley, another picturesque destination that owed its fame chiefly to Gilpin. James, two years after Jane's death and four months before his own, kept a journal of a trip through the south-west in which he alludes to Gilpin's 'On Picturesque Travel' and everywhere reveals debts to his school.[4]

James's connoisseurship in the reading of landscape is apparent in the many topographical pieces that form the larger part of his poetic output, but one recurrent theme in these – and one his sister would have approved – is the importance of keeping an open mind to the varied appeal of different kinds of natural scene. Only the more timid camp-followers of Gilpin and Price (both of whom insisted on the value of preserving a catholic taste) are happy to fall back on a set of rules. As a seasoned old hand, James rejoices in the holiday-makers who respond unselfconsciously:

> Everything around
> Delights them; & though haply never taught
> By Gilpin or by Price to judge by rule,
> To praise where praise is due, & regulate
> Their admiration by the Canon law
> Of orthodox & genuine taste; they find
> Sufficient to admire in all they see.[5]

Though James is delighted most by 'nature's wilder scenes' such as the classically Gilpinesque 'clos'd topp'd mountain, & the cliff abrupt', he

---

[2] 'Biographical Notice', v, p. 7.

[3] To Francis Austen, 25 Sept. 1813, *Letters*, p. 230. In the same letter Austen notes that her nephew Edward at Godmersham was 'no Enthusiast in the beauties of Nature', and that he was unlike his father in this respect.

[4] In his 'Journal of a Tour through Hampshire to Salisbury' (dated 10 Aug. 1819), James Austen enlarges on the reasons that Gilpin gives for travel in his *Three Essays* (1792), p. 41. Considering the effects that different backdrops would have on Stonehenge, James suggests that the New Forest would make the circle an object of beauty rather than awe, and concludes that while the actual setting of bald moorland strictly puts the monument outside the category of the picturesque, it is no less impressive for that. See his Journal, HRO 60/3/1, ff. 6–8.

[5] 'The Œconomy of Rural Life' (1819). HRO 60/3/2. References to James Austen's verse are to this manuscript unless otherwise stated.

refuses to dismiss the utilitarian as 'waste and barren all', putting in a plea for the attractions of cultivated land, and for other vistas that fail the requirements of 'composition pure & picturesque'.[6] This tolerant attitude was no doubt reinforced by Austen's mockery of picturesque jargon in *Sense and Sensibility* and by her defence there of utility – for which Price, too, had spoken up.[7] Apart from these qualifications, James has only praise for a movement that has turned the landscape into an object of pleasure for all, bypassing the proprietor:

> But most I prize
> And cultivate that taste for nature's charms
> Which teaches me to view her simplest scenes
> With high & indescribable delight.
> This makes me Lord of all I see around:
> My neighbour's lawns, & fields, & woods are mine;
> Mine, by the title deeds of genuine taste.[8]

An aesthetic stake in the countryside is the reward of every initiate, and elsewhere James Austen points to the strongly urban base of those addicted to things green when he describes city-dwellers who are starved of all but 'a plant in brown glazed pot', and 'office pent / For six long days; upon the seventh emerge, / And take their weekly portion of fresh air / With double relish'.[9] His insight into both the demography of the scenic movement and its comparative transcendence of social barriers surely owes much to *Pride and Prejudice*, where the Gardiners plan their Gilpinesque trip from the heartland of the City, arrive in due course at a Pemberley open to visitors, and find themselves shown round the estate by an obliging steward. Jane Austen, in her turn, would certainly have benefited from a family unusually well-versed in the discourse of the picturesque, who if they retained some scepticism towards its 'Canon law' nevertheless remained lifelong members of its broad church.

Gilpin is listed in 'The History of England' among the 'first of Men', one of whom is a fictional villain, but the fifteen-year-old Jane pays a firmer compliment to her hero when she steals a joke from the *Observations* (1786), adapting a passage on Cromwell's 'masterly hand' at creating picturesque ruins to Henry VIII's sacking of the monasteries, which was 'of infinite

---

[6] See 'Lines Written in the Autumn of 1817', and 'Morning – to Edward' (1814).
[7] *Sense and Sensibility*, pp. 92, 96–8; for a discussion of the importance of cultivation in Price's scheme of things see Stephen Daniels and Charles Watkins, 'Picturesque Landscaping and Estate Management: Uvedale Price at Foxley', in Stephen Copley and Peter Garside, eds., *The Politics of the Picturesque* (Cambridge, 1994), pp. 13–41.
[8] 'Lines Written in Autumn 1817'.   [9] 'The Œconomy of Rural Life'.

use to the landscape' (142–3).[10] Iconoclasm played a part in the inspiration of both Jane and her mentor. Gilpin had levelled his sights at a narrow, received idea of beauty reinforced in his day by Burke's influential separation of emotive responses into the sharply opposed categories of the beautiful and the sublime. Where, for Burke, beauty had the effect of pacifying the subject, while the sublime provoked awe and astonishment, the new category of the 'picturesque' encompassed an intermediary range of affects, so redeeming more of the natural and everyday world for aesthetic recognition. The ploy of defining the picturesque as that which would do well in a picture concealed some circularity, for the selection of landscape painting was inevitably prescriptive, and the intention was really to prize the vision of a Claude or Salvator Rosa over that of a Wilson or Devis. Central to the pictorial metaphor was the conception of a frame, but this, too, was to prove disposable, for it conflicted (as Wordsworth was to observe)[11] with the actual experience of a scene, a point graphically illustrated in *Volume the Second* by the ardent Fanny whose sketches in Wales are somewhat blurred by her habit of sketching on the run (176).

Formal landscaping is one of Gilpin's favourite targets in his campaign against the conventionally beautiful, and what he calls the 'garden-scene' frequently comes under fire for embodying everything that the picturesque is not.[12] 'Why', he asks in the first of his *Three Essays*, 'does an elegant piece of garden-ground make no figure on canvas?', and he proceeds to deck out his garden-scene with aesthetic features borrowed from the earlier part of the century:

The shape is pleasing; the combinations of objects, harmonious; and the winding of the walk in the very line of beauty. All this is true; but the *smoothness* of the whole . . . offends in picture [sic]. Turn the lawn into a piece of broken ground: plant rugged oaks instead of flowering shrubs: break the edges of the walk: give it the rudeness of a road: mark it with wheel tracks; and scatter around a few stones, and brushwood; in a word, instead of making the whole *smooth*, make it *rough*; and you make it *picturesque*.[13]

In the course of his writing, the injunction 'make it *rough*' is fleshed out by a range of associated antinomies – the irregular against the geometric,

---

[10] See William Gilpin, *Observations on Cumberland and Westmoreland* (1786, facs. edn Poole, 1996), II, 122–3.

[11] See Wordsworth's note to line 347 of *Descriptive Sketches*, and on this point Hugh Sykes Davies, *Wordsworth and the Worth of Words*, ed. John Kerrigan and Jonathan Wordsworth (Cambridge, 1986), p. 240.

[12] The campaign is already under way in *Observations on the River Wye* (1782) where Gilpin pronounces that 'garden-scenes are never *picturesque*' – principally because they aspire to 'smoothness'; see 5th edn (1800), p. 98.

[13] See 'Picturesque Beauty' in *Three Essays*, p. 8.

the abrupt against the rounded, the bold and free against the carefully finished; above all, perhaps, by a contrast between the dynamic and the static, for 'who does not admire the Laocoon more than the Antinous?'[14] Capability Brown was a particular boon to Gilpin, for his clumped trees, neatly impaled paddocks, sweeps of bare gravel, and belts of mown lawn conveniently epitomized all that was most inimical in the standard idiom of landscaping. And from such practices there flowed – it now seemed clear – a host of far-reaching implications.

Jane Austen embarked on an exploration of these when she began her *Volume the Third* with 'Evelyn' (1792), a story that opens with a Mr Gower passing through a village in Sussex, the Evelyn of the title, which the first sentence identifies as one of 'the most beautiful Spots in the south of England'. There Mr Gower is struck by the 'benevolence which character- izes the inhabitants', and his desire to settle among them is realized when the Webb family instantly make him a present of their house, the situation of which he finds particularly gratifying:

It was in the exact centre of a small circular paddock, which was enclosed by a regular paling, & bordered with a plantation of Lombardy poplars, & Spruce firs alternatively placed in three rows. A gravel walk ran through this beautiful Shrubbery, and as the remainder of the paddock was unincumbered with any other Timber, the surface of it perfectly even & smooth, and grazed by four white Cows which were disposed at equal distances from each other, the whole appearance of the place as Mr Gower entered the Paddock was uncommonly striking. A beautifully- rounded, gravel road without any turn or interruption led immediately to the house.[15]

The four equidistant cows, along with the rest of the scene, are straight out of Gilpin,[16] but where, of course, Mr Gower is rapturous, Gilpin's attitude is well summed up in a passage from 'Picturesque Travel':

[The traveller] is frequently disgusted also, when art aims more at beauty, than she ought. How flat, and insipid is often the garden-scene! how puerile and absurd! the banks of the river how smooth, and parallel! the lawn, and its boundaries how unlike nature![17]

But what does Jane Austen make of Mr Gower? The serene and dreamlike opening of 'Evelyn' soon yields to more disturbing scenes: Mr Gower, after accepting the house, its grounds, a meal and a gift of money without demur, shows that there are no limits to what he will take for granted. He now

---

[14] Ibid., p. 12.   [15] *Minor Works*, p. 181.

[16] Foursomes were famously proscribed in Gilpin's discussion of the aesthetics of grouping cattle; see *Cumberland and Westmoreland*, endnotes xii–xiii.

[17] In 'Picturesque Travel', the essay to which James, much later, alludes: see *Three Essays*, p. 57.

asks for a handsome dowry and for the eldest daughter – 'the lovely Miss Webb, who seemed however to refer herself to her father & Mother':

> *They* looked delighted at each other – At length Mrs Webb breaking silence, said – 'We bend under a weight of obligations to you which we can never repay. Take our girl, take our Maria, and on her must the difficult task fall, of endeavouring to make some return to so much Benefiscence.' (183)

Like Sir Charles Grandison to whom he is later adroitly compared (when Maria, tending his gout, shines in the character of a nurse), Gower exists at the centre of a world that seems specially arranged to satisfy his every need, and the orderliness of the setting makes the arrangement appear preordained. Indeed, the awful self-effacing politeness of the Webbs comes over as the proper expression of their setting, for even their speech falls into formal patterns: 'Welcome best of Men – Welcome to this House, & to everything it contains . . . It is yours, from this moment it is yours' (182–3). A mysterious social mechanism evidently aggrandizes the visitor to Evelyn, but its wheels are oiled by smooth manners, and its workings are kept out of sight.

The story undergoes a dramatic change of key when Mr Gower is reminded by four equidistant roses in the Webbs' garden of his sister Rose, who – as a thirteenth daughter of the family, left back in Carlisle – moves in a sphere altogether antipodean. Where in balmy Evelyn, misery, ill-health, and vice seem absent (181), up north, passion and misfortune are rife. Where Maria exists for the reader in the vague blur of one who is 'lovely and deserving', Rose is given a vivid individuality – clear skin, brilliant eyes, and a fine head of hair. Where Maria has no say in the matter of her marriage, and no regret at having none, Rose falls in love with a man whose rank and wealth spell trouble from his family. Withstanding all their interventions, Rose survives the drowning of her lover in a shipwreck, and when she too is gone, Gower pays a visit to the stubborn parents to elicit a blessing for the dead. Unsurprisingly the castle in which they live is not to his taste, not at least without the mediations of Brown:

> There was an irregularity in the fall of the ground, and a profusion of old Timber which appeared to him illsuited to the stile of the Castle, for it being a building of a very ancient date, he thought it required the Paddock of Evelyn lodge to form a Contrast, and enliven the structure. The gloomy appearance of the old Castle frowning on him as he followed its winding approach, struck him with terror. Nor did he think himself safe, till he was introduced into the Drawing room where the Family were assembled to tea. (187)

Gower is so discomposed by the intense feelings of the family (the mother overcome with grief, the father rancorously implacable) that he flees into the night, abandoning all plans for a reconciliation, and the story breaks off as he gallops in panic through a moonlit wood with his eyes tight closed. In a piece written earlier in the same year, Austen had peopled a castle with two robust daughters who provide a complete contrast to the submissive loveliness of the heroine of Evelyn, more especially as perceived by their petite and much rouged mother-in-law on a visit from the West End:

I already heartily repent that I ever left our charming House in Portman-Square for such a dismal old Weather-beaten Castle as this. You can form no idea sufficiently hideous, of its dungeon-like form . . . But as soon as I once found myself safely arrived in the inside of this tremendous building, I comforted myself with the hope of having my spirits revived, by the sight of the two beautifull Girls, such as the Miss Lesleys had been represented to me, at Edinburgh. But here again, I met with nothing but Disappointment and Surprise. Matilda and Margaret Lesley are two great, tall, out of the way, over-grown Girls, just of a proper size to inhabit a Castle almost as Large in comparison as themselves. I wish my dear Charlotte that you could but behold these Scotch Giants; I am sure they would frighten you out of your wits. (123)

Out of this joke of fitting physiques to settings arose the more subtle conception that rival theories of taste were full of psychological and social implication. This is the idea explored in 'Evelyn' where beauty of a conventional sort is associated with repression.

In 1794 Uvedale Price came up with the treatise in which he formulated the tenets underlying Gilpin's practical aesthetics, and worked out their relation to Burke's influential theory. In it he coined the word 'picturesqueness' and this abstraction led him, two years later, to a much wider application of the 'general principles' at which he had already arrived. In his new edition of the *Essay* (1796) he argues that the 'qualities which make objects picturesque, are not only as distinct as those which make them beautiful or sublime, but are equally extended to all our sensations, by whatever organs they are received'.[18] So a movement by Scarlatti or Haydn might, just as much as a scene in nature, belong to the category by virtue of its 'sudden, unexpected, and abrupt transitions, – from a certain playful wildness of character and appearance of irregularity'.[19] With a typical neglect of the boundaries between life and art, Price proceeds to enlist a range of activities and phenomena under the banner of the picturesque,

---

[18] Uvedale Price, *An Essay on the Picturesque: A New Edition*, 2 vols. (1796), I, 53.
[19] Ibid., p. 55.

shifting his criterion away from the object itself to the quality of physiological response, and installing as his touchstone, as did later theorists, the excitatory, the attention-provoking, even the irritating. Here, in a nutshell, was the secret of the new taste. Traditionally, the subject had been either calmed by the beautiful which induced 'an inward sense of melting and languor', or stunned by the sublime which had the effect of 'stretching the fibres beyond their usual tone', but here was a further realm.[20] Predictably, Price found his prototype for the *natural* heightening of impulse in sexual arousal, and in a much cited passage called the picturesque 'the coquetry of nature':

it makes beauty more amusing, more varied, more playful, but also,
> 'Less winning soft, less amiably mild'.

Again, by its variety, its intricacy, its partial concealments, it excites that active curiosity which gives play to the mind, loosening those iron bonds, with which astonishment chains up its faculties.[21]

The quotation from *Paradise Lost* describes not Eve, but *Adam* as first glimpsed by Eve, her own reflection providing the ground for comparison,[22] and though there may be a homoerotic streak in Price's aesthetics (as there certainly is in Richard Payne Knight's) that is not of immediate relevance here. What Price is intimating is that received ideals of feminine beauty (and all that is implied in them) are much too confined, and that their extension would make for greater freedom. Some of his readers would have spotted a similarity in this move to Wollstonecraft's contention that it was necessary for women to reclaim qualities that had been appropriated as essentially masculine by men.

Arguing that attractiveness in women is something distinct from 'beauty', and archly invoking the French as the arbiters on such matters, Price finds an approximation for the picturesque in the word 'piquant'. This he glosses intriguingly as 'an uncertain idea of some character . . . which, from whatever causes, produces striking and pleasing effects'. He then moves on to make the extraordinary claim that his entire theory is embodied in the heroine and plotting of a tale by Marmontel:

The amusing history of Roxalana and the Sultan, is at the same time the history of the picturesque or the *piquant*, both in regard to person and manners, and also of its effects. Marmontel certainly did not intend to give the *petit nez retroussé* as a beautiful feature, but to shew how much such a striking *irregularity*, might accord and co-operate with the same sort of irregularity in the character of the mind.

[20] Ibid., pp. 104–5.   [21] Ibid., pp. 105–6.   [22] *Paradise Lost*, IV, line 479.

The playful, unequal, coquettish Roxalana, full of sudden turns and caprices, is opposed to the beautiful, tender, and constant Elvira; and the effects of irritation, to those of softness and languor: the tendency of the qualities of beauty alone towards monotony, are no less happily insinuated.[23]

Price could rely on his reader's knowledge of Isaac Bickerstaffe's *The Sultan*, a dramatized version of the comic oriental tale by the famed *encyclopédiste*.[24] The play had enjoyed a good run on the London stage before being published in 1784, and was sufficiently provocative to catch the eyes of the young Austens. Eliza de Feuillide reports that it was put on at Steventon during the winter season of 1788–9, with Miss Cooper (a cousin) in the part of Roxalana and Henry as the Sultan. Soon after its performance, Jane followed up her earlier playlet 'The Mystery' with her two-act 'The Visit', which contains a quotation from another farce performed over that Christmas.[25] *The Sultan* seems to have incubated in her mind for longer, for it surely ranks among the literary germs that went into the shaping of *Pride and Prejudice*.[26]

What Price refers to as the piece's overall *effect* is neatly summed up in James's epilogue where Roxalana boasts that her story shows 'an Empire's fixed laws by a laugh overturned'.[27] James responds to *The Sultan* partly as a demonstration of western cultural hegemony, arguing that it reduces 'a proud Turk to Christian obedience' (in fact, it ends – unusually among eighteenth-century Turkish pieces, and in defiance of Voltaire's tragic *Zaïre* – in a cross-cultural marriage). But his verse centres attention on the play as a statement about the changing status of women. Indeed, the occasion provided him with a sequel to his epilogue from the previous year for Susanna Centlivre's *The Wonder*, where he looks back at a passing age characterized by a denial of 'all female claim' by the 'possessors of the sword and pen'. *The Sultan* is unusual, again, among plays of its type in its single-minded focus on the emancipation of the heroine, who begins quite conventionally as an English slave newly arrived at the harem. Because Roxalana finds a true lover in the Sultan himself rather than in a disguised European visitor or fellow-captive, romance is kept at the centre of the stage where it takes on some of the fire of the Janissary theme. 'Love

---

[23] *An Essay*, 1, 88–9.
[24] Though Price no doubt knew 'Solyman le Second' from the *Contes moraux* (1761), his anglicizing of *Roxalane* and *Elmire* suggests that Bickerstaffe's play coloured his description.
[25] Le Faye, *A Family Record*, pp. 63–4.
[26] Penny Gay arrives at the same conclusion in her recent book, *Jane Austen and the Theatre* (Cambridge, 2002), where she points to other verbal parallels, see pp. 73–4, 88–9.
[27] *Poems and Verse*, ed. Selwyn, pp. 40–1.

and anger often go together', Roxalana reminds the Sultan who impotently attempts to retrieve himself by pondering the dignity of his position. But his anger has its source in the fact that he is weary of subservience, and secretly riveted by the spectacle of subversion. At the opening of the play he admits his disenchantment with the seraglio, which he disbands, finally, for his sole empress, Roxalana. The price of supremacy is boredom which dulls even his trysts with the beautiful Elmira who studiously conforms to the stereotype of the alluring slave:

ELMIRA: I don't presume to complain; for your image is so imprinted on my heart, that you are always present to my mind.
SULTAN: (impatiently) Nay, dear Elmira, I have not the least doubt.
ELMIRA: How does my sovereign like this robe which I have put on, on purpose to please him?
SULTAN: Oh, (yawning) Elmira, you love music – I have sent for the Persian slave, who I am told sings so well.[28]

Roxalana's spirit of 'caprice and independence' undoes all his attempts to shun her, or to meet her on his own terms. And though she speaks in defence of her rights as a 'free-born woman', her most effective weapons prove to be irony and mimicry, for she is able to voice unspoken norms in the very process of inverting them, as when she declares: 'Men were born for no other purpose under heaven, but to amuse us; and he who succeeds best, perfectly answers the end of his creation.'[29]

Despite its baldness and poverty of dialogue, *The Sultan* was found sufficiently ground-breaking by Price in 1796 to provide a model for his cherished concept of the picturesque, and it left a lasting mark on 'First Impressions' which was begun in October of the same year. In *Pride and Prejudice* the physical complementarity of Elizabeth and her conventionally beautiful sister Jane responds to the contrast between Roxalana with 'her laughing eyes, and the play of her features' and 'the more soft and more majestic Elmira'.[30] For this there were certainly other models, but the play's influence seems unmistakable when Elizabeth herself explains to Darcy how something more than liveliness of mind sparked off his fascination:

You may as well call it impertinence at once. It was very little less. The fact is, that you were sick of civility, of deference, of officious attention. You were disgusted with the women who were always speaking and looking, and thinking for *your* approbation alone. I roused, and interested you, because I was so unlike *them*. (380)

---

[28] *The Sultan; or, A Peep into the Seraglio* in *Supplement* to *Bell's British Theatre* (n.d.), pp. 319–28; p. 313.
[29] Ibid., p. 315. [30] Ibid., pp. 315–16.

In retrospect, Darcy's objection to Jane as a partner for his friend Bingley, on the grounds of her 'constant complacency' (208), is reinforced by this diagnosis, for his respect for simplicity is slow to develop. The straight looks and easy nature that Jane and Bingley share set off the complexity of the central couple, and while Elizabeth tells Bingley to his face that 'a deep, intricate character' is no more estimable than his own, she has the force of the narrative behind her when she insists that, at least, 'intricate characters are the *most* amusing' (42). Though there is no lack of comic precedent for the contrast between the two couples, or – come to that – for Elizabeth and Darcy's unwitting and unwilling attraction, for their wit, or readiness to give and take offence, Jane Austen goes out of her way to embed the language of their characterization in the discourse of the picturesque. Intricacy, for example, is a favourite term with Gilpin, and a *sine qua non* for Price who defines it as 'that disposition of objects which, by a partial and uncertain concealment, excites and nourishes curiosity'.[31]

'Abrupt' is another word that supplies a good instance of this bilingualism. Pemberley is approached by a road that winds with 'some abruptness', and over the page the estate 'where natural beauty had been so little counteracted' is given the stamp of the picturesque when seen from the house:

The hill, crowned with wood, from which they had descended, receiving increased abruptness from the distance, was a beautiful object. (246)

This echoes Gilpin, analysing mountain shapes in Derbyshire and Cumberland:

abruptness itself is sometimes a source of beauty, either when it is in contrast with other parts of the line; or when rocks, or other objects, account naturally for it.[32]

When Darcy unexpectedly materializes, forcing an unavoidable encounter and the deepest of blushes, his presence is semantically linked to the landscape ('so abrupt was his appearance', 251) in a way reminiscent of 'Evelyn'. His 'shocking rudeness', his staring and his silence are all symptomatic of a social abrasiveness that equates with the requisite 'roughness' of the new taste.

Elizabeth, for her part, is repeatedly associated with the word 'energy'. Her physical exuberance which leads on occasion to a trail of present participles (as in 'jumping', 'springing', 'glowing', 32) is one aspect of the 'wildness' by which she is regularly characterized – though the play of her (asymmetrical) features points to a deeper source, a delight in expressing herself at

---

[31] *An Essay*, I, 26.   [32] See Gilpin, *Cumberland and Westmoreland*, I, vi; and p. 84.

the risk of transgression. Though she does her best to cover the damage, her four-mile walk to Netherfield ends in dirty ankles and a muddied petticoat. While Darcy is struck by the flush given to her skin by the exercise, the guardians of household propriety are scandalized. Uvedale Price used to complain ruefully that he had been accused of having only one idea, which was to 'wet everybody in high green grass, tear their clothes with brambles and briars, – and send them up to their knees through dirty lanes between two cart-ruts'.[33] That Caroline Bingley can get away with describing Elizabeth's walk as an *abominable* show of 'conceited independence' points to its being a real breach of decorum (36). Even Marianne Dashwood's beloved Cowper had expressly ruled out winter hikes for women:

> When Winter soaks the fields, and female feet,
> Too weak to struggle with tenacious clay,
> Or ford the rivulets, are best at home,
> The task of new discoveries falls on me.[34]

On this point he was followed by James Austen who speaks of 'deep miry lanes / To female feet impervious'.[35] But Elizabeth's violation of taboo, however much underlined, only causes Darcy to remark on the way her eyes have been brightened by exercise; and his sense of being 'bewitched' and in 'some danger' is hardly dispelled when, at the chapter's end, Elizabeth refuses his company with the remark, 'The picturesque would be spoilt by admitting a fourth', before gaily running off (53).[36]

Though the picturesque was sometimes strategically aligned with the cult of sensibility by Anti-Jacobin satirists, the two movements were in fact distinct to the point of being contrary, the one proving as tough-minded as the other was sentimental. In 'Love and Freindship' (1790), the brusque Augusta is inspired to visit Scotland by Gilpin's *Tour of the Highlands* (105), but she remains devoid of all 'interesting Sensibility' in the eyes of the exquisite 'freinds', and an outsider in a plot engineered to mock the novel of sentiment with a long roster of domestic crimes. A trace of the same satire lingers on in Caroline Bingley who, after the exodus from Netherfield, expediently brushes off Jane in a letter full of high-flown expressions that rouses in Elizabeth no more than 'the insensibility of distrust' (117). If Jane Austen really believed that *Pride and Prejudice* wanted more shade to

---

33 Uvedale Price, *A Letter to H. Repton* (1795), 2nd edn (Hereford, 1798), p. 121.
34 *The Task*, I, lines 266–9. *Poems of William Cowper* (1813–14), II, 13.
35 'Lines written at Steventon in the Autumn of 1814, after refusing to exchange that Living for Marsh Gibbon.'
36 See n. 16 above, p. 77.

set off 'the playfulness & Epigrammatism of the general stile',[37] she had underestimated the novel's frequent disclosure of lustreless depths.

COURTSHIP AND THE PICTURESQUE

Given the feverish climate of the times, 'First Impressions' (turned down unseen by Cadell in November 1797) would have raised the eyebrows of some for its embrace of the picturesque. The *Anti-Jacobin* (1797–8) levelled the charge of political anarchism against the movement as a whole, and in 'Loves of the Triangles' took particular issue with the stadial framework of Richard Payne Knight's *The Progress of Civil Society*, together with the Linnaean sex of Erasmus Darwin's *The Loves of the Plants*. Though Knight was an innovator, social evolution was no more new to the picturesque than was the focus on sex in the natural world. Gilpin had drawn on the stadial schemes of the Scottish Enlightenment, and delighted in *banditti*. Price, pursuing further Gilpin's interest in the painterly possibilities of the rough and shaggy (and careless as always of category mistakes), had found a paradigm of the picturesque in wild beasts 'when inflamed with anger or with desire'. Hovering on the anthropomorphic, Price moves on to sexually aroused birds:

the first symptoms appear in their ruffled plumage: the game cock, when he attacks his rival, raises the feathers of his neck: the purple pheasant his crest; and the peacock, when he feels the return of spring, shews his passion in the same manner,
        And every feather shivers with delight.[38]

Though Price complained that his enemies portrayed him as 'a sort of tyger who pass my life in a jungle', praise of physical exuberance runs deep in his work, and his claims for the natural are often unequivocal as when he writes: 'the effect of all high polish on the character of scenery, as on that of the human mind, is to diminish variety and energy'.[39] His growl, however, was arguably worse than his bite, and when it came to treatise writing, he and his fellow propagandists tended to ignore the injunction to make it rough, Repton setting the fashion for expository heroic couplets. Naturalness was, indeed, to prove a very relative term. In *Mansfield Park* Fanny Price solaces herself with the blank verse of Cowper when she visualizes the havoc that will ensue if Repton is given his way with improvements at Sotherton (55–7).

---

[37] To Cassandra, 4 Feb. 1813, *Letters*, p. 203.
[38] *An Essay*, I, 77–8.   [39] Uvedale Price, *A Letter to H. Repton*, pp. 137, 67.

Following in the tracks of Repton who had claimed that Price's taste in landscape implied a notion of government based 'on the uncontrouled opinions of man in a savage state', the *Anti-Jacobin* accused Richard Payne Knight of wishing to remove all fetters on man's 'primal purity and excellence'.[40] Knight's primitivism was, in fact, not of this soft kind at all, and it is interesting that the Anti-Jacobin satirists distorted it, in the hope perhaps of preserving a monopoly of hard-nosed attitudes for themselves. What sympathy had been to the cult of sensibility, priapism was to prove for Knight's version of the picturesque. In *The Progress of Civil Society* sexual attraction is the force that spurs individuals, by nature deeply selfish, into developing as social beings. Knight draws on Adam Smith's theory of the four stages, on his own study of phallic rites, and on his love of ruggedness, to sketch a complex view of social evolution in which sex is both the creative prime mover, and an energy to be contained. For while the primal desire initiates all that 'changed the wandering brute to social man', it is also the source of deep antagonism:

> First native lust the rugged savage led
> To the rank pleasures of his lawless bed: –
> Promiscuous glow'd the fierce instinctive flame,
> Uncheck'd by reason, and unawed by shame,
> Till, often cloy'd with what he oft desired,
> His passions sicken'd, and his nerves grew tired.[41]

Only through the curbing of sexual passion (or perhaps through satiety) can the higher impulses initiate that 'converse of the soul' that forms family bonds and weaves a civil fabric from them. Since every individual is the theatre of a racial history, courtship rehearses, in its small way, the great drama of sociability. The instinctual life that survives from prehistory remains continuous with – and yet in essence distinct from – the life of civil refinement, and both come into play, uneasily saddled together – in the quest for a social partner. In a revealing passage from his later *Analytical Inquiry* (1805), Knight points to the way dancing straddles these divided worlds, for while it releases animal energies, it works as a 'natural expression of refined or elevated sentiment', this last impulse being visible even in its primitive forms, for 'the attitudes and gestures of savages' are grace and dignity itself.[42] In adolescence, however, animal desire combines with the

---

[40] 'Mr Repton's Letter to Mr Price' prefixed to Uvedale Price's *A Letter to H. Repton*, p. 10. See 'Letter' (16 Apr. 1798) introducing 'The Loves of the Triangles', in *Poetry of the Anti-Jacobin*, 4th edn (1801), p. 120.

[41] *The Progress of Civil Society: A Didactic Poem in Six Books* (1796), I, lines 131–6.

[42] *An Analytical Inquiry into the Principles of Taste*, 4th edn (1808); see particularly I,iii,2, and II,ii,58–62, 88; and p. 213.

idealism of romance to form unstable fantasies, 'pictures of perfection' (the phrase is evidently not Austen's alone)[43] that can only lead (without the aid of satire) to cynicism or disillusion. Knight insists, in sum, that the psyche of the modern beau is two-tiered, and that the experience of wooing, so much taken for granted, is a bewildering process, inevitably ridden with tension.

A similar sense of intrinsic irony pervades the central courtship of *Pride and Prejudice*, and it surfaces early at the evening party hosted by Sir William Lucas who, with an avuncular eye on matchmaking, tries to persuade Darcy to dance:

> 'What a charming amusement for young people this is, Mr Darcy! – There is nothing like dancing after all. – I consider it as one of the first refinements of polished societies.'
> 'Certainly, Sir; – and it has the advantage also of being in vogue amongst the less polished societies of the world. – Every savage can dance.'
> Sir William only smiled. 'Your friend performs delightfully;' he continued after a pause, on seeing Bingley join the group; – 'and I doubt not that you are an adept in the science yourself, Mr Darcy.'
> 'You saw me dance at Meryton, I believe, Sir.' (25)

Every savage can dance, and so can Darcy who carelessly betrays a pride in his performance at Meryton, while puncturing Sir William's pretence. His refusal to dance, dressed up as a principle, rises from a determination to avoid entanglement in what he primly considers to be inappropriate company, and belongs to the same mood of self-denial that causes him to find fault with Elizabeth's looks while admitting to her beauty and attractiveness. When the gauche Sir William seizes on Elizabeth to offer her up as a partner, Darcy – despite being 'extremely surprised' by the present of her snatched hand – finds himself 'not unwilling to receive it' (26). When he does ask for the dance, Elizabeth, still stung by his earlier rejection of her, refuses him, but her refusal restores the possibility of civility between them, while at the same time reawakening Darcy to the great pleasure of her presence.

Like Coleridge's water-insect, Elizabeth and Darcy's relationship moves forward by fits and starts, gathering from every setback the energy for a new break. In retrospect it appears to Elizabeth that they have each 'improved in civility', but reproachful behaviour seems to have speeded them on their way (367). Sexual attraction and civility make uneasy bedfellows, for if 'incivility' towards the outside world is 'the very essence of love' (an aphorism

---

[43] To Fanny Knight, 23–5 Mar. 1817, *Letters*, p. 335.

based on Adam Smith),[44] it is also a condition that afflicts lovers themselves. Elizabeth's 'deeply-rooted dislike' of Darcy has its rational side, and the reasons for it, good as well as bad, mount fast. Darcy's offensive haughtiness provides a fertile breeding-ground for Wickham's skilfully implanted slanders, and there is the real injury of his removing Jane as a partner for Bingley, news of which Colonel Fitzwilliam lets slip. All this is more than enough to account for Elizabeth's refusal of Darcy, but the particular outrage of the proposal, when it comes, points to a strong undertow of the irrational in their relationship. Elizabeth with her usual flair for articulation goes some way to identifying this when she asks Darcy if he can deny

a design of offending and insulting me [when] you chose to tell me that you liked me against your will, against your reason, and even against your character? Was not this some excuse for incivility, if I *was* uncivil? (190)

Darcy's only rational cause of dislike for Elizabeth is tied up with his recoil from bad 'connections', but it seems that the presence of a desire that resists conscious control is itself a cause of irritation to him. And when Elizabeth admits to 'taking so decided a dislike to him, without any reason' – for the sake, as she says, of giving free rein to her wit (225–6) – her own explanation is not to be trusted. Though she does indeed revel, Beatrice-like, in the role of a licensed taunter, there is much else ado. For her, as much as for Darcy, dislike masks an underlying attraction.

On the subject of sexual allure *Pride and Prejudice* is as eloquent as it is inexplicit. Beyond a fairly conventional sort of report on how characters look and are perceived to look, the narrator has little directly to offer. But the reader is made to see almost from the start that Elizabeth and Darcy are marked out for courtship, and this knowledge is superimposed on their apparent inability to get on with each other, standing in, as it were, for the attraction they refuse to acknowledge themselves. With an inspired reticence and tact Jane Austen succeeds in enclosing the unconscious feelings which impel her promising couple, who are alike in being unafraid of dislike. One early clue to their attachment comes in the after-dinner scene at Netherfield, when Darcy – after studiously burying himself in a book to avoid the sycophantic arabesques of Caroline Bingley – makes an unconscious gesture on hearing her ask Elizabeth to join in a turn about the room:

---

[44] *Pride and Prejudice*, p. 141; 'though a lover may be good company to his mistress, he is so to nobody else': Adam Smith, *TMS*, p. 31, but see the whole section of 1.ii.2.1.

Elizabeth was surprised, but agreed to it immediately. Miss Bingley succeeded no less in the real object of her civility; Mr Darcy looked up. He was as much awake to the novelty of attention in that quarter as Elizabeth herself could be, and unconsciously closed his book. (56)

Under the cover of civility Caroline sets in train a self-serving and knowing ploy. Using Elizabeth to bait her own hook, she shows herself more conscious of the real object of Darcy's interest than he does himself, for his distracted and telltale closing of the book is partly rationalized as curiosity over Caroline's out-of-the-way behaviour. But where Caroline senses potential depths from the start, the Bennets are so blind that Jane has to ask Elizabeth, after she has accepted Darcy, how long she has been in love, to which she replies, 'I hardly know when it began' (373). Twice she insists that it has been quite 'unconsciously' that she has inspired feelings in Darcy (190, 193), a situation reciprocated by the almost compulsive teasing that his presence inspires in her. The evening party at Hunsford is particularly revealing here, for it shows Elizabeth's feelings of anger and indignation for 'that abominable Darcy' (144), newly refuelled by proof of Wickham's accuracy on the character of Lady Catherine (84, 162), yielding to a manner that is bantering and flirtatious. Colonel Fitzwilliam gives Elizabeth a lead when he playfully inquires how Darcy behaves among strangers:

'You shall hear then – but prepare yourself for something very dreadful. The first time of my ever seeing him in Hertfordshire, you must know, was at a ball – and at this ball what do you think he did? He danced only four dances! I am sorry to pain you – but so it was. He danced only four dances, though gentlemen were scarce; and, to my certain knowledge, more than one young lady was sitting down in want of a partner. Mr Darcy, you cannot deny the fact.' (175)

Wickham's grave charges of misconduct pale away before the sprightly comedy that Elizabeth improvises round the uncomfortable memory of the ball at the Meryton assembly, and Darcy's lame plea that he needs to be introduced to strangers plays into her hands, allowing her to stage-manage a post-mortem on the original scene:

'Shall we ask your cousin the reason of this?' said Elizabeth, still addressing Colonel Fitzwilliam. 'Shall we ask him why a man of sense and education, and who has lived in the world, is ill qualified to recommend himself to strangers?' (175)

When Darcy confesses to a lack of social ease on such occasions, Elizabeth retorts, from the piano, that such skill is as much acquired by practice as mastery of the keyboard, and that his trouble is that he has never taken the pains to learn. Her whole bearing to Darcy proves, when face to face, to be out of key with her more composed sense of his moral outrage, but while this is a sign of her unacknowledged fixation on him, her assured replaying of the moment of her humiliation at the assembly shows that she is not only determined but more than able to keep the upper hand.

James Thompson has argued that Austen typically validates emotional depth through a sort of linguistic restraint: 'by claiming a presence beyond the limits of language', by pointing to what cannot be directly described, she fills out and gives form to 'an imaginative world of inner experience'.[45] This method of containment presents some obvious parallels to the ways draughtsmen and painters suggest volume and recession through the scantiest of interventions. The art of scumbling, stumping, or of leaving gaps was a major resource in early Romantic landscapes which aspired to the freshness of the sketch. But owing to the hallowed status of nature itself, the same tradition allowed room for highly detailed mimesis also. In a digression on picturesque painting in his long poem *The Landscape* (1794), Richard Payne Knight insists that while the component parts of a canvas should be copied from nature 'with the most minute and scrupulous exactitude', the overall emotive effect lies in a striking combination and arrangement of them.[46] And here, as Price so frequently insists, the ruling principle is *intricacy*: transitions should be 'sudden, unexpected, and abrupt', tension reaching a height when lines 'cross each other in a sudden and broken manner'.[47] The way in which Jane Austen conveys the perplexed feelings of her central couple is very much in keeping with these precepts. Her juxtaposition of clashing attitudes, recorded in finely observed scenes, continually opens up a new and arresting perspective on the complexities of courtship.

The plotting of *Pride and Prejudice* is in keeping with this aesthetic too. Unexpected disclosures and ironic reversals abound, so that the narrator's remark on Lady Catherine's last-ditch attempt to railroad through her matrimonial schemes, has a wide application: 'its effect had been exactly contrariwise' (367). Obstacles in the path of true love have always been the stuff of comedy, but in *Pride and Prejudice* the obstacles take on a life of their own, adding momentum to the subversive career of passion. At Pemberley Elizabeth wistfully notes that had she married Darcy she would not be enjoying the company of the Gardiners. But it is in fact the Gardiners – a byword for 'low connections' since they live in Cheapside (36) – who are the immediate means of reuniting them and of sustaining

[45] James Thompson, *Between Self and World: The Novels of Jane Austen* (1988), p. 101.
[46] Richard Payne Knight, *The Landscape: A Didactic Poem, addressed to Uvedale Price*, 2nd edn (1795), p. 47.
[47] *An Essay*, 1, 55, 58.

the connection. Indeed Darcy in his second trip to London becomes so closely associated with them that his good deeds are for some time mistaken for theirs. Lydia's elopement with Wickham provides a further twist in this ironic bonding. Before the event itself, Caroline – hoping to embarrass Elizabeth at Pemberley – comments that the withdrawal of the militia from Meryton must be a blow to her family, but Darcy is in fact stung by her remark which reminds him of Wickham's attempted seduction of his sister Georgiana, a secret he and Elizabeth share (269). Though Wickham's seduction of her own sister confirms Elizabeth in the view that all is lost between herself and Darcy, the effect of this supposed unattainability is to make him an object of supreme desire as never before (312). And Darcy, on his side, making amends for the damage done by Wickham, finally rids himself of his social legacy of intolerance when he turns sleuth in the East End to track down – and haggle with – the scandal-rousing couple.

Whereas Elizabeth comes to a new realization of her feelings in Derbyshire – a setting wilder in some respects than the Lakes in Gilpin's view, Darcy's shift of attitude can be traced on the map of London. Darcy, the proud incumbent of St James who can be counted on having no truck with the City and would, as Elizabeth says, 'hardly think a month's ablution enough to cleanse him from its impurities' (141), is soon at home in St Clement's Parish, where he picks up the trail from a disreputable boarding house in Edward Street. For Elizabeth, the final icon of his humbled pride and the last word on the matter of connections, is his presence at her sister's wedding at St Clement's Eastcheap. The choice of a fine Wren church at the heart of the City is in keeping with the warm portrayal of the East End all along.

Darcy feels responsible for Lydia because he has sworn to conceal Wickham's past in order to protect Georgiana's reputation (321, 324). But the leaking of this secret, like the promise Lydia breaks when she blurts out that he was at the wedding (319), proves to be immediately fruitful. Here as elsewhere the plot rewards the miscarriage of plan, accident over contrivance. And so Elizabeth who consoles herself for not taking in the Lakes, as originally planned, with the thought that she may at least return from Derbyshire with a pocketful of the spars made famous by Gilpin (239),[48] gives thanks in the end for one of a long list of coincidences that include, of course, Collins's link with Lady Catherine and the Gardiners' with Pemberley (382).

---

[48] Gilpin, *Cumberland and Westmoreland*, II, 217–18.

But the conflict between plan and happenstance is at its most glaring in the novel's presentation of courtship itself. Nowhere else does Jane Austen present quite such a broad spectrum of possible alliances, and situated at the furthest extreme from Elizabeth and Darcy are the dynastic pairings that the Bennet daughters seem born to frustrate. The most dismal of these is the engagement foreseen by Lady Catherine between Darcy and her daughter, Miss de Bourgh, whose sickly looks give some pleasure to Elizabeth, though Darcy seems, in fact, not seriously to be in the running for this interfamilial marriage that boils down to the union of two estates (158, 83). He is into the business of advantageous matchmaking nonetheless, and has his sister earmarked for Bingley, which gives him a certain susceptibility, by way of trade-off, to the advances of Caroline. Marriages of convenience come in many different shades in *Pride and Prejudice*. While a match that begins in infatuation (the Bennets') can end in convenience, another that begins in convenience (the Collinses') holds the alarming possibility of blossoming into lust on one side.[49] And in the case of Lydia and Wickham, lust and convenience coexist, despite an unequal partnership, and seem set to survive.

At Hunsford, halfway through the novel, what the narrator calls the 'stateliness of money and rank' (161) appears in full parade and is shown, too, in action. Though Darcy's disastrous proposal is, as he explains, a triumph of impulse over will, it reeks of hauteur and snobbery. Shortly before hearing it Elizabeth learns, moreover, of his blatant interventions to stop the progress of Bingley and Jane's romance. Even Darcy's companion at Rosings, the steadfast Colonel Fitzwilliam has to confess to Elizabeth – whom he openly admires – that as the younger son of an Earl he will not be able to choose a wife 'without some attention to money' (183). It is Elizabeth's taste of life with the Collinses, however, that conveys most immediately the stifling quality of a marriage without affection, and the view from the Parsonage – nestled against the palings of Rosings Park – gives further insight into an existence lived in the shadow of 'the stateliness of money and rank'. Lady Catherine's estate stands in exact and pointed contrast to Pemberley, and finds just the sort of appreciation for which it was intended in the response of Collins who, gazing out at it from his own neat plot, exacts his visitor's praise:

---

[49] Elizabeth admires the 'command of countenance' Charlotte shows when speaking of the healthy exercise that her husband gets from gardening: 'she owned that she encouraged it as much as possible'. At the same time she reduces contact in the house by choosing a room at the back for her living room, Collins being committed to a view of the road (156, 168). Roger Gard elaborates on these innuendos in his amusing and insightful book, *Jane Austen's Novels: The Art of Clarity* (1992), pp. 112–13.

every view was pointed out with a minuteness which left beauty entirely behind. He could number the fields in every direction, and could tell how many trees there were in the most distant clump. (156)

Collins's aim is to quantify Lady Catherine's grandeur, a chief point of which is 'the prospect of Rosings, afforded by an opening in the trees' (156). The last phrase is picked up later in a description of the grounds at Pemberley that brings home the very different role granted to lovers of the picturesque:

They entered the woods, and bidding adieu to the river for a while, ascended some of the higher grounds; whence, in spots where the opening of the trees gave the eye power to wander, were many charming views of the valley, the opposite hills, with the long range of woods overspreading many, and occasionally part of the stream. (253)

Where at Pemberley the view from the house itself unfolds intricately from room to room – trees and slopes 'taking different positions' (246), at Rosings it is a case of 'the view' for which all are summoned to a window (162). Far from being self-empowered, the gaze of visitors to the Park is directed centripetally towards the presence of Lady Catherine who, in the interests of having 'the distinction of rank preserved', frowns on conversation and is happiest when her guests dress down for dinner. The implications of her baroquely inflated despotism are boldly drawn out by the *points fixes* of comedy. Lady Catherine not only speaks of her nephew being *destined* from his earliest hours for his cousin, but *dictates* opinions and *determines* the next day's weather. She is aptly stationed in an estate which – though a little less symmetrical than that of the Webbs in 'Evelyn' – owes its layout to the genius of Capability Brown. Elizabeth on her walks through the Park favours 'an open grove' tucked away at the edge with a sheltered path 'which no one seemed to value but herself' (169). And though perhaps no one but Collins would have counted the number of trees in a 'clump' (any more than they would the windows of Rosings), with four mentions of palings, and eight of gates Austen makes the fingerprints of a specific style impossible to mistake.

Price, in attacking the school of Brown, turned the clump into an object of contention, and his account of its genesis in his *Essay* has an intriguing bearing on the social ethos of Hunsford. Trees, in Brown's scheme, were reserved for an encircling belt round the perimeter of the park (at Rosings this border is breached to allow a vista of the house, 156), and were otherwise confined to separate groups whose purpose was to emphasize the clear and smooth sweep of grassy land. In the job of clearance, Price argues, 'the giant sons of the forest' were often left standing to form the nucleus of clumps while lesser trees and scrub were swept away, but on these the whole effect of the natural scene depended:

often some of the most beautiful groups, owe the playful variety of their form, and their happy connection with other groups, to some apparently insignificant, and to many eyes, even ugly trees.[50]

Accusing Brown of regimentation, he compares his clumps (which were commonly fenced off) to platoons on parade, and by such means builds a political dimension into his protest against the taste that had already won the status of a national style. Connection rapidly shifts from a visual term, in his hands, to a sociological one: he uses the word to embroil the liberal, Anglo-Scottish idea of a social fabric woven of local loyalties. In his letter to Repton who had labelled him an anarchist, he equates connection in a landscape to a community which owes its good relations to a sense of reciprocal responsibility. Repton's breach of this principle is brought home in *Mansfield Park* where the alterations to Thornton Lacey suggested by Henry Crawford (who is a devotee of his school) involve a total reorientation that would 'shut out' all traces of the vicarage's social context – the adjoining farmyard and blacksmith's shop (241–2). In the plates of several of Repton's books such excision was enacted with the help of raisable flaps, one of which notoriously disposed of a beggar.[51] Brown's even more drastic clearances – which often entailed eviction – and stemmed from a love of the 'distinct, hard, and unconnected', spelt out a proud isolationism that rejoiced in the severance of ties with lower ranks;[52] and his improvements seemed, in the troubled climate of the mid-nineties, to be a conspicuous symbol of an aristocracy that refused to acknowledge the source of its riches, islanding itself in an ocean of mown grass.

Though Lady Catherine is the high-priestess of 'connection' – a word that re-echoes throughout the novel, what she really means by the word is dis-connection as her ready recourse to the metaphor of pollution shows. If she is brought to visit Pemberley after the wedding it is in spite of the

---

[50] *Essays* (1810), I, 255.

[51] Repton began this practice in his Red Books; the begging war-veteran appears on the flap of a plate entitled 'View Fom My Own Cottage, In Essex'. *Fragments on the Theory and Practice of Landscape Gardening* (1816), facing p. 232. For a valuable discussion of Austen's relation to Repton's work see Alistair M. Duckworth, *The Improvement of the Estate: A Study of Jane Austen's Novels* (Baltimore, 1971), pp. 39–52.

[52] See *A Letter to H. Repton*, p. 163; and for some valuable commentary on the implications of Brown's 'style of disconnection' see Stephen Daniels and Charles Watkins in Copley and Garside, eds., *Picturesque*, p. 21.

taint that its 'woods had received, not merely from the presence of such a mistress, but the visits of her uncle and aunt from the city' (388). When it comes to courtship Lady Catherine is the clumper *par excellence*, her incestuous outlook being formed not only by the wish to keep wealth within the family but by the premiss that her family is the best possible connection. These family attitudes also run deep in Darcy who has, by his own admission, been taught from an early age 'to be selfish and overbearing, to care for none beyond my own family circle, to think meanly of all the rest of the world' (369). Darcy changes, however, and though he frequently and bluntly reverts to the 'inferiority' of Elizabeth's connections (52, 189, 192), he does ultimately learn, in her phrase, 'to get the better of himself' (327). He undergoes a radical transformation in the course of the novel, powered by the spell of Elizabeth and by all that disposes him to her, and no other character alters as much. Critics who press the novel into an Anti-Jacobin mould tend to compress or discard this basic feature, concentrating instead on Elizabeth's change of heart, treated in some cases as though it were a religious conversion. In fact, the Butlerian stereotype of the sprightly heroine who renounces her independence of mind in order to conform to a received view of the world is peculiarly ill-suited to the character of Elizabeth Bennet who suffers no diminishment of either liberty or sprightliness in her process of maturation. Indeed, such a reading is deliberately blocked by the narrator on the novel's last page:

Georgiana had the highest opinion in the world of Elizabeth; though at first she often listened with an astonishment bordering on alarm, at her lively, sportive, manner of talking to her brother. He, who had always inspired in herself a respect which almost overcame her affection, she now saw the object of open pleasantry. Her mind received knowledge which had never before fallen in her way. (387–8)

'Self-abasing' Elizabeth never is,[53] and though her mortification over being duped by Wickham leads to genuine remorse, this seems to reflect her generous spirit, for Mrs Gardiner is also deceived despite her much longer acquaintance with Wickham, and it is with good cause that Darcy holds himself responsible for covering up his history. Elizabeth is really never under any illusion about the superficiality of her feelings for a man who lacks the capacity to arouse her hate (149).

Hunsford and Pemberley are rival headquarters in that crucial conflict of world view that Jane Austen plays out through the novel's comedy of courtship. If Hunsford uses the idiom of Brown to throw an aura of

---

[53] Butler, *War of Ideas*, p. 209.

inviolability round social privilege, and to mystify the acquisition of power, Pemberley displays the principle of connectedness both in its landscape and in the field of social relations. It is there that Darcy, on a winding path under a 'hanging wood' of 'scattered trees', learns of the identity of the Gardiners and finds himself pleasantly *'surprised* by the connexion' (254–5). And though Austen refrains from using the term in Price's sense – either because the linkage remained unconscious for her, or because the term itself smacked too much of the treatise – the word is nonetheless used to denote complex mental association as when we are told of Elizabeth that 'with the mention of Derbyshire, there were many ideas connected' (239).

When the theoreticians of the picturesque extrapolated from aesthetics to the fabric of society they were guided by a notion of organic form. Price, for example, points to the way that the loss of a single tree can be of 'infinite consequence to the effect of a place, by making an irreparable breach in the outline of a principal wood'.[54] His respect for the natural is tied up with his sense of a mysterious self-regulating process that allows competing individual forms to adapt jointly to forces like the wind, and to make the optimum use of resources such as air and light. What he sees in the picturesque setting where 'the small connecting ties and bonds' are allowed to develop,[55] is something equivalent to Adam Smith's idea of 'the invisible hand', an idea that comes in for special praise, unsurprisingly, in Knight's *Progress of Civil Society* where it surfaces after the division of labour which 'Taught men each other's talents to employ':

> As mutual wants and appetites required,
> What one rejected, others still desired;
> And shares unequal, tended to arrange
> The just equality of just exchange.[56]

From this understanding of a social order that is self-creating rather than preordained, there flows a deep regard for individual enterprise and a suspicion of power:

> Thus fix'd, the sense of public good excites,
> Its best support, respect for private rights,
> Connects the many, to repress the wrong
> Which oft the feeble suffer'd from the strong.[57]

Such a view had clear implications for private life, and particularly for courtship where the essential thing was a bond of affection as involuntary

---

[54] *Essays* (1810), I, 255.   [55] Ibid., I, 238.
[56] *The Progress of Civil Society*, IV, lines 52–5.   [57] Ibid., I, lines 436–9, p. 20.

and as intractable as individuality itself.[58] An absence of 'particular regard', for instance, makes it clear to Elizabeth that the very plausible pairing of Bingley and Georgiana poses no threat to her sister Jane (262). Because affection was a *sine qua non* of happiness, it was a consideration altogether distinct from issues of prudence, and likely to be put at risk by coercion. Moreover, since marriage was, as Henry Tilney puts it in *Northanger Abbey*, as much 'a contract' between two individuals as any dance (76), equality was its essence, and female expressivity an essential means to it. Hence the challenging piquancy of Roxalana in *The Sultan*, the heroine whom Price singled out as an icon of the picturesque. Hence, too, the far more supple Elizabeth Bennet who provides Darcy's repressed sister (267) with a model of the free-spirited wife.

But while there was a radical aspect to picturesque theory, the movement had more than one face. Foremost was a non-interventionist attitude which received support from the latent idea of an invisible hand busily at work shaping both nature and society. The precept of laissez-faire carried a threat to vested interests in the old pre-mercantile order: it could be associated with the energies of a rising middle class or with casual dismissal of the authority of church and state. On the other hand, the deeply *conservationist* tendencies of the movement could be used to tease out a quite contrary message, and it is amusing to watch Price resorting to this ploy when defending himself against the charge of Jacobinism.[59] Answering Repton, who argued that Price's work took the short route to French republicanism, Knight, for his part, disowns any link between 'picturesque composition and political confusion', and sarcastically begs his readers not to assume that 'the preservation of trees and terraces has any connection with the destruction of states and kingdoms'.[60] In fact, the links with revolutionary sentiment were sometimes explicit. Knight in the first edition of *The Landscape* (1794) describes a dam that breaks, its stagnant waters tearing up soil that settles at length into rich agricultural land: 'So when rebellion breaks the despot's chain, / First wasteful ruin marks the rabble's reign / . . . Then temperate order from confusion springs.'[61] But to the second edition of his georgic he added a passage championing the rising in the Vendée, and a sympathetic vignette of the imprisoned Marie-Antoinette, describing the government

---

[58] 'Anything is to be preferred or endured rather than marrying without Affection'; To Fanny Knight, 18–20 Nov. 1814, *Letters*, p. 280.

[59] See, for example, his *Letter to H. Repton*, pp. 163–4.

[60] Part of his comment on Repton's 'Letter to Price' in the 'Postscript' to his *The Landscape* (1795), p. 104.

[61] *The Landscape*, ii, lines 395–8. For a reading of Knight as a more conservative figure see Tim Fulford, *Landscape, Liberty, and Authority* (Cambridge, 1996), pp. 130–4.

in France as a military despotism.[62] By the time that Jane Austen started on 'First Impressions' the school of the picturesque had taken on the character of a reformist rather than radical movement. While openly monarchical its watchword was freedom, and the political tenets of both Price and Knight seem to have been closely allied to those of their friend, the Whig leader Charles James Fox.

The stadial and Smithian framework of *The Progress of Civil Society* (1796) lent itself to an essentially reformist view of political change, and was a logical development of the earlier ideas on landscape. Where Brown had aspired to fixity, and to the stasis of art, Gilpin and Price enthused over natural change, holding up the process of ageing as a paradigm of the picturesque, and insisting that even dead and stricken trees had a place in their scheme of things. And if reverence was due to organic growth, historical accretions obviously counted for something too. Avenues and formal gardens surrounding old houses were to be preserved at all costs.[63] What, then, of societal institutions inherited from the past? The answer seems to have been twofold. Knight in his *Progress* attributes the stability of society to the maintenance of customs and laws, arguing that wherever 'tradition's lengthening chain descends, / Order connected spreads and rule extends'. On the other hand tradition was, by virtue of its piecemeal design, ever-evolving and subject to one refining precept in particular, 'respect for private rights'.[64] This added up, in all, to a respect for the past that fell far short of a Burkean sanction of it, for where nature could be counted on to change itself, society was the product of conflicting interests, some of which were entrenched and opposed to change. The 'invisible hand' could not do its work if it was tied.

Where Anti-Jacobin satirists attempt to invest social *mores* with a kind of quasi-religious sanctity, the picturesque writers, from Gilpin onwards, take a far more pragmatic stance towards the operations of social lore. So, too, did Jane Austen, who remarked in her teens that ancient customs should be regarded as sacred – unless 'prejudicial to Happiness', a formulation that agrees with Adam Smith's 'two principles' of governance in his *Theory of Moral Sentiments*, the first of which prescribes a reverence for the already established, providing that it remains consistent with the

---

[62] See *The Landscape* (1795), p. 92.

[63] When Jane Austen's brother Edward took over Chawton House in 1798, he seems to have attempted to restore some of the walled gardens and enclosures swept away by a landscape designer of the Brown school. See Lesley Garner, 'A Literary Landscape: Chawton House', *Gardens Illustrated* (Mar. 2001), 74–80.

[64] See *The Progress of Civil Society*, I, lines 375–6, 437, pp. 17, 20.

second – 'an earnest desire to render the condition of our fellow-citizens as safe, respectable, and as happy as we can'.[65] In *Pride and Prejudice* a good test case is provided, on a domestic scale, by the sexual union of Lydia and Wickham which flourishes for some time without the benefit of clergy. This breach of code is taken seriously, and the language of 'wildness' is applied to Lydia's blithe disregard for the claims of society, but the spirit of analysis remains overwhelmingly secular. Collins may refer on one occasion to Lydia's guilt, but the real issue is the shame brought on her family, and its ruinous effects on the marriage prospects of the other daughters. Unlike many of her contemporaries, Jane Austen writes about shame unblinkingly, exposing its devastating impact and its power of involving the innocent. She shows that shame matters, and that it is a rudimentary social force, albeit one that cries out for humane mediation. Humour has a part to play in its remission, and the way Lydia herself remains untouched (and radiantly self-centred) is a source of rich comedy. But the storm that rages around her is real enough, and Mr Bennet is at his most facile when he shrugs off Elizabeth's warnings about Lydia: 'What, has she frightened away some of your lovers? Poor little Lizzy! . . . Such squeamish youths as cannot bear to be connected with a little absurdity, are not worth a regret' (231). This underestimation is on a par with the rest of his paternal reticence, though the shortcomings of the Bennet parents have, in retrospect, more to do with a neglect of the younger daughters' education than with any reluctance to intervene on their behalf. It is precisely Mrs Bennet's relentless matchmaking that seals Lydia's fate by putting her into Wickham's hands, her pandering on this occasion nearly destroying the hopes of her two eldest daughters for a second time.

Thanks to Darcy's deft rescue bid, Lydia's scandal soon blows over, and the stigma of her transgression is quick to heal. Collins, however, does his best to keep the wound open, arguing that since the 'heinous offence' is eternal, Lydia and Wickham should be ostracized forever, to which he adds that had he been rector of Longbourne he would have rejected any approach as 'an encouragement of vice' (364). In fact, Collins has a bifocal attitude towards his professional duties at Rosings where he acts as the stooge of Lady Catherine as well as the scourge of the Lord. His advice to the Bennets is accordingly tailored to his patron's interest (363), and his tone and bearing at such points have numerous precedents among

---

[65] Jane Austen wrote in the margin to her copy of Goldsmith's *History of England*: 'Every ancient custom ought to be Sacred, unless it is prejudicial to Happiness.' See Mary-Augusta Austen-Leigh, *Personal Aspects* (1920), p. 28. And see Adam Smith, *TMS*, VI.ii.2.11–12, 231–2.

Church-and-King parsons in the 'Jacobin' novels against which Austen is so often assumed to have warred.

BAGE, BURKE, AND WOLLSTONECRAFT

One forbear of Collins who particularly repays scrutiny is the rector in *Hermsprong*, for Jane Austen not only owned a copy of this quasi-radical novel by Robert Bage which appeared early in 1796, but seems, from a variety of internal evidence, to have read it before starting on 'First Impressions' later in the same year.[66] Though she would have been aware of several contexts in which the linkage 'pride and prejudice' occurs,[67] Bage's use of the phrase has a special pertinence for it is his shorthand for the social snobbery that threatens to destroy the relationship between his lovers, the outspokenly democratic Hermsprong and Caroline Campinet, daughter of the autocratic Lord Grondale. The theme of 'low connections' comes into play in other ways as well, for Lord Grondale spurns his aunt Mrs Garnet, a paragon of civility, who has married into trade; and he is tormented by the sprightly Miss Fluart, his daughter's bosom-friend who is a veritable 'child of commerce'. Miss Fluart (applauded by Mary Wollstonecraft, and compared since to Elizabeth Bennet)[68] succeeds in her scheme of uniting the lovers, despite being opposed by the Reverend Dr Blick who, as his patron's staunch ally, moves heaven and hell to keep them apart.

In Dr Blick, a sworn enemy to reform and 'lenity', Bage provides a political caricature of the diehard Church-and-King parson of the mid-nineties. Blick preaches against infidelity whether in pulpit or pub, condemns religious tolerance and is angered by the exercise of charity.[69] He dismisses his curate on the grounds that he is 'tainted with principles almost republican', and rehashes Burke when developing his attack on 'the abominable doctrines of the rights of man'.[70] With Burke he is again linked through the way he came by his patronage at a borough election. Gerrymandering on Lord Grondale's behalf, he escapes prosecution only by refuging himself in that legal grey area of 'prescription' which Burke had famously championed.[71] A passage from *A Letter to a Noble Lord* (1796) in which

---

[66] See Gilson, *Bibliography*, pp. 437–8. Begun in October of 1796, 'First Impressions' was offered for publication to Cadell in November 1797.

[67] Notably Fanny Burney's *Cecilia* in which the phrase is capitalized; see R. W. Chapman's appendix to *Pride and Prejudice*, pp. 408–9.

[68] See Stuart Tave's Introduction to the facsimile reprint of Robert Bage, *Hermsprong; or, Man as he is Not*, 3 vols in one (1982), pp. 1–2. All references are to this edition (and to the original pagination of 1796).

[69] Ibid., I, 127.   [70] Ibid., I, 139; II, 36.   [71] Ibid., I, 134–5.

Burke returns to this brief, gives a fair sample of the sharply straitened tone of mid-decade reaction:

The duke of Bedford [a notable friend to the French cause] will stand as long as prescriptive[72] law endures; as long as the great stable laws of property common to us with all civilized nations, are kept in their integrity, and without the smallest intermixture of laws, maxims, principles, or precedents of the grand revolution. They are secure against all changes but one. The whole revolutionary system, institutes, digest, code, novels, text, gloss, comment, are, not only not the same, but they are the very reverse, and the reverse fundamentally, of all the laws, on which civil life has hitherto been upheld in all the governments of the world. The learned professors of the rights of man regard prescription, not as a title to bar all claim, set up against old possession – but they look on prescription as itself a bar against the possessor and the proprietor.

To the Burke of Jane Austen's adolescence even unwritten laws are sacrosanct, a part of that 'well compacted structure of our church and state' that he drapes in sacral language ('the sanctuary, the holy of holies'), and thus puts far beyond the reach of any improving hand. In keeping with his view that the smallest departure from tradition leads to cataclysm, the elderly Burke attributes the Revolution to the leniency of the Enlightenment. Not *l'infâme* but *douce humanité* has confounded the French gentry who 'could not bear the punishment of the mildest laws on the greatest criminals', having become so soft that the 'slightest severity of justice made their flesh creep'.[73] Several critics have dwelt on the cultural rift that separates Austen from Burke who did much to revive the cult of sensibility in the nineties, and set a standard for highly figured rhetoric. Marilyn Butler remarks that 'in manner they were antithetical'.[74] In politics they differed too, as is all the more apparent when due allowance is made for Burke's immense debt to the Anglo-Scottish discourse on civility.

In *Hermsprong* Dr Blick is all severity to his parishioners, but to his patron he presents another face, and in this he anticipates that great comic creation, Collins. An adept at the 'art of assentation', Blick is as 'cringing to superiors' as he is otherwise overbearing, living proof of his maxim that it is 'scarce possible a Lord should be wrong at any time'.[75] This makes for

---

[72] The claiming of a right through long usage; see *The Works of the Right Honourable Edmund Burke*, 8 vols. (1803), VIII, 48–9; and for the relevant passage from *Reflections on the Revolution in France*, V, 275–7.

[73] *Works of Edmund Burke*, VIII, 53.

[74] Butler, *War of Ideas*, p. 95. Claudia L. Johnson sees Austen as an opponent of the effeminizing tendencies of Burke's revival of chivalry, see *Equivocal Beings*, pp. 1–22, 191–203. From a different standpoint, Janet Todd has stressed Austen's distance from the whole tradition of romanticized sensibility in 'Politics and Sensibility', pp. 71–87.

[75] *Hermsprong*, I, 42, 229; I, 107; II, 9.

a loyalty, however, that is provisional rather than personal, so that when Lord Grondale takes second place to Hermsprong (who turns out to be the rightful heir) Blick is swift to change tack, turning his hand to a 'copious epistle, in a stile of pompous humiliation'.[76] Collins goes through a similar contortion after Elizabeth's engagement, wind of which comes through Mr Bennet: 'Console Lady Catherine as well as you can. But, if I were you, I would stand by the nephew. He has more to give' – advice so graciously taken that Darcy is soon 'exposed to all the parading and obsequious civility' that Collins can muster (383–4).

Underlying both these portrayals of the sycophantic parson is an idea boldly enunciated by Mary Wollstonecraft in a discussion of the way individual character is moulded by profession. In *Hermsprong* Bage frequently cites the *Vindication*, and in the course of long debates on education and sexual equality summarizes its arguments.[77] From this novel alone Austen would have had a clear sense of what Wollstonecraft stood for, but there can be little doubt that she knew the book in any case. Isobel Armstrong has pointed to the way the characterization of Wickham accords with an arresting passage from the *Vindication* on the effeminacy of army officers, and the same passage provides a sketch of the clerical disposition. In both fields a 'great subordination of rank' takes its toll on independence, bishops consequently being exempt:

The blind submission imposed at colleges to forms of belief serves as a novitiate to the curate, who must obsequiously respect the opinion of his rector or patron, if he mean to rise in his profession. Perhaps there cannot be a more forcible contrast than between the servile dependent gait of a poor curate and the courtly mien of a bishop.[78]

Bage clearly alludes to this in *Hermsprong* when the narrator closes a conversation between Blick and Lord Grondale on the respect due to property and rank:

There are men – classes of men, I believe, to whom no human attainment is so useful and profitable as assentation. It is for the benefit of young beginners in this respectable art, that I have recorded this dialogue. Dr Blick was an adept. He cannot be a bishop.[79]

As a novelist Bage interprets Wollstonecraft's analysis with some latitude for his curate of 'liberal opinions' does indeed stand up to his rector – though

---

[76] Ibid., III, 264.   [77] Ibid., II, 168–77.

[78] Wickham 'simpers and smirks', and enjoys the cross-dressing of his friend Chamberlayne (330, 221). See Isobel Armstrong's Introduction, xxiv–xxv; and Mary Wollstonecraft's *Vindication of the Rights of Woman* in *Political Writings*, ed. Janet Todd (1993), p. 87.

[79] *Hermsprong*, I, 229.

at the price of his job – and he includes a third charitably minded parson to show that Blicks are by no means universal.

Jane Austen appears to take a passing glance at Wollstonecraft also, but only in the act of demonstrating that Collins is larger than any stereotype: 'far from dreading a rebuke either from the Archbishop, or Lady Catherine de Bourgh', he leaps at the opportunity of attending the Netherfield ball, booking Elizabeth for the first two dances (87). Though Collins is as importunate in courtship as he is obsequious in the affairs of his parish, his conduct carries the mould-marks of social conditioning all along, for he relies on the submission of women as blindly and habitually as he submits to the yoke himself.

Austen's great brilliance in conceiving Collins was to conjoin two seemingly incompatible stock-in-trades – the toadying lackey and the presumptuous lover – and reveal their congruence. Her conflation of fictional types is readily illustrated from *Hermsprong* where Collins has a forerunner not only in Dr Blick but in Sir Philip Chestrum, the physically repellent and thick-skinned suitor whom Lord Grondale has earmarked for his unwilling daughter. Though the match is backed by Dr Blick, the sprightly Miss Campinet puts in a spoke wherever she can, and in a memorable passage tries to argue Sir Philip into accepting the principle that it takes two to make a couple:

'Does Miss Campinet's fancy and your's hit?'
'I can fancy she, if she can fancy me.'
'Well, I have told you that I could fancy you, if you could fancy me. But you can't, you know; and you say that's a good reason for not having me. Now what's a good reason for you, may be a good reason for Miss Campinet.'[80]

Collins perseveres in a wilful self-deception that is based, like Sir Philip's, on the premiss that daughters have no other role than to please. When Elizabeth tries to break through the assurance that causes him to take her refusals as a mere tease, she resorts to language that has the exact ring of Wollstonecraft's: 'Do not consider me now as an elegant female intending to plague you, but as a rational creature speaking the truth from her heart' (109). But the *Vindication* has already made its presence felt in the scene in which Collins, taking it upon himself to read to the Bennet daughters, discards a novel from the circulating library in favour of Fordyce's sermons. Wollstonecraft had devoted an entire section of her tract to the mischief done by this stand-by of the young woman's library, no doubt because it so perfectly exemplified an attitude – associated with Rousseau and the

[80] Ibid., III, 94.

sentimental school – that she was out to attack.[81] Quoting lavishly from the work, she notes an insistence on the physical feebleness of women ('They are timid and want to be defended. They are frail . . .'),[82] and a formulaic reduction of all marital unhappiness to a lack of proper compliance. This taken with a procrustean stress on the softness and patience of the female sex adds up in her view to 'the portrait of a house slave'. Wollstonecraft sums up her scathing analysis with the remark that such a counsel of submission might be calculated to have the opposite effect to the one intended: 'Dr Fordyce must have very little acquaintance with the human heart, if he really supposed that such conduct would bring back wandering love, instead of exciting contempt.'[83] When Lydia boisterously cuts across Collins after three pages-worth of sermon to arrange an excuse to get within range of the militia, she is treated, along with the other sisters, to a spluttering admonition which would have caused readers of Wollstonecraft to smile. Collins is amazed that young ladies can be unmindful of a work, 'written solely for their benefit', and of such manifest advantage to them (69).

Fordyce wrote, it is clearly implied, for the benefit of the likes of Collins, for the Collins, that is, who finds in Charlotte just the sort of prudent and uncomplaining wife who – looking for no more in marriage than a 'preservative from want' (123) – measures up to the specifications of *Sermons to Young Women* (1766). But the sexual politics of the Hunsford parish do not end there. *Pride and Prejudice* is a novel in which strong-willed women are dominant. Whereas Bage sees to it that his buoyant Miss Fluart is bested by the modest and demure Miss Campinet who wins the hero, Jane Austen champions Elizabeth Bennet, so that generations of Anna Howes, Charlotte Grandisons and Miss Fluarts come at last into their own. And on Collins, Austen practises a sly novelistic revenge. Triumph over Charlotte Lucas as he may, Collins is in the thrall of the patron whom he blissfully serves as a parish drudge. A comparison with Dr Blick's attendance on Lord Grondale brings out the particularly humble role allotted to Collins – Blick, for example, is encouraged to become a Justice of the Peace in order to be of use in upholding the game laws or in seeing off a political rival.[84] But Lady Catherine's control of her domain extends even to the smallest domestic arrangements at the parsonage where, if she accepts a meal it is only to make sure that the joint of meat is not too large. Collins's job as a cat's-paw is correspondingly limited: he merely works as a spy, reporting the complaints that Lady Catherine silences:

[81] *Vindication*, ch. 5, sect. ii.   [82] Ibid., p. 175.
[83] Ibid., pp. 177–8.   [84] *Hermsprong*, I, 42.

Elizabeth soon perceived that though this great lady was not in the commission of the peace for the county, she was a most active magistrate in her own parish, the minutest concerns of which were carried to her by Mr Collins; and whenever any of the cottagers were disposed to be quarrelsome, discontented or too poor, she sallied forth into the village to settle their differences, silence their complaints, and scold them into harmony and plenty. (169)

Though the tone is comic, the perception of a sort of policing partnership between patron and parson is acute, and of finer edge than the joke, from 'Henry and Eliza', about Sir George and Lady Harcourt's cudgel (33). Whereas testimony to good relations comes unsolicited from the tenants and workers at Pemberley, at Rosings (as might be expected of a conspicuously dis-connected estate) Lady Catherine is the sole authorized speaker and her words the only form of redress.

Though Jane Austen seems to have been influenced by the radical argument that the structure of society had a determining effect on the formation of character, she was not sufficiently impressed by the idea to abandon belief in social hierarchy. And in this she was in company with other liberal novelists of the later nineties who directed their attention to reform within the status quo, recognizing that such reform would lead to new kinds of social dispensation. Where in the early nineties Godwin in *Caleb Williams* had effectively collapsed the distinction between a good and bad squirearchy by pointing to the overriding force of positional corruption, a novelist like Bage returns to the distinction with renewed vigour, possessed with a sense that a difference in outlook within the landed gentry had immediate and lasting significance. His hero Hermsprong, who represents a model of the new man, is ultimately (by the old trick of romance) seeded into the aristocracy where he displaces Lord Grondale, who epitomizes the old regime. The same rhythm of comparison runs through *Pride and Prejudice*, informing the contrast between the ethos of Rosings and Pemberley, but expressing itself most subtly through Fitzwilliam Darcy, whose character refracts into a variety of images – not only because he is misrepresented as well as being misread, but because he matures.

The 'Noble Lord' to whom Burke addressed the most reactionary of all his works was William Fitzwilliam, the second Earl Fitzwilliam. And it is a strange fact, as D. J. Greene once pointed out, that the only Earl mentioned in Austen's fiction should carry this name.[85] Her choice may have begun as a private joke: the Leighs on her mother's side were distantly connected to the Wentworths and through them to the Fitzwilliams, and Jane at the

[85] D. J. Greene, 'Jane Austen and the Peerage', *PMLA*, 68 (1953), 1017–31; see pp. 1024–5.

age of nine had assigned herself to a Fitzwilliam in the wedding register at Steventon. But by the time of the novel's publication the choice had become inspired, for by then the Fitzwilliam family had moved through a dramatic range of political positions. In *Pride and Prejudice* the Earl is brother to Lady Catherine de Bourgh, and uncle to Darcy who is christened Fitzwilliam after him; and this shadowy background character corresponds historically to the second Earl Fitzwilliam (1748–1833) who was not only Burke's dedicatee but later the editor of his collected works, and by the late nineties a byword for reaction. His son Lord Milton (1786–1857), on the other hand, who later inherited the earldom, outgrew an unpromising debut to become an ardent reformer some time before his election to parliament in 1807. The gap between the generations is particularly well brought home by their respective attitudes to the slave trade. Where Fitzwilliam, after siding with the Portland Whigs, turned against the cause of abolition, his son stood by Fox, and became an active associate of Wilberforce.[86] Differences in outlook were not simply reducible to a social matrix after the manner of Godwin, when they so patently existed within the same position.

The least flattering version of Darcy that filters through to the reader comes from Wickham who seductively presents the companion of his boyhood as a sort of latter-day Falkland, the aristocratic anti-hero of *Caleb Williams*. Darcy, on this account, is driven exclusively by the desire of maintaining a spotless reputation. His conspicuous generosity is accordingly no more than the symptom of an inordinate family pride, and his virtues can be defined negatively since they amount to no more than a fear of detection in vice: 'Not to appear to disgrace his family, to degenerate from the popular qualities, or lose the influence of the Pemberley House, is a powerful motive' (81–2). While Elizabeth finds enough support from appearances to take up Wickham's construction of a feudal Darcy, it becomes clear at Hunsford – where everything is indeed 'built for envious show' – that Darcy's pride is partly a proper pride in that it has less to do with reputation than with self-esteem, in which he has to reckon with an impartial spectator very much like Elizabeth Bennet. All the same, Darcy's pride is, by his own admission, partly conditioned, for he has been taught ever since childhood to downgrade everyone beyond his immediate circle, or – more tellingly – 'to *wish* at least to think meanly of their sense and worth compared with my own' (369).

[86] See Roger Anstey, *The Atlantic Slave Trade and British Abolition, 1760–1810* (1975), pp. 398–9, and fn. 35; and see *DNB* entry on Charles William Wentworth (1786–1857), the third Earl. In a report of his election dinner, *The Times* of 15 June 1807 (p. 3a), hailed Lord Milton as 'an ardent friend to the cause of Liberty'; Fox was toasted on this occasion and a speech given by Sheridan.

No matter what the brand of aristocratic constitution (whether de Bourgh/Falkland-like or in a more modern style of egotism), high estate in *Pride and Prejudice* spells out a social pride that disdains connection. And while it is precisely against this dis-connection that the courtship plot of the novel is pitted, its romantic energies are, we have seen, deeply rooted in a system of belief fostered by the picturesque. In the writings of this school, imagery of emancipation abounds; Price speaks of loosening iron bonds and unchaining the faculties, Knight of the gusto experienced by the 'unfetter'd mind'.[87] Sustaining this reformist politics was a powerful (and by no means unproblematic) mantra, related to Adam Smith's 'invisible hand', which held that order, rather than being preordained and fixed, was continuously created by the expression of individual being. *Pride and Prejudice* is shaped by this libertarian idea.

[87] *An Essay*, I, 105–6; *The Landscape* (1795), pp. 2–3.

CHAPTER 3

Northanger Abbey *and the liberal historians*

Few controversies can have struck more resonant chords than the feud begun in 1766 by Samuel Sharp with his jaundiced travel-book, *Letters from Italy*. In 1805 Coleridge noted that travellers came in two kinds, 'both bad', but found in favour of the Sharpians.[1] In 1807 Jane Austen reminded Cassandra of an old quarrel on this score, admitting to some change in her view:

We are reading Barretti's other book, & find him dreadfully abusive of poor Mr Sharpe. I can no longer take his part against you, as I did nine years ago.[2]

That it was nine years back that 'Susan' took shape may have helped her date the argument with her sister, for Barretti's *Journey from London to Genoa* (1770), the better tempered of his replies to Sharp, intersects with the novel finally published as *Northanger Abbey*.

Baretti addresses the account of his native Italy to the English, and sums up his theme in the slogan, 'it is in your country as in all others'.[3] His aim is to oust the fashion for disparaging travels set by Sharp and Smollett, recently lampooned by Sterne in the figure of *Smelfungus*.[4] With Shandean guile, he preludes his continental trip with a tale of 'petty tyranny' that exposes a horrendous underside to 'the rural beauties of Devonshire'. A land-agent maliciously ruins the business of an innkeeper after being rejected by his daughter, and his case cuts clean to the nub of contention:

Now, ye Englishmen, said I to myself, behold! Here as well as elsewhere, the whale swallows up the small fishes, whatever you may say of your laws, which you think so antidotal against all sorts of tyranny. Your laws you say, are an adamantine shield

---

[1] *The Notebooks of Samuel Taylor Coleridge*, ed. Kathleen Coburn, II: *1804–1808* (Princeton, 1961), 2719, 2719n.
[2] 20–2 Feb. 1807, *Letters*, p. 124. 'Susan' was probably begun in August 1798.
[3] Joseph Baretti, *A Journey from London to Genoa*, 2 vols. (1770), I, 29; see also II, letter 57, 'All men alike', pp. 1–6.
[4] *A Sentimental Journey* (1768), 'In the Street' (ii).

that covers your whole island. No oppression is here of any kind; no: not the least shadow of it. But go to mine hostess gentlemen, and you will hear another story. You will hear that it is in your country as in all others; I mean that no such laws can be thought on by mortal legislators, as perfectly to screen the weak against the strong, or the poor against the rich; especially when the subject of complaint is not so great as to draw the public attention, which is generally the case in those many oppressions that the little endure from the great.[5]

Insisting on the limits of legal regulation, Baretti echoes the maxim of his friend Samuel Johnson, 'How small, of all that human hearts endure / That part which laws or kings can cause or cure'; and though a lapsed Catholic, he goes on to invoke the sovereignty of divine law, attributing the chauvinistic attitudes of his opponents to a facile humanism.[6] Sharp, a surgeon by profession, had certainly left no doubts about the secular nature of his outlook: a visit to Voltaire features prominently in his opening pages, and mockery of religious ritual alternates with passages on the violence and squalor of Italian life.

Distance from Italy is a firm index of political position in the travellers' debate, and when Baretti engages with English society many topical issues are brought into play. He traces the superciliousness of his debunking opponents to their confidence in social progress, for which he holds Whig history to blame. He seeks, in particular, to drive a wedge between commerce and social justice, ideas commonly linked by liberal writers in the comparison of national development:

The very dullest amongst them, thinks himself equal to the task of proving that the Italians, because less industrious, must of course be less happy than the English or the Dutch, who are the modern patterns of industry. But let us notice, that in the dictionary of traders and politicians, riches and happiness are made perfectly synonymous, though they are not strictly so in the lexicon of philosophers; and let us reflect above all, that it is impossible to enrich the hundredth part of the inhabitants of any country, but through the hard and incessant labour of the other ninety nine parts.[7]

Though Baretti later makes some conciliatory gestures to his adopted country, his answer to Sharp is a radical critique of modernization, in which he points not only to the inadequacy of law, and to its fragility in the face of unconstrained power, but also to the stark inequalities of industrial society.

That Jane Austen sided with Baretti in 1798 by no means implies that she shared his position overall; in fact she was far from doing so. For a

[5] Baretti, *A Journey*, I, 28–9.   [6] Lines 429–30 of Goldsmith's *The Traveller*.
[7] *A Journey*, I, 35–6.

start, she would have recognized that the social polarities to which he pointed had long been a critical issue for many thinkers of an enlightened persuasion. Adam Ferguson, for one, had anticipated Baretti in deploring the inequality of fortune that seemed inevitably to flow from the division of labour, bringing with it a widespread demoralization.[8] If modernization had brought a higher standard of living to the poor, it was nevertheless at a real cost: 'In every commercial state, notwithstanding any pretension to equal rights, the exaltation of a few must depress the many.' To which Ferguson adds that the commodity-orientated nature of the new society reinforces social division, by making 'the separation of ranks more sensible'.[9] *Northanger Abbey* has everything to do with the nastiness of acts of 'petty tyranny', and it exposes (within its own range) the profound difference between being deemed to have and being deemed not to have. Though written from a cooler and more detached vantage-point than *Pride and Prejudice*, it still adheres to the same school of thought. Baretti's protest is integrated into a social vision that owes much, as we shall see, to the liberal historians who come in for special praise in what Jane Austen planned to be her first published novel. But the debate over Italy sheds light on some of the more enigmatic stances of her characters there, and gives a recognizable location to the whole Radcliffean shenanigans at the Abbey.

The famous speech in which Henry Tilney scolds Catherine for imagining that his father is a murderer both answers Baretti and introduces a series of concessions to his point of view. It begins with an assertion of cultural difference – 'Remember the country and the age in which we live. Remember that we are English', but the case for a special modern civility is not allowed to rest solely on claims for civil law. In keeping with the Anglo-Scottish tradition, stress is laid on the concept of a social fabric woven of many strands, ranging from the psychological to the material:

Does our education prepare us for such atrocities? Do our laws connive at them? Could they be perpetrated without being known, in a country like this, where social and literary intercourse is on such a footing; where every man is surrounded by a neighbourhood of voluntary spies, and where roads and newspapers lay every thing open? (197–8)

Henry appeals to what we would now call 'the public sphere', to a lively culture sufficiently powerful, in view of its developed infrastructure and

---

[8] Adam Ferguson is frequently explicit on this point, for example: 'In the result of commercial arts, inequalities of fortune are greatly increased.' See *An Essay on the History of Civil Society* (1767), ed. Duncan Forbes (Edinburgh, 1966), p. 217; also pp. xxxiii, 183, 186. For the influence of Adam Ferguson on *The Loiterer*, and perhaps on *Catharine*, see pp. 63–7. above.

[9] *An Essay*, pp. 186, 248.

press, to breach the walls protecting privilege and secrecy.[10] He also invokes a world in which individuals strive for approbation under the eyes of real or of impartial spectators – and of some, perhaps, on the payroll as well.[11] Certainly his harangue is lightened, as it develops, by touches of irony that gradually rid his rite of exorcism of its Panglossian air. In due course his counsel is adopted by Catherine who remorsefully consigns her gothicizing to Italy and other southern realms, urging herself to believe that there is security even for the unloved 'in the central part of England' (200).

By now the imperative to 'remember the country' has taken on the force of a recognizable trope, one of those injunctions made only to be broken, and, sure enough, news instantly arrives of what has been waived as unthinkable – James reports on the way Isabella has swept aside their forthcoming marriage by becoming engaged to Frederick Tilney. Tied in with this surprise is Henry's own defaulting on the advice he gives Catherine apropos his brother: that conduct is seldom benign and nothing more blinding than good nature (133, 152). The task of coming to grips with the motives of Isabella and of General Tilney consequently becomes a training in 'the apprehension of evil' (237), and Catherine's gothic prefiguring of Henry's father as a Montoni turns out to have an imaginative truth, as she herself is again brought round to see when she reflects that in suspecting him 'of either murdering or shutting up his wife, she had scarcely sinned against his character, or magnified his cruelty' (247). Though the General breaks no law, his dealings – grounded in a ruthless greed – epitomize the antisocial, which makes him just the figure to give life to Baretti's critique of unofficial oppression. While the thrust of the novel's burlesque is in line with Sharp, the ironic re-adaptation of gothic inclines the other way, picking out the features of a menace that passes without name.

RADCLIFFE AND RECIDIVISM

Catherine is lured into reading her world in depth through Mrs Radcliffe who casts deep shadows over daily routines at the modernized Abbey. This seems strange in a novel noted for its send-up of the gothic. But there is further paradox in the fact that Radcliffe undoubtedly ranks among the followers of Sharp – she specializes in historical and exotic settings

[10] See Jürgen Habermas, *The Structural Transformation of the Public Sphere: An Inquiry into a Category of Bourgeois Society*, trans. Thomas Burger (Cambridge, 1989).
[11] See B. C. Southam, '"Regulated Hatred" Revisited', in his *Jane Austen: Northanger Abbey and Persuasion: A Casebook* (1976), pp. 122–7; and Robert Hopkins, 'General Tilney and Affairs of State', *Philological Quarterly*, 57 (1978), 213–24.

that are deliberately made remote and unfamiliar. In *Udolpho* crossings of the Alps and Pyrenees have all the effect of time-travel. The state of anarchy ascribed to society on the far side actually belongs, as Dobrée once observed, to an era far earlier than the sixteenth century.[12] And when Radcliffe chooses a contemporary setting, she relies on special means to underline the lawlessness of the ultramontane. So *The Italian* begins with a party of English travellers watching in stunned disbelief as an assassin takes asylum in a church where he will receive both food and shelter. Unsurprisingly the material for this scene comes from Sharp who strongly censures the sanctuary afforded to delinquents in holy places.[13] 'If we were to shew no mercy to such unfortunate persons', Radcliffe has a Florentine helpfully explain, 'assassinations are so frequent, that our cities would be half depopulated'.[14] The Inquisition, as pictured by her later in the novel, is well on its way to taking care of the other half.

Radcliffe's anachronisms and simplifications play their part in a tactical scheme – her celebration of what she terms in *Udolpho* 'the civil story', the rise of a peaceful order from the ruins of feudalism.[15] The telescoping of this social narrative is eased in her fiction by central characters who, as Coleridge acutely notes, 'give so much the air of modern manners'.[16] The lovers in *Udolpho* are straight from the novel of sensibility but find themselves at the mercy of an older dispensation. What Emily sees in Italy – as if through the eyes of the reader – is a 'tumultuous situation . . . every petty state was at war with its neighbour, and even every castle liable to the attack of an invader'.[17] The timescale effectively reaches from the present back to the collapse of the Roman Empire, a range that compares with that of Enlightenment histories such as William Robertson's *Charles V* (1769). In a climactic chapter Radcliffe equates a band of cut-throat smugglers, at large in the Pyrenees, to the warlords of a vanished era, comparing one of their number to the sort of scowling vandal responsible for the sack of Rome.[18] It transpires, at the end, that the same gang have used Chateau-Le-Blanc as their hide-out all along, and are identical with the novel's famous ghosts.[19] With this brilliant move Radcliffe clinches her sense of a precarious order haunted by a violent past, the magnetism of which is manifest in the content of her work. The peaks of the Pyrenees, glimpsed rivetingly from the haven

---

[12] Ann Radcliffe, *The Mysteries of Udolpho*, introd. Bonamy Dobrée (1980), p. viii.

[13] Samuel Sharp, *Letters from Italy* (1766), pp. 283–5.

[14] Ann Radcliffe, *The Italian*, ed. Frederick Garber (Oxford, 1981), pp. 2–3.

[15] Ibid., pp. 602–4.   [16] *Coleridge's Miscellaneous Criticism*, ed. T. M. Raysor (1936), p. 357.

[17] *Udolpho*, ed. Garber, p. 145.   [18] Ibid., pp. 604, 610.   [19] Ibid., p. 633.

of La Vallée at the start – 'awful forms, seen, and lost again', point to the treacherous ways of history and of the psyche.

Though Radcliffe deals in the vexed relations between old and new, acknowledging the threat of recidivism, she remains optimistic about social development, and in her travelogue of a trip through northern Europe made in the year *Udolpho* appeared, she commits herself to an abrasively confident brand of Whig history. Remarking on the way the Dutch have 'prepared their country to become a medium of commerce', she spells out 'the gradations, through which all human advances must be made', choosing as her model of stagnation the baronial states of Germany where feudal despotism still holds sway.[20] Holland and England are singled out (*pace* Baretti) as the countries which best exemplify the happiness that springs from the civilizing effects of trade:

Frequent opportunities of gain, and the habit of comparing them, sharpens intellects, which might otherwise never be exercised. In a commercial country, the humblest persons have opportunities of profiting by their qualifications; they are, therefore, in some degree, prepared for better conditions, and do not feel that angry envy of others, which arises from the consciousness of some irremediable distinction.[21]

Plainly discernible here is the presence of Adam Smith and also of David Hume who writes on the emancipatory effects of trade in a similar vein, praising the achievements of the English and Dutch at the expense of the Italians.[22] To the same tradition Radcliffe owes her pervasive sense of the intimate ties between government and quality of life. In Germany she associates sullenness and even stuffy rooms with a prevailing lack of freedom, and in the countryside traces 'sallow countenances' to the practices of exploitative land-barons.[23] Her enthusiasm for social and constitutional reform never wavers, even though she is a witness to the violence of the Revolutionary army, and once back in England she pays homage to a monument to the Glorious Revolution, omitting no 'act of veneration to the blessing of this event'.[24] Diametrically opposed to Baretti, Radcliffe attributes to ancient regimes and their lawlessness the oppression which she condemns as much as he. It is characteristic, however, of gothic fiction

---

[20] Ann Radcliffe, *A Journey Made in the Summer of 1794* (1795), pp. 13, 33.

[21] Ibid., p. 345.

[22] 'Of Civil Liberty' in *David Hume: Political Essays*, ed. Knud Haakonssen (1994), p. 52.

[23] Ibid., pp. 97–8, 100.

[24] Her husband, the journalist William Radcliffe, wrote in support of the early stages of the French Revolution in the *English Chronicle*; and see *A Journey*, p. 389.

that its drama and excitement are out of bounds, morally speaking, so that the genre resembles one of its storm-blasted trees, a ravaged head tearing away from the bole.[25]

At first sight, Austen's quarrel with Radcliffe is elusive. Eleanor Tilney finds *Udolpho* 'a most interesting work'; her brother Henry reads the novels 'with great pleasure' (108, 106). *Northanger Abbey* itself is as much concerned with the theme of civility as the gothic romances it parodies; and it too dwells on the cultural gap between present and past (or between England and contemporary Italy), even if less emphatically. Some irony tinctures the report of Catherine's new-found reservations about Mrs Radcliffe's works:

> it was not in them perhaps that human nature, at least in the midland counties of England, was to be looked for. Of the Alps and Pyrenees, with their pine forests and their vices, they might give a faithful delineation; and Italy, Switzerland, and the South of France, might be as fruitful in horrors as they were there represented. Catherine dared not doubt beyond her own country, and even of that, if hard pressed, would have yielded the northern and western extremities. (200)

In that 'dared not doubt' there is more than a hint that the perception of separateness rests on imaginative fatigue. It is Radcliffe's own, deliberately exaggerated sense of historical distance that makes her a dangerous influence on a reader like Catherine who resists the perennial truth that character everywhere is a 'general though unequal mixture of good and bad' (200), and thinks in terms of angels and devils. In so far as Radcliffe has a benign effect on Catherine it is, indeed, by disrupting her bland projection of benevolence. Austen's stress here on the way otherness is always mediated by human nature is thoroughly typical of the liberal school. Henry Tilney's formula, 'human nature in a civilized state' (109), arrived at in talking of history, marks out her accord with a writer like David Hume who, while he presents cultural and psychological forces in a state of perpetual interaction, insists that the 'principles of human nature' are mixed, part wolf and part dove.[26] Though a less conspicuous champion of progress than Radcliffe, Austen is ultimately a truer exponent of the Anglo-Scottish school. Her concern with exactitude and with probability, even her demur over Radcliffe's historicist melodrama, are all facets of a thoroughgoing empiricism.

---

[25] Thus, after exposing the cruelties of life in a convent, Radcliffe writes, 'such horrible perversions of human reason make the blood thrill and the teeth chatter', *A Journey*, p. 109.

[26] David Hume, *EPM*, 9.1., 147.

THE NEW WELL-TEMPERED GENRE

Though the passage about historians in *Northanger Abbey* fills more space than the famous set-piece in praise of the novel, many critics have failed to get beyond Catherine's caustic aside ('the men all so good for nothing, and hardly any women at all', 108), often inferring from it that Austen's attitude was one of dismissal also.[27] Lack of historical sense is the condition, however, of Catherine's quixotry. With the same assurance that allows her to transport Beechen Cliff to the south of France, she expects the portrait of Eleanor's mother to look just like Eleanor, for surely 'a face once taken was taken for generations' (106, 191). Her passion for ruin and abbey is fuelled, throughout the first volume, by the thwarted expedition to Blaise Castle, a brand-new folly. And history pointedly presents itself as a topic just after she has betrayed the naive quality of her absorption in Mrs Radcliffe.

The prevalent view that Jane Austen had no time for historians flies in the face not only of contemporary report, but of her known reading. Her brother Henry's claim that she had a 'very extensive' knowledge of the field – made in the note that prefaced the first edition of *Northanger Abbey* – is borne out, in any case, by the novel's internal reference. Catherine's complaints fall in with the manifesto material of the liberal historians themselves. If she is bored by all the good-for-nothing men, or 'by the quarrels of popes and kings, with wars or pestilences, in every page' (108), she is in company with Voltaire who set a new trend in historiography with the preface to his *Charles XII* – a copy of which belonged either to Jane or to her brother James. There the influential historian takes earlier chroniclers to task for concentrating on useless 'Popes and Kings', on princes whose 'lives furnish so little matter either for imitation, or instruction, that they are not worthy of notice', or who are to be remembered only like 'fires, plagues and inundations'.[28] Though Voltaire's narrative of the swashbuckling Swedish King took him only a little way down the road to a history grounded in the experience of ordinary life, some of his later works were known to Austen also. From the *Essai sur les mœurs* she cites the example of the powerful sorceress Galigai de Concini, paraphrasing from the speech Voltaire

---

[27] This canard seems to have been launched by Jocelyn Harris, *Art of Memory*, in the course of a valuable discussion of *Northanger Abbey*, pp. 26–7.

[28] Voltaire, *The History of Charles XII King of Sweden*, trans. from the French, 6th edn (1735), iv, v. A copy of this edition, signed J A, is still in the possession of the family; see Gilson, *Bibliography*, p. 434. Jane Austen mentions Charles XII in a letter to Frank, 3 July 1813.

gives his heroine: 'It is the Influence of Strength over Weakness indeed.'[29] Catherine's reading is perhaps confined to old-fashioned school history, for what she is looking for is very much in line with what the innovators had to offer. Women figure centrally, for example, in Robertson's popular *History of Scotland* (1759) dominated (as the narrator of 'The History of England' would claim for her own piece) by the story of the two rival Queens. Ultimately, the new history would swerve towards essay-form and away from storytelling. So Robert Henry's *History of Great Britain* (1771–85) surveys each period in turn, under seven separate social aspects – as if designed for nightly reading, Jane Austen once drily noted.[30]

Nevertheless, Catherine's concluding remarks bring history into firm relation with the novel ('other books'), and answering her complaint that the speeches given to historical characters are, like much else, mere invention, Eleanor touches on a number of hotly debated issues that bear on the practice of fiction. In defending the historians, she raises the key question of what status attaches to experience that lies beyond the individual's immediate sphere:

In the principal facts they have sources of intelligence in former histories and records, which may be as much depended on, I conclude, as any thing that does not actually pass under one's own observation. (109)

Eleanor refers here to the hypersceptical 'Pyrrhonist' rejection of ancient testimony (on the grounds that it must be as distorted as the sounds in a whispering gallery), and to its rebuttal by numerous Enlightenment figures ranging from Voltaire, Hume, and Gibbon to Austen's favourite divine, the egregiously empirical Thomas Sherlock.[31] Theories of probability, central to the period's philosophy of history, were honed on this debate; and from it there emerged a clear-cut distinction between written evidence and oral tradition – the latter only classed as untrustworthy. But for Hume, in particular, questions of internal probability were paramount. In place of the Pyrrhonist premiss that 'belief consist[s] only in a certain vivacity,

---

29 'Mon sortilège a été le pouvoir que les âmes fortes doivent avoir sur les esprits faibles', *Oeuvres complètes de Voltaire*, 12 (Paris, 1878), *Essai sur les mœurs*, 11, 577; and see To Anne Sharp, 22 May 1817, *Letters*, p. 341.
30 To Martha Lloyd, 12–13 Nov. 1800, *Letters*, p. 59.
31 For an excellent account of this debate see David Wootton, 'Hume's "Of Miracles": Probability and Irreligion', in M. A. Stewart, ed., *Studies in the Philosophy of the Scottish Enlightenment* (1990), pp. 191–229. For Jane Austen on Sherlock see To Anna Austen, 28 Sept. 1814, *Letters*, p. 278; Hugh Blair singled out Sherlock as an exemplar of Anglican rationalism (see the first *Edinburgh Review* (1755–6), 1, Appendix, article 1; 11, article 9.

convey'd from an original impression', he installs the touchstone: fidelity to 'the general course of things'.[32]

Though the visions of romance never are quite over in *Northanger Abbey*, Jane Austen is careful not to exceed the sort of expectations characterized by Hume. Indeed, phrases like 'the natural course of things', 'the ordinary course of events', 'the ordinary course of life', run through the novel like a reproving refrain; and the word 'probability' tolls constant warning bells. At the same time, the way Catherine sets about demonizing the General, conscripting almost any fact to her purpose (187, 200), gives full showing to Hume's analysis of our 'remarkable propensity to believe'.[33] In other ways, too, the plot responds to an empiricist sense of things. At the root of trouble (a happy disordering though it proves) is 'error', or unreliable hearsay. Isabella is led to her scheme of trapping the Morlands in marriage by her brother's yarns of their great prospects; and further trouble flows from the extraordinary version of this story that John Thorpe concocts for General Tilney out of sheer vanity:

as his intimacy with any acquaintance grew, so regularly grew their fortune. The expectations of his friend Morland, therefore, from the first over-rated, had ever since his introduction to Isabella, been gradually increasing; and by merely adding twice as much for the grandeur of the moment, by doubling what he chose to think the amount of Mr Morland's preferment, trebling his private fortune, bestowing a rich aunt, and sinking half the children, he was able to represent the whole family to the General in a most respectable light. (245)

These word-of-mouth histories, which Jane Austen found so rich a source of comedy throughout her career, were also deeply intriguing to Hume. The world of *Pride and Prejudice* is at hand when the philosopher remarks on the power of credulity in small communities: 'There is no kind of report, which rises so easily, and spreads so quickly, especially in country places and provincial towns, as those concerning marriages; insomuch that two young persons of equal condition never see each other twice, but the whole neighbourhood immediately join them together.'[34]

In choosing to centre the discussion of history in *Northanger Abbey* on the propriety of invented speeches, Austen points to the openly admitted role of fiction in a sister genre which was not only solemn, as Catherine has

---

[32] David Hume, *THN*, 1.iii.xiii, 145, and see also 1.iii.iv; 83–4; 'Of Commerce', in Hume, *Political Essays*, p. 94.

[33] *THN*, 1.iii.ix; 113; also 1.ii.viii.

[34] 'Of Miracles', *Enquiry Concerning Human Understanding*, ed. Tom L. Beauchamp (1999), 10,2, p. 176.

it, but had recently been canonized.[35] Indeed Hume was well aware that
the speeches he included in his narrative served to advertise his continuity
with the great writers of classical history, a gesture that many moderns had
felt bound to eschew.[36] Ironically, it was his scepticism that earned him the
right to this easy familiarity with fiction: as a philosopher he had shown
how integral 'fiction' was to the forming of such basic ideas as identity,
or cause-and-effect – the honest course was to make an admission of its
pervasiveness. In 'Of the Study of History' he propagandizes for his subject
by insisting on the way it resembles other forms of literature in its power
to move. He tells how he passed off Plutarch's *Lives* as a novel to a friend
who would read nothing else, and his model for the ideal history is a sort
of drama that is not only true to the past but that will make it come alive.
History, in sum, is an 'invention, which extends our experience to all past
ages, and to the most distant nations; making them contribute as much
to our improvement in wisdom, as if they had actually lain under our
observation'.[37] When Eleanor defends the sort of historians who 'display
imagination', she echoes this last phrase, but finds a special virtue in the
quality of representation itself – in the exercise, that is, of a fine and up-
to-date intelligence. Speeches, she claims, may have all the more value for
being 'the production of Mr Hume or Mr Robertson than if the genuine
words of Caractacus, Agricola, or Alfred the Great' (109).

Though no historian could vie with Jane Austen in the choice of a heroine
as ordinary as Catherine Morland or of experience as apparently dull, the
programme of the new history tallies in several important respects with her
manifesto for the novel. Both forms are envisaged as educative but popular,
and engaging to young women especially. While human nature and its
social vicissitudes are taken to be focal, the medium itself is crucial, instinct
with what Austen calls, more than half-seriously, 'the greatest powers of
the mind' (38); and the mental habit is evidently analytical, aphoristic,
and alive to irony. A key to Jane Austen's sense of the new comes, at the
close of the passage, in a curiously curt dismissal of the *Spectator*, judged
so full of improbable circumstance, unnatural characterization, and coarse
language 'as to give no very favourable idea of the age that could endure
it'. This confidence in the recent progress of intellect is itself, of course, a

[35] Dugald Stewart, for example, remarks that Hume and Robertson 'divide between them the honour
      of having supplied an important blank in English Literature'; see introductory Life (1801) to the
      Works of William Robertson, 10 vols. (1821), I, 31.
[36] See Philip Hicks, *Neoclassical History and English Culture: From Clarendon to Hume* (1996), pp. 180–2.
[37] See 'Of the Study of History', in *David Hume: Philosophical Historian*, ed. David Norton and Richard
      Popkin (Indianapolis, 1965), p. 38.

feature of the liberal historian's stance. If Eleanor Tilney prefers the voices of Robertson and Hume to the voices of the past, she is merely upholding their general sense of a civilization that has been lucky enough to attain, by hook or by crook, ever greater levels of refinement. Something of this is hinted, indeed, in her mention of Caractacus, Agricola, and Alfred. For these names taken together invoke the main theme of liberal historiography; they spell out a 'civil story' such as Hume uses to open his *History of England* (1754–63).

Hume's opening account of an unsteady cultural ascent culminates in the figure of Alfred, one of the great heroes of his work, who is seen to combine the best of his own Germanic traditions with what he draws from Jerusalem and Rome. The scene is set for this successful, eclectic set-up by the Roman defeat of the Britons under the generous-spirited Caractacus, the consolidation of Roman rule by Agricola who 'introduced laws and civility among the Britons',[38] and by the subsequent decline of Roman power and British morale, enabling the gradual supremacy of the Saxons. But while Hume heaps every kind of praise on the great Philosopher-King, he unceasingly stresses the brutality of Saxon society. Alfred's laws amount to little more than an attempt to regulate feuding, and curb the power of warlords. In language that looks forward to Radcliffean gothic, Hume describes how 'gangs of robbers much disturbed the peace of the country', noting that 'a tribe of banditti, consisting of between seven and thirty-five persons' was a legally recognized entity. Though Alfred vowed that the English should be as free as their thoughts, crimes such as Catherine Morland imputes to General Tilney, would not, on Hume's account, have come to law. The conclusion drawn from this is that social harmony is the product of civilized nations, and that the morality sustaining it flourishes only 'where a good education becomes general'.[39] There is much in the *History* on these lines, and when Henry Tilney picks up the conversation from his sister, he chimes in with Hume in his defence of the way education – and particularly the reading of history – cannot be divorced from the idea of 'human nature in a civilized state', a point he returns to when reproaching Catherine for her alarms (109, 197–8).

If the new history brought lustre to the present by exposing a tarnished past, the new novel was occupied, on the face of it, only with the present. Austen's narrator has scornful words for books 'which no longer concern any

---

[38] Hume, *History*, I, 10. A more fully drawn Caractacus is to be found in Goldsmith's version where he is given a speech in praise of Rome.
[39] Ibid., I, 178–9.

one living' (38), but *Northanger Abbey* holds the modern in constant relation to the ancient as if by sleight of hand. Settings are strategically juxtaposed: the refurbished but largely intact abbey of the second volume follows on the modish and new city of Bath, where, aptly enough, Austen was probably given her set of Hume's *History*, nine months before she began work on the novel.[40] The modernity of the resort is brought out through contrast with the small country village from which Catherine comes ('retired' unlike the 'populous' and shop-filled Woodston), and the treatment of her initial dislocation condenses much of that influential distinction to be made later by Ferdinand Tönnies between *Gemeinschaft* (communal society) and *Gesellschaft* (associational society). Catherine is chilled, at first, by the sea of unknown faces, by the press of crowds that carry her along, and by the fear she may not be found to conform, but the lively and colourful scene instantly excites her. The comparisons she is led to make by Henry are all in disfavour of the 'sameness' of country life, and her confession that she 'never was so happy before' points in part to the amenity of a social fabric raised on specialism, hence her insistent harping on the 'variety of amusements', 'variety of things to be seen', 'variety of people in every street' (51, 78–9). At Bath even the most time-honoured activities are caught in a new light; marriage as well as dancing is said by Henry to be a contract formed between man and woman 'for the advantage of each' (77); the evening card-game is 'Commerce' (89); 'civility' is the word repeatedly used to convey the tone of chit-chat and everyday encounter.

The second volume perplexes this confident view of the present, however, by opening a long temporal perspective that goes back beyond the Reformation. The Tilney fortunate enough to have a 'richly-endowed' convent *fall into his hands* (142), is all too plainly related to the General who is on the lookout for fresh sources of endowment, and patronizes Catherine until he finds she has less than ample means. A prodigy of greed displaces the image of cloistered and collegiate life, twice tantalizingly conjured up by the actual 'traces of cells' (183, 188). This brief but bold historical superimposition was missed by G. K. Chesterton who complained of the novel that Catherine Morland 'never found the real crime' – which was no other than 'the crucial crime of the sixteenth century, when all the institutions of the poor were savagely seized to be the private possessions of the rich'.[41] As soon as the General, who appears to be a paragon of *civility* despite the lack of ease

[40] Gilson, *Bibliography*, pp. 442–3.
[41] 'The Evolution of *Emma*', in Littlewood, ed., *Critical Assessments*, I, 444. As a Catholic, Chesterton was quick to attribute what he took to be Jane Austen's silence on the topic to her being 'supremely irreligious'. But her overall attitude to the dissolution probably resembled that of her brother James,

that he inspires, proves to be 'grossly uncivil' (72, 129–30, 185, 225–6), the reader is faced with the question that Baretti posed. Does the success of the commercial society amount to anything more than a skilful concealment of the cruelties that it has the power to multiply? At the climax of the novel Catherine is absorbed in the contemplation of an 'actual and natural evil' that assumes an almost palpable form:

> That room, in which her disturbed imagination had tormented her on her first arrival, was again the scene of agitated spirits and unquiet slumbers. Yet how different now the source of her inquietude from what it had been then – how mournfully superior in reality and substance! Her anxiety had foundation in fact, her fears in probability. (227)

Though her recognition shows up the limits of civility, the influence of social change is nonetheless implicit (even in the very different feel of her wakefulness), and her insight itself is approximated to the order of science.

Jane Austen's admission of perplexity was in any case typical of the new analytic school, which frequently vaunted its refusal to be partisan. Historical distortion was traced time and again to the interests of Party, and unexamined loyalties identified as the main breeding-ground of myth and untruth. Though Hume once owned to his generally Whiggish leanings,[42] he delighted in defending Tory positions, and his *History* first won notoriety for its complex contextualizing of Stuart autocracy. On broad issues such as the Roman conquest, the dissolution of the monasteries, or the Puritan revolution, he invariably found things to say on both sides of the question. An early reviewer named him 'a patron of toleration' for his habit of making free with the vices of every party.[43] An apology for this approach was put forward by Robertson in the preface to his *History of Scotland*, a work which Jane Austen seems to have read in her teens.[44] There he explains that practically all the documents about Mary Queen of Scots descend from either of two camps 'animated against each other with the fiercest political hatred embittered by religious zeal':

who in his poem 'Selbourne Hanger' makes a plea for the social value of the monasteries as places of refuge for the unworldly and serious-minded: 'Let not these enlightened days / Deny some little meed of praise / To those who thus, for what they thought / Religion, here retirement sought'.
[42] See David Wootton, 'David Hume, "The Historian"', in David Fate Norton, ed., *The Cambridge Companion to Hume* (Cambridge, 1993), p. 300.
[43] *The Critical Review* (Apr. 1759), p. 292.
[44] In 'The History of England' the date for the eve of Queen Mary's execution ('Wednesday the 8th of Feb. – 1586') seems to come from Robertson, for neither Whitaker, Goldsmith, nor Hume attach a day to the date; the year is wrongly given, no doubt on purpose.

Truth was not the sole object of these authors. Blinded by prejudices, and heated by the part which they themselves had acted in the scenes they describe, they wrote an apology for a faction, rather than the history of their country.[45]

While Austen's 'History of England' has recently been interpreted as an attempt to redress Whig and masculine bias,[46] its satiric concern with fanatical one-sidedness has escaped notice, despite the brash persona – the 'partial, prejudiced, & ignorant Historian' of the subtitle – whose one idea is 'to vent my Spleen *against*, & shew my Hatred *to* all those people whose parties or principles do not suit with mine, & not to give information' (138, 140). Even the great heroine of the piece has finally to take second place to her historian:

indeed the recital of any Events (except what I make myself) is uninteresting to me; my principal reason for undertaking the History of England being to prove the innocence of the Queen of Scotland, which I flatter myself with having effectually done, and to abuse Elizabeth. (149)

To read the squib as a sort of salute to the Stuarts (Charles, in the last sentence, is spared the 'Reproach of Arbitrary & tyrannical Government' for the simple reason 'he was a Stuart') is to miss the point and half the fun. Such reading is based, of course, on young Jane's irate margin notes to Goldsmith's *History*, but these scribbles only underline the point, for Goldsmith's selective plagiarism of Hume's work is so slanted as to exemplify parochial history at its worst.

The project of freeing history from political and religious sectarianism had some striking formal consequences. A chief aim was to produce a discourse that would throw the fictive shaping indulged in by earlier writers into bold relief. Hume takes a delight in consigning 'giants, enchanters, dragons, spells' to the pages of romance, and states that it is his policy to reject the miraculous, and to doubt the marvellous.[47] Robertson follows suit, gently mocking 'the amazing credulity' of his sources, and pooh-poohing such sensational stories as the poisoning of the four French Deputies.[48] This does not, however, rule out the search for a realistic basis to the mythical, as when Hume ascribes the supernatural events surrounding Joan of Arc to court propaganda, but simultaneously insists on personal qualities that are in their own right 'extraordinary'.[49] Such displacement

45 In *Works of William Robertson* (1821), I, v–vi.
46 See Christopher Kent, 'Learning History with, and from, Jane Austen', in J. David Grey, ed., *Jane Austen's Beginnings* (Ann Arbor, 1989), pp. 59–72; and Margaret Anne Doody's Introduction to *Catharine and Other Writings*, xxvi.
47 *History*, I, 487; II, 389.   48 *Works*, I, 359.   49 *History*, II, 398–9.

is an often-remarked feature of the gothic burlesque in *Northanger Abbey*, a text designed like the histories to hold received fictions in suspension. Indeed, the playful juxtaposing and cancelling of well-worn ploys – particularly the juggling with stereotypes in the opening chapters – bears some resemblance to a method for which Robertson was famous. In a work very familiar to the adolescent Jane, William Gilpin (whose distaste for the smooth extended even to storytelling) admires the way the Scot would make a parade of the well-worn narratives, before breaking through to a more realistic version of his own:

He first states the facts; and shews the almost impossibility of either supposition. When he has brought his readers into this dilemma, who knows what to think of the matter, he takes up the facts again – throws a new light upon them, on *another supposition.*[50]

In the *History of Scotland*, Robertson virtually conjures with his *idées reçus*, devising a characteristic syntax for the trick – a run of balanced disjunctives.[51] With her usual lightness of touch, Austen adopts this style in constructing the experience of Catherine:

Whether she thought of him so much, while she drank her warm wine and water, and prepared herself for bed, as to dream of him when there, cannot be ascertained; but I hope it was no more than in a slight slumber, or a morning doze at most; for if it be true, as a celebrated writer has maintained, that no young lady can be justified in falling in love before the gentleman's love is declared, it must be very improper that a young lady should dream of a gentleman before the gentleman is first known to have dreamt of her. (29–30)

A subversively disengaged narrator plays havoc with the old authorities, including the grandest of her precursors, Samuel Richardson.

It has been said that Hume's determinedly 'bifocal view' of history proved too subtle for his critics.[52] A reluctance to concede complexity certainly bedevils many accounts of *Northanger Abbey*, the 'reversible ironies' of which (in Edward Neill's phrase) have only recently been delved into.[53] At the heart of the novel there is a debate between two prevailing cultural forms (each, as it happens, of a liberal provenance), and too often the assumption has been that Austen is wholly partisan. On the one hand is the philosophy of the picturesque, a movement that begins in aesthetics

---

[50] William Gilpin, *Observations Relative Chiefly to Picturesque Beauty* (1789), pp. 109–10.
[51] An example of this recurring form: 'But whether . . . or whether . . . it is impossible, amidst the contradictions of historians and the defectiveness of records, positively to determine', *Works*, II, 74.
[52] Duncan Forbes, *Hume's Philosophical Politics* (Cambridge, 1975), pp. 284, 291.
[53] See Edward Neill, 'The Secret of *Northanger Abbey*', *Essays in Criticism*, 47 (1997), 13–32, 14.

but reaches to 'disquisition on the state of the nation', as Henry Tilney shows (III). On the other is the school of utility – or of progress through the 'mechanical arts', represented by the General, but implicit, too, in the burlesque of gothic. The Abbey is the site of intricately pleached arguments for and against.

Catherine is predisposed to the picturesque, but her feelings for it are heightened by her reading of Mrs Radcliffe, and more especially by Henry's résumé of Gilpin's ideas at Beechen Cliff. When she voluntarily rejects the whole city of Bath from that summit, Austen underlines the narrowness of the original visual theory, remembering perhaps the moment at which Gilpin, cresting Highgate Hill, averted his gaze from London 'and all those disgusting ideas, with which its great avenues abound'.[54] But Henry proceeds to draw on a more inclusive, and compassionate work by his mentor. The sequence of his talk, as he moves from the image of a withered oak-tree on a crag, to the oak in general, and from there 'to forests, the inclosure of them, waste lands, crown lands and government' (III) is designed to recall *Remarks on Forest Scenery* (1791), the book in which Gilpin turned his hand to a history of his local Hampshire.[55] Taking a leaf from his much admired Dr Robertson, Gilpin adopts a sceptical view of his sources on the New Forest, and diffidently offsets his own account of forest-law with an appendix by a dissenting hand, who accuses him, not without cause, of spreading revolutionary ideas. Gilpin moves from the Norman enclosure of the New Forest with its dismantling of villages and chapels for the sake of what Prince Rufus 'called his garden', to the later displacement of forest-law by game-law, with the consequence that 'a thousand tyrants started up instead of one'. Pointing to the unsatisfactory state of the crown-owned forests in the present, with their mixture of waste areas, inherited leasehold, and informal squatting, Gilpin sides with the view that sale of the land would provide the best solution, a remedy already being put into effect – as he must have known – across the channel.[56] The politics that lead to silence – and beyond that to talk of riots (via the joke at Catherine's expense) – are concerned with the distribution of land. And Henry, far from being the reactionary of critical orthodoxy, is aligned with a scheme – comparable to the auctioning of *biens nationaux* in France – aimed at launching peasant

---

[54] Gilpin, *Cumberland and Westmoreland*, II, 267.

[55] William Gilpin, *Remarks on Forest Scenery* (Richmond, 1973 facs. edn). For a plate of the blasted or 'withered' oak see I, 14–15, 31; for the essay on the oak, I, 21–31; for the history and politics of enclosure, see II, 1–49. The dedicatee is the historian William Mitford who has shown 'the crimes of antiquity' in their true colours, p. vi.

[56] Ibid., II, 7, ii; II, 14; II, 42–3.

proprietors. Much has been made of Jane Austen's defence of the Stuarts in her copy of Goldsmith's *History*, but one note – attached to a story illustrating extreme destitution in the countryside – reveals a less explored facet of her character: 'How much are the poor to be pitied, and the rich to be Blamed!'[57]

Attacks on 'improved' abbeys are a recurring feature in Gilpin's books, and it is not surprising to find that censure of the renovations at Northanger comes chiefly from the quarter of the picturesque. Catherine reminds herself of her lesson in such taste as she starts her walk round the grounds (177), but although she feels cheated at having to defer her initiation into the mysteries of the house, the state-of-the-art kitchen-garden proves, in fact, to be the scene of her closest brush with the eerie: 'The walls seemed countless in number, endless in length; a village of hot-houses seemed to arise among them, and a whole parish to be at work within the inclosure' (178). The trance-like vista of infinite scale is also a route into the past. Much that Hume remarks about the way 'whole estates were laid waste by inclosures' in the aftermath of monastic dissolution,[58] and about the way their occupants were rendered dependent, is compressed in Austen's potent image. Village and parish have gone; villagers and parishioners remain, conscripted into a new rite of praise to the glory of a singularly unfit object. The shift is ironically noted in a dry aside on the General's alterations to the Abbey kitchen: 'His endowment of this spot alone might at any time have placed him high among the benefactors of the convent' (183). Though the novel does nothing to confer individuality on the servants of the Abbey (a far cry from Pemberley), it does convey a weird sense of the anonymity of their labour, and more than a hint, too, of its perversity. The General's vegetable garden swallows up a 'whole parish'; and his domestic staff seem to be drained of assurance even in the privacy of their own quarters (184).

Jane Austen was not the only novelist of the nineties to use the picturesque as a means of indicting sybaritism – the vice that Baretti identified as the particular bugbear of the commercial scene. Charlotte Smith, whose work she knew, invents a series of gardens in *Desmond* (1792), the first of her radical works, to draw out the inner traits of her characters: the heroine feels most at home in a garden dating from the Glorious Revolution that has fallen into exquisite decay; an ill-natured Justice of the Peace is said, like General Tilney, to have the best garden in the country where 'his men do more work – his crops are more luxuriant'; and a wicked lawyer ruins a

---

[57] Mary-Augusta Austen-Leigh, *Personal Aspects of Jane Austen* (1920), p. 33.
[58] *History*, III, 369.

natural coppice by introducing 'an immense range of forcing and succession houses' given over to pineapples and the arts of early ripening.[59] Perhaps the succession-house (to which there are no references earlier than the nineties) received part of its symbolic resonance from the fact that Hume, in 'Of Refinement in the Arts', had selected as his chief example of 'vicious luxury' a dish of *Christmas* peas requiring 'the same care and toil' that would give bread to a family for six months.[60] Hume refuses, however, to let the abuse of commodities check his thesis that progress in humanity and knowledge is linked to advances in the 'mechanical arts'. So, too, he argues in his *History* that Henry VIII's suppression of the monasteries had the long-term effect of delivering a blow to 'the fetters on liberty and industry'.[61]

Where Jane Austen differs from a writer like Charlotte Smith is in her unwillingness to stick by tidy dichotomies, or, indeed, to leave an earlier position unexamined. Though she again celebrates the natural, the well-aged, the self-expressive, and other qualities associated with the picturesque, she reopens debate in *Northanger Abbey* and searches out the movement's shortcomings as reflected in popular taste. She points, for example, to the quaint selectiveness of Catherine's response to the Abbey: to the way she spurns any furniture from a date later than the fifteenth century (182), prefers 'dirt and cobwebs' to panes that are large, clear, and light (set in windows that the General has preserved 'with reverential care', 162), and entirely overlooks 'comfort and elegance', or the 'modern' and 'habitable' (185, 173). In the garden Catherine has eyes only for the gloomy grove and its winding path; in the kitchen she focuses on 'the massy walls and smoke of former days' to the neglect of 'the stoves and hot closets of the present'. Her blind spots exactly coincide with the General's particular fixations, so that his craze for the freshly invented and newly manufactured goes frustratingly unacknowledged, except by the narrator who picks out the technology in uncustomary detail, alighting in particular on the fireplace by Rumford (162), and on the striking cooking installations that are also after his design.[62]

Count Rumford's reputation, at its height in the late nineties, was not only as an inventor but as a philanthropist. Recently risen to the rank of general, he had applied science to great effect throughout his military career, developing an experimental vegetable garden in Munich to feed his troops,

[59] Charlotte Smith, *Desmond*, ed. Antje Blank and Janet Todd (1997), pp. 333–4, 167–8.
[60] *Political Essays*, p. 113.   [61] *History*, III, 227.
[62] Compare the 'stoves and hot closets' of the Abbey (pp. 183–4) with those described and illustrated in *The Annual Register*, 1798 (pp. 397–400) for the kitchen designed by Rumford at the Foundling Hospital.

while caring for their welfare in many other ingenious ways. His credo, set out in numerous cheaply published essays, was that the application of science to manufacture, and to a range of domestic processes besides, could bring about a revolution in the standard of living. The pamphlets which the General reads late into the night, blinding his eyes, as he boasts, 'for the good of others', are no less likely to be Rumford's for being about 'the affairs of the nation' (187), for Rumford dedicated his works 'to the public good' and took on topics like 'the real situation of the Poor'.[63] In 1798 a review of the kitchen he fitted out for the Foundling Hospital describes 'the consequent increase of comfort and accommodation of the poor' as so great as to make 'the encouragement and promotion of these valuable inventions a national object'.[64] Some strains of this discourse are heard at the Abbey, when Catherine is just about to be overcome with picturesquely inspired pique. Fuming inwardly at the removal of outbuildings (as who wouldn't?), she is led to fix on 'mere domestic economy' by the General who is

convinced, that, to a mind like Miss Morland's, a view of the accommodations and comforts, by which the labours of her inferiors were softened, must always be gratifying. (184)

His confidence is borne out by what we are shown of the interior: 'every modern invention to facilitate the labour of the cooks, had been adopted within this, their spacious theatre; and, when the genius of others had failed, his own had often produced the perfection wanted'. Here it is easy to believe Rumford's brag that, on the new principles, less heat would be needed to cook a dinner for fifty than was used elsewhere to boil a kettle. Though vanity is clearly the motivating force at Northanger, and the General the person with most to gain, the benefits of Rumford's economies of scale are seen to reach all – even if the General's staff themselves, caught behind scenes, appear cowed. Catherine is brought round to see the virtues of convenience, roominess, and specialism, and moved to reflect on the comparatively 'comfortless' arrangements for staff at Fullerton. She is nudged, also, into her first criticism of Mrs Radcliffe, recalling 'abbeys and castles, in which, though certainly larger than Northanger, all the dirty work of the house was to be done by two pair of female hands'. This insight into the ways of gothic chic is a major step in Catherine's development, and prepares us for the heroine who is soon to fall for the rectory at Woodston, 'new-built'

[63] Benjamin Thompson, *Essays, Political, Economical, and Philosophical,* 4 vols. (1796), I, 5, 180.
[64] *The Annual Register,* 1798, p. 399.

and with windows cut to the floor. There Catherine saves an outhouse from an improver, but her house-to-be represents a marriage of the picturesque and utilitarian: though 'well-*connected*' to her eyes (the specialist landscape term seems right for a recent initiate),[65] its walled kitchen-garden is the creation of the General (183–4, 175–6, 212–14).

Woodston Parsonage, that terminus of the courtship plot, reaches into the heart of Jane Austen's sense of how things come about – far from being the construct of a single will, it is the meeting-point of opposing influences. Her vision of history and of the society to which it gives birth, is along these lines also. As a novelist she is especially sensitive to what rival traditions exact, aware of their disjunction, suspicious of the supremacy to which they pretend. In *Northanger Abbey* she created a taut contrapuntal work that includes voices as disparate as those of Baretti and Sharp, Gilpin and Rumford. The inclusiveness is enabled by the play of an unsparingly critical intelligence, and it is here that her links to the sceptical historians with their refusal to underwrite the claims of clan are most enduring. No doubt this broad-minded outlook won her the championship of later liberal writers. Perhaps Macaulay, a notable architect of her nineteenth-century reputation, had *Northanger Abbey* at the back of his mind when he caricatured the blackballing of technology on grounds that were purely aesthetic: 'And what is this way? To stand on a hill, to look at a cottage and a factory, and to see which is the prettier.'[66] Jane Austen constantly switches from one perspective to another, and reserves her sharpest satire for characters who voluntarily reject part of the view.

---

[65] The term is Uvedale Price's, see above, p. 94.
[66] 'Southey's Colloquies' (1830) in Thomas Babington Macaulay, *Critical and Historical Essays*, 3 vols. (1891), I, 233. It was in 1831 that Macaulay 'praised Miss Austen to the skies'.

CHAPTER 4

Sense and Sensibility *and the philosophers*

On one site or another Godwin has been made to supply most of the shuttering for that dismal construct, Jane Austen the Anti-Jacobin. Remove the premiss that the two writers are so exactly opposed as to be complementary and such production should, in theory, stumble to a halt. If Austen is primarily a satirist who set out 'to emulate and refute' the radical fiction of the early nineties,[1] it makes good sense, admittedly, to fix on *Caleb Williams* (1794) as the anti-type to her work, and there are, indeed, some limited gains to be had from the move. Above the din of those warring typologies for the Austen and Godwin novel that Marilyn Butler draws from Godwin's early masterpiece, one or two narrative antiphonies do make themselves heard. Catherine Morland's discovery of a cotton counterpane gains in hollowness when set against the chest that gives away the secret of Falkland, and the process by which Elizabeth Bennet breaks through her first impressions of Darcy and Wickham recalls – while it reverses – the changing status of Falkland and Caleb.[2] But a few retorts like these hardly add up to a brief for political reaction, and to use Godwin's revolutionary classic as a yardstick for novels drafted in the late nineties is in any case to skew the record. Debate moved on rapidly through the decade, until – by its second half – Jacobin allegiances were so widely shunned that the term Anti-Jacobin becomes indefinite and misleading.

If Jane Austen is to be placed on the political spectrum, it should be borne in mind that Godwin himself underwent a number of broad shifts in outlook after 1795. These second thoughts, together with the fiction of his middle period, belong to the forefront in any comparison of the two writers that is alive to context. Between Godwin's *St Leon*, in particular,

---

[1] Gary Kelly, *The English Jacobin Novel, 1780–1805* (Oxford, 1976), p. 268.
[2] The question posed in each case is which of the two figures is the good man, and the answer runs contrary to general opinion. Congruence is further underlined by the fact that at Pemberley Wickham is the steward's son, while Caleb looks on Falkland's steward as his father. Though chests abound in gothic fiction, Godwin's novel was dramatized as *The Iron Chest* (1796).

and *Sense and Sensibility* – the novel often taken to be the most doctrinaire of the six – there exist a variety of striking parallels that point to the moderate, even liberal character of Jane Austen's stance among her contemporaries.

In practice, the Anti-Jacobin historicist readings have a way of resisting ordinary means of disproof. Typically, the focus on Austen as an active opponent of revolutionary ideology sets up a presumption of antagonism that overrides direct inference from fact. If Austen appears to resemble Godwin, for example, in her commitment to reason and objectivity, it is only because she assumes (mistakenly or perhaps cunningly) that sensibility and subjectivity are the heartland of the radical case.[3] If Burke, on the other hand, champions sensibility it is because he 'adapts the characteristic tools of the progressive' in order to add lustre to the conservative case.[4] This theory of political mimicry is stretched so far by Marilyn Butler as to give complete cover to her assignment of certain values to certain causes, principally her bracketing of sensibility with liberalism, though in fact the relation between these was complex, as we have seen, even by the 1780s.[5] But the see-saw tactics continue to be applied when it comes to interpreting individual texts. In *Sense and Sensibility*, sense has it all the way, and sense, in a usage more restricted than Austen's, is seen to preside in all the other novels, where – for the majority of heroines – 'moral progress consists in discerning, and submitting to, the claims of the society around them'.[6] It is interesting to see how closely the last summary matches Marianne's sarcastic account of her sister's 'doctrine', noting at the same time Elinor's reply:

'I thought our judgments were given us merely to be subservient to those of our neighbours. This has always been your doctrine, I am sure.'

'No, Marianne, never. My doctrine has never aimed at the subjection of the understanding . . . I am guilty, I confess, of having often wished you to treat our acquaintance in general with greater attention; but when have I advised you to adopt their sentiments or conform to their judgment in serious matters?' (94)

The novels emerge from such reading as a row of Procrustes beds, each a member of that class of contemporary fiction designed to sap 'the individual's reliance on himself'. And against this paradigm of the conservative novel there is pitted a view of the radical novel as a vindication of self, a

---

3 Marilyn Butler, *War of Ideas*, see particularly p. 33.   4 Ibid., p. 37.
5 For a fuller and excellent account of this complexity see John Mullan's *Sentiment and Sociability: The Language of Feeling in the Eighteenth Century* (Oxford, 1988).
6 Butler, *War of Ideas*, p. 1.

vehicle for the 'steady championing of Individual Man against a corrupt society'.[7] No mention in all this of the leftist revival of the 'public good', or of Rousseau's massively influential 'general will'.

In other ways also, the rage for polarity leads to damaging simplification. Butler treats *Caleb Williams* as 'the prototype of a series of six fictions so similar in their essential features that it is as meaningful to speak of the Godwin novel as of the Austen novel',[8] but what makes Godwin's masterpiece of 1794 a persuasive standard for the radical novel on her terms – its formal endorsement of the rational thought-processes of its beset but steadfast hero – is far less true of the others: *St Leon* (1799) carries on its title page the subscript, 'Ferdinand Mendez Pinto was but a type of thee, thou liar of the first magnitude'; and the first-person narrator of *Fleetwood* (1805) exists for much of the time in a state of total delusion. The effect of this prototyping is to foreshorten the aftermath of Revolution, a period highly eventful by any reckoning. Novels like *St Leon* and *Sense and Sensibility* – which took shape more or less concurrently[9] – need to be treated, however, as *Post*-Jacobin.

When Elinor protests to Marianne that she is guided not by the judgement of society but by her understanding, she falls back on a moral vocabulary that owes on the whole rather more to empirical philosophy than to the sermon. If Austen's use of keywords from the liberal tradition has not been widely recognized, the Anti-Jacobin cloak is chiefly to blame. But she does draw insistently on terms which, though used by latitudinarians or by outspoken churchmen like Sydney Smith, won their currency largely from writing of the Enlightenment. Phrases like 'unaffected benevolence' or 'general benevolence' – and pivotal they are to her work – are the butt of satire in the pages of the *Anti-Jacobin*,[10] and much the same goes for her 'utility', or her 'liberty and independence' – that catchphrase so central to the historical writing of William Robertson and David Hume.

Jane Austen's engagement with the liberal tenets of a previous generation is fairly typical of writers of the centre in the years she began on her mature fiction, and seems to have been obscured by historicist criticism for two

---

[7] Ibid., pp. 101, 32.

[8] In her introduction to the *Collected Novels and Memoirs of William Godwin*, ed. Mark Philp, 8 vols. (1992), I, 26.

[9] Godwin mentions 'The Adept', from which *St Leon* evolved, as early as January 1796. 'Elinor and Marianne' probably dates from 1795, but was radically redrafted after November 1797.

[10] The only contributor to the *Review* ever mentioned by Austen was Anne Lefroy's brother Sir Samuel Egerton Brydges, about whom she is broadly dismissive. See letter to Cassandra, 25 Nov. 1798, *Letters*, p. 22. There is, in fact, no external evidence whatever to support the idea that Jane Austen held right-wing views.

chief reasons. First, there has been a tendency to trade-in the overt themes of the novels for an account of rhetorical warfare that treats ideas not as the stuff of war but as illusory amd shifting, epiphenomena of the underlying conflict, a sort of street-theatre on the battlefield. Content is thus emptied so as not to meddle with the all-important business of contest, as when Butler – dismayed by the appearance of accord among rival camps – complains of the radicals, 'their advocacy of reason and restraint often makes them read like their opponents'.[11] It takes a humbler kind of history to restore the perspective of the common reader, or to credit the idea that *Sense and Sensibility* 'really is about the relations between Sense and Sensibility': about the relations, that is, 'between Head and Heart, Thought and Feeling, Judgement and Emotion, or Sensibleness and Sensitiveness', as Gilbert Ryle once observed.[12] It was in language similar to this that Godwin introduced *St Leon* to his public, and we shall see that his probing of such terms not only runs in parallel to Austen's but draws on many of the same cultural sources.

But a second cause of confusion has been a reluctance to admit how widespread the concern with social stability was in the post-revolutionary period, and how fully coexistent it was with an active belief in the need for reform. Austen has frequently been coupled with Burke on the grounds that she is a party to 'the organicist political theory that was a counter to the radical ideology of the Revolution'.[13] But theory of this type was by no means limited to Burke, and was far from being the exclusive property of reaction. It was the legacy of an Anglo-Scottish tradition in sociology that was sympathetic – indeed even integral – to the constitution of 1789. Nor for that matter was the spectre of social anarchy that Burke so deftly uses as a goad to his conservatism in the *Reflections* (and that Jane Austen deflates in *Northanger Abbey*) of his own making either. The view that a libertarian culture had been installed in France in a fashion needlessly destructive of the social fabric was broadly held, and reinforced daily by the received picture – often vehemently projected – of a strife-torn citizenry, haunted by distrust and fear. Wordsworth's retrospective sketch of a Paris transformed nightly into a place 'defenceless as a wood where tigers roam' exactly captured this raw sense, and out of it there materialized a question. Was an absence of social order not actually implied by the individualism of

[11] Butler, *War of Ideas*, p. 45.
[12] 'Jane Austen and the Moralists', in B. C. Southam, ed., *Critical Essays on Jane Austen* (1968), p. 107.
[13] Warren Roberts, *Jane Austen and the French Revolution* (1979), p. 6.

the liberal creed? Writers who responded to this anxiety in a constructive way – and Austen is among them – returned to that central issue of debate in the Enlightenment, the problem of how sociability was constituted and engendered.

Unfortunately for Austen criticism, it has been the contribution of Burke that has monopolized attention here; and certainly the spirit of counter-revolution is never more clear in the *Reflections* than when Burke urges, in a revealing glide of metaphor, that 'to love the little platoon we belong to in society, is the first principle (the germ as it were) of publick affections'.[14] But the 'little platoon' is his adaptation of a phrase repeatedly used by Adam Smith in a similar, though politically distinct, context when he defends local loyalties against the old Stoic suspicion of partiality:

By Nature the events which immediately affect that *little department* in which we ourselves have some little management and direction, which immediately affect ourselves, our friends, our country, are the events which interest us the most, and which chiefly excite our desires and aversions, our hopes and fears, our joys and sorrows. (my italics)[15]

The passage was written for the final version of *The Theory of Moral Sentiments* (1759) which came out in January 1790, not long before Burke began cogitating on his *Reflections*. Revisions for this edition included an entire new part, and comprised an important (and now oddly neglected) document in the Revolution debate. Strategically keyed into the controversy at a number of points,[16] the fresh material is devoted largely to questions of self-transcendence. Starting from the proposition that 'every man [is] first and principally recommended to his own care', Smith argues that it is out of attachments that are primary and habitual that the habit of sympathy is born. While there is much that anticipates Burke on this score – particularly the stress on the benefits to be drawn from the natural process of becoming 'endeared' to the familiar, Smith both relativizes the idea of social bonding through a comparison of different kinds of social order, and acknowledges the need for periods of radical innovation. The caveats which he issues against instant 'new-modelling' have to be read in conjunction with his specific recommendations in *The Wealth of Nations* for wholesale reforms in France, many of which had already come before the National Assembly.

---

[14] *Reflections on the Revolution in France* (1790), p. 68 (*Works*, v, 100).
[15] Adam Smith, *TMS*, VII.ii.1.44–5, 292.   [16] Ibid., see VI.2.2.4, and 12–18.

Smith has uniformly been identified as one of Jane Austen's spiritual antagonists by her Anti-Jacobin interpreters: for Butler he epitomizes the spirit of intellectual independence which Austen is determined to oppose; for Duckworth he is the source of the 'sensibility' which she refutes.[17] We shall see, however, that Smith is not only a pervasive presence in *Sense and Sensibility*, but that his understanding of sympathetic imagination, distorted in Marianne, is taken up and developed by the narrator. First, though, we need to return briefly to the issue of Austen's comparative position in the late nineties, and a good place to start is with the influence of Hume and Smith on *St Leon* (1799), Godwin's major work from the period.[18]

EMPIRICISM REVISITED

Even though Godwin was to claim that there was still 'too little given to the passions', three successive overhauls of his *Enquiry* left the stark rationalism of his original political theorizing modified almost beyond recognition.[19] Basic to the first edition of 1793 is the axiom that the intellectual perception of truth carries a charge sufficient to motivate action.[20] But this confident belief in the power of reason and in its sweeping jurisdiction (moral concerns are compared to geometry) was soon to yield to strictures on its role as an instigator. The chapter 'Of Self-Love and Benevolence' added in 1796 revokes the view that altruism rises, fully formed, from 'the decisions of the intellect', offering instead an account grounded in empiricist psychology, and deeply indebted to Smith as reference to an 'impartial spectator' shows. Here benevolence is born in self-gratification, and grows, through habit, into a reflective faculty.[21]

For *St Leon* Godwin devised a plot that simultaneously turns on the frailty of reason and eulogizes, as he says in the preface, the 'culture of the heart'. The last phrase derives from Francis Hutcheson and was taken from

[17] Butler, *War of Ideas*, p. xv; and Alistair M. Duckworth, *Improvement*, pp. 98–100.

[18] Jane Austen's antagonism towards Godwin has frequently been inferred from her use of the word 'raffish' for one of his admirers. For a discussion of the contexts of this remark, lexical and otherwise, see my article 'What Jane Austen Meant by "Raffish"', pp. 105–8. Austen enjoyed the company of the man she so described, and *The Loiterer* deplores the snobbish dismissal of townsmen by gownsmen as 'raff', arguing that commerce is the cornerstone of civil society, and that collegiate existence depends on 'these very *Raffs*', many of whom have endowed the university only to be held 'in the most utter Contempt by the Objects of their Bounty' (no. 24, 11 July 1789).

[19] Peter H. Marshall, *William Godwin* (New Haven, 1984), p. 199.

[20] *Enquiry concerning Political Justice*, ed. F. E. L. Priestley (1946). For this section of the 1793 text – bk iv, ch. viii – see III, 309; and for commentary on its replacement, III, 90.

[21] *Enquiry*, I, 427; III, 315.

the posthumously published *The Wrongs of Woman* in which Wollstonecraft reinstated the claims of feeling, particularly of ready sympathy.[22] Godwin encouraged the view that St Leon's long-suffering wife Marguerite was an elegiac portrait of Wollstonecraft, and his central couple embody the novel's major theme which is that 'the domestic and private affections' are the mainspring of a wider benevolence. Because these passions offer a training ground for every form of sociability, they constitute 'the true school of humanity'.[23] Twice St Leon and Marguerite approach the ideal of the simple good life when surrounded by their family in a country setting, but on each occasion St Leon, despite his determination to preserve his happiness, takes a decision that leads to misery for them all. The second of these self-betrayals bears a striking resemblance to Willoughby's account of how he came to desert Marianne immediately after 'firmly resolv[ing] within myself of doing right', and a number of other textual echoes suggest that Austen invited her readers to notice the parallel.[24]

Where St Leon's about-face dramatically undermines Godwin's earlier maxim that men always do that which they think to be correct, Willoughby's 'vindication' overlays and complicates Colonel Brandon's view of him as the typically demonized rake of the eighteenth-century novel. But in both cases it is something dispositional, the surfacing of a latent social ethos, that causes them to capitulate. Willoughby, who finds himself deeply inured to a life of fashion, comes from the same stable as St Leon who declares that 'vanity and ostentation were habits wrought into my soul, and might be said to form part of its essence'.[25] Godwin's switch to a passional system of motivation left his insistence on individualism problematic, for with it there came an associationist understanding of the *relational* matrix of most feeling – hence his comparison of the human mind to a barometer 'directed in its variations by the atmosphere which surrounds it'.[26] *St Leon* might be said, indeed, to be less concerned with the battle between Individual Man and Society than with the presence of society in the individual man, and the same perception was of long standing for Jane Austen.

---

[22] See William Leechman's preface to Francis Hutcheson's posthumous *A System of Moral Philosophy*, 2 vols. (1755), I, xxxi; and see Mary Wollstonecraft, *'Mary' and 'The Wrongs of Woman'*, ed. Gary Kelly (1991), especially p. 115, also pp. 76, 79, 98.

[23] William Godwin, *St Leon*, ed. Pamela Clemit (Oxford, 1994), pp. xxxiii–xxxiv, 49.

[24] See *Sense and Sensibility*, pp. 321, 324, and *St Leon*, pp. 136–7. Apart from their sudden U-turns, Willoughby and St Leon share the same slang and a romantic obsession with the death-like features of those they have betrayed. For further details of the parallel, see my article 'Sense and Sensibility, Godwin and the Empiricists', *The Cambridge Quarterly*, 27 (1998), especially pp. 188–95.

[25] *St Leon*, p. 99.

[26] William Godwin, *Thoughts Occasioned by the Perusal of Dr Parr's Spital Sermon* (1801), p. 9.

One crucial difference in the outlook of the two writers is pinpointed by their divergent relation to that most potent of eighteenth-century social theorists, Bernard Mandeville. Shortly after completing the first *Enquiry*, Godwin reread *The Fable of the Bees*,[27] and the 'Second Dialogue' attached to the fable seems to have contributed significantly to *Caleb Williams*, particularly to the figure of Falkland. Here Mandeville illustrates his view that pride is of all qualities the one most beneficial to society: he draws the picture of a nobleman who passes for a paragon of taste and virtue, but who turns out to be motivated entirely by the desire for social esteem, when – contrary to every principle of his devout and law-abiding character – he opts to duel rather than lose face. In *Caleb* Godwin similarly uses the duel (that 'vilest of all egotisms') to underline the way his aristocratic idol is no more than 'the fool of honour and fame'. So Falkland can afford to avoid a fight when the insult inflicted on him by Count Malvesi goes unseen, but, when subjected to public humiliation by Tyrrel, he resorts to murder; and though the deed is again unseen, he is poisoned by it, because it deprives him of the only rite that can remove his stain.[28] The parallel only holds over a certain distance however. For where Mandeville extracts a general human trait from the conduct of his nobleman, Godwin historicizes Falkland's love of praise as the passing afterglow of a vanished era. And if *St Leon* represents a more sympathetic reappraisal of the chivalric hero (as some contemporaries noted), the thirst for approval appears there as a universal motive only intermittently – as when the narrator remarks that 'self-applause is our principal support in every liberal and elevated act of virtue'.[29] Fellow-feeling is what now chiefly redeems knight-errantry, and the novel contrives through comparison of its many shifting settings to place a premium on the non-competitive passions.

In *Pride and Prejudice* the accent is different. When Wickham holds Elizabeth spellbound with his slander of Darcy, a cleverly modish part of his strategy is to pass Darcy off as a sort of Falkland figure, an aristocrat obsessed with the maintenance of image (72–3). Pride, on this reckoning, is a specific construct, a behavioural aberration, but Elizabeth brings a quite contrary understanding of it into play when she retorts that she is surprised that pride alone was not enough to keep Darcy honest and just. Though she

---

[27] See *The Fable of the Bees*, ed. F. B. Kaye, 2 vols. (Oxford, 1924), II, 438.
[28] *Caleb Williams*, ed. David McCracken (Oxford, 1986), pp. 15, 97–88, 102, 120.
[29] *St Leon*, p. 137.

distinguishes between proper and improper kinds of pride, Elizabeth shares Mandeville's sense of the social benefits that derive from the virtuous vice, and this sense is endorsed by the novel overall.[30] In common with latter-day exponents of the 'experimental method', like Hume and Smith, Jane Austen upheld a pull-me push-you idea of motivation: the 'natural virtues', founded in sympathy, were one inducement to decency, but the care of self-image was the more familiar goad. So it is that sympathy and pride are twinned as motives when Jane Bennet exclaims of the evil fathered on Darcy by Wickham, 'No man of common humanity, no man who had any value for his character, could be capable of it', or when Elizabeth imagines Darcy's rescue of Lydia to be doubly inspired by 'compassion and honour', though it strikes the reader as no worse for being prompted by his attachment to herself (85, 327). This duality in Austen's vision – while it reflects her belief in a 'mixed' human nature – answers to two separate traditions which are reconciled (though still often distinct) in the writing of Hume and Smith, despite the last's much vaunted 'problem'. On the one hand, there is the view popularized by Shaftesbury and Hutcheson, that human nature is itself sufficiently benevolent to supply the foundation for morals; on the other, the insight, deriving chiefly from Mandeville, that the forces of self-love are capable of providing the groundwork of polity on their own. Sociability, according to this last account, depends on a spontaneously generated framework of conventions and laws, Hume's 'artificial virtues', or Mandeville's 'joynt Labour of many Ages' – in each case an ever-evolving system of codes honed by utility.[31]

Manners took on a central role in this evolutionary reading of society, for if, as Mandeville claimed, it was 'the Work of Ages to find out the true Use of the Passions',[32] skilful control of their expression was of the essence. Pride, the *Fable* warns, is capable not only of blinding the self but also of inflaming the other. Both points were taken up by the Scottish school, and are put to the proof, together, when Jane Austen has Darcy brashly boast that 'where there is a real superiority of mind, pride will be always under good regulation' (57). To function as a social cement pride had to be 'well-regulated' in Hume's phrase, or even well concealed, and in this connection Smith had noted that the high self-esteem of others, even when well-founded, 'mortifies our own' – a caveat turned by Elizabeth to

---

[30] For a fuller account of these themes in *Pride and Prejudice* see my essay, 'The Philosophical Context' in the *Commentaries* volume to the Cambridge edition of Jane Austen (forthcoming).
[31] *Fable*, II, 128.   [32] Ibid., 319.

epigram when she says of Darcy, 'I could easily forgive *his* pride, if he had not mortified *mine*' (20).[33] Though Darcy is right to point out later that Bingley's apparent humility in calling attention to the speed and careless rapture of his letter-writing is entirely deceitful, Bingley (unlike himself) proves to be a true adept at masking a show of what he takes to be a flattering trait (48–9). Typically this lively scene, though it glances at conduct-book material and at Dr Johnson's strictures on hurried composition, is true to 'the experimental method' in constantly returning to the question of human nature. Though Mandeville's ideas would have reached Jane Austen through many channels, it is quite likely that she was familiar with *The Fable*, and recalled its advice on how to deny pride so as to make ourselves 'acceptable to others, with as little Prejudice to ourselves as is possible'.[34]

Jane Austen never grew tired of exposing the motives lurking behind social concealment, however habitual or necessary. One of her perennial goals as a writer of comedy was to leave her readers less deceived. Particularly rich in satiric reward were those polite affectations that seem designed to erase all trace of egoism, and throughout her career she specialized in dealing out the most self-sacrificial of creeds to the most assertive of characters. Following a lead from Hume, her brother James had noted a sort of commodifying of affect in the commercial society where reliance on external status had partly given place to the urge 'to make ourselves conspicuous by appearing to possess qualities in a superior degree to the generality of those around us'.[35] When Jane Austen turned her attention to the cult of fine-feeling in *Sense and Sensibility* it was to restore recognition of a tabooed competitiveness, and it is telling that Marianne is shown never to be more proud than when she declares that she has no pride at all (189, 191). True to the two-tiered morality of the sceptical Enlightenment, Jane Austen believed in fine-feeling nonetheless, and in Marianne's special capacity for it; and the novel, for all its overt mockery of sensibility, shares with *St Leon* the aim of celebrating the 'natural virtues'. It explores a crux at the heart of empiricist philosophy – how sociability is to be explained on the materialist premiss of a self-serving ego; and it develops in the process a comedy that has a constructive as well as a satiric dimension.

---

33 *THN*, II.iii.ii, 600; *TMS*, VI.iii.22, 246. This last parallel was remarked on by Kenneth Moler, 'Bennet Girls', p. 568.

34 *Fable*, II, 147. Mary Crawford's irreligious joke about the sacrifices performed by returning heathen heroes (108) tallies well with Mandeville's scoffing account of 'the many Hecatombs that have been offer'd after Victories' in his *Fifth Dialogue*, II, 214–17. Claudia L. Johnson in her dense essay, 'Jane Austen and Dr Johnson Again' notes the presence of Dr Johnson in this scene, see Littlewood, ed., *Critical Assessments*, II, 141.

35 *The Loiterer*, 33 and 50; and pp. 60–1 above.

SENSIBILITY RECLAIMED

Comedy, by virtue of its form alone, deals in the interplay between individual and society, and this appears to have made the genre particularly attractive to writers of a liberal persuasion, as its remarkable hold on the nineteenth-century novel suggests. There is, however, an alternative account, implicit in the view that Austen's adoption of the 'standard courtship plot' proceeds from 'a limited, unduly acquiescent or unduly commercial outlook upon life', a course sidestepped in her time by such stalwart spirits as Maria Edgeworth.[36] What is glaringly missing from the attempt to read comedy as a covert means of shoring up the status quo, is an acknowledgement that comic endings are about fresh starts. An 'evolution of social sensibility within an accepted culture' – so Allan Rodway sums up Jane Austen's contribution to her age – but the phrase applies equally to the structure of the works themselves. All the mature novels answer, in some degree, to Northrop Frye's notion of the New Comedy as a mode that 'moves towards the crystallization of a new society', a grouping in which readers take an imaginative part.[37] Though the endings vary in regard to how much the lovers hold in common with their wider circle, and how far they deviate from external norms, the sense of a new-found social identity is basic to them all. In each, moreover, at least one central figure undergoes a process of enlightenment in which self-knowledge is tied to a widening recognition of adjacent lives. The reader's induction into the varied doings of the '3 or 4 Families in a Country Village' subtly counterpoints this internal course of discovery.

   The limits that Jane Austen put upon her scope as a novelist belong with her commitment to an almost uniquely realistic mode of classical comedy, in which festive celebration is muted, domestic living far from golden, and individuality fiercely preserved. In this recalcitrant world it seems fitting that abstract nostrums about society should be exposed to scepticism, and for the most part they are. Hartley's theory that an associational mechanism does the work of converting self-interest into a love of mankind, comes under sceptical scrutiny as early as the juvenilia.[38] But, in one instance, Austen goes out of her way to build into her text a standard item from the store of contemporary social theory.

   The idea is from the opening chapters of *The Theory of Moral Sentiments* (1759–90), and represents Adam Smith's particular refinement upon the

---

[36] Butler, *War of Ideas*, xxxvii.   [37] Northrop Frye, *A Natural Perspective* (1965), p. 92.
[38] See the discussion of 'Love and Freindship' above, p. 56.

powerful account of sympathy offered by Hume in the *Treatise* (1739). In that early work, sympathy stands primarily for an involuntary transfer of feeling, an almost magnetic influence that draws one person into the mental orbit of another.[39] Because it not only sustains all 'natural' moral activity but also reinforces the 'artificial' forms arising from self-interest, it is the great cohesive force responsible for social bonding. Smith, in his ethics, offers an account that is more orientated to the self, partly because he draws on a more stable sense of identity than that given by the *Treatise*.[40] He looks, particularly, at the way sympathy relates to approval, and he often uses the term, in a distinctive way, to denote a specific correspondence of feeling between individuals. But both writers resort to metaphors from music to express the operation of this all-important faculty. Hume describes the mysterious passage of fellow-feeling through the phenomenon of sympathetic vibration on a stringed instrument:

As in strings equally wound up, the motion of one communicates itself to the rest, so all the affections readily pass from one person to another, and beget correspondent movements in every human creature.[41]

Smith, pursuing a relational model, speaks of concord and dissonance between his subjects, of falling in and out of time, of lowering and sharpening pitch. While his main interest is in the degree of accord established between subjects whose experience differs, he puts forward the simpler case of two people confronted by the same object. In such an instance a like response implies sympathy between the two, but also a reciprocal (if limited) approbation:

To approve of the passions of another, therefore, as suitable to their objects, is the same thing as to observe that we entirely sympathize with them; and not to approve of them as such, is the same thing as to observe that we do not entirely sympathize with them . . . He who admires the same poem, or the same picture, and admires them exactly as I do, must surely allow the justness of my admiration . . . On the contrary, the person who . . . either feels no such emotion as that which I feel, or feels none that bears any proportion to mine, cannot avoid disapproving my sentiments on account of their dissonance with his own.[42]

Response to the object and judgement of the other go hand in hand. Reverting to his duo, Smith concludes: 'according as there is more or less

---

[39] *THN*, iii.iii.ii; 592.
[40] For a valuable comparison of Hume's and Smith's idea of sympathy, see John Mullan, *Sentiment*, pp. 43–56.
[41] *THN*, iii.iii.i; 575–6.   [42] *TMS*, i.i.3.1, 16.

disproportion between his sentiments and mine, I must incur a greater or lesser degree of his disapprobation'.[43]

Austen works back to this formulation of Smith's in the opening chapters of *Sense and Sensibility*. Marianne, after itemizing Edward Ferrars's defects, spells out her own specifications for a lover – which turn out to be the ones usually found in a heroine of sensibility: not only must his taste coincide at every point with her own, but he 'must enter into all my feelings; the same books, the same music must charm us both' (17). Music – as is already clear from the order in which Edward's deficiencies are listed – proves to be Marianne's main touchstone of all that is meritorious. Though Willoughby makes his entrance in the approved way of romantic heroes, rescue is not the key thing – not at least to her eyes:

From Willoughby their expression was at first held back, by the embarrasssment which the remembrance of his assistance created. But . . . when she saw that to the perfect good-breeding of the gentleman, he united frankness and vivacity, and above all, when she heard him declare that of music and dancing he was passionately fond, she gave him such a look of approbation as secured the largest share of his discourse to herself for the rest of his stay. (46)

Once Willoughby's considerable 'musical talents' are in evidence, the couple enjoy an intensity of feeling appropriate to their 'conformity of judgment' (47), and their total absorption receives added point from Marianne's recent experience of playing after dinner at the Middletons, where – for all the loud praise – only Colonel Brandon listens to her:

she felt a respect for him on the occasion . . . His pleasure in music, though it amounted not to that extatic delight which alone could sympathize with her own, was estimable. (35)

Though his rating may not be very high, Brandon stands out sufficiently from the rest of the party (whose inattention to the music spells out a 'horrible insensibility') to move Marianne into making some allowance, in his case, for the blunted faculties of age. But, in precisely Smith's terms, it is only the responses of herself and of Willoughby that entirely *sympathize*.

However wry its handling, the Smithian sympathy-assay does yield reliable results within its sphere. Though critics have argued that Jane Austen intended to discount the rapport that comes from shared tastes (along with physical attraction) as a proper criterion for marriage,[44] no such didactic goal appears to be in view. Far from being undermined, Marianne and Willoughby's special compatibility is kept resonating almost to the end, so

---

[43] *TMS*, i.i.3.1, 17.   [44] Butler, *War of Ideas*, p. 194.

that when Mrs Dashwood pleads that Brandon, despite being less hand-some, will prove 'much more accordant with [Marianne's] real disposition', Elinor remains silent, withholding her assent (338). On one plane Brandon's own qualifications as a hero of sensibility – which include a temperament both warm and sympathetic (336) – easily outweigh those of his rival, but they do not displace them. Jane Austen is truthful in charting the motions of the heart, ruthless in witnessing the forces that lead to its betrayal.

Music and idiom drawn from it play a large part in *Sense and Sensibility*. The tense scene in which Lucy Steele tells Elinor of her betrothal as they sit in 'the utmost harmony engaged in forwarding the same work' owes much both atmospherically and dramatically to the *fortissimo* accompaniment of a 'very magnificent concerto' from Marianne, whose feelings about her sister's rival would be confirmed by Lucy's calculated use of the 'shelter of its noise' (145, 149). At her own piano she spends hours 'alternately singing and crying' after Willoughby's desertion of her (83), and the last stage of her recovery is signalled by her brave, though at first futile, attempt at practice (342). These poignant episodes give a special savour to the novel's concluding statement on the unholy alliance of Lucy and Robert Ferrars, Mrs Ferrars and John and Fanny Dashwood: 'nothing could exceed the harmony in which they all lived together' (377).

The Smithian analysis of emotional bonding carries over to those who are not noted for emotion, as when the narrator remarks of the curious tie that forms between Mrs John Dashwood and Lady Middleton (who gives up the piano once securely married) that 'they sympathised with each other', naturally attracted by a 'kind of cold hearted selfishness' (229). This 'selfishness' becomes a keyword, as Marilyn Butler has pointed out, in the closing volume of the novel, where a fault-line begins to open between the two sets of characters who are reported (with varying reliability, in view of Mrs Ferrars's volatile temper) to live happily ever after. The judgement that Willoughby is 'selfish', together with his confession to 'vanity' and 'dissi-pation', links him with the group who exclude themselves from the circle that takes shape round the Delaford living. The alignment is underscored, moreover, by a number of scenes which expose the mercenary outlook that governs every aspect of the Ferrars's world, above all marriage. These range from the comic hyperbole of Mrs Ferrars's notion that suitors are inter-changeable but for status (297), to Robert's sordid ruminations on how the jilted Marianne stands in the market – 'five or six hundred a-year, at the utmost' (227). Within this social field, Willoughby's desertion of Marianne for a Miss Grey is a fact of no consequence.

To suppose, however, that Austen's attack on the money-grubbing set is a standard conservative rally against economic individualism, as Butler does,[45] is to misconstrue the axis of debate. It is the gentry rather than Smith's commercial world who come under fire, as is clear from the readiness with which the nasty-Dashwoods accept Lady Middleton, and spurn her mother on the grounds that Mr Jennings's money was got by trade (228). Nor is Austen's criticism directed merely at decadence within the landed class, for it takes on board such persistent features of its economy as land enclosure, duelling, and the shirking of profession (225, 233, 102–3). The values sustaining this critique are of a liberal provenance, fairly summed up, in fact, by 'sensibility' – though at some distance from the modish idea of the term.

Crucial to the voicing of this ethos is the scene in which the Delaford living is first put on the map, and begins to assume its symbolic role as eye-of-the-needle. The humble vicarage with its poor pasturage, and still sparser stipend that so opportunely repels Lucy Steele, is a gift to Edward Ferrars from Colonel Brandon, who chooses Elinor as his go-between. On the meeting of these two friends, Jane Austen lavishes (in a way she was never to repeat) all the contrivance of a comic scene from Shakespeare, but the themes addressed are altogether contemporary. That Mrs Jennings is able to persist in reading what passes between Brandon and Elinor as a proposal of marriage, in the face of ever-mounting obstacles, shows the power of her sympathy; Colonel Brandon's scheme springs from association. His memory of Eliza Williams is revived by the news that Mrs Ferrars has cut off her eldest son for persevering in his engagement to Lucy Steele (282), and this old story, while it echoes the fortunes of the Ferrars sons, also reflects the violence done to Marianne (205), as does its sequel, the betrayal of the second Eliza by Willoughby. These histories run, palpably, into the ganglion of feeling that fires Brandon's generosity towards Edward whom he has met only 'two or three times', but this in no way modifies Elinor's respect for a sympathy (or improvidence, as Robert Ferrars calls it) that goes far beyond ordinary claims. And the extent of her own altruism is shown in the way her pleasure at Edward's good luck – intense enough to be mistaken for joy – outdistances the thought of Lucy's now improved hopes:

Her emotion was such as Mrs Jennings had attributed to a very different cause; – but whatever minor feelings less pure, less pleasing, might have a share in that emotion, her esteem for the general benevolence, and her gratitude for the particular friendship, which together prompted Colonel Brandon to this act, were strongly felt, and warmly expressed. (283)

---

45 Ibid., pp. 194, 9–11.

Earlier, when John Dashwood mentions his wife's 'benevolence' in putting up the Steeles, we recall that they were invited to keep the Dashwood sisters at bay (266), but there is nothing equivocal about the motive that prompts the disposal of the Delaford living.

Austen's treatment of benevolence gives, in fact, a good sense of her whereabouts in the post-Revolutionary debate. Few qualities were regarded with greater suspicion, or more frequently targeted by the Anti-Jacobin camp, and what draws particular fire is the notion of a moral imperative that goes beyond personal or local loyalties. Typically, the dispersive aspects of benevolence are at the centre of attack. Canning in his deft and contemptuous portrait of 'French Philanthropy' shows a figure vaporously diffusing 'general love of all mankind': 'through the extended globe his feelings run / As broad and general as the unbounded sun!'[46] Behind this satire lies Dr Johnson's conceit on the impotence of 'general benevolence' which, if 'not compressed into a narrower compass, would vanish like elemental fire, in boundless evaporation'.[47] By 1800 the ideal was so beset that Dr Parr could back Godwin into a corner by merely citing his notorious remark about saving Fénelon from a fire in preference to his mother. So reluctant, indeed, is Parr to admit the possibility of even *wishing* well of 'those with whom we are not connected' that he was rebuked by Sydney Smith for passing off the desire for general good as 'a pardonable weakness, rather than a fundamental principle of ethics'.[48] Sydney Smith is moved to defend Godwin 'as unquestionably right', taking issue only over the matter of particular affections, so that his own position coincides with Godwin's revised one. In a field of argument so contracted, the essential point of difference is well exposed by Sydney Smith when he accuses Parr of leaving us 'to suppose that the particular affections are themselves ultimate principles of action, instead of convenient instruments of a more general principle'.[49] Jane Austen's reference, twice over, to Brandon's 'general benevolence', together with the distinction she draws between it and 'particular friendship', clearly place her with the expansionists, an outlook possibly masked by, but quite compatible with, her penchant for minute scale.

To apply the magnifying glass is second nature to the empiricist, and Austen shares a rationale with Adam Smith in her intentful focus on the family scene. In his *Theory* Smith had treated the sibling bond as the germ of all social relation, raising a model from those 'earliest friendships, the

---

[46] See 'New Morality', in *Poetry of the Anti-Jacobin*, p. 238.
[47] *The Rambler*, ed. W. J. Bate and Albrecht Strauss (New Haven, 1969), no. 99, II, 166.
[48] *Dr Parr*, from *Edinburgh Review* (1802), in *The Works of the Rev. Sydney Smith*, 4 vols. (1839), I, 5.
[49] Ibid., I, 5, 7.

friendships which are naturally contracted when the heart is most suscep-tible', but he noted, at the same time, that such bonds could prove to be of no account.[50] There is a similar gist to the famous statement made in *Mansfield Park* about the potentially unique power of such ties: to Fanny Price it seems that the 'same first associations and habits' keep alive a 'sen-timent in all its prime and freshness', providing an epitome of union, but the narrator reminds us that in other circumstances the attachment can be 'worse than nothing' (234–5).

Though Jane Austen makes a tough candidate for any school of sensibil-ity, her concern with fellow-feeling in *Sense and Sensibility* is as all-pervading as it is hard-headed. The opening sequences of the novel – the pages that marked her debut on the literary scene (and include the caustic sketch of the newly endowed but stingy Dashwoods) – warn of the meagre yields to be expected from charity while they underline the need for principles and for law. Self-interest is the dominant fact in her fiction, but it is faced for the most part in a spirit of constructive acceptance. Energy is linked to self-assertiveness, and selfish intentions are seen to have ironic outcomes. Perhaps there is a playful, half-mocking glance at Adam Smith's concept of 'the invisible hand' in the way Lucy Steele's 'unceasing attention to self-interest' so obligingly precipitates the novel's happy ending (376). Certainly Austen's heroines move in that world memorably evoked by Smith's caveat to the soft-minded in the *Wealth of Nations*: 'it is not from the benevolence of the butcher, the brewer, or the baker, that we expect our dinner, but from their regard to their own interest'.[51] Her characters breathe an ordinary air, and the sensitivities they convey are the more robust for being free of the usual romantic ether. Typical in this respect is the choice of Mrs Jennings to illustrate the fine workings of sympathy; her feelings are brought into focus as she tends to the once-contemptuous Marianne at the crisis of her fever:

Her heart was really grieved. The rapid decay, the early death of a girl so young, so lovely as Marianne, must have struck a less interested person with concern. On Mrs Jennings's compassion she had other claims. She had been for three months her companion, was still under her care, and she was known to have been greatly injured, and long unhappy. The distress of her sister too, particularly a favourite, was before her; – and as for their mother, when Mrs Jennings considered that Marianne might probably be to *her* what Charlotte was to herself, her sympathy in *her* sufferings was very sincere. (313)

---

[50] *TMS*, VI.ii.1.4 and 7, 219–20.   [51] *WN*, I.ii.2, 26–7.

First, Austen underlines the natural transference of feeling that requires no particular 'interest'; second, she indicates how Mrs Jennings's feelings are intensified by manifold associations with the Dashwood family; and third, she shows that Mrs Jennings's grief is redoubled by the way she thinks herself into Mrs Dashwood's position. This last imaginative construction of 'what we ourselves should feel in the like situation' is Smith's special contribution to theory, though it coexists in his treatise with associative explanations and with Hume's idea of automatic influence.[52] And indeed this mirror-like finding of the other in the self – so graphically mimed by Austen's syntax and italics – throws light on the form of *Sense and Sensibility* as a whole.

In his model, Smith posits an 'attentive spectator' to engage with the experiencing agent, 'the person concerned'.[53] To the end of maximizing the sympathy between these two consciousnesses, he extrapolates a set of virtues proper to each. So the bystander will have to be exceptionally sensitive, the sufferer unusually stoic in order for the optimum level of concord to be reached. The 'amiable virtues' appropriate to the spectator are summed up in the term 'sensibility'; to the agent, on the other hand, belong 'the awful and respectable virtues' most often shorthanded as 'self-command'.

The relevance of these categories to the initial placing of the two heroines is suggestive – we hear almost as much of Elinor's self-command as we do of Marianne's sensibility. But the plot works in such a way as to complicate and test these attributes. Each sister is, in Smith's terms, both an agent and a spectator of the other, and for each of them, the special endowment is complemented by its contrary, so that Marianne is 'sensible' as well as amiable, and Elinor has 'good heart' in addition to her sense. Each, moreover, on Smith's model, is to find herself out of role with regard to the evolving action. Marianne is soon to become 'the person concerned' for her sufferings turn out to be the more extreme, as Elinor sees, and more rapidly come to their height. Elinor's sympathies, on the other hand, are stretched from the moment she assumes the part of bystander, and our sense of her character is as much moulded by her mental and practical interventions as by her immediate affairs. But if Elinor emerges as almost a paragon of attentiveness, Marianne – on any *social* reckoning of the amiable virtues – gets off to a very slow start, hampered as she is by a received culture that puts a high premium on exclusivity, and by a plot that connives at her detachment from Elinor's real situation by masking it with a vow of secrecy.

---

[52] *TMS*, 1.i.1.2 and 1.i.1.6, 9–11.   [53] Ibid., 1.i.1.4, 10.

Sense and Sensibility centres, as its title signals, in the relationship of the sisters – hence no doubt the recurring criticism that its heroes are drawn, for once, short of full length. In place of the usually even-tenored ways of confidantes, Jane Austen unfolds a relationship that itself undergoes great strain, responding beneath its polite surface to the old Terentian maxim that lovers fall in only after they have fallen out. Things come to their lowest ebb between the sisters when Marianne blurts out her 'mortifying conviction', long held, that Elinor's feelings are weak, and her self-command, therefore, of little consequence (104, 263). Each accuses the other, at different times, of concealment (79, 170), and the pain of each is heightened by a privacy unbroken by the small change of daily contact. But here there is a significant distinction between them. Where Marianne, for the sake of the purest possible apperception, cultivates silence and absorption – or 'idleness' as the narrator, following Johnson, acidly remarks (104)[54] – Elinor busies herself, keeping up the usual pretences and civilities, without ever quite losing touch with her sorrow. In so far as Elinor finds solace by this route, she embodies Smith's type of the agent who 'exert[s] that recollection and self-command which constitute the dignity of every passion, and which bring it down to what others can enter into'.[55] Marianne, on the other hand, corresponds to the anti-type who, sacrificing 'equality of temper' to a 'sense of honour', is 'apt to sit brooding at home over either grief or resentment'.[56] Indeed the language applied to the sisters in this context is often highly reminiscent of the *Theory*, as is the gist of the narrator's clinching observation that by 'brooding over her sorrows in silence, [Marianne] gave more pain to her sister than could have been communicated by the most open and most frequent confession of them' (212).

Smith's notion of 'matching' emotional tone in the interests of promoting both social and individual harmony runs through the novel. After Marianne is rebuffed by Willoughby at the party, the sisters are described 'in joint affliction', Elinor's fits of tears 'scarcely less violent than Marianne's' (182). More vividly, at the climax of Marianne's illness, Austen produces a special prose, full of dashes and asyndeton, to convey the 'anxious flutter' of her unofficially sensitive heroine (314–15). While the obvious parallels that unfold between the two courtships make an irony of the emotional distance that subsists between the sisters for much of the time, they account also for the strength of their final intimacy. Marianne's cry of remorse – 'how

---

[54] To Mrs Thrale, 17 Mar. 1773, *The Letters of Samuel Johnson*, ed. Bruce Redford, 3 vols. (Oxford, 1992), II, 21.
[55] *TMS*, I.i.5.3, 24.   [56] Ibid., I.i.4.10, 23.

barbarous have I been to you' (264), her heroic intervention on Elinor's behalf in the Dashwoods' drawing room (235–6), or her later anguished reception of the misleading news of the Ferrars marriage (353), all carry the stamp of her own agony. But it is the differences in situation that draw out the rational, harder-sought aspect of the sympathizing faculty. Thus Elinor in London is moved to 'the deepest concern' when she perceives that Marianne's feelings of loss are troubled, as hers with respect to Edward are not, by Willoughby's destruction of all ground for esteem (179).

If Elinor emerges as the novel's chief exponent of sensibility, a point noticed by a reviewer soon after publication,[57] Marianne, whose natural tenderness is never in doubt, is only partially implicated in the satire of sensibility. Austen distinguishes between the social virtue and the reigning cult, which she observes, with relish, to have evolved into something like its antithesis, as the case of the two Ferrars brothers shows. Edward, who is deficient only in the parade of sensibility, has an 'open affectionate heart' (where Willoughby has 'open affectionate manners', 15, 48), and his values are very much of a kind with those celebrated by Godwin in the Lake Constance episode of *St Leon*. His neglect of fame, of 'great men or barouches', his inclination for 'low company' and his lack of ease among 'strangers of gentility' are backed by a high regard for the life of domestic affection (16, 94). The 'small parsonage-house' and the social duties that await him there provide his brother Robert with just the foil to show off his wit and 'sensibility' by turns – the last in a demonstration of his shock at Edward's disgrace (298–9). The 'delicacy' that Robert exhibits in his long-drawn-out choice of a toothpick-case is as much designed to impress as the trinket itself (220–1) – toothpicks and tweezer-cases are singled out by Smith to illustrate the cachet of useless purchases.[58] That the wealthy set think of the amiable virtue as a commodity indispensable to *bon ton* is clear not only from the obligatory simperings of Fanny Dashwood (a specialist in the art of shrinking sympathies), but from Robert Ferrars's verbal arabesques on the ideal cottage – which seats eighteen couples for dinner (252, 371). While such gross appropriation of Rousseauesque motifs is at some remove from the practice of Willoughby and Marianne, a continuity is nevertheless visible. Willoughby's boast that he would love to pull down Combe Magna and rebuild it on the plan of the Dashwoods' dwelling, smoking chimney

---

[57] The anonymous reviewer twice attributes 'sensibility' to Elinor, and compares her 'patience and tenderness' with the antisocial tendencies of her sister. *Critical Review* (Feb. 1812), in Southam, ed., *Critical Heritage*, [1], pp. 36, 38.

[58] *TMS*, IV.1.8, 182.

and all (72–3), is – like his protest against the few alterations intended by Mrs Dashwood – half a pretence, as his more serious scheme for revamping Allenham shows. Marianne flirts in a similar way with the same aesthetic. 'What have wealth and grandeur to do with happiness', she exclaims before admitting to a 'competence' that exceeds Elinor's modest idea of wealth (91). Included in her gloss of pastoral chic is all the equipage ('a proper establishment of servants, a carriage, perhaps two, and hunters') that Mrs Jennings imagines a reformed Willoughby doing without, in the cause of his devotion (194).

The ease with which 'sensibility' is divorced from its primary significances points to a fatal flaw in the sort of creed jointly upheld by Marianne and Willoughby. 'Sympathy', in their case, signifies correspondence of feeling – their own feeling, and it begins and ends – such is their boast – with themselves. Mrs Dashwood unwittingly supplies an intriguing clue to this deficit when she claims to recognize 'no sentiment of approbation inferior to love' (16). The discounting of esteem in all but the love relationship is basic to the outlook of Austen's self-adulatory couple, who trusting in their shared intuitions turn a blind eye to the outer world, and in doing so leave themselves peculiarly defenceless to its inroads. Marianne, after Willoughby's desertion, finds herself in a social context which she has emptied of all meaning, and which she continues to suppose more treacherous than her betrayer (188–9). Willoughby, for his part, gives away a split in his make-up when he admits, in his hour of remorse, that he put Marianne through their final meeting at the cottage because he shrank from the thought that the Dashwoods, 'or the rest of the neighbourhood', might guess that he had fallen out with Mrs Smith (324). This hankering after general esteem runs entirely counter to the lovers' self-assumed character, and proves to have all the more power for its suppression. Like St Leon torn from Marguerite by the force of disposition, Willoughby capitulates to a need that rises, so to speak, from an unconscious that is irremediably *social*. Readers would have had no difficulty in connecting this need to the drive for social status widely described (though by no means always applauded) by liberal theorists. Specially apt in view of the stress laid on Willoughby's worldly aspirations, is Smith's idea that the more exalted ranks of society naturally attract admiration and that social stability is born of such instincts. But though Smith stood by this view, he was increasingly struck by the corruptive effects of imitation, and in his edition of 1790 pictures the realm of wisdom and virtue as foreign to that of wealth and power – 'the road which leads to the one, and that which leads to the other, lie sometimes in very opposite directions'.[59] Both Godwin and Austen begin where Smith leaves off. They observe his diverging roads, but enlarge greatly on his critique of a materialist ethos. Approbation emerges as a far from straightforward social instrument in *Sense and Sensibility*. In place of Smith's regulator and diffuser of social mores, Austen presents something uncomfortably two-edged. Mr Palmer, for example, is driven by his thirst for applause to a veritable vaudeville act of antisocial feats (115–16).

Though no warts are removed, the minor characters (barring the exclusive London set) make deeper claims on the reader's respect in the last volume. This 'softening' of attitude may well be the result of revision, as Roger Gard has noted,[60] but it has its strategic side. Satire and caricature recede, as Marianne is gradually brought into more extroverted relation to her immediate world. Solidity returns as she prepares to join that (briefly glimpsed) society in which she will soon be 'submitting to new attachments', and, as patroness, 'entering on new duties' (379). The change in her outlook is signalled by the phrase 'affectionate sensibility' and by her adoption of the word 'esteem' which she has previously considered taboo. What underlies her earlier social estrangement is that excess of sensibility noted at the novel's start, a trait that bears comparison with Adam Smith's term 'excessive self-estimation'.[61] In ethics, self-approval was usually understood to make up for the experience of taking on others' pain. But Austen exhibits a school where the compensatory part seems poised to take over. Marianne prides herself on the intensities of her distress. She seeks out solitude to 'augment and fix her sorrow', savours an 'invaluable misery', or cherishes an 'irritable refinement' (104, 303, 201). Her self-absorption kills 'every exertion of duty or friendship' – 'scarcely allowing', as she later admits, 'sorrow to exist but with me' (346). This quality of self-enclosure is vividly captured when she takes her leave of Norland ('could you know what I suffer[!]'), or congratulates herself on having feelings sufficiently strong to love a sister whose affections are merely calm (27, 104). And her isolation in the first volume is comically exaggerated by the huge family web that Austen weaves round her in Devon – where Middletons, Dashwoods, Palmers, and Steeles are all interconnected. She meets her perfect anti-type in that overwhelming social convenor Sir John ('Benevolent, philanthropic man!'), who cannot bear to 'keep a third cousin to himself' (119). A refreshingly practical philanthropist, Sir John is among those characters

[59] Ibid., i.iii.3.8, 64. The tone of such discussion in *The Wealth of Nations* is often sterner still, see e.g. iii.iv.10, 418–19.
[60] Roger Gard, *Novels*, pp. 85–6.   [61] *TMS*, vi.iii.31, 253.

who grow more likeable with rereading: his shocking geniality loses some edge.

Though unparalleled in its penetration and lightness of touch, Jane Austen's criticism of period 'sensibility' is by no means unique. Coleridge, for one, entertained a similar scepticism towards this peculiarly literary virtue. At the height of a short friendship he commended Charles Lloyd for a 'benevolence enlivened, but not sicklied, by sensibility'.[62] But before Lloyd came to write his own portrait of corrupt sensibility in *Edmund Oliver*, his explicitly Anti-Jacobin *roman-à-clef*, Coleridge got in a parody of Lloyd's mawkish style in a sonnet that hinges on the phrase, 'But, alas! Most of *Myself* I thought.'[63] Closer in some respects, however, is Godwin's full-length study of the man of feeling in *Fleetwood* (1805).

This novel, though in its time widely (and in some quarters wilfully) misunderstood,[64] owing to the oblique irony of its first-person narration, charts the increasingly antisocial course embarked upon by a hero dedicated to the pursuit of fine-feeling. Fleetwood is haunted, from motherless childhood on, by the thought that he stands alone. He pictures himself at one point – with a surreal brilliance that looks forward to Dickens – as an empty and disused industrial plant (263).[65] Drawing on the language of empiricist ethics,[66] he singles out sympathy as the only force that can animate this dreary automatism (150). In line with liberal theory again, he admits to the part played by 'attachment and approbation' in the making of the self, adding the proviso that he needs to find 'other persons in the world of the same sect as himself' – and there lies the rub, for he has found none. Abandoning politics and reverting to the life of fashion, the connoisseur of feeling becomes a prey to ennui and to nausea (140, 263). His life enters a new phase in the Lake District, however, when he meets Macneil, a thoroughgoing 'philanthropist' who lectures him on the need for human attachment. After making up a parable about a 'fastidious misanthropist' who is shipwrecked only to find, to his surprise, every kind of resource in the company of a quite ordinary sailor, Macneil unwisely encourages Fleetwood to marry his daughter. Misanthropy dies hard, and Godwin's

---

[62] To Thomas Poole, 24 Sept. 1796, *Collected Letters*, ed. E. L. Griggs (1956–71) I, 236.

[63] First of the 'Sonnets Attempted In The Manner Of Contemporary Writers', in *Coleridge: Poems*, ed. John Beer (1974), p. 124.

[64] See Walter Scott's brilliant but disingenuous piece on the novel in *The Edinburgh Review*, 6 (Apr. 1805), pp. 182–93.

[65] *Fleetwood*, in *Collected Novels and Memoirs of William Godwin*, v, ed. Pamela Clemit (1992); references are given in the text.

[66] Compare, for example, *TMS*, I.i.1.2–3.

anti-hero persists in one crass error after another, propelling his wife, through a third volume, to the brink of an early grave. A far cry from the public-spirited hero celebrated by Mackenzie, Godwin's 'man of feeling' is a creature in ever-faster flight from reason and all social relation.

In the aftermath of Revolution, sensibility drew fire generally, and the attack came, as has often been noted, from quite different quarters. That Austen's satiric treatment of it has been linked with the Anti-Jacobin front, says something about the great fame of Gillray, Canning and the *Review*, something too about the relative obscurity of other critiques, but precious little about her work. In a survey of the field Janet Todd remarks on the way the Anti-Jacobin satirists 'worked to bind sensibility to radicalism'.[67] Context is all-important in determining the direction of the many critical assaults that were then current. In *Sense and Sensibility* Marianne's doctrine is associated with wealth and a face-saving materialism, and found wanting when pitted against a classical account of the social virtues, conspicuously grounded in the Enlightenment. That Marianne is made vulnerable by her studied indifference to matters of contract (witness her disregard of engagement) tallies closely, at the same time, with Wollstonecraft's warnings to women on the blinkering of sensibility. But, for Austen, neither the amiable virtue nor its counterfeits are by any means specific to gender. In Gillray's cartoon of the Theophilanthropes (Coleridge and Godwin are among them) Sensibility, complete with tricolor, is flanked by the gross and menacingly swollen figure of Philanthropy. Austen and Godwin make their relative positions clear when they bring in 'philanthropists' (however distinct) to show just how lacking in sociability their official figures of fine-feeling are.

[67] Janet Todd, *Sensibility: An Introduction* (1986), p. 130.

PART TWO

Engaging with the new age

CHAPTER 5

Diffraction

By most accounts the Age of Enlightenment drew to a close with the unfolding of the Revolution in France, but reports of its extinction are sometimes exaggerated. If the movement fell victim to the cultural terrorism of the nineties, it went on to enjoy a long (and often suitably unorthodox) afterlife, perplexed by much shape-shifting. Though spurned in some quarters altogether, it found fresh heirs in the new century who were happy to advertise their enlightened descent, while many old hands changed tack significantly without wholly surrendering allegiance to it. This continuity has been masked, however, by a tendency among literary historians to polarize the period into the two camps of Jacobin and Anti-Jacobin, and to focus somewhat exclusively on the way a national mood of political reaction was fuelled by fears of domestic upheaval, and by the onset of war.

Austen criticism, in particular, has been prominent in explication of this sort. Marilyn Butler's famous study provided, when it appeared, a valuable corrective to views of tradition that were all but devoid of social content, and her 'war of ideas' has proved to be an asset to historiography of the nineteenth century ever since.[1] But the 'Anti-Jacobin' label (all question of its applicability aside) is peculiarly unfortunate in the context of the times, for in the years that Austen came before her public the term received its colour chiefly from *The Anti-Jacobin Review and Magazine* (1798–1821), the angry follow-up to the organ founded by Canning. After proclaiming that Jacobinism was a perpetually self-renewing monster,[2] the *Review* proceeded, monthly, to milk its fearsome Hydra in order to envenom attacks on feminism, the abolition of the slave trade, evangelicalism, philanthropy, and 'philosophy' – on anything that moved and smelt of reform. Its tactic of emptying the middle ground looks forward to the later critical strategy

---

[1] The term is adopted by Boyd Hilton in his important study *The Age of Atonement: the Influence of Evangelicalism on Social and Economic Thought, 1785–1865* (Oxford, 1988), p. 3, 3n., and *passim*.

[2] See 'Prefatory Address', *The Anti-Jacobin Review and Magazine*, 1 (July 1798).

of lumping together all but the most radical voices as 'Anti-Jacobin', so it is as well to keep in mind that the *Review* was far from typical of contemporary periodicals. At its outset, indeed, it was the only right-wing monthly and it continued to be heavily outnumbered – and outperformed – by more liberal journals for as long as it survived.[3] Some of these it is true could accurately be described as 'Anti-Jacobin' in view of their opposition to, say, republicanism or a universal franchise, but a good proportion favoured constitutional change, and none matched the *Review* in defiant dismissal of the Enlightenment. While many critics who have applied the Anti-Jacobin label to writers of this period have shown themselves aware of such distinctions, the elision from Austen-the-Anti-Jacobin to the *Anti-Jacobin Review* has frequently been made, even by the most magisterial of historians.[4] It seems unfair that Jane Austen whose daily newspaper was the Foxite *Morning Chronicle* should pay this special historicist tax at so high a rate.[5]

Because of its deep, initial association with the *philosophes* and their British counterparts, the French Revolution was embroiled in every later intellectual response to the Enlightenment. And for some, reappraisal led to almost total repudiation. Coleridge, famously, switched from empiricism to idealism after his political recantation, and compensated for naming his first son Hartley by christening his second Berkeley. Hannah More, in a series of homilies, identified liberty and equality as the enemies of piety, and traced a host of social evils to the 'irradiation' of modern ideas.[6] For the most part, however, reactions were more elliptical and circumspect. Thus it was frequently argued that the Enlightenment had been betrayed by its inheritors. Southey in an 'Anti-Jacobin' poem (which Jane Austen read with 'much approbation' on the whole)[7] came up with an effective formula for objectifying apostasy: 'They had the Light, and from the Light they turn'd.'[8] The portrayal of contemporary France as a warmongering despotism was an aspect of Southey's Waterloo poem that Jane Austen probably approved, for the same contention is central to a political tract by Charles Pasley which she rated very highly.[9] Whatever the merit of such arguments, the

---

3 See Derek Roper, *Reviewing Before the Edinburgh, 1788–1802* (Cranbury, NJ, 1978), pp. 180–2.
4 See Porter, *Enlightenment*, p. 293.
5 See To Cassandra, 29 Jan. 1813, *Letters*, pp. 201, 411; and see Gilson, *Bibliography*, pp. 24, 641.
6 William Roberts, *Memoirs of the Life and Correspondence of Mrs Hannah More*, 4 vols. (1834), III, 100.
7 To Alethea Brigg, 24 Jan. 1817, *Letters*, pp. 327–8.
8 *The Poet's Pilgrimage to Waterloo*, IV, stanza 12; *The Poetical Works of Robert Southey* (1845), X, 93.
9 Francis Austen certainly shared Pasley's view of France. He writes of Boulogne: 'The inhabitants are French, subjects to Napoleon the First, lately exalted to the Imperial dignity by the unanimous suffrages of himself and his creatures.' See J. H. and E. C. Hubback, *Jane Austen's Sailor Brothers* (Stroud, 1986) p. 122; and Tucker, *Woman*, p. 77n.

implicit appeal to Enlightenment values is an indication of their staying power. And yet in the case of Southey, as of others, the celebration of light was far from unqualified, and sometimes all too visibly exacted by the need to defend an earlier career. One common line of defence was to insist that debate had moved on since the nineties. So Southey, after the embarrassing exhumation of his unpublished early Jacobin play *Wat Tyler*, remarked of Napoleon's sympathizers: 'They had turned their faces towards the east in the morning to worship the rising sun, and in the evening they were looking eastward still, obstinately affirming that still the sun was there. I, on the contrary, altered my position as the sun went round.'[10] Hazlitt finding the chink in this defence – Southey had surely altered his ideals along with his affiliations – retorted: 'The sun, indeed, passes from the East to the West, but it rises in the East again; yet Mr Southey is still looking in the West – for his pension.'[11] But the retort did not prevent Hazlitt himself from falling back on the image of the vanished dawn, when he confessed, a decade later, that his political hopes had fled with his youth: 'I little dreamed that long before mine was set, the sun of liberty would turn to blood, or set once more in the night of despotism.'[12]

In *The Poet's Pilgrimage to Waterloo*, the long poem that won Jane Austen's approval, Southey took stock of the recent turbulent and bitter course of history which Napoleon's defeat promised finally to check. Officially the work is a laureate's ode of national thanksgiving, but Southey was unprepared for the suffering that he witnessed on his visit to the hospital at the site of the battle – privately describing it as 'the real face of war', and the *Pilgrimage* unfolds his struggle with a deeply invasive experience of desolation before returning to a festive major key. In keeping with this positive mood, the poem moves from realism to allegory, from descriptions of Flanders and the scene of war to a visionary part II dominated by the rival figures of Wisdom and the Heavenly Muse. To Wisdom, a latter-day spokesman for the Enlightenment, falls the task of evoking the disillusion and ruin that have followed in the wake of the glorious days of Revolution. To Urania, who fills the poet with a spirit of renewal (anticipating in this respect Keats's tragic Moneta from *Hyperion*), goes the brief of restoring faith in a benign providence and the power of mystery. But despite the high

---

[10] See 'A Letter to William Smith' (1817), in *The Life and Correspondence of Robert Southey*, ed. C. C. Southey, 6 vols. (1850), IV, 382. Southey is quoting his own earlier words from 1809.

[11] See David Bromwich, *Hazlitt: the Mind of the Critic* (Oxford, 1983), p. 284.

[12] 'On the Feeling of Immortality in Youth' in *Winterslow* (1902 edn), p. 50. Hazlitt must have forgotten that Southey had given almost exactly the same image to his evil prophet in the *Pilgrimage*, see II, stanza 5.

drama of the poet's conversion, the poem's most remembered lines come from its evil prophet who pictures a universe as callous and imperfect as man:

> The winds which have in viewless heaven their birth,
>   The waves which in their fury meet the clouds,
> The central storms which shake the solid earth,
>   And from volcanoes burst in fiery floods,
> Are not more vague and purportless and blind,
> Than is the course of things among mankind![13]

History seems to have conspired against the overt optimism of the *Pilgrimage*, for the glowing scene of family reunion with which the poem opens was overshadowed, shortly after publication, by the death of Southey's only son. The news was widely known, and coloured the reception of the poem for many, including Jane Austen.[14]

Southey designed his poem to celebrate not merely British victory over the French but the triumph of religion over 'gross material philosophy'.[15] Yet for all its would-be refutation of Enlightenment thought, *The Poet's Pilgrimage to Waterloo* relies heavily on the tenets of liberal history. As the villain of the piece, Napoleon is made to exhibit every evil of absolutist rule, and his 'barbarian dream of empire' is seen to set the clock back, his tyranny being thrown into relief through frequent comparison with England as a model of the modern state. Even in France his accession to power is understood to spell out political regression: in Aix, it is noted, a figure of Liberty was demolished on the night of his investiture (Liberty having died, it was said, in giving birth to an Emperor).[16] On social freedom the entire stadial advance of society is taken to depend, but it is the necessary condition, also, of the well-being of the individual. Southey tactfully quotes from a radical poem written on the eve of Revolution to stress the liberal basis of this belief:

> 'Where Freedom is not, there no Virtue is',
> Where Virtue is not, there no Happiness.[17]

'Full emancipation [from] bodily and mental bondage' is upheld as the ideal of civilized life, and conversely slavery in all its forms is seen as the

---

[13] Ibid., II, stanza 20; X, 74.

[14] After singling out the Proem as 'very beautiful', Austen adds, 'one cannot but grieve for the loss of the Son so fondly described': see To Alethea Bigg, 24 Jan. 1817, *Letters*, p. 328.

[15] 'Argument', *Poetical Works*, X, 1.   [16] Ibid., X, 130–1.

[17] Ibid., IV, stanza 14; X, 93. The quoted line is from the loco-descriptive poem *Lewesdon Hill* (1788) by William Crowe, the 'ultra-Whig' fellow of New College, Oxford, who supported the French Revolution in its early phase.

product of an outmoded political system that finds its ugliest expression in the slave trade – hence the apostrophes to Wilberforce and Clarkson, and the plea for total abolition. In sum, Southey, in attacking material philosophy, shows himself sufficiently wedded to its principles to justify both his later boast that he had remained true to his early idealism, and his vow that he would continue to fight social evil 'with all the resources of science, and all the ardour of enlightened and enlarged benevolence'.[18] So wholehearted is the silent appropriation of Anglo-Scottish sociology in *The Poet's Pilgrimage to Waterloo* that it could well cast doubt on the precise content of Southey's Christian faith. Even his rechristening of the theory of the four stages as Progress, or his attempt to sacramentalize his insistent imagery of light by invoking the presence of God, seems to boil down in the end to a rather backward-looking Enlightenment confidence in the benevolence of nature's laws.

Though the theodicial and other doctrinal aspects of Southey's poem are likely to strike readers today as the least satisfactory part of it, there can be little question that they appealed to Jane Austen. Nine months before Napoleon's defeat she ventured a view on the providential guidance of war very similar to that in the *Pilgrimage*. Writing to the wife-to-be of Francis, the elder of her two sailor brothers, she holds out for eventual victory over America on the grounds that Britain has the stronger 'claim to the protection of Heaven, as a Religious Nation, a Nation inspite of much Evil improving in Religion'.[19] Even in the heyday of the Enlightenment such views enjoyed wide currency. The great liberal historian William Robertson suggested, for instance, that the hand of Providence was evident in the way the Reformation had grown, against mighty odds, 'to an amazing degree of vigour and maturity'[20] – like many other members of the Scottish school, Robertson came from a strongly non-conformist background to which he remained attached. All the same, there is an urgency in Austen's hope of divine intervention, and a raw nationalism in her plea, that have the authentic ring of her times. And in this connection it is interesting to note that Wilberforce had complained in his *Practical View* that Robertson (for whom he had a high regard) had not done enough in his treatment of the Reformation in *Charles V* to make God's purposes sufficiently plain.[21]

Austen's nation 'improving in Religion' is a clear reference to the religious revival that gathered momentum throughout the country in the first decade of the century, and particularly through the years 1807–11. Though critical

---

[18] See 'Letter to William Smith', *Correspondence*, IV, 388.
[19] To Martha Lloyd, 2 Sept. 1814, *Letters*, pp. 273–4.
[20] For a discussion of this see Pocock's *Barbarism and Religion* (1999), II, 291–3.
[21] William Wilberforce, *A Practical View*, 16th edn (1827), p. 244.

of the movement (and never strictly an Evangelical herself), Jane Austen witnessed its huge impact on Anglicanism, and was herself touched by the new energies that galvanized a wide range of belief. Through her family (at least two of whom became outrightly Evangelical) she read widely in the literature of the more moderate flank of the sect, and was well placed to observe what was to prove the most important of all cultural movements of the dawning era. Paradoxically it was the darkness of the times that spurred on faith in a divine presence, and the same darkness shaped an understanding of that presence. The natural theology of Paley seemed far too benign to mediate the experience of a decade that had been plunged into the terrors of revolution and war. Nor did the harsh facts of food shortages, economic blockade, and national debt, together with the prospect of internal uprising, invasion, and Malthusian famine, belong to the kind-hearted cosmos implied by natural religion. That bleak universe conjured up by the sinister figure of Wisdom in Southey's *Pilgrimage*, only to be cheerily dismissed by the sanguine Urania, would not go away. And the only means of incorporating it within a religious system was to change the image of the divine, to replace the benevolent cypher of rational belief with a personal, punishing, patriarchal God. In Southey's poem, Wisdom presents the picture of a fearsome landscape torn by catastrophe as an image of the world without God, but the same landscape could be made to carry a divine sanction; and so it does in a passage by Thomas Gisborne, an Evangelical writer, one of whose works pleased Jane Austen:[22]

The earth, as to its exterior strata, is not at present in the same condition in which it was when it came forth from the hand of its Creator; but has manifestly undergone universal and violent and overwhelming convulsions of such a nature as to spread general destruction among the animated inhabitants of its surface at the time of the catastrophe.

Gisborne proceeds to supply the only possible explanation for this 'state of desolation and ruin':

a moral change calling for such an event had taken place in that portion of the inhabitants of the earth, which was endued with moral agency and responsibility; in other words, that mankind had offended their Creator, by transgressions of his laws, and had brought upon themselves penal consequences of disobedience.[23]

---

[22] Austen remarks of a work by Gisborne (which is not clear), 'having begun, I am pleased with it'; see To Cassandra, 30 Aug. 1805, *Letters*, p. 112. Gisborne was the most cultivated spokesman of the Clapham sect, a keen abolitionist who wrote poetry in the vein of Cowper, and contributed to the utilitarian ethics of the Enlightenment. Though a key figure in the Bible Society, he was a moderate.

[23] Thomas Gisborne, *The Testimony of Natural Theology to Christianity* (1818), pp. 64–5.

In her teens Jane Austen had read Percival on the dangers of attributing providential design to natural causes in his *Tales*, a book she remembered affectionately in middle age, and scourging by disaster can safely be numbered among the Evangelical beliefs that she refused to subscribe to. But the prevailing sense of a darker and more cruel world, and of the moral strength that can be won from struggling against it, worked its way deeply into *Mansfield Park*, which she began planning at Chawton in 1811, after she had already revised *Sense and Sensibility* for publication, and was bringing *Pride and Prejudice* to a final stage of completion. The new novel was the first she had begun since the nineties – with the exception of the unfinished *Watsons* which in some ways anticipates it, both in the painful situation of its heroine and in its caustic exposure of a worldly grandeur that was also (on Cassandra's evidence) to be sold short by the plot.[24] The choice of an evangelically inclined central couple for *Mansfield Park* offered the chance not only to move beyond the sphere of the relatively light, bright, and sparkling, but to engage in a direct way with what was crucial to the new age.

EVANGELICALISM AND THE ENLIGHTENMENT

However remote from the *philosophes*, the Evangelical movement was to prove at length an important vehicle for the Enlightenment. In view of the unqualified hostility of many of its spokesmen, this debt is certainly an unexpected one. That it was incurred at all has probably to do with the revival's determination, on the one hand, to deal with the real world, and with the Enlightenment's success, on the other, in convincing the public of the truth of their empirical account of it. Wilberforce led the way with frequent citations from Adam Smith in *A Practical View* (1797), his attack on an effete, 'nominal' Christianity that had lost sight of the 'guilt and evil of sin'.[25] At a time when Smith's ideas were regarded as having 'a revolutionary tendency' in the words of his first biographer (and when criticism of his work was protectively withheld by one ardent admirer), Wilberforce's open annexations of Smith's ethics showed considerable daring, extending as they did even to his theory of duty and conscience.[26] Audacious, too, was the

---

[24] Emma Watson was to reject the proposal of the vain and vacuous Lord Osborne and accept Mr Howard, rector of the parish, after he had shaken off Lady Osborne, a glamorous fifty-year-old widow – perhaps Lady Susan fifteen years on; see *Minor Works*, p. 363.

[25] *Practical View* (1827), p. 181.

[26] See Anand C. Chitnis, *The Scottish Enlightenment, and Early Victorian English Society* (1986), pp. 26, 118; and see *Practical View*, pp. 165–6, 68, 182, 248.

successful intervention of the Scottish Evangelicals at Edinburgh University in 1805 in the notorious case of John Leslie, a layman whom the moderate Presbyterians had attempted to bar from the Chair of Mathematics on the grounds that he endorsed Hume's notions of causality.[27] One commentator on this affair remarks on how ready the Evangelicals were to appreciate 'that even the so-called "scepticism" of Hume might be woven into the fabric of Christian apologetics'.[28] The sort of rationalism that stressed the limits of reason clearly suited the book of a movement that set great store by beliefs, inner lights, and intuition.

If the Evangelical reliance on Enlightenment psychology is accountable on these terms, their wholesale appropriation of political economy seems at first sight more puzzling. Adam Smith, after all, had supplied a fairly optimistic view of the fine balance that resulted from the free play of market forces, even though he entertained doubts about the effects of commercial enterprise on culture, and acknowledged the need for various kinds of state intervention. But by the start of the new century his economic system had been placed against a lowering backdrop by the revisionism of his disciple Malthus. Though Smith had already addressed the problem of an expanding population outrunning food supply, and noted that 'scantiness of subsistence' was only held in check by infant mortality,[29] Malthus's idea of the drastically uneven growth rates of humans and their resources not only shattered the perfectibilianism of liberals like Godwin, but made even the everyday business of earning a living seem a cut-throat affair. So there emerged the unacceptable face of political economy, and to the Evangelicals nothing seemed more acceptable. If the world had been created as a 'moral ordination' for the individual soul, as one of their apologists put it, the more trials and tribulations that were on offer the better.[30] Smith's system with its Malthusian revisions was not only taken aboard, but soon accepted as the right instrument by which the devout should steer. Given its divine sanction, political economy took on the inflexibility of a religious doctrine. Boyd Hilton sums up the matter well in *The Age of Atonement*, his definitive study of the economic aspects of Evangelical thought: 'Barriers to Free Trade, like monopolies, protective duties, and preferences, not only offended the unprivileged, but were elements of friction obscuring God's

---

[27] See Chitnis, *Scottish Enlightenment*, p. 25; and Boyd Hilton, *Atonement*, pp. 24–5.
[28] Ian D. L. Clark, quoted in Boyd Hilton, *Atonement*, p. 25.
[29] *WN*, I.viii.38–9, 97–8.
[30] See Thomas Chalmers, *On the Power, Wisdom, and Goodness of God*, quoted by Boyd Hilton, *Atonement*, p. 84.

clockwork providence.'[31] This doctrinaire approach to political economy, entirely alien to the spirit of its founder, was to have grim consequences in the public sphere. Official and private relief to the poor was frequently curbed on the grounds that it amounted to interference with the vast riddling machine that the Creator had designed and put into use for the moral benefit of man.

These ties with the past formed by the Evangelicals in the new century go back, in fact, to a much earlier alliance between non-conformists and rationalists on the issue of slavery. Emancipist pamphleteering, in which Quakers and Methodists were always to the fore, drew from the first on the political philosophy of the Enlightenment. Anthony Benezet quoted Montesquieu at length, and John Wesley knew, if only at second-hand, his Rousseau. Wilberforce referred to Hume and Smith in his speeches, and was fed information for them by William Robertson, famous for his praise of the way Christianity had virtually extirpated slavery from western Europe in the fourteenth century.[32] In his history of the abolition, Thomas Clarkson dwells on the contribution of empiricists, citing Hartley, Kames, Hutcheson, and Millar in addition to Robertson and Hume; indeed, so impressed was he by the 'Glasgow professors' that when he came to map the course of the entire movement as a river, in an interleaved plate, he made over a whole tributary to the Scottish Enlightenment. In the run-up to the critical parliamentary bills of 1806–7, the Clapham sect worked in close co-operation with the Whig grandees of Holland House, a powerhouse of liberal ideas, so that what began as loose association ended as political pact.[33] Unity of purpose did something to disguise the very different premisses on which the two camps proceeded. While enlightened thinkers generally thought in terms of human rights, Evangelicals looked to free agency as a necessary condition of salvation, the first step in a broader process of deliverance, 'emancipation from the power of sin'.[34]

We know that Jane Austen was well up in these matters. In January 1813, at about midpoint in her drafting of *Mansfield Park*, she put Clarkson's name first when listing writers she had been 'in love with'; Claudius Buchanan, the Evangelical missionary, is another. But her loyalties to these, she playfully confessed to Cassandra, have paled away before her

[31] Ibid., p. 69.
[32] See Dugald Stewart's introductory Life to William Robertson's *Works*, I, 192–4; Thomas Clarkson's *History of the Abolition of the Slave Trade*, 2 vols. (1808), p. 88; and Robertson's *Charles V*, in *Works*, IV, 44–5, 298–305.
[33] See Chitnis, *Scottish Enlightenment*, p. 85.
[34] Wilberforce to Ralph Creyke, 8 Jan. 1803, *The Correspondence of William Wilberforce*, ed. R. I. and S. Wilberforce, 2 vols. (1840), I, 253.

enthusiasm for the hawkish Charles Pasley, a writer steeped in Adam Smith and other Enlightenment mentors. Emancipation is a recurring theme in the *Essay on the Military Policy and Institutions of the British Empire* (1810) where Pasley parades the evils of Napoleonic despotism while upholding the liberties of the governed at home and abroad. But the book is entirely without religious trimmings, which suggests that Austen's interest in liberty needed no devotional bush, and that she approached Clarkson's great classic for what it was – a *History of the Abolition*.[35] Her concern was shared by her brothers. James, as we have seen, propagandized in *The Loiterer* for the Abolition Bill that came before parliament in 1789. And Francis, when in St Helena in 1808, noticed with approval the legal restraints that had been placed on the treatment of slaves, confirming (as an eyewitness) the 'harshness and despotism which has been so justly attributed to the conduct of the Land-holders, or their managers in the West India Islands'. To this he adds that 'Slavery however it may be modified is still Slavery', while calling for an end to the institution in all countries 'dependant on England, or colonized by her subjects'. So much has often been quoted, but there is a further sentence in the manuscript, dropped without indication in the extract given by the Hubbacks, and unnoticed since by any of Austen's biographers or critics:

Jealous as she [England] has ever been of her own liberty, she should pay equal attention to the inalienable rights of all the nations, of what colour so ever they may be, and in particular should take care that the blessing be fully and equally distributed to all who live subject to her own sway.[36]

The talk here of 'inalienable rights' and racial equality was strong meat even in the early days of the nineteenth century, and by the start of the next not easy to bear.

Francis Austen's comments date from within a year of the Abolition Bill, and are typical of the mood of idealism that swept through the country after it became law. Its passage through parliament was a triumph for the Evangelicals (the vote was carried by 114 against 15 in the House), and resulted in a huge increase in the number of their MPs between 1807 and 1811. But the movement gained in general influence in these years as much as in political power, for abolition had become a thoroughly popular cause.

---

[35] See To Cassandra, 24 Jan. 1813, *Letters*, p. 198. Chapman mistakenly supposed that Clarkson's work referred to here was the *Life of William Penn* (1813); chronology rules this out in view of Austen's 'as I ever was [in love with]'.

[36] Francis William Austen, 'Remarks on the Island of St Helena' (Apr. 1808). Greenwich, AUS/6, ff. 52–8; see ff. 53–4. See J. H. and E. C. Hubback, *Sailor Brothers*, p. 192.

This last fact was noticed by many commentators at the time, Coleridge contending, for one, that the Bill was forced on the politicians by public opinion and that the main opposition to it came from the Cabinet of the Whig Ministry of Talents.[37] Taking advantage of the high ground, the Evangelicals pressed home their claim to moral leadership of the nation, and were increasingly successful in setting a new and more solemn tone. Indeed, the success of the revival bred a mounting confidence bordering at times on the chiliastic, one of its apologists (known to Jane Austen) declaring that Christianity had at last recovered the spirit of its foundation.[38] Not since the dawn of the French Revolution had such optimistic sentiments been voiced, and it is interesting to note that the classical imagery of illumination so often then in use came back into fashion, though invariably given a religious slant. In the debate on the Abolition Bill the Lord Chancellor could speak of Britain as 'the morning star of enlightened Europe whose boast and glory was to grant liberty and life', or Southey hail the nation's will 'to spread the sphere of happiness and light', just as he looked back on the Revolution as the moment 'when the Morning Star / Of Freedom on rejoicing France arose'.[39] But when Claudius Buchanan identifies Indian missionary activity as the second star of Bethlehem in his sermon 'The Star in the East' (1808), and proceeds to herald a new age of light, his borrowings are meant to taunt and put the age of reason in its place.

Though the Evangelicals' attempt to institutionalize missionary work in India predates abolition, there is no doubt that it drew strength from it. As early as 1805 Buchanan was deploring the absence of chaplains in the East India Company, and calling for the foundation of a Christian establishment in the colonies; by 1808 his plea was being taken up by many, including Francis Austen who, making the same points, complains that it was a matter of deep regret that the Company 'which provides so amply for the temporal wants of everyone engaged in its service' should have taken no care of religious instruction.[40] After the Company renewed its charter in

---

[37] See Review of Thomas Clarkson's *History of the Abolition* in the *Edinburgh Review*, 13 (July 1808), p. 372. It has been argued that Jane Austen's irritation with this ministry over the Popham affair is a mark of her conservatism (Brian Southam, *Jane Austen and the Navy* (2000), ch. 7). But the ministry was widely unpopular, and attacked by the likes of Leigh Hunt and Sheridan. Coleridge's remarks give further reason for its poor image: 'A majority of the cabinet, it is believed, were hostile to the abolition.'

[38] Claudius Buchanan writes: 'the vital spirit . . . of our religion has revived and is producing the fruits of the first century', see *Christian Researches in Asia* (1812), p. 449.

[39] Thomas Erskine quoted in Thomas, *Slave Trade*, p. 552; and Southey, *Poet's Pilgrimage to Waterloo*, IV, stanza 30, II, stanza 4; *Poetical Works*, X, 97, 70.

[40] *Remarks*, AUS/6 ff. 57–8.

1813, its former policy of keeping religion at bay was reversed, and regular chaplains and missionary societies became part of its ordinance.[41] We can be sure that the Austen family were fully aware of how contentious this move was, for their friend and patron Warren Hastings took the lead in opposing it, remarking before the House of Commons on how dangerous and misguided it was 'to force our religion on the consciences of the people of India'.[42] But Claudius Buchanan, the prime mover behind the plan for the Church in Asia, was clearly an influence too, so that the issue must have provided fertile ground for debate in the period that *Mansfield Park* was being written. To judge from the external evidence, Jane's allegiances might have gone either way, for in 1813 she records, on the one hand, her pleasure in hearing of Hastings's praise of *Pride and Prejudice* ('I am quite delighted with what such a Man writes about it'), and notes, on the other, her respect for the writings of Buchanan, while lauding Pasley.[43]

A divergence of attitude on these matters is reflected in *Mansfield Park* when Mary Crawford scoffs, much to Edmund's irritation, that he is all set to make his mark as 'a celebrated preacher in some great society of Methodists, or as a missionary into foreign parts' (458). We shall see that the novel's pungent if sparse references to the East, as well as to the West, are part of its canvassing of 'the global moralism' that was a chief legacy of the Evangelicals. It was Wilberforce, after all, who remarked, at the height of his parliamentary triumph, that the Christian conversion of India was even more important than the bringing of liberty to African slaves.[44] Tellingly, the revival's apology for this proselytizing often deferred to the authority of the Enlightenment itself, dwelling in particular on the better conditions enjoyed by women in Christian societies – despite its own backward-looking record in this sphere! So Buchanan insisted that it was true of all pagans that women were treated as 'an inferior race: and, in general, confined to the house for life, like irrational creatures'.[45] Here he built on Wilberforce who, making the same claim in his *Practical View*, propped it up by referring his readers to a section in William Robertson's *History of America* on the 'Condition of Women'.[46]

[41] See Philip Lawson, *The East India Company* (1993), p. 150.
[42] Robin Furneaux, *William Wilberforce* (1974), p. 324. In a letter to Hastings, Henry Austen speaks, in the most glowing terms, of the way he has been revered by his family from childhood through the period of his trial to the present day. See Letter of 5 June 1802, BM 29,178, f. 213; and *Austen Papers*, pp. 176–8.
[43] See To Cassandra, 24 Jan. and 15–16 Sept. 1813, *Letters*, pp. 198, 218.
[44] Ford K. Brown, *Fathers of the Victorians* (Cambridge, 1961), p. 261.
[45] *Christian Researches in Asia*, pp. 116–17.
[46] *Practical View*, p. 20; William Robertson, *History of America*, bk. IV, section 2; *Works*, VII, 356–63.

EVANGELICALISM AND THE AUSTENS

Jane Austen's attitude to the religious revival has been the subject of much conjecture and debate. But the conviction shared by many critics that she became an Evangelical, or at least a fellow-traveller, generally proceeds from a sense of Edmund Bertram and Fanny Price's clear revivalist traits and of her apparent sympathy with them. Remarks on the movement in her letters do not, when read in context, give any support to the thesis that she was gradually brought round to the sect. Though she often changed her first impressions of writers, Austen's initial ridicule of Hannah More's *Cœlebs*, which prompted her to protest in 1809, 'I do not like Evangelicals', seems only to have hardened into disapproval, for the book is given Mrs Percival's imprimatur in the revisions she made to *Catharine* some time after 1811.[47] Her reasons for disliking the novel that Sydney Smith compared to a 'dramatic sermon' may well have been touched on by her brother James in a bluffer's guide to conversing about popular successes:

> Much praise, & slightly blame the book
> Where every pious female cook,
> May learn, while Cœlebs they peruse,
> To blend Religion with ragouts.[48]

The allusion here is to the scene in which More finds fault with a family of bluestockings for serving a badly cooked dinner to her Christian hero who proves on this occasion utterly unforgiving. Women's first duty, after all, is to be helpmeets for men – indeed the novel opens with a Miltonic reminder on the role of consort: 'nothing lovelier can be found / In woman, than to study household good'.[49] Such are the sentiments also of Catharine's guardian Mrs Percival, though it was perhaps rather her fanatical conservatism that put Jane Austen in mind of Hannah More. In the very speech where Catharine's aunt offers her a copy of *Cœlebs in Search of a Wife* she delivers her standard complaint, 'everything is going to sixes & sevens and all order will soon be at an end throughout the Kingdom' (232). Though the character of Mrs Percival pre-dates this revision, it certainly made a

---

[47] See *Catharine and Other Writings*, pp. 353, 357.
[48] 'Morning – to Edward', dated July 1814. HRO 60/3/2.
[49] Sydney Smith makes great play of the bad dinner in his hostile piece on *Cœlebs* in the *Edinburgh Review*, 14 (Apr. 1809), pp. 145–51, 147. For the text itself see *Cœlebs in Search of a Wife*, introd. Mary Waldron (Bristol, 1995), pp. 18–20, 9–12; *Paradise Lost*, IX, lines 233–4.

happy match for the writer who hoped that her work would have the effect of 'assuring the subordination of the poor'.[50]

Austen kept up the mockery of More, in a veiled way, through her remarks on the Webb sisters in her letters. In 1814 she bids a fond farewell to the family whom she first found buried in a copy of *Practical Piety*:

> The Webbs are really gone. When I saw the Waggons at the door, & thought of all the trouble they must have in moving, I began to reproach myself for not having liked them better – but since the Waggons have disappeared, my Conscience has been closed again – & I am excessively glad they are gone.[51]

Throughout the period of her imputedly new-found piety – what was known as 'seriousness' – Jane Austen's sense of mischief remains irrepressible. She characterizes visits to the most devout of Henry's Evangelical friends as 'quiet Tea-drinkings with the Tilsons' (and notes their readiness to chop down trees), or remarks that 'Mr Brecknell is very religious, & has got black Whiskers.'[52] Such light-heartedness had no place in the evangelical scheme of things, failing even to conform to any recognized style of sin. The same could not be said of Jane Austen's unabashed delight in theatre-going, a vice that even the moderate Wilberforce had decried in all its forms on the grounds that the God-fearing would not wish to set foot in places 'congenial to the debauchee'.[53] Given the climate of the time, the deliberation in *Mansfield Park* over whether plays are good or bad, suitable or not, amounts to a defence of theatre. Sydney Smith did not exaggerate unduly when he exclaimed of Hannah More: 'There is something in the word *Playhouse*, which seems so closely connected, in the minds of these people, with sin, and Satan, – that it stands in their vocabulary for every species of abomination.'[54] One evil frequently attributed to the theatre by the Evangelicals was radicalism: Wilberforce liked to pretend that Jacobinism and the Stage went hand in hand; John Styles was even more sweeping – 'a man must have studied in the schools of Hume, Voltaire, and Kotzebue, who can plead in behalf of theatre'.[55]

The famous quotation from the letters on which Jane Austen's reputation as a Saint largely rests needs to be taken in its context. Her niece Fanny

---

[50] So Brown approvingly (and accurately) summarizes Hannah More's argument in her tract *The Delegate* (1816): see *Fathers*, p. 251.

[51] To Anna Austen, 28 Sept. 1814, *Letters*, p. 278; and see pp. 191, 196.

[52] See To Martha Lloyd, 2 Sept. 1814; and To Cassandra, 30 Apr. and 6 June 1811: *Letters*, pp. 273, 193, 186–7.

[53] *Practical View*, see pp. 194–6.

[54] Review of *Cœlebs*, *Edinburgh Review*, 14 (Apr. 1809), p. 149.

[55] See Review of John Styles's *Strictures*, *Edinburgh Review*, 14 (Apr. 1809), p. 40.

Knight – who sought advice from her aunt on all her suitors – had formed a serious relationship with an evangelically minded young Cambridge graduate. Was this difference between them in religion, she asked, not a cause for breaking it off? Fanny had enjoyed the confidence of her aunt Jane for some years, and the fact that she could even put such a question to her is sufficient evidence in itself that Jane Austen was not an Evangelical. Jane, for her part, was obviously unwilling to bear the responsibility for putting a young couple asunder, and told Fanny plainly to rely on 'your own feelings & none but your own'.[56] She was determined, moreover, to make it clear to Fanny that she did not approve of her citing her lover's 'goodness' as a reason for incompatibility, replying to her in November 1814: 'I cannot admit *that*. I am by no means convinced that we ought not all to be Evangelicals, & am at least persuaded that they who are so from Reason & Feeling must be happiest and safest.'[57]

Jane Austen's general respect for the revival is clear from this, and there is no reason to doubt the sincerity of her claims for the efficacy of Evangelical belief. Yet she later voiced a not inconsistent dislike of the Evangelical tenor of her cousin the Reverend Edward Cooper's new volume of sermons – 'fuller of Regeneration & Conversion than ever – with the addition of his zeal in the cause of the Bible Society'.[58] It has been claimed that Austen's criticism of the Evangelicals is really aimed at Methodism rather than its more moderate forms, but Cooper was the mildest of Evangelicals,[59] and the Bible Society, disapprovingly mentioned in connection with him, was a thriving institution even within the Anglican domain. It would indeed have been difficult for the most moderate of Evangelicals to have stood out against a society headed by the Clapham sect and supported increasingly by Anglicans of almost every shade. Not untypical is the case of Dr Herbert Marsh, Professor of Divinity at Cambridge and initially a vociferous detractor, who recanted in 1812, remarking that he might as well try to stop a volcano.[60] Among those who remained critical to the end was Jane's clerical brother James, and his position provides a much needed corrective to the widely held view that the entire family fell under the spell of Evangelicalism.[61] In a talk given in 1814 James adds his voice to the objection

---

[56] 30 Nov. 1814, *Letters*, p. 285. Mary Waldron writes clinchingly on this point, see *Fiction of her Time*, pp. 85–6.
[57] 18–20 Nov. 1814, *Letters*, p. 280.
[58] To Cassandra, 8–9 Sept. 1816, *Letters*, p. 322.
[59] For some discussion of Edward Cooper's sermons, see Jarvis, *Jane Austen and Religion*, pp. 20–3.
[60] W. Canton, *History of the British Bible Society*, 2 vols. (1904), 1, 303.
[61] Even MacDonagh assumes that the younger Austen generation, James included, was Evangelically inclined, see *Real and Imagined Worlds*, pp. 3–5.

most commonly made against the Bible Society: that its practice of distributing Scripture without the mediation of *The Book of Common Prayer* was imprudent and unsound.[62] His tone is fairly equable here, but when he returns to the topic in the last pages of the poem he left unfinished at his death, it is with scarcely suppressed exasperation that he insists that only the prayerbook 'may preserve / From Calvin's harsh bewildering image / And heart-appalling views, that humble mind / Of the unletter'd Christian'. He seizes with particular venom on *The Methodist Magazine* (on which *The Evangelical Magazine* had so exactly modelled itself as to be virtually indistinguishable), and proceeds to denounce what Jane Austen shorthands as 'Conversion and Regeneration':

> From the shelf
> Which his small tatter'd library contains
> Banish the fanatic, schismatic tract
> Which monthly issues from th'all honour'd press,
> Stitched in blue paper; where in frontispiece
> Stare the harsh features of some saintly man,
> Some self-appointed preacher of dissent,
> Whose page too oft contains the poisonous creed
> Of Antinomian error, or at best
> Perverts the mind by the delusive hope
> Of strong assurance – inwards – and the tale,
> The wondrous tale, of childhood's premature
> Devout *experience* – both the dying words
> Of suckling confessors & embryo saints.[63]

James's lines are very much in keeping with the campaign against Evangelicalism conducted by Sydney Smith in the *Edinburgh Review*, which reserved some of its sharpest fire for the two magazines that it lumped together.[64] Smith remarked on the high circulation of these monthlies (20,000 in 1807) and on their wide distribution, noting that in one issue readers were exhorted to fling 'one shilling worth of these tracts out of the chaise window' for every pound they spent on the road.[65] Like James Austen, Smith is disturbed by the antinomian emphasis of the teaching ('they say a great deal about faith, and little about works'), above all, by what he names 'the doctrine of inward impulse and emotions', and illustrates by

---

[62] See 'Intended to be spoken at the first Meeting of the Branch of the Society for the promoting of Christian Knowledge at Basingstoke, 1814', Chawton MS, pp. 195–7.

[63] 'The Œconomy of Rural Life' (1819).

[64] See his review of Robert Ingram's *Causes of the Increase of Methodism* in the *Edinburgh Review*, 12 (Jan. 1808), pp. 341–62.

[65] *Edinburgh Review*, 12 (Jan. 1808), p. 350.

quoting the testimonies of sudden conversion that were standard fare in both magazines.

Sydney Smith, like many critics of revivalism, understood that John Wesley was really the founding figure of the movement, and that what lay at the heart of the new religion was his belief that the individual's innate wickedness could be waived once for all through an act of faith. The paradox of Wesley's system was that it simultaneously demonized human existence by insisting on man's natural depravity, and at the same time held out the prospect of perfectibility for its own élite. Cynics might argue that this was a dogma designed to maximize the advantage of belief, but then Wesley himself was quite ready, when the numbers of converted took a downward turn, to upbraid his followers for not making enough of the purity of the regenerate state.

Reviewing Hannah More's *Cœlebs*, Sydney Smith clinches why it was that Evangelicalism, despite its obsession with sin, should favour art forms that were not only didactic but dominated by figures of shining virtue. In taking Wesleyan preachers to task for averting their gaze from human weakness, he had already insisted that good clergymen realize that it is much easier 'to give credit to doctrines, than to live well', and so concern themselves most with 'those points where human nature is the most liable to prove defective'.[66] If human impurities were removed, on the other hand, by the sudden chemistry of conversion, nothing much remained to be done but to record the properties of true faith. So Hannah More's impeccable hero models the set of beliefs at which he has long arrived, in the knowledge that religious correctness is all. Incomplete only in his celibacy, Cœlebs searches for a wife who can complement (and compliment) his male virtues, but this involves him in the rejection of a small queue of women, female perfection being hard to come by. At last, however, the daughter of an exemplary family wins through, bringing the novel's extended trial-by-opinion to a close. In his review Smith notes More's timidity as a moralist (it is a 'bad rule never to quit the house for fear of catching cold'), and he relates her clear preference for 'temples to friendship and virtue' over flesh and blood, to her revivalist belief in the unassailable goodness of the reborn. It is an overweening moral self-confidence – with which we may compare James's 'delusive hope of strong assurance' – that leads More, in his view, to fix on 'very pure models'.[67] And in thus turning the novel into a 'dramatic sermon', she loses touch with the real world.

---

[66] Ibid., p. 357.   [67] *Edinburgh Review*, 14 (Apr. 1809), pp. 145–51.

Though Jane Austen is unlikely to have been in total agreement with her brother James on the subject of the Evangelicals, she would certainly have been fully aware of criticism of the sort that he voices. And to judge from her letters alone, her position was much closer to his than to either Francis or Henry's. Though Francis relies, as we have seen, on the enlightened language of rights and equality, his championship of Buchanan appears to have been thorough, and he was probably too much of an Evangelical to have shared Jane's suspicions about 'Conversion and Regeneration'. Henry, on the other hand, was a strict adherent of the sect, or so at least he became, for in the text of a series of lectures on Genesis that he gave in 1818, a year after his ordination, he stands in bold and diametric opposition to his brother James, asserting that the Bible needs no mediation, and insisting that religion – which should rest purely on revelation – has been distorted by 'the tradition of men'. Scripture unlike the prayerbook passes the 'test of inspiration'; even the details of its narrative – such as the creation of Eve from Adam's rib – are to be taken as literal fact, as is the direct intervention of the Devil. At a far cry from his enlightened *Loiterer* days, he now briskly dismisses the sciences, praises Cromwell, and pours scorn over the Restoration and the Stuarts.[68] No doubt the 'Biographical Notice' (1817), with its sketch of his sister's character, owes much of its beatifying and didactic tone to this conversion. Jane seems herself, in fact, to have been rather sceptical of the effects on young women of Evangelical instruction, predicting that her cousin Edward Cooper's daughters would turn out, in fifteen years' time, to be 'fine, jolly, handsome, ignorant girls'.[69] James's elegy on his sister, though as full of praise as Henry's, unfolds a more sharply focused portrait:

> A Temper, even, calm & sweet:
> Though quick & keen her mental eye
> Poor Nature's foibles to espy
> And seemed for ever on the watch,
> Some traits of ridicule to catch.[70]

Whether the image of a pious Austen would have persisted so long had her character been introduced to the public by James, remains an empty speculation; it had fallen to her London-based, and more extrovert brother to look after the business side of her publishing almost from the first.[71]

---

68 Henry Austen, *Lectures upon Some Important Passages in the Book of Genesis* (1820); see also *A Sermon in Aid of the Fund Raising for the Vaudois* (1826).

69 To Cassandra, 21–3 Jan. 1799, *Letters*, p. 37.   70 Le Faye, *A Family Record*, p. 232.

71 George Tucker, *A Goodly Heritage: A History of Jane Austen's Family* (Manchester, 1983), pp. 142–3.

As far as Austen's critical reception goes, the main casualty of her Evangelical image has been the misreading of *Mansfield Park*, and there is an irony here seeing that the novel really is about the revival and the change of cultural climate that followed in its wake. About it, but not of it, for far from being a didactic work, offering pictures of perfection, *Mansfield Park* is merciless in exposing the weaknesses of its hero and heroine. Yet to suggest that it supplies a critique of the revival from an Enlightenment perspective would be a simplification, for it reappraises certain aspects of the Enlightenment too. What can be said, is that the whole thrust of the novel's commentary is profoundly secular, that its concern with religion centres in conduct, and that human happiness is integral to its morality (93, 467, 471). Dispositions rather than doctrines are at its core, as are works rather than faith. At the period it was produced writers did not feel obliged to be Evangelical in order to comment on Evangelicalism. Some attacked the movement head-on like Eliza Hamilton who, in *The Cottagers of Glenburnie* (1808), mocks 'the self-conceit, and presumption [of] these professors of evangelical righteousness'; and it is surely an indication of Jane Austen's own feelings of scepticism that she was delighted to hear that *Sense and Sensibility* had been attributed to 'such a respectable' author.[72] Others were won round to a grudging admiration for the Clapham sect after the triumphant passing of the Abolition Bill. Even Sydney Smith, perhaps the most dangerous of the movement's critics, voted for Wilberforce in the parliamentary elections of 1807, and in a fulsome letter of praise tried to involve him in Irish politics as a friend of the oppressed. On Southey who once owned that his Christianity was essentially social, the revival made so lasting an impression that he devoted himself to a monumental *Life of Wesley*, followed by a full-scale edition of Cowper. No end of models exist for an engagement with the new age that was sympathetic without being uncritical. And perhaps there is no better corrective epigraph for *Mansfield Park* than the criticism Southey honourably recorded of his Methodist heroes: 'you know not your own hearts'.[73]

---

[72] To Cassandra, 6–7 Nov. 1813, *Letters*, p. 252.
[73] Robert Southey, *Life of Wesley*, 2 vols. (1820), I, 351.

CHAPTER 6

Mansfield Park: *charting the religious revival*

Jane Austen's appeal as a writer has often been said to lie in her creation of safe havens. In fact the atmosphere of stability and calm that prevails in the novels drafted at Steventon is invariably shown to be illusory, and this disclosure is all the more unsettling for arising, in each case, out of what is ordinary and accepted – from laws that dictate dispossession, from trusted stereotypes that disguise evil, or from benign first impressions that defer its recognition. In *Mansfield Park*, however, the illusion of natural harmony is continuously under assault, so that Fanny Price, window-gazing on a starlit summer's night, breaks off her rhapsody to invoke the wickedness and sorrow of the world (113). The novel opens, significantly, not with the Park itself but with Portsmouth, and the sketch of the 'large and still increasing' Price family – who have to make do on the 'very small income' of their disabled father in the Marines – sets the tone for a narrative in which struggle and hardship are dominant motifs. Even the seemingly unassailable prosperity of the Bertram family is shaken when losses on their West Indian estate prove severe enough to suggest that, as a relief from the expense of her support, the newly adopted Fanny be given over to the care of her aunt Mrs Norris (24), a fate reserved in the end for her cousin Maria. William, the Prices' eldest child, for whom shift has to be made at an early age, joins the navy, and as a midshipman, without the necessary strings for promotion, accustoms himself to social slights and to the endless prospect of 'bad weather and hard living' (249).

Malthus seems to have been the first writer to use the phrase 'struggle for existence' which became so seminal in the nineteenth century, and though Jane Austen does not use the phrase herself, the concept is very much alive in *Mansfield Park*.[1] That she had some knowledge of the *Essay on Population* is certain for it is cited and fully summarized by her much admired Pasley.[2]

---

[1] See Thomas Malthus, *Essay on Population* (1798), ed. James Bonar (facs. edn, 1926), pp. 47–9.
[2] See Charles Pasley, *Essay on the Military Policy and Institutions of the British Empire*, 2nd edn (1811), pp. 503–6.

She was aware too, if only in a general way, of the new field of city studies, first made statistical through the actuarial research of Richard Price, but going back to Hume and Smith, and to the philanthropist whom she called the 'famous Dr Percival of Manchester'.[3] Her brother James, who particularly praised the Portsmouth scenes of *Mansfield Park*, and wrote about urban poverty himself, seems also to have been familiar with such work.[4] Taking up a point made by Smith who argued in the *Wealth of Nations* that the needy often suffer from a lack of community in the metropolis where they find themselves 'sunk in obscurity and darkness', James dwells on the way the 'Alleys dark / And garrets high, shut out their inmates poor / From public notice', with the result that 'One half of the world, alas, but little know / The sufferings of the other. They who live / In cities least of all.'[5] Though the Prices are members of the middle class, making a respectable turn-out at church on Sundays, they are sufficiently stricken by circumstance (eleven mouths to be fed on a single reduced wage) to be so only in name; and if they remain gregarious they are at least lost to sight from the eminence of the Park for eleven years. Jane Austen seems to have been particularly alert to the unhealthiness of crowded conditions (which both Percival and Price supported with tables of mortality), and to the effects of urban pollution, for Fanny's 'delicate and puny' frame is soon to benefit on her arrival at the Park from 'change of air' (11). Infant death rates prompted Price, as Percival records, to describe large towns as 'the graves of mankind',[6] and his figures were touted in the *Essay*. Over the Price family Malthus seems to hover when we are told of its increasing size and dwindling resources or – in the narrator's crisp phrase – of its 'superfluity of children, and such a want of almost every thing else' (5). Many writers felt the impact of Malthus's appalling idea that food supply could not keep pace with the expansion of populations without either adopting his diagnosis (that constraint was independent of social ordering) or his remedy (to let the poor go to the wall). Jane Austen's feelings on the last point are clear from the account of how Mary Price bequeathed the silver knife to her elder sister Susan two hours before she died, a scene which with its grave epilogue, 'she was taken away from evil to come', looks forward to Dickens in everything but its remarkable compression (386–7).

Malthus exercised, it is clear, a strong influence on the rise of Evangelical thought, but it is likely that he was influenced by it in his turn. In the

[3] To Cassandra, 7–9 Oct. 1808, *Letters*, p. 145.   [4] *Minor Works*, p. 432.
[5] *WN*, v.i.g.12, 795; and see 'The Œconomy of Rural Life', HRO 60/3/2.
[6] Thomas Percival, *Observations on the State of Population in Manchester* (n.d.), p. 31.

later editions of the *Essay*, the original sociological theory is progressively moralized, in a way that lends itself to the theodicial arguments of revivalists.[7] In consequence the public heard less about how God had invited too many mortals to nature's feast, and more about the moral and psychological benefits of constraint and struggle. If the world had turned out to be far crueller than Paley had bargained for, it was meant to be so, for it was a place of trial. Struggle produced character; without exertion there was no mind; necessity was preordained to sharpen human faculties: such were the lessons to be learnt from a harsh universe taken to be informed by God's design.

A belief in Providence might have inclined Jane Austen to fall in with the view that hardship and disorder were all part of a 'moral ordination'. The view is certainly on offer in *Mansfield Park*, most conspicuously in Sir Thomas's solemn retrospect on the action from which he reads 'the advantages of early hardship and discipline, and the consciousness of being born to struggle and endure' (473). But the novel stops far short of endorsing it. Sir Thomas's maxim is not only prefixed by a firm reminder of his subjectivity ('Sir Thomas saw . . .'), but wrapped up also in flagrant self-praise – the patriarch finds 'repeated, and for ever repeated reason to rejoice in what he had done for them all'. By any standards this is complacent, for Sir Thomas can hardly congratulate himself on being responsible for the most painful of Fanny's many ordeals.

Born to struggle and endure Fanny undoubtedly is, and she seems herself to adopt the view that hardship is destinal when she finds words to comfort her brother William in a moment of despondency (249). She is conscious too of the need to fight against the misery that repeatedly overwhelms her ('the great black word *miserable*' becomes her byword) partly because she is afraid of appearing ungrateful, chiefly because there is little to admire, as Edmund has it, in 'the mind which does not struggle against itself' (13, 320, 88). The struggle for existence which the Portsmouth scenes register as an elemental fact is echoed throughout the novel, on the moral plane, by internal conflicts from which perhaps only Lady Bertram is exempt. And in the description of these, the word 'struggle' loses none of its physical force, for we hear of a 'struggle in Edmund's cheerfulness', of how Fanny 'struggled for speech', even of 'her struggling sobs'.[8] Although this falls in well with the Evangelical stress on suffering as an instrument of redemption, and

---

[7] See Boyd Hilton, *Atonement*, ch. 3: 'Poverty and Passionate Flesh'.

[8] See pp. 273, 268, 374. The word 'struggle' occurs at least twelve times in *Mansfield Park*, in *Northanger Abbey* only twice.

contributes to the reader's sense of Fanny as a revivalist heroine, it really belongs to a wider period preoccupation with the darker face of human experience. Austen has something in common here with Keats, who rejected the providentially ordained 'vale of tears', while holding out for the 'vale of soul-making' – that world of pains and troubles which could 'school an Intelligence and make it a soul'.[9]

Fanny's anxieties and perturbations are the medium of her growth, and it is not surprising, in view of this urgency, that Austen should have developed new means for their realization. The ebb and flow of Fanny's thought and feelings are made vivid by a narrator who surrenders neither affection nor detachment. And in a way comparable to free indirect speech with its blend of interiority and third person, the cold East room – to which Fanny withdraws after a particularly fraught session of casting for *Lovers' Vows* – is seen at once from outside and through her eyes. Its clutter is selectively lit up as it touches, object by object, her consciousness, picking out an intricate web of obligations and social ties. So the reader responds to the slight absurdity of the sketch of William's ship with 'HMS Antwerp' at the bottom in letters as tall as the main-mast, while absorbing Fanny's sisterly pride, and catches the condescension inscribed in Tom's repeated gift of workboxes that involuntarily trigger instincts of dependence. Through this alternating focus Austen is able both to encourage a respect for Fanny's growing ability to organize her feelings and moral perceptions, and at the same time to underline what she excludes. That Fanny prefers, as Dr Johnson alleged of Clarissa, almost anything to the exact truth, holds true mainly of one area of her vision, but that is enough to warp many of her judgements.

Despite her centrality to the plot and her hold on our sympathies, Fanny has a decidedly smaller share in the spirit of the novel, overall, than is the case with Austen's other heroines. Her unrelieved solemnity (redoubled in her duos with Edmund who has, as he owns, no wit in his nature) stands out not only against the empty frivolity of her female cousins, and Mary Crawford's 'talents for the light and lively' (81), but against the variegated grain of the narrative itself. Owing to the sheer vitality of Austen's invention which is at its very highest point throughout the first volume of *Mansfield Park*, Mary Crawford's rapturous retrospect on the theatricals is more likely to strike a chord with the reader than Fanny's 'it was all misery *now*' (358, 157). Indeed, Austen probably hit on the theatricals as a particularly telling way of dramatizing the Evangelical sympathies of Edmund and

---

[9] *The Letters of John Keats*, ed. H. E. Rollins, 2 vols. (1958), II, 101–2.

Fanny, and her selection of *Lovers' Vows* (a play which may well have been acted by her brother Henry and his circle)[10] was certainly designed to draw out the contemporary reaction against the stage in full. Fanny seems to have been intended not simply as a revivalist but as a born one, and her recoil from acting is only one aspect of what appears to be her natural disposition for 'the serious'. No sooner has she arrived at the Park than we hear that she has no desire to learn either music or drawing, and that she takes no interest in the duets played by her cousins (19, 14). Her disinclination is modified later – we are told that she would (if invisible) like to listen to Mary on the harp, and that she respects good acting – but only once the main lines of her character have been drawn, and then perhaps chiefly to guard against giving over-zealous readers a sanction for philistinism.

For her creation of Fanny, Austen probably drew on Gisborne, and perhaps too on Clarkson, for we know that she had been reading both. In his *Enquiry into the Duties of the Female Sex* Gisborne stops short of a total condemnation of the theatre, warning against amateur acting on the grounds that it breeds immodesty,[11] but elsewhere he elegized (and eulogized) Cowper, and wrote on scenery in the picturesque tradition – a combination of interests which coincides with Fanny's, and which seems to have been fairly typical of the revivalist movement as a whole, establishing itself across differences in denomination. If Thomas Clarkson's *Portraiture of Quakerism* (1807) reveals a similar profile, and one that bears an uncanny resemblance to Fanny's, that goes to show just how representative a character she is. Though the taboos against theatre, music, and dancing are all very much softened in Fanny's case (and are carefully mediated, too, by Clarkson's commentary), the praise of stillness and quietness, the stress on subjugating the passions, and the suspicion of self-gratification are all of a piece with her temperament. So also is the attitude of reverence attaching to all living creatures and especially to the unspoilt countryside.[12] Fanny who stands at the window rhapsodizing over the beauty of the starlit night rather than joining the glee, who worries that her mare may be stressed by too much riding, who quotes Cowper in defence of the old avenue at Sotherton, apostrophizes the evergreen, and marvels at the beauty of the changing seasons at the Park, is foreshadowed at almost every point by the

---

[10] See Deirdre Le Faye's interpretation of a recurring reference to a Frederick in Austen's letters from *Letters*, pp. 256, 258, 262, and the note, p. 429.

[11] Bradbrook, *Predecessors*, p. 36.

[12] See Thomas Clarkson's *A Portraiture of Quakerism*, 3 vols. (1807), I, chs. 3, 4, 5, and pp. 33, 116; II, pp. 49–52.

Quaker portrait,[13] and Clarkson had particular programmatic reasons for underlining the tender-mindedness of the sect.

Portraiture was the run-up to Clarkson's monumental history of the abolition. He wrote it partly as a tribute, always keeping in sight both the Quakers' unblemished record on slavery, and their courage in conducting the campaign, and so composed his portrait round a single theme – the life devoted to emancipation. The work was timed to appear just after the Abolition Bill became law, and Clarkson wrote in the awareness that the sudden and popular overthrow of what had for so long been accepted as ineradicable meant that customary practices of all kinds were brought under review and exposed to a raking light. His study amounted to something more than an account of Quaker beliefs and manners: it had the air of a blueprint. His portraiture was really of a new society, and at its centre was the modern woman.

THE VIRTUE OF INDEPENDENCE

Readers today need to recognize that *Mansfield Park* is consciously set in the post-abolition period, in a world that had the aura of a dawning epoch, but which held for many the urgent sense that emancipation still pended. Slavery continued to flourish in British dominions, and would do so until the Act of 1833, but the illegitimizing of the trade (reinforced by further punitive legislation in 1811) struck at its base, and had the effect of calling other oppressive institutions into question. Emancipation is the theme closest to the heart of *Mansfield Park*, and as might be expected from a title that enshrines the name of the judge who pronounced that there could be no slave on British soil, the novel examines domestic forms of subjection against the distant backdrop of the international trade. In *Emma* Austen was to hint at a parallel between the lot of the unmonied single woman and the sale of human flesh, Jane Fairfax remarking wryly that although there was a wide difference in the guilt of those who brokered jobs for governesses and those who ran the slave trade, misery in either case was the unfailing result (300–1).[14] In *Mansfield Park* a similar sense of equivalence, ranging

---

[13] Quakers, Clarkson reminds his readers, have shown that even the barrier between man and the animals is an artificial one, for man 'can anticipate and know their feelings by his own'; see *Portraiture*, I, 151.

[14] A similar analogy is drawn by Wollstonecraft, without the pointing of irony, in *The Wrongs of Woman* where it is said of Mrs Venables that 'no slave in the West Indies had [a master] more despotic', see *'Mary' and 'The Wrongs of Woman'*, p. 171.

over differences in both degree and legitimacy, is brought into play by the pointed use of Sir Thomas's Antiguan estate as a counter in the opening narrative of Fanny's fortunes. It is the estate which prompts Mrs Price to overcome her pride and break the long silence to ask her sister whether her son William might be found employment on it, and the outcome of the evidently negative answer is that Fanny is selected for adoption at the Park. Fanny's prospects are again linked with the estate, when its losses, five years on, threaten her with the care of her aunt Norris, chief architect of her subservient role, who shares her name – as has frequently been pointed out – with one of the most treacherous slave-dealers excoriated by Clarkson.[15] Finally, it falls to Fanny to question Sir Thomas about the slave trade on his return from Antigua, and though we learn from Edmund that his father is eager to be forthcoming, Fanny herself is silenced by the unresponsiveness of the rest of the family (198). The reader is left in no doubt, however, about her views on the subject; they are implied not only by the tender-mindedness which is central to her outlook, but by her absorption in Cowper (famously dubbed the poet laureate of abolition by Clarkson) through whose spectacles she looks not only at the threatened trees at Sotherton but at the cruel family separation integral to boarding schools (56, 431).

Although entire essays have been written on the politics of *Mansfield Park* without any mention being made of the Abolition Bill, and much debate expended on the exact chronology of the novel's action, Austen puts her readers in command of the post-abolitionist setting of *Mansfield Park* from the start. 'About thirty years ago', the book opens, establishing a firm present tense at publication time, and with the next paragraph the first reference to the West Indian estate is automatically clipped into a historic frame. The post-abolitionist perspective is there no matter whether Sir Thomas's visit to Antigua post- or pre-dates the passage of the law, and his outgoing voyage has variously been placed at 1810, 1807, and 1805.[16] In fact, Jane Austen carefully laid out a scheme, making only one departure from it. Everything in the opening chapters is precisely consistent with Sir Thomas's visit to Antigua taking place between the autumns of 1807 and 1809. And since 'thirty years ago' puts the marriage of the Bertrams in 1784, and another 'half dozen' years go by before Fanny's parents marry and start their large family

---

[15] Frank Gibbon seems to have been the first critic to make a point of the names Mansfield and Norris; see his ground-breaking article 'The Antiguan Connection: Some New Light on *Mansfield Park*', *Cambridge Quarterly*, 12 (1982), 298–305, 303.

[16] See, respectively, Brian Southam's 'The Silence of the Bertrams', *TLS* (17 Feb. 1995), 13–14; Chapman's 'Chronology of *Mansfield Park*', *Works*, III, 554–7; and Warren Roberts, *French Revolution*, p. 97.

(1790), and another twelve years pass before Fanny, just turned ten, moves to the Park (1802), and another five before Sir Thomas is called away, placing him in Antigua over the critical period of transition, it looks very much as if Austen arranged her narrative round the date of abolition – the bill became law early in the summer of 1807.[17] But she seems also to have gone out of her way to underline the contemporaneity of the novel's world, as if to insist on the presence of the modern. At Sotherton the party amuse themselves with 'chit-chat and Quarterly Reviews', which seeing that the *Quarterly* was founded in February 1809, while the visit belongs to mid-August of the same year, is right up-to-date. Appropriately, during the theatricals a few months later, Fanny retires to the East room to get on with her reading of Macartney's 'great book' on China, which had appeared in splendid quarto in 1807, but on her table there is also a copy of 'Crabbe's Tales' (156), though the work of that title had only appeared in 1812 as Jane Austen well knew. This seems, however, to be the only anachronism in the novel, and perhaps in this instance Austen thought she could have her cake and eat it too, for Crabbe's work had been shorthanded as 'tales' ever since *The Parish Register* (1807), and the reference to Fanny's book is made in direct speech by Edmund.

Some other pointers to the newness of the novel's setting have been missed by commentators. After seven years of absence in the *Antwerp*, William is amazed to find his sister decked out in the trim hairdo that had spread from France at the turn of the century ('when I first heard of such things being done in England I could not believe it'), but he is soon completely won round (235). Charles Austen had opted to wear his hair unpowdered and cropped in January 1799, though news of this was kept from Edward, the proud inheritor of Godmersham, who happened to be unwell at the time, on the grounds that it might 'fall on his spirits and retard his recovery'. Jane Austen reported great things of this transformation, and clearly approved of it herself, remarking to Cassandra that Charles 'appears to far more advantage [now] than he did at Godmersham, not surrounded by strangers and neither oppressed by a pain in his face or powder in his

[17] For the lapse of five years, see p. 25. Further corroboration for the consistency of the scheme outlined here is supplied by Tom's being seventeen at the time of Fanny's arrival at the Park (a good fit for the Bertrams' marriage in 1784), and by Fanny turning seventeen in July of the second year of Sir Thomas's absence which is what she would be in 1809 (p. 40). From the date of the Ball (Thursday 22 December) it is clear that Jane Austen was using an almanac for 1808 (unless as has been argued for 1814, which might not easily have been available at the time she was planning the novel). To have been in accord with her scheme she should have used one for the following year, though it is highly questionable whether she would have thought this discrepancy mattered.

hair'.[18] Needless to say, the in-look was also a key to outlook. Though Jane Austen may have disliked *Lovers' Vows* (in company with Coleridge and others), she was certainly at odds with the reviewer in the *Anti-Jacobin* (October 1798) who, taking particular exception to a Count Cassel with a 'Jacobin cropped head without *powder*', spat out: 'It is disgusting enough to see so many of these heads among the audience, but the actor who displays such a head, especially when in violation of all the rules of propriety and decorum, deserves to be hissed from the stage.'[19]

William Price undoubtedly owes much to the naval brothers, but Austen's adaptations of biography invariably reveal strokes of invention that underline her themes. While the *Thrush* which William joins as Lieutenant at Portsmouth echoes the *Lark* in which Francis had served in the same rank, it was a real boat, not the fiction that has been supposed: a small sloop of that name had been newly refitted in 1808 when it may well have been seen by the Austen sisters at Spithead, much in the way that it was watched for by William's friends at Portsmouth.[20] The 'freshness' of William's uniform – which matches the 'freshness of its wearer's feelings' – chimes in well with the revamped vessel which, in the novel, sails out to much excitement at dawn, 'the finest sloop in the service' (368). Again, while it has often been noticed that William's gift to Fanny of an amber cross looks back at the topaz ones that Charles Austen bought for his sisters with prize money in 1801, the fictional gift is said to have been brought from Sicily (254),[21] famous as the launching place for a spectacular defeat inflicted on Napoleon's infantry in 1806 – 'such a thing', wrote a French officer, 'has not been seen since the Revolution!'.[22] The promise of this military success was certainly not lost on Jane Austen who also knew from Pasley that Sicily had been considered as a bridgehead for an invasion of Italy, and hence for conquest of the entire Empire, which she too probably saw as 'an uniform system of slavery and oppression'.[23] Her brother Francis certainly shared Pasley's view; writing from Boulogne, he scoffs at the way Napoleon had exalted himself 'to the Imperial dignity by the unanimous suffrages of

---

[18] 21–3 Jan. 1799, *Letters*, pp. 38, 37. For further discussion of the 'crop' hairstyle see my article 'What Jane Austen Meant by "Raffish"', pp. 105–8.

[19] *The Anti-Jacobin Review and Magazine*, 1 (Oct. 1798), pp. 479–80.

[20] The *Thrush* was docked and masted at Spithead from May to mid-July 1808; Cassandra visited the Isle of Wight from Southampton some time in June, and Jane was back in Southampton on 8 July. See *Log of Thrush*, National Maritime Museum, Greenwich, ADM//L/T/270.

[21] There is no record of where Charles bought the topaz crosses while voyaging in the Mediterranean on the *Endymion*, but the change of gem suggests that there may also have been a change of origin.

[22] See the account of the victory of Maida in Arthur Bryant, *Years of Victory 1802–1812* (1945), pp. 226–8.

[23] Pasley, *Military Policy*, pp. 347–60, 479.

himself and his creatures'.[24] The betrayal of the cause of abolition by the French (dwelt on at length by Clarkson) – let alone the cynical reimplementation of old slave laws by Napoleon in 1802 – set the empire at the opposite pole from Francis's ideal of a dominion that would 'pay equal attention to the unalienable rights of all the nations, of what colour so ever they may be'.[25]

A global scene

Sir Thomas Bertram's long visit to his West Indian estate in the period immediately following the abolition of the slave trade was sufficiently typical to carry a recognizable stamp. The journals of those years carry many reviews and reports about the islands, and of the steps being taken to address the sudden stop to the import of slaves, as well as to deal with the recent sugar glut which was partly the result of war measures, including further annexation of land. Even the most hardbitten of plantation managers had to knuckle down to the task of improving conditions in order to ensure a rise in the birth rate of those who laboured for them, and a widely used remedy was to replace inferior cane plantations (and low-yield practices such as coppicing) with fruit and vegetables for home consumption. It can safely be inferred that Sir Thomas, on his return, owes his 'burnt, fagged worn look of fatigue' not to lust (an attractive option for film-makers) but to humdrum activities of this kind, and his ameliorative impulses appear to be genuine – unusually so, since MPs with a West Indian interest happy to hear favourable things of abolition were indeed few. In choosing the name Bertram, Austen may have had at the back of her mind the parliamentarian Barham (praised by Clarkson), an unsaintly but vocal supporter of the Act who illustrated his tracts and speeches with reference to his Jamaican estates over the crisis.[26] But with the Act once passed there is a surprising conformity of opinion over the direction that the West Indies should take, and discussion on all sides is dominated by the shade of Adam Smith, whose view that slavery was as inefficient as it was iniquitous had been a boon to abolitionists all along.

In a particularly influential chapter from *The Wealth of Nations* Smith compared European colonies of his day to those of Rome, arguing that the

---

[24] See J. H. and E. C. Hubback, *Sailor Brothers*, p. 122.

[25] See above p. 164; Clarkson, *History of the Abolition*, pp. 141, 166; and Hugh Thomas, *Slave Trade*, pp. 546–7.

[26] See Seymour Drescher, *Econocide: British Slavery in the Era of Abolition* (Pittsburgh, 1977), p. 139 and his note 38; and Clarkson, *History of the Abolition*, p. 522.

ancient Greek version of colonization provided a model far more consistent with modern economic theory. Whereas the typical Roman colony began as conquered territory manned by a garrison and remained in a state of total subjugation, the Doric equivalent was considered by the mother city 'as an emancipated child, over whom she pretended to claim no direct authority or jurisdiction'.[27] The liberation rhetoric in which he clothes this distinction is strategic, for it leads straight to his central contention that slavery and mercantilism belong to the same mind-set and need to be jettisoned together. To underscore the point further, Smith describes the many protectionist devices imposed by Europe on trade with its American colonies as 'a manifest violation of the most sacred rights of mankind' and refers to them as the 'badges of slavery'.[28] It was no accident that Lord Mansfield, after pronouncing the slave James Somerset free in 1772, went on two years later to make another epoch-making judgement in the case of Campbell *versus* Hall which defended the right of the Grenada Assembly to refuse to pay export duty to Britain, and so struck at the root of the mercantilist system.[29]

In a pamphlet of 1810 Joseph Barham took up Smith's argument, insisting that if the West Indies were to be saved from economic ruin there should be instant deregulation, for restrictions on local manufacture, on shipping, and on the import of raw materials belonged to the bad old days of the triangular route. His objection to the 'subservient' role of the colonies is later fleshed out in a piece that dwells on Westminster's overruling of the attempt by South Carolina to prohibit the further importation of slaves in 1760, and on the similar fate met by Jamaican attempts at limitation in 1765.[30] Not all slave-owners made as liberal an impression as Barham; the case of Gilbert Mathison who wrote up his visit to Jamaica in 1808 after an absence of fifteen years is more representative, but even Mathison pays lip-service to the new order, while never losing an opportunity – as a *Quarterly* reviewer noted – of dredging up the criticisms that were originally levelled against it.[31] It is interesting to see, all the same, that the *Quarterly* adopts the Smithian position wholesale, arguing that the West Indies can no longer be 'thwarted and shackled' by mercantilist measures; a similar line was pursued by the *Edinburgh Review* in a series of pieces by Henry

[27] *WN*, IV.vii.a.1, 556.   [28] *WN*, IV.vii.b.39–44, 580–2, see also IV.vii.c.66, 616–17.

[29] See Vincent Harlow, 'The New Imperial System, 1783–1815', *Cambridge History of the British Empire*, II (Cambridge, 1940), pp. 153–4.

[30] Joseph Barham, *Considerations on the Abolition of Negro Slavery* (1823), pp. 28–9.

[31] Gilbert Mathison, *Notices Respecting Jamaica* (1811); reviewed in *Quarterly Review* (Oct. 1811), p. 149.

Brougham.[32] Pasley, again, takes his cue from the *Wealth of Nations* when he identifies Napoleon's regime with Roman colonization, and compares French rule to that of the Carthaginians who

instead of endeavouring to civilise, and grant such privileges to their new subjects, as would give them a national feeling and an interest in the state, treated them always as a conquered people; thinking them, perhaps, too brutish and stupid to be worthy of being put on a footing with themselves; without considering, that the character of nations is stamped by the way in which they are treated.[33]

This is the thinking that underlies Pasley's argument for the secession of the West Indian colonies, and backs his warning that French conquest would lead to 'a second race of imperial monsters and idiots', ending in a 'renewal of the history of the dark ages'.[34]

Although emancipation was a concept so fully aired in the years immediately following abolition that even slave-owners talked about their own liberation, it turned out to mean very different things to different people. Over the issue of colonialism, particularly, a deep division set in between those who believed in the virtues of autonomous development and those who were all for an interventionist regime. The second camp, soon to prove itself victorious in India with the inauguration of an official religious presence in 1813, was headed by the Evangelicals, for whom emancipation meant in the end only one thing, conversion to their creed. It was clearly in the Evangelical interest to insist on the otherness and inferiority of those over whom they assumed jurisdiction, for how were they otherwise justified to evangelize?

Jane Austen was fully aware of this division. She had read (as already noted) Claudius Buchanan, a chief apostle of the new colonialism, who not only demonized the Hindu religion in his tract *Christian Researches in Asia* (1811) but sneered at the 'orientalists' who had fostered respect for native arts and culture – including Warren Hastings, whom she and her family venerated.[35] In *Mansfield Park* we hear of British colonies in both the Indies – either might provide the solution to Mrs Price's Malthusian problem of catering to an overcrowded house ('or how could a boy be sent

---

[32] As early as 1807, Brougham traces the 'state of extraordinary calamity' in the islands not only to the conditions of war but to slavery and to the strengthening of monopolies; see *Edinburgh Review*, II (1807), 145–67. See also 13 (Jan. 1809), 382–413; and 14 (Apr. 1809), 95–106.
[33] *Military Policy*, p. 478.   [34] Ibid., pp. 448, 467, 477–9.
[35] From a letter written by Henry to Warren Hastings on 5 June 1802, it appears that certain of Hastings's manuscripts were in the possession of George Austen who 'continually offer'd [them] as objects of imitation' to his children at Steventon. See Add. MS 29,178, f. 213.

out to the East?', 5), and we hear of trade with the Orient (Lady Bertram commissions two scarves from William), and of missionary activity from a sarcastic Mary Crawford. But it is ultimately through a literary reference that Jane Austen manages to insert a signpost to her position in the colonial debate. The fact that Fanny is reading Macartney's journal of the embassy to China rather than one of Buchanan's works (which started to come out at the same time) is itself significant, for though Macartney was no friend to Hastings, he was strongly committed to the Enlightenment ideal of reciprocal exchange in international relations, and fascinated too by the exotic. His gaze penetrated beyond the rituals of mandarin life, and early on his trip he was moved to exclaim 'brave new world' by the sight of happy sailors and a vigorous peasantry, questioning whether 'all the authority and all the address of the Tartar Government will be able much longer to stifle the energies of their Chinese subjects'.[36] His notorious refusal to kowtow was a challenge to the would-be global suzerainty of the Manchu regime which tolerated trade only under the guise of tribute, and assumed that all foreign nations were vassals. The lack of interest displayed in the embassy's commercial overtures, or in the scientific instruments that were brought as gifts bore, in his view, the mark of a feudal arrogance that was all too familiar at home.

On the home front

A geopolitical scaffolding surrounds the central construction of *Mansfield Park*. And in a way comparable with her working of the West Indian setting, Austen puts the Macartney allusion to a dramatic use that draws out a parallel between the personal and political. The book is introduced at the crisis that provides the climax to the first volume, for at the very instant that Edmund tells Fanny of his sudden about-face, of his decision to take part in the theatricals after all, we see him attempting to cover his shame by opening up the volume on her table, and remarking in a bumbling way: 'when we meet at breakfast we shall be all in high good humour at the prospect of acting the fool together with such unanimity. *You* in the meanwhile will be taking a trip into China, I suppose. How does Lord Macartney go on?' (156). Macartney's journal had given a vivid account of the pressures put on him and his party to kowtow, and after its publication his name became synonymous with intransigence. Austen was aware of this:

---

[36] 'A Journal of an Embassy', in *Some Account of the Public Life, and a Selection from the Unpublished Writings of the Earl of Macartney*, ed. John Barrow, 2 vols. (1807), II, 365.

both Macartney and Barrow (who wrote his own account of the embassy) are mentioned in her letters, and her brother Francis had conspicuously followed in the Earl's footsteps when, on a diplomatic mission in China in 1810, he spiritedly refused to buckle to cavalier treatment from the Viceroy of Canton, defending his action to the Admiralty in terms that echo the Journal's.[37]

Fanny Price finds herself less advantageously placed, however. For her there is to be 'no reading, no China, no composure', and before long she is dragooned into taking a minor role in *Lovers' Vows*. She owes her discomposure partly to her shock over Edmund's capitulation (to which her jealousy of Mary is tied), but also to the knowledge that without his protection she is at the mercy of the rest of the group. With brilliant compression, Austen uses this backstage business to expose both the forces that hold Fanny in a servile position and the qualities that enable her to kindle a spirit of independence. Twice in the course of the apology given for his decision, Edmund begs for his cousin's 'approbation', and deprived of Edmund's backing, Fanny is equally disturbed. Thus Austen points not only to the *social* foundations of her serious couple's moral sense, but to that classical interaction of approbation and sympathy that she had explored in its original Smithian context in *Sense and Sensibility*. Such accounting is at a far remove from the orthodox Evangelical idea of conscience as a sort of inner mechanism, impervious as a Harrison chronometer to all weathers. Without impugning the integrity of Fanny's judgement, Austen shows that it rides unsteadily on a sea of 'discontent and envy' or of 'jealousy and agitation' (74, 159). Tellingly Fanny is ready to give at least the appearance of approval to Edmund until he asks her to sympathize with the plight of Mary, at which point – and not before – she is immediately stopped short by her 'conscience' (156). But even when Edmund and Fanny's judgements are at fault, the very fact that they judge (typically grading behaviour as 'very wrong', 'improper', or 'not quite right') gives them a valuable purchase over their world, freeing them from conformity to it. Even so Austen is concerned to show how fragile their bond is, and how easily moral enterprise can collapse in the face of group-forged attitudes. The moment at which Fanny is first pressed into reading the part of the Cottager's Wife, a role given to the Governess at Ravenshaw, and variously described at the Park as an 'insult', 'a nothing of a part, a mere nothing', reveals the almost conscious assumption by the Bertram family that their cousin is a servant at heart:

[37] See my article 'Fanny Price Refuses to Kowtow', *Review of English Studies*, 47 (1996), 212–17.

'Fanny,' cried Tom Bertram, from the other table, where the conference was eagerly carrying on, and the conversation incessant, 'we want your services.'

Fanny was up in a moment, expecting some errand, for the habit of employing her in that way was not yet overcome, in spite of all that Edmund could do.

'Oh! we do not want to disturb you from your seat. We do not want your *present* services. We shall only want you in our play. You must be Cottager's wife.'

'Me!' cried Fanny, sitting down again with a most frightened look. (145)

The focus on Fanny's movements here, on her reflex jumping up and obedient return to her chair, shows just how deep the sense of herself as an object of use goes, and the impression is confirmed when she seeks to excuse herself on the sole grounds that she 'can't act' – as if nothing short of physical incapacity would do. In previous scenes we have seen her reduced to a useful body round the house when Lady Bertram has need of a pair of hands, or when Tom Bertram escapes from a rubber with Mrs Norris by seizing on her as a dancing partner without neglecting to tell her why (119–20). It is telling that the greatest cruelties to Fanny are initiated by Tom Bertram, always abetted by his chivvying aunt, shortly after his return from the Antiguan plantation.

In his tract on abolition, the liberally minded Jamaican estate-owner Joseph Barham posed the question: 'If to change the character of a people by law be in any case the most difficult problem in political science, what must it be in that strange anomaly of human society, which the Colonies now present to our view?' His answer was that 'customs, manners, and opinions' were all embroiled in the old status quo, and that real change required 'deep prejudices to be rooted out'.[38] In *Mansfield Park* Jane Austen uses the brightly ameliorist *Lovers' Vows* to set off her own darker drama of an emancipation streaked with recidivism. Sir Thomas returns from the his two-year spell in the West Indies a less forbidding man, ready to admit fault, eager to talk of his experiences abroad, but when Fanny asks about the slave trade she is stonewalled by the rest of the family, and despite her longing to learn more dries up herself. A similar predicament is the subject of the first tale in the volume by Crabbe that keeps company with Macartney on Fanny's table. In 'The Dumb Orators' an eloquent Justice is struck dumb when he finds himself at an assembly of Jacobins, and later has his revenge when one of their number is rendered mute at a dinner of parsons; from the poem the reviewer in the *Edinburgh* extracted the moral 'that a man's fluency and force and intrepidity of speech depends very much upon his confidence and the approbation of his auditors'.[39]

---

[38] *Considerations on the Abolition* (1823), p. 10.   [39] *Edinburgh Review*, 20 (Nov. 1812), p. 281.

Fanny's defeat is again at the hand of an unsympathetic group that over-comes the benign influence of Edmund and his father, but it is from Sir Thomas himself that the most daunting challenge to her sense of self-respect is to come.

Although Henry Crawford's determination to woo Fanny begins in – and never quite transcends – his Lovelace-like plan to subdue a seemingly impenetrable heart, it wins the support of the entire Bertram family, who read Fanny's principled rejection of his proposal and her exercise of the most elementary of rights, as a breach of convention. Sir Thomas leads the way in this, and finding himself crossed, turns into a monster of imperiousness (recalling at times Macartney's Qianlong)[40] who coaxes and cajoles his niece by turns, and sends her back to Portsmouth to mend her views when warming fires and fiery words have failed. His case against Fanny is that she represents a desire for independence which 'in young women is offensive, and disgusting beyond all common offence' (318). But with the help of her strong (if never fully self-admitted) passion for Edmund, Fanny succeeds in staving off the advances of Henry and standing up for herself, so demonstrating her full claim to the vice that the relapsed Sir Thomas finds symptomatic of the modern age.

Though Fanny's piety plays an important part in the growth of her confidence and moral stature, Jane Austen's analysis of her growth owes nothing to Evangelical belief. Indeed, the emancipatory tenets for which the revival was famous are applied throughout *Mansfield Park* in a way that is often contrary to its spirit. They are applied, in the first place, to the domestic sphere where paternal authority was seldom challenged,[41] and beyond that to the whole class system which the 'serious' mostly under-stood to be preordained. There is no novel written before *Mansfield Park* (and few after it) which can begin to match its account of the power of nurture – a concept central to the Anglo-Scottish school but virtually ignored by the Clapham sect who tied identity to rebirth and divine elec-tion. It is an account honed by a thoroughgoing scepticism that makes continual allowance for 'disposition' and 'nature', and that never invites us to conceive of a world without hierarchy. No doubt Jane Austen held no brief for a classless society – the point has been asserted *ad nauseam* – but

---

[40] Like the Emperor whom Barrow describes as engaged in the 'experiment' of starving – or fêting – the legation into compliance (accommodation, food, and heating were all made conditional on their behaviour), Sir Thomas curbs his 'experiment' of 'starv[ing Fanny], both mind and body' into submission for fear 'she might die under the cure'. See *Mansfield Park*, pp. 315–16, 369, 413; and see *Some Account*, ed. Barrow, II, 209, 213, 221, 294, 297, 302.

[41] See Bradbrook, *Predecessors*, pp. 90–1.

she clearly regarded it as her province to show just how social class affects individual behaviour.

While the global reference of *Mansfield Park* draws out the novel's concern with independence and emancipation, the contrast between its two English settings is repeatedly used to highlight the hugely formative role of the socioeconomic forces summed up in the word 'circumstance'. By pointing up the close resemblance in temperament and appearance between Lady Bertram and her sister Frances who makes the bad marriage, Austen lays on a sort of demonstration of the power of class (377, 390, 408). From the first we hear not only about the hardships and ill-health of the Price household but of the resentment they feel towards the 'pride' of Sir Thomas, and of the breach between the two families that results. On Fanny's move back to Portsmouth, much is made of the crowded conditions under which the family live, of the uncleanliness and clutter which require a personality more disciplined than Frances's to remedy, and, above all, of the absence of codes that make for considerateness or disguise its deficit. Austen avoids a deterministic frame of reference, freely allotting blame, but she leaves no doubt that William and Fanny can only have benefited (as Susan will) from the mediation of some institution external to the family. But the overriding sense that the episode leaves is one of sheer wonder at the arbitrariness of social fortune, an insight borne in on Fanny when she reflects with pain on how alike her mother and Lady Bertram really are: 'to think of the contrast between them – to think that where nature had made so little difference, circumstances should have made so much' (408). The occasion for this is the spruce family turn-out for morning service at the Garrison Chapel, where the narrator's language is tinged for a moment by fairy-tale, if we remember the heroine of Charles Perrault's 'Peau d'Ane' who has the same beauty whether she is clothed in her dirty weekday skin or in her Sunday best: 'Nature had given them no inconsiderable share of beauty, and every Sunday dressed them in their cleanest skins and best attire.'[42] Later, in another sequence that touches on parable, Fanny resolves the long and bitter quarrel between Betsey and Susan over possession of the silver knife left to Susan by their dead sister, when she buys a second one. Though the two knives are quite different – Fanny's is bought from pocket money and has only newness in its favour – that proves not to be serious, for it is the equality of status that matters.

---

[42] On Sundays the Princess removes her filthy donkey-skin and washes herself; see Charles Perrault, 'Peau d'Ane' in *Contes* (Paris, 1967), p. 66.

The Park itself, however, is the novel's main forum for exhibiting the force of class, for Sir Thomas, as a matter of policy, accords a lesser rank to his newly adopted niece than to his daughters, and to this decision can be traced a distinct reticence in Fanny (*naturally* timid in any case) that makes for low self-esteem and a mood of dejection. Sir Thomas is wrong to suppose that his declaration that 'they cannot be equals' can be free of the effect of 'depressing her spirits too far' (11). Fanny soon feels that she 'can never be important to any one' for reasons that seem to her to be self-evident: 'Every thing – my situation – my foolishness and awkwardness' (26); and her assumption of inferiority runs so deep that she is blind to its causes. She normalizes her position, taking for granted even the grossest condescension towards her, thinking 'too lowly of her own claims to feel injured by it' (20). Austen exposes the constitutive power of social attitudes in two main ways. On the one hand, Fanny's Portsmouth background becomes the occasion for a parade of class prejudice, so that before her arrival the Bertrams anticipate 'gross ignorance', 'meanness of opinions', 'vulgarity of manners', even the possibility of a disposition 'really bad', and are on their guard against contagion. After her arrival, Fanny's puny stature, delicate health, and lack of general knowledge provide the family with the gratifying hard evidence for Bertram superiority, or for what the narrator wryly calls later, in the case of Maria, 'so very hurtful a degree of self-consequence' (466). On the other hand, we are shown how the effects of class difference are used to induce a sense of deficiency. Regardless of her claims, the adopted Fanny is continually thrust back into the mould of the poor relation by the entire family with the exception of Edmund. If the Bertram sisters hold her cheap for her lack of sashes, or eagerly exclaim over her unfamiliarity with the Roman emperors or the planets, she is made to feel that these shortcomings are a reflection of her *nature*, and that she lacks, as Lady Bertram genially explains, resourcefulness, intelligence, and memory. The whole process casts a reflexive light on the way accomplishments – and particularly factual knowledge – can be used to entrench social position.

Fanny's vulnerability in the first stages of her life at the Park comes over very vividly, and this is owing in part to some hidden means that look forward, despite Austen's realism, to the shrinking and growing potions of Lewis Carroll's Alice. As the eldest Price daughter, Fanny moves from the densely crowded spaces of her family home to find herself the youngest child (by two years) in a house of comparatively massive size. While she is small and weak for her age, her cousins are well-grown and full of the rude health and assurance that come from a diet that is the equivalent of

royal jelly. We see Fanny diminished by 'the grandeur' of rooms too large
for her to move in with ease, while a flow of passive verbs ('disheartened',
'awed', 'overcome', 'wondered at', 'sneered at') underlines her cowed spirits and the freezing of her confidence (12–15). Austen inverts this gambit
when Fanny, on her return to Portsmouth, is disoriented by the smallness
of the rooms, but enjoys for the first time 'the office of authority' (377,
396). Back home William's absence and her mother's poor housekeeping
have the effect of prompting her to act off her own bat, and after joining
the local circulating library, where she finds herself 'amazed at being anything *in propria persona*', Fanny takes on the education of Susan, whose
respect for her is the cause of further surprise (398). The answer to Mary
Crawford's query, in early days, as to whether Miss Price is 'in or out',
is that Fanny only comes out fully when she leaves the Park, and critics
who strive to identify her with the house need to recall that she is destined to leave it, once for all, after she is married. If she finally welcomes
the patronage of the Park, that is because it has silently been fashioned to
her image (471–3).

What really brings Fanny into intimate relation with Susan – from whom
she stands at first aloof – is her judgement that her conduct is 'at times very
wrong' (396). The phrase carries Edmund's stamp, and it is noticeable
that in tutoring her younger sister Fanny enjoys a reversal of role, but the
judgement itself emboldens her, and the same has already held true of the
censure that she and Edmund so freely dispense at the Park. The appeal
to an absolute realm gives her the power to discount or at least distance
the circumstantial one, and given Fanny's world this process has real value.
All the same, Austen is not the sort of novelist who speaks through her
characters and it is part of her brief to show that moral judgements can
be wide of the mark. Edmund and Fanny are *meant* to seem priggish for
much of the time, and – even less attractively – their *obiter dicta* often
fall visibly short of disinterestedness. Sexual jealousy causes Edmund, on
hearing that Mary is to get in Charles Maddox to play Anhalt to her Amelia,
to pronounce in favour of acting after all; and envy frequently gives an edge
to Fanny's many depreciations of her rival. Her repeated objection to Mary's
amusing and perfectly innocent satire on the letters written by brothers
(seldom even a page) is somewhat queered when she has to report to Mary
that Edmund himself has written 'but a few lines' (59, 64, 288). Still less
deserved is the rap over the knuckles that Mary receives, in absentia, when
her remarks on her uncle are found 'very wrong – very indecorous', since
her diagnosis of family ills is exactly in line with the summary already given
by the narrator. We are left to wonder whether it is really Mary's candour

that shocks, or her exculpation of her aunt at the expense of her uncle, for Fanny is curiously reluctant to exclude Mrs Crawford from blame. Indeed, in an inversion of visiting the sins of the parents, she argues that Mary's impropriety in defending her aunt shows that her aunt lacked propriety as well (40–1, 63–4).

It is usually true of Fanny that her display of a 'serious' trait is coupled with some unacknowledged motive or emotion. Pangs of jealousy, roused by the sight of Edmund taking Mary's hand in the Grants' meadow, provide the accompaniment to her worry that her mare may be overstretched by its double round of exercise (67–8). A desire to keep Edmund to herself underscores her rapturous praise of the night, delivered at a window, while Mary prepares to lead the rest of the party in a glee. Indeed, her rhapsodic deixis, 'Here's harmony . . . Here's repose,' comes in answer to a repeated 'There goes' from Edmund praising Mary's physical grace. And as the scene unfolds, Fanny's starlit presence becomes increasingly exposed to a more earthly source of light. The ambiguity is perfectly caught in her wish to see Cassiopeia, for while this constellation which never sets is in keeping with her love of constancy (like the evergreens in the shrubbery), it is also invisible from the house and so entails a visit to the lawn. When Edmund postpones this to join in the singing, Fanny's boast of an all-absorbing sublimity is punctured by a sense of incompletion. Left alone in the cold, she sighs (113).[43]

Readers today who expect to find a paragon of virtue in Fanny are likely to overlook the complexity of her treatment. But contemporaries who were versed in the criticism of the revivalist movement would have found it difficult to miss. Particularly sensitizing was the common charge that Evangelicals repressed their emotions, and indulged in moral absolutism at the cost of self-knowledge. If the sympathetic portrait that Thomas Clarkson drew of Quakerism provides a recognizable profile of Fanny, the accusation levelled against the sect by Francis Jeffrey in his review of the book finds a parallel in the novel too. To a 'self-denying principle' underlying the entire creed, Jeffrey traced the recoil from sensual pleasure, the prohibitions on entertainment, and the suspicion, in particular, of all forms of impersonation. And why, he demands, should a good Christian 'be more still and sedate than his innocence and natural gaiety incline him to be'?[44] This argument was taken further by Sydney Smith in later numbers of

---

[43] For a fuller account of this scene see my article 'Jane Austen's Nocturnal and Anne Finch', *English Language Notes*, 39 (Mar. 2002), 41–54.

[44] Review of Thomas Clarkson's *A Portraiture of Quakerism* (1806), *Edinburgh Review*, 10 (Apr. 1807), p. 91.

the *Edinburgh Review* and applied to Evangelicalism *tout court*, much being made not only of the denial of 'pleasures and amusements', and of a related unsociability, but also of the way suppressed desires were often found to lurk 'under the garb of piety'.[45] Smith calls attention, too, to a standoffishness that flows from the belief that the converted are 'a chosen and separate people, living in a land of atheists and voluptuaries',[46] an attitude that compares with Fanny's tight-lipped intolerance of the Crawfords, even – as has been pointed out – when they are at their closest to reform.[47]

The stress in these critiques on the psychological repression common to dissenting Christianity develops out of an earlier analysis linking the movement to political repression. In the *Wealth of Nations* Adam Smith had divided religious sects into two groups, the strict and the liberal, arguing that straitened social conditions favoured beliefs that were rigorous and austere. Levity, luxury, and intemperance were all serious liabilities to the underclass, enough 'to undo a poor workman for ever', and were accordingly made the object of strenuous reprobation by the devout.[48] When Hazlitt said of his own Dissenter forbears that 'from being proscribed themselves, they learn to proscribe others' he was building on such foundations.[49] *Mansfield Park* unfolds its own searching etiology of revivalism through Fanny, whose lack of self-knowledge is linked to a lack of self-confidence that goes back, in its turn, to that sense of social 'nothingness' imparted by the denial of her equality in the Bertram family. The strict creed which she develops jointly with Edmund (who seems to have revivalist connections, perhaps through the Owens with whom he stays over his ordination)[50] proves to be the instrument by which she wins back self-esteem and social status. Once she is able to act with authority, she becomes noticeably more open about her feelings for Edmund. But Jane Austen does not allow us to forget that Fanny's creed has implications that go a long way beyond the personal. Though it is not the only system of belief committed to emancipation, and though it runs counter, at crucial points, to the claims of honesty and independence, it is a creed that merits respect.

As a foil to her gauche but worthy central couple Austen lays on the Crawfords who are seductive but ultimately vapid. Through them she gives depth

---

[45] *Edinburgh Review*, 14 (Apr. 1809), p. 44.   [46] *Edinburgh Review*, 12 (Jan. 1808), p. 350.
[47] Waldron, *Fiction of her Time*, pp. 107–9.   [48] *WN*, v.i.g.10, 794.
[49] Catherine Maclean, *Born Under Saturn* (1953), p. 385.
[50] The Owen family with its two devout males – father and son both 'clergymen together' (287–9) – and three 'pleasant, good-humoured, unaffected girls' (355) sounds rather like the Coopers, with both father and son in the church, and three daughters who would turn, Austen predicted in 1799, into 'fine, jolly, handsome, ignorant girls', see To Cassandra, 21–3 Jan. 1799, *Letters*, p. 37.

to her enlightened critique of the Evangelical by showing how Enlightenment values can themselves become nugatory. Mary Crawford answers to Adam Smith's picture of the liberal Christian whose indulgence extends even to 'wanton' mirth, unchastity, and luxury,[51] but she embodies this old-fashioned stereotype in an unflattering way, speaking with scorn of the 'cloth' while upholding the sermons of Blair (92). Mary's other authors are Pope and Voltaire, the latter by now probably the worst-weathered of all the *philosophes*, his anti-clericalism and weakness for universal monarchy having long drawn criticism – Cowper's dispraise of the 'brilliant Frenchman' is quoted from in *Sanditon*.[52] Mary's comparison of herself to his Genoese Doge who saw nothing at Versailles as remarkable as his own presence there, adds an exquisite air of absolutism to her usual self-regard.[53] Indeed, the allusion neatly sums up the Crawfords' ruling passion which is a hunger for self-aggrandizement with no holds barred. Mary's playful pretension to an unremediable selfishness turns out to be the whole truth, and even more telling is her trotting out of the 'London maxim, that every thing is to be got with money' (68, 58). Warnings against the uncurbed mercenary spirit were a feature of Enlightenment writing from the time of Adam Smith, and are amplified by many of the movement's nineteenth-century heirs. To her portrait of the Crawfords, Austen added a background detail used by Southey when evoking the effects of commercialism in his *Letters from England* which she had read in 1808. The worship of money, Southey argues, breeds contempt for all other kinds of endeavour, including the achievements of the past; indeed, the monied 'new gentry' look to improvements on their estates only as a record of their grandeur:

He who has no paternal oaks has reason to prefer the poplars of his own planting, and may well like to expatiate upon the inconvenience of an old family house, long galleries, huge halls, and windows which none but the assessor can count, in his own villa, which is built to the pattern of the last tax upon light, and where the stucco upon the walls is hardly dry.[54]

Henry, leading the party of improvers at Sotherton (where the main avenue is under threat) gravely shakes his head after visiting 'more rooms than could be supposed to be of any other use than to contribute to the window tax'.[55] And Mary, on the same occasion, rates the giving up of

---

[51] *WN*, v.i.g.10, 794.   [52] *Minor Works*, p. 370; and see Cowper's *Truth*, lines 302–36.
[53] *Mansfield Park*, p. 209; Voltaire, *Louis XIV, Works*, VII, 91.
[54] Robert Southey, *Letters from England* (1807), ed. Jack Simmons (1951), p. 367.
[55] Austen devises a loose participial construction at this point to reflect the prevalent view of the party, see *Mansfield Park*, p. 85.

services in the family chapel as among the 'improvements' there. The modernism that the Crawfords represent makes a clean sweep of anything that threatens immediate pleasure, making no allowance, at a conscious level at least, for what Hume would have called the 'artificial virtues'. Austen's criticism of this raw hedonism is neither puritanical nor unenlightened. It is in line with the observation made by her much admired Pasley that where money becomes the measure of all things, valour and learning are trampled underfoot, and with them all 'liberality of mind'.[56] But this is the commercial spirit carried to excess, and Pasley preludes his attack by reaffirming the old precept advanced by Hume that 'the luxury of individuals is infinitely more beneficial than dangerous to the state'.[57] Even in Fanny's case, it is a fortune of a kind – £10 – that enables her to join that most enlightened of institutions, a circulating library, causing her to feel for the first time that she is a person in her own right, and to exclaim that 'wealth is luxurious and daring'.[58]

---

[56] *Military Policy*, pp. 474–5.

[57] Ibid., p. 473; Pasley's argument at this juncture closely follows the sixth and seventh paragraphs of David Hume's essay 'Of Commerce', though the last point is made more trenchantly in 'Of Refinement in the Arts'. See *Political Essays*, ed. Knud Haakonssen, pp. 95–7, 110–14.

[58] *Mansfield Park*, p. 398. Fanny would have been left with lots to spare: a Southampton circulating library (possibly used by Jane Austen in 1808) charged three shillings for a season, and half a guinea for the year; a three-novel volume at this period could be twice as much – more than Mrs Norris's much-vaunted gift to William, which Jane Austen privately confided to be £1. See Christopher Skelton-Foord, 'To Buy or to Borrow? Circulating Libraries and Novel Reading in Britain, 1778–1828', *Library Review*, 47 (1998), 348–54, 352.

CHAPTER 7

Emma, *and the flaws of sovereignty*

Jane Austen began *Emma* shortly before the hiatus in the war with France that followed on Napoleon's abdication in April 1814, and she finished it in March 1815 just at the moment that the deposed Emperor was resuming power. The peace may have been an illusory one, but if Austen wrote with the prospect of peace in view her timing was impeccable for Waterloo was history and Napoleon already on St Helena when the novel finally appeared. It was *Pride and Prejudice* that caused Winston Churchill to exclaim over the benignly becalmed lives led by Austen's characters, and in many ways *Emma* marks a return to the pacific settings of the earlier fiction. It also picks up on many of the earlier themes with a directness that suggests that Austen was consciously engaging in a rite of restoration. Indeed, at first sight the novel seems, for all its brilliance and intricacy, to be a summation of the work initially drafted in the nineties, but although the old Enlightenment motifs recur, many prove on closer inspection to have undergone a subtle sea change.

Emma, the imaginist, springs (to an extent seldom realized) from the same eighteenth-century tradition of female quixotry that gave birth to the heroine of *Northanger Abbey,* for her plots owe as much to romance fiction as do the frenzied perceptions of Catherine Morland, even if their source is relatively concealed. Where Catherine transposes *Udolpho,* Emma's pre-occupation with the type of the noble orphan and with the erotic fruits of heroic rescue are fully prefigured by *The Romance of the Forest,* its imme-diate predecessor.[1] There is more than a hint that Harriet's high regard for this book is shared by her mentor, since it is while apologizing for Robert

---

[1] On her mother's death, Adeline is sent to a convent at the age of seven, and later falls in love with Theodore who dramatically rescues her from the clutches of an evil Marquis. It turns out that she is the daughter of the Marquis's long-murdered elder brother. See *The Romance of the Forest,* ed. Chloe Chard (Oxford, 1986), pp. 35–6, 167, 346. The relevance of this novel to Harriet's situation has recently (and independently) been commented on by Richard Cronin and Dorothy McMillan in a valuable note that also draws out parallels with another of Harriet's books, Regina Roche's *The Children of the Abbey:* see 'Harriet's Smith's Reading', *Notes and Queries,* 49 (2002), 449–50.

Martin's interest in books such as *The Vicar of Wakefield* (which Emma 'would not think any thing of') that Harriet speaks of her plan to get Robert to read the Radcliffe which he has – perhaps unsurprisingly – forgotten to borrow (34).[2] But the matter is left open, and the relative detachment of fantasy from its literary source has its point, for it accords with the novel's premiss that there is fiction in the very air that the characters breathe. Already in *Northanger Abbey* Catherine's fanciful constructions are a lot more plausible than the strained leaps of Charlotte Lennox's heroine, making the novel's quixotry more domestic than female. Catherine's daily muster of new evidence to fit her case provides a demonstration, however dramatic, of a quite normal cognitive process – and one much fixed upon by sceptical philosophers. Thus David Hume insisted on the ubiquity of 'fictions', and on how our 'remarkable propensity to believe' generates its own momentum, so that 'any train of thinking is apt to continue, even when its object fails it, and like a galley put in motion by the oars, carries on its course without any new impulse'.[3]

In *Emma* quixotry is generalized further than in *Northanger Abbey*, for we are shown that it is not only heroines that 'can see nothing that does not answer'. Mr Woodhouse, for one, turns out to be as much of an imaginist as his daughter, unconsciously attributing many of his own feelings and expressions to Mr Perry; and the scrupulously accurate Miss Bates is puzzled to find that she has visualized Mr Dixon as a look-alike of John Knightley, explaining that 'one takes up a notion, and runs away with it' (233, 107, 176). If George Knightley has a better idea of what is going forward than the other characters, it is because he is unusually ready to make allowance for what he projects. And when he self-reprovingly quotes from Cowper, 'Myself creating what I saw', he somewhat overcorrects his wish to think badly of Frank Churchill, for the tender look Frank has given Jane Fairfax is, indeed, a telltale one.[4] Even Mr Knightley's judgements are liable to warp, however, as we see when Frank Churchill suddenly begins to rise in his estimation after Emma has said that she never loved him (433).

---

[2] Jane Austen's preference for the Goldsmith seems very clear here, which is odd, perhaps, in view of her earlier respect for Radcliffe. *The Romance of the Forest* is, however, a considerably less interesting novel than *Udolpho*, as Claudia L. Johnson concludes in her sensitive account of it (*Equivocal Beings*, pp. 73–93). It is as well to keep in mind that Radcliffe's reputation had declined significantly in the decade after her death, see my '"Strange Fits of Passion": Wordsworth and Ann Radcliffe', *Notes and Queries*, 45 (1998), 188–9.
[3] *THN*, I.iii.ix,113; I.iv.ii,198; see also I.ii.viii.
[4] Cowper, *The Task*, IV, 'The Winter Evening', line 290; *Emma*, p. 344.

Not content with generalizing mental waywardness in *Emma* through a wide cast of imaginists, Jane Austen is out to show that her reader is an imaginist too. Where plot is collapsed in *Northanger Abbey* and Catherine's extravagant construction round the figure of Montoni continually exposed to the daylight of 'probability' and the 'natural course of things', in *Emma* the reader is as much in the dark as the characters themselves, and kept guessing about outcomes. Emma's own ideas on what is in the offing are quite in line, moreover, with the resolutions provided by many of Austen's fellow-novelists and found acceptable by the audience she shared with them. Only Austen's refusal to understate the mercenariness of the marriage market makes a non-starter of Emma's darling scheme of uniting Harriet to Mr Elton, whose love of money (with only a small deflection of character) might well have been subdued by lust. As she wrote Austen must have realized that she had it in her power to supply sufficient substantiation to make many of Emma's fantasies come true. But the snuffing out of fictive plots also conveys the sense that the ways of reality are deep and intractable, uniquely right like the answers to riddles. Emma and Harriet's much talked-up collection of these provides the reader with a clue to the nature of the novel's plot, a clue confirmed on second reading when the solution to Emma's puzzle over why Jane Fairfax should be enduring Highbury for so long – 'She is a riddle, quite a riddle!' – seems blindingly simple (285). A successful riddle poses a question to which there appears to be no possible answer, usually because its component clauses are, on the face of it, incompatible, and in *Emma* this obfuscatory function is performed by the various fictions that grow up around the secretly engaged couple. Frank himself, in the first place, makes a show of flirting with Emma 'in order to assist a concealment so essential to me', even if this may seem a rather suspect rationalization for his habitual coquetry (438). And Emma, for her part, assigns Jane to Mr Dixon, providing an adulterous attachment for her rival at which Frank mischievously connives, before she goes on to assign Frank to Harriet, after the episode with the gypsies. Even if some of these fictions obviously ring false they are enough to put the reader off track, so that the union of Frank and Jane is lost on all but the most disciplined of imaginists.

Once the novel's central riddle is resolved, the disclosure has a knock-on effect. Emma is not left to worry for long over the imaginary grief of Harriet, and the discovery that it is Mr Knightley whom Harriet has set her heart on rather than Frank, precipitates the recognition that she wishes to marry Mr Knightley herself. Jane Austen compresses what must rate as one of the most superbly managed of all denouements into a few pages, and simultaneously clinches a central and pervasive theme: that blindness is the reward of assuming a godlike control. Harriet breezily asks Emma, once the secret of the engaged couple is out, if *she* at least had had no idea of it – 'You, perhaps, might. – You (blushing as she spoke) who can see into everybody's heart; but nobody else.' In fact it is 'with her own heart' that Emma has, for the first time, to come to terms (404, 407). And her moment of truth, which is treated to the heightened language of a formal recognition scene ('With insufferable vanity . . . with unpardonable arrogance . . .'), brings with it the perception that in being deceived about others she has also deceived herself (412). At a relational level it is the accident of her manipulation of her puppet-like companion into the posture of a potentially serious rival – for hasn't she already told Mr Knightley that Harriet is just the right wife for him? – that breaks the spell of her dominance, and suddenly calls into question what she has presumed to be her special right – 'to arrange everybody's destiny' (413).

The forces that underpin Emma's exercise of sovereignty will occupy us later, but the immediate point to grasp is that Emma's fictions are themselves shaped by her habitual stage-managing. The context of her description as an 'imaginist' is suggestive here, for it is the news of Harriet's rescue by Frank that sets her planning once again, and rescue of one kind or another is at the root of all her imaginings. It is the account of how Dixon saved Jane at Weymouth from being dashed into the sea 'by the sudden whirling round of something or other among the sails' that gives her the germ for her graphic and ever-expanding story of their affair (160), and it is rescue that holds the key to her adoption of Harriet whom she yearns to raise from obscurity to a position of eminence through matchmaking. It would be wrong to suppose that Jane Austen had no time for the 'preserver' motif. Indeed, it is put to work in *Emma* when Colonel Campbell takes the orphaned Jane under his care out of gratitude for having been saved from death during a camp-fever by her father (163). But it is characteristic, all the same, that the rescue that carries the most weight in the novel is Mr Knightley's unobtrusive act of kindness to Harriet after she has been cruelly snubbed by Mr Elton at the ball, an act 'much more precious' than Frank's dashing intervention on the scene with the gypsies (328, 406). But the special attraction of rescue for Emma – what stamps it as her personal motif – is that she finds particular enjoyment in a role (whether vicarious or not) which safeguards her supremacy by allowing her to be the obliger rather than the obliged.

If the novel's concern with fiction is bound to questions of rank, this is true also of its treatment of sociability. Thus a theme of Austen's earlier career is, again, given a new direction in *Emma*, and one continuous with the analysis of social position that is so conspicuous in *Mansfield Park*, only from the opposite point of view, since Emma occupies a place as exalted as Fanny's is lowly. Though these two novels – which together represent the climax of Austen's career – are strikingly different, they are given a complementarity by their joint concern with the psychological effects of circumstance. This, too, as much as the analysis of imagination, and of group-bonding, is a traditional Enlightenment concern, though we shall see that Austen's treatment of it is as individual as ever. While still on the subject of plot, however, we should first look at the relation between Emma's development and her shifting attitudes towards the social life of Highbury.

Emma's fitful movement towards self-knowledge is tied, as is the case with the sisters in *Sense and Sensibility*, to her widening recognition of adjacent lives, so that she is involved in a process of discovery loosely analogous to the reader's, a ploy that was to become increasingly standard for the liberal novelist. But included in this inbuilt paradigm (always at risk from her vitality) is a gradual alteration in the way she thinks about herself. Social position is of the utmost importance to Emma at the novel's start. Her arrangements of destiny have everything to do with the articulation and preservation of rank. Her decision to patronize Harriet ('delightful inferiority') rather than befriend Jane, is in keeping with Alexander Pope's dictum on Atossa: 'Superiors? death! and Equals? what a curse! / But an Inferior not dependant? worse'.[5] And her chagrin at having to stand second to Mrs Elton on the dance floor, or hear her assume equality with Mr Knightley, is intensified by the way she has collapsed any alternative scale of value by repeatedly pronouncing on the priority of rank over worth. So Robert Martin is dismissed for his want of gentility and 'air', regardless of the quality of his letter, and Harriet is informed – despite all professions of lasting regard – that under the name of Mrs Robert Martin she can receive no visit (32, 53). It is Emma's remorse over her rudeness to Miss Bates at Box Hill that at last provides the turning-point in this unhealthy scheme of things. The choice of Miss Bates is significant not simply because as an unmonied spinster she is a type of the socially defenceless, but because she is particularly richly endowed with 'universal good-will', a virtue that comes in for high praise throughout *Emma* (21). Austen returns here to a debate of the nineties in which, as we have seen, she earlier took part, and she once again upholds a belief in philanthropy while distinguishing between it and personal affection.[6] It is while reflecting on Mr Weston's undiscriminating attentions to all his acquaintance that Emma is brought

---

[5] Pope, *Epistle to a Lady*, lines 135–6; *Emma*, p. 38.   [6] See above, pp. 143–4.

to realize that 'General benevolence, but not general friendship, made a man what he ought to be', and her remark, while it recalls her insight into the overlooked merits of 'tenderness of heart' in Harriet and her father, clearly points forward to a growing appreciation of those who are actively well-disposed, whether that be Mr Knightley or the 'good-humoured and obliging' Robert Martin (320, 269, 28).

The concern with benevolence in *Emma* marks a return to specifically Enlightenment themes, for though the term was sometimes used by latitudinarian divines, it was with a consciousness of its original provenance in the writing of the sentimental philosophers. When Joseph Butler speaks of 'a natural principle of attraction in man towards man' so strong that even the bare fact of membership of a community is sufficient to create a bond, he echoes a passage in which Francis Hutcheson compares 'universal Benevolence' to the 'Principle of Gravitation' because of the way its power increases with propinquity to form 'strong Ties of *Friendship*, *Acquaintance*, *Neighbourhood*, *Partnership*; which are exceedingly necessary to the Order and Happiness of human Society'.[7] Later thinkers who distrusted the optimism of the Shaftesbury school were nevertheless deeply impressed by the force of this conception, and took it further. So David Hume, while insisting that social sympathies are, in practice, never enough to curb an innate selfishness, argues hypothetically, in the *Treatise*, that were 'the benevolence of men or the bounty of nature' to be increased to a sufficient degree, justice would be rendered useless.[8] Roy Porter once observed that it was in the equivalent to Ferdinand Tönnies's notion of *Gemeinschaft* as opposed to *Gesellschaft* (i.e. in a communal society) that the Enlightenment found its chief answer to the question of how individual expression could coexist with moral order.[9]

Sensitive to the different kinds of sociability afforded by different kinds of grouping and circumstance, many Enlightenment writers commented on the relatively tight weave of the social fabric in country districts, so that the country often emerges, ironically enough, as the best model on offer of the civil. Jane Austen's much quoted recipe for novels of courtship – '3 or 4 Families in a Country Village' – falls in well with Anglo-Scottish theory on the makings of sociability, more especially when taken in context, for she was busy at the time with *Emma*,[10] the demographics of which are plotted

[7] Joseph Butler, *Fifteen Sermons* (1726) (Edinburgh, n.d.), sermon 1, p. 41; Francis Hutcheson, *An Inquiry into the Original of Our Ideas of Beauty and Virtue* (1725), II.v.ii, 220.
[8] *THN*, III.ii.ii; 494–5.
[9] 'The Enlightenment in England', in Porter and Teich, *The Enlightenment*, p. 15.
[10] To Anna Austen, 9–18 Sept. 1814, *Letters*, p. 275.

in John Knightley's remark at a late stage to Emma: 'Your neighbourhood is increasing, and you mix more with it' (311–12). But if Emma is slow to develop sympathies, and risks 'being left in solitary grandeur', it is through fear of acting out of character rather than through lack of empathy. Her natural considerateness is early brought home by the dinner at which she humours her father's anxieties about eating while silently ensuring that the guests are well fed, as also by her unconditional (though by no means unpatronizing) care for the poor. But this sensitivity is disrupted by the priority she attaches to rank, in defence of which she sacrifices the chance of winning the confidence of Jane Fairfax. It has been pointed out that Highbury poses a particular challenge to Emma's social sympathies by virtue of its sheer limitedness; 'in so compressed a society', Oliver MacDonagh remarks, 'personal preference could not safely be indulged'.[11]

The lesson of Highbury is not that you have to learn to like everybody, but rather that you have to get on with people you do not like, and that these will never be in short supply. Of the six novels *Emma* is the one most concerned with the provisions and skills that make for affable contact and easy accord, and Austen once again relies on the framework of empiricist psychology for her exposition. In keeping with Adam Smith's notion of 'attunement', the narrator observes how her male characters on entering Mrs Weston's drawing room have to temper mood and temperament to the prevailing atmosphere:

Mr Elton must compose his joyous looks, and Mr John Knightley disperse his ill-humour. Mr Elton must smile less, and Mr John Knightley more, to fit them for the place. (117)

And the converse process is observed at Box Hill where a 'want of union' amounting to a 'principle of separation' spoils the enjoyment of all (367), setting the scene for a competitively egotistical display from Frank and Emma that proves hurtful to Jane Fairfax and Miss Bates. When it comes to more intimate relations, Smith's belief that approbation and a flow of feeling go hand in hand is evident in the treatment of each courtship. Emma takes it as a danger signal that Robert Martin is 'always mentioned with approbation' by Harriet, and later flatters Mr Elton in Harriet's hearing by declaring that his gallantry can only win 'every woman's approbation', though she is herself left a little uncertain that the 'balance of approbation' is in his favour (28, 82, 111). When Emma and Mr Knightley fall out over Robert Martin, the jarring sensations of their discord are dwelt on, and

---

[11] MacDonagh, *Real and Imagined Worlds*, p. 134.

they are both left after the fray to take stock of their 'self-approbation' (67). On the other hand, when Mr Knightley arrives at the Westons' party in a carriage (rather than as usual on foot, for he keeps no horse) Emma is so delighted at the sight of him accoutred as a gentleman that she speaks 'her approbation, while warm from the heart'; a response that pleases him, despite his brusque reprimand of her snobbery (213–14). So highly does Emma come to value Mr Knightley's approval that he figures for her as the nearest thing to an 'impartial spectator', as when she imagines him seeing into her heart and finding no blemish in her dealings with Jane Fairfax (391). But to an extent that is unique in Austen's fiction, the central characters in *Emma* are continually and extensively represented in relation to the many lives that make up the existence of their parish, and the focus on Highbury is never allowed to stray to another setting. So intertwined with place is Emma and Mr Knightley's relationship, that even gifts of food in the village can readily be accepted as a part of their story. Originating from Hartfield, the hindquarter of pork that Mr Woodhouse ineffectually attempts to reduce to a leg, and that looks set to provide Mrs Bates with a roast and Mrs Goddard with a stew before it is salted, becomes inextricably wrapped up with the news of Mr Elton's engagement (172–7). And the apples from Donwell Abbey that Mr Woodhouse eats baked three times over and the Bateses in partial deference to his opinion only twice, and that Jane enjoys fresh, provide a small clue to her secret engagement, when she tries to prevent Mr Knightley from gallantly (as she supposes) renewing the supply (238–9).

If that, however, was all there was to Austen's representation of the social scene, there might be justice in the claim that the novels made the squirearchy appear, as Leslie Stephen complained, 'an essential part of the order of things'.[12]

RANK, COURTSHIP, AND GENDER: ADAM SMITH AND WOLLSTONECRAFT

The political thrust of Adam Smith's theory of approbation is that there is no excuse for authoritarian rule. Human beings are such that the thirst for approval and the avoidance of dispraise make for a natural social order which, though its success will depend on various kinds of governmental intervention and institutional support, is likely to be more just than a

---

[12] Leslie Stephen, 'Humour', *Cornhill Magazine* (1876), collected in Southam, ed., *Critical Heritage*, II, *1870–1940*, pp. 174–5.

society engineered according to a plan, or put under the control of an absolute monarch or Leviathan. Rank, however, appears to Smith to be an inevitable feature of any social formation, more particularly of societies in the commercial phase, and rank in itself automatically attracts approbation. The desire to gain in rank is thus universal but it proves nonetheless to be something of a delusion, for neither health nor happiness enter into it. 'To be observed, to be attended to, to be taken notice of with sympathy, complacency, and approbation' – *that* is what underlies the itch for social betterment.[13] And there is a further paradox in the fact that the approbation that goes with high position has a dulling effect on ambition, so that achievements that count for something almost invariably come from those of middle or lower rank. Smith notices as a regrettable but inevitable fact that 'the man of rank and distinction' whose glory consists in 'the propriety of his ordinary behaviour' is essentially static, without the motive to find the resolution necessary to take on tasks 'attended either with difficulty or distress' (55).

Strictly Emma belongs to the middle rank of society, but Highbury is parochial enough to constitute its own world, and in this world Emma holds a position that is supreme. Though the grounds of Hartfield are modest enough to prompt Mrs Elton to compare them to the 'extensive grounds' of Maple Grove (and to cause Emma to reflect that those richly endowed with land seldom have much interest in the estates of others), the Woodhouses have enough money and are of a family sufficiently long-settled and ancient to enjoy a status second to none. Blessed in addition with beauty, blooming health and intelligence, Emma has only to *be* in order to reap universal adulation, and, on the face of it, that is all she wants. If she dismisses the idea of marriage, the solitariness that she looks forward to is of a regal kind, well summed up in Mr Elton's veiled and thrice-repeated description of her in his charade: 'And woman, lovely woman, reigns alone' (71, 72, 73). Only when she sees that her decision to refuse the Coles' invitation and teach them a lesson about keeping their place entails 'being left in solitary grandeur', or when a summer storm and the thought of having lost Mr Knightley to Harriet, lead to a 'reign' of loneliness and melancholy at Hartfield, does she have any clear misgivings about her sovereignty (424).[14] The reader, however, is alerted from the first to 'the real evils of Emma's situation', to the evils of a supremacy intensified by the special circumstances of her domestic history. These include the early

---

[13] *TMS*, I.iii.2.2, 50.
[14] James Thompson comments shrewdly on this use of 'reign' in his *Self and World*, p. 173.

loss of her mother, and an escape from the 'shadow of authority' made all the more emphatic by the weakness of her father, the dullness of her elder sister, and the compliance of her governess. No one can doubt that Emma owes much of her energy and sunniness to the chance events that enable her to become – from the time that she is twelve – 'mistress of the house, and of you all' (37), but the freedom to assume control brings in its train a variety of impediments that appear, from a brighter perspective, to be the regalia of her rule.

Emma's education and talents are the first-mentioned casualties of that state of self-sufficiency that is encouraged by her rank. Only a few pages after the references to *The Romance of the Forest*, we hear of the many elaborate reading lists that Emma has been in the habit of drawing up since her early teens, but also of the reason why she has never applied herself to them. 'She will never submit to any thing requiring industry and patience', Mr Knightley observes, returning to the same verb later in the conversation when he wryly remarks to Mrs Weston that as Emma's tutor she must have received a training in 'the very material matrimonial point of submitting your own will' (38). When in the next chapter the question is raised of why Emma with her exceptional talents for both drawing and music has fallen well short of what she might have attained, the answer again lies in her reluctance to take pains, in the 'so little labour as she would ever submit to' (44). The potential for real accomplishments is hinted at here, for a review of Emma's drawings and paintings follows, and the narrator applies to her the full-blown phrase 'to the steady eyes of the artist', though Emma's self-parodying commentary on her work betrays a lack of 'steadiness', just as later her deficiencies as a pianist are thrown into relief by Jane Fairfax's hard-earned musicianship. And there is more than a suggestion that the energies that she puts into matchmaking properly belong to more taxing kinds of 'labour', as when we are told that she finds it 'much easier to chat than to study; much pleasanter to let her imagination range and work at Harriet's fortune, than to be labouring to enlarge her comprehension or exercise it on sober facts' (69), where the blending of possessive pronouns is itself indicative of a relaxed agency. Indeed the compensatory nature of Emma's applied art is well brought home by Mr Knightley's remark, 'if Elton is the man, I think it will be all labour in vain' (66).

When Mr Knightley complains, while on the subject of reading, that Emma shows a resistance to any 'subjection of the fancy to the under-standing' (37), he echoes, presumably unwittingly, a key point from Mary Wollstonecraft's critique of women's education. The question of how and why the 'cultivation of the female understanding' has been subverted in contemporary society is the subject of a much quoted chapter from the *Vindication*, which grows out of the observation that women have been taught to respect the 'graceful before the heroic virtues'. Wollstonecraft's exposition of the social forces that underpin this state of affairs is based on Adam Smith's account of approbation, from which she quotes freely. At the heart of her thesis is the bold proposition that 'the whole female sex are, till their character is formed, in the same condition as the rich', the reason for this being that they are automatically accorded a chivalrous deference which saves them from the need to 'ever think of works of supererogation'.[15] Men are responsible for the far-from-disinterested pretence that women are in themselves complete, loveliness requiring no further addition, least of all in the sphere of intellect. The thesis is cleverly demonstrated by applying to women a passage on Louis XIV that Smith had used to illustrate the automatic attachment of approbation to high rank. Just as the Sun King had no need for 'unwearied and unrelenting application', no need even for exceptional judgement, learning or valour, but excelled in his role simply by cultivating a graceful manner and majestic presence, so women in modern society, Wollstonecraft contends, are most likely to succeed. But the argument goes one step further, for Wollstonecraft directly attributes the rise of the chivalric and sentimental attitude towards women to the spread of courtly manners from Versailles, thereby associating it – and the related effeminization of men – with the politics of absolutism.[16] Her own republican position affords her a mental vantage-point outside this entire structure, so that her critique of the shielded condition of women is aimed also at social hierarchy. Remove the privilege of rank, and remove the treacherous 'privilege' of gender, and all citizens will enjoy the benefit of experiencing a real thirst for approbation.

Though Austen may well have been stimulated by Wollstonecraft's brilliant idea of the wholesale court-ifying of women, she is likely to have found it both too idealistic and too sweeping. In giving Emma sovereign status, she cuts directly to the quick of the notion that high rank has inherently limiting effects, without committing herself to the view that female gender equates with social privilege when it comes to motivation. If she responds to the idea, she at least diversifies it. Jane Fairfax's situation is a reminder

---

[15] See *A Vindication of the Rights of Woman*, p. 133. For Jane Austen's knowledge of the *Vindication*, see above, p. 102.

[16] For a full account of this aspect of Wollstonecraft's thought, and its relation to Austen, see Claudia L. Johnson, *Equivocal Beings*, pp. 13–18, 34–6, 202–3. See also Carol Kay's seminal essay, 'Canon, Ideology, and Gender: Mary Wollstonecraft's Critique of Adam Smith', *New Political Science*, 15 (1986), 63–76, especially pp. 69–72.

that there are women who have to make their way in a masculine world without the ordinary shield of provision, though her readiness to achieve can be taken as a corollary to Wollstonecraft's theorem. Miss Bates, on the other hand, as a low-ranking spinster, presents the case of a woman who lacks the talent necessary to compete in any intellectual way, but merits respect, nonetheless, for her benign disposition. But on one point Austen comes very close to the *Vindication* – to its argument about courtship, which preludes in fact the bold (and apparently *ad hoc*) contention that we have been examining. It is the sudden and conspicuous elevation of women during the period that they are eligible for marriage that brings up the larger issue of the culturally contrived status of the female sex. Though courtship offers only a temporary reign, the values it instils have a lasting effect, and one that reduces the chance of compensating for the advance of age, or of finding relief from the relatively subservient role of wife. Hence the remark that young women are 'treated like queens only to be deluded by hollow respect', or her quotation of lines from Anna Aikin:

> In beauty's empire is no mean,
> And woman, either slave or queen,
> Is quickly scorn'd when not ador'd.[17]

In fact Wollstonecraft draws in this section of the *Vindication* on a tradition of satiric commentary that goes back beyond Mrs Barbauld (as Aikin became) to Samuel Richardson,[18] but her emphasis is distinctive and the language she uses often chimes in with *Emma*, as when she claims that 'the sovereignty of beauty' has proved to be a bitter legacy, its inheritors having 'chosen rather to be short-lived queens than labour to obtain the sober pleasures that arise from equality'.[19]

The charade on *court-ship* that Mr Elton writes for Harriet's riddle-book but intends for Emma, pictures exactly the sort of courtship that Wollstonecraft has in mind, only from a masculine viewpoint. Each of the two syllables is encoded in a way that underlines the sovereignty of men:

> My first displays the wealth and pomp of kings,
> Lords of the earth! their luxury and ease.
> Another view of man, my second brings,
> Behold him there, the monarch of the seas!

---

[17] *Vindication*, pp. 131–2, and note.
[18] So in *Clarissa*, for example, Anna Howe complains that women are 'courted as Princesses for a few weeks, in order to be treated as Slaves for the rest of our lives'; see the Shakespeare Head Edition (Oxford, 1930), I, 191.
[19] *Vindication*, pp. 130–1.

In paying court, however, all is turned topsy-turvy – men now play the part of slaves, women become queens:

> But, ah! united, what reverse we have!
>   Man's boasted power and freedom, all are flown;
> Lord of the earth and sea, he bends a slave,
>   And woman, lovely woman, reigns alone.
>
> (73)

Had Emma realized that the lines were for her, she might have reacted to the hint that the reign of woman is valid only for the duration of courtship (Mr Elton is soon to discover that her sense of superiority is not conferred), but she is perfectly happy to watch Harriet being raised high on the see-saw of conventional gallantry. Indeed, so long as it is not herself that is concerned (she demurs somewhat at what it would be like to be the 'principal'), she is happy to find Mr Elton's show of 'love and complaisance' admirable, and the two of them embark on a joint exposition of courtship, made all the more stark as well as comic by their misunderstanding. Emma finds a flattering pose for Harriet, and sets about sketching her at full-length, improving the look of her eyes, while adding to her height. And the more she ennobles her sitter, the more Mr Elton is obliged to insist dotingly on the likeness she has caught, so determined is he that 'nothing that did not breathe a compliment to the sex should pass his lips' (70). Nor is the tableau of courtship that they jointly put on, much put out by the mistake about who loves whom, for person counts for little, it is plain, in Mr Elton's quest for a wife. Emma can later note that she was right all along. Her devoted admirer never had any real feelings for her, and since he only wanted 'to aggrandize and enrich himself', and has now failed to ensnare the heiress with thirty thousand pounds, he can soon be counted on to 'try for Miss Somebody else with twenty, or with ten' (135).

But in other ways Emma has got it wrong. She, too, is taken in by the charm and courtly babble of the man she chooses for Harriet, duped by him to such an extent that she can cite him in preference to Mr Knightley as a paragon of manners, or can call for a Hartfield edition of Shakespeare that seems likely to delete one letter from the line, 'The course of true love never did run smooth' (34, 75). Smoothness is a cardinal virtue for Emma in the heyday of her matchmaking – ever since her boast, in fact, of having 'smoothed many little matters' in supervising the Westons' growing acquaintance (13). And Mr Elton is a prime example of the smooth wooer who tirelessly upholds a pretence of adulation: he 'sigh[s] and languish[es] and stud[ies] for compliments', and on departing 'smile[s] himself off' like the Cheshire cat, but though his desire to please is, in a sense, willed, it is indelibly ingrained in his whole bearing towards the eligible part of the sex, for whom his 'every feature works' (49, III).

It is altogether apt that Jane Austen should introduce this brand of courtship in the context of a game and under the title CHARADE, for though the pattern of conduct to which Mr Elton subscribes is so entrenched as to count as a cultural form, we are constantly reminded of its artificiality. What begins as fiction, ends as fiction too. When Mr Elton, in fulfilment of Emma's prediction, succeeds in attaching Augusta Hawkins (the ten thousand pounds) much play is made of the fact that he finds a chief source of satisfaction in the way 'the story told well'. And the story *is* told in one of the longest and funniest sentences Austen ever wrote, though 'the wind-up of the history' has to be borrowed from the more imposing marriage of Mrs Elton's elder sister to the owner of Maple Grove (181–2, 183).

Austen's contemporaries could be relied on to recognize the underlying contours of a stereotype in the character whose 'gallantry [is] always on the alert' in mixed company, or who displays, as Emma admiringly says, 'the tenderest spirit of gallantry towards us all' (49, 77), for the word so repeatedly applied to Frank Churchill as well as to Mr Elton was replete with cultural clues. Samuel Johnson recorded its French origin in the Dictionary, where he singled out the sense of 'refined address to women', and in his famous story about the unhappy ride to his wedding laid the blame for an extravagant instance of sexual pedestalling on the currency of 'the old romances'.[20] David Hume had noted that modern gallantry was the true descendant of feudal chivalry,[21] and in a dialogue known to Wollstonecraft had commented on its ascendancy in the France of his time, remarking, in particular, on the way the courtly elevation of women effected a change in general manners – a premium being placed on politeness and gaiety, at the cost of simplicity and good sense.[22] Attention has often been drawn to the association of Frank Churchill's style with things French, originally by critics in search of Austen the Anti-Jacobin, but the gallicism in question has nothing whatever to do with the Revolution. When Mr Knightley remarks that Frank (aptly named) can be 'amiable only in French not in English' because he has the 'smooth, plausible manners' that rate as '*aimable*' while lacking real sensitivity to the feelings of others, his distinction is closely

---

[20] 'She had read the old romances, and had got into her head the fantastical notion that a woman of spirit should use her lover like a dog'; see James Boswell, *The Life of Samuel Johnson*, ed. Roger Ingpen, 2 vols. (1925), I, 42.
[21] *History of England*, I, 486–7.   [22] *A Dialogue*, *Essays* II, 300, 302.

allied to the one made by Hume, and draws on an issue much contested by the Enlightenment (149). While most historians of civil society treated the original chivalric rescue of women from a subjugated state as a landmark of social development, the *revivalist* chivalry of Versailles, of the latter-day romance, or of Edmund Burke's highly coloured championship of Marie-Antoinette was quite a different matter, smacking suspiciously of anachronism. Claudia Johnson in her account of the way the sentimental tradition was assailed by women writers of Austen's period, convincingly relates the portrayal of Frank Churchill and Mr Elton to Wollstonecraft's critique of the effeminized male, even if the perspective somewhat diminishes – or at times blurs – the sustaining context of enlightened debate.[23]

If Frank Churchill and Mr Elton are linked by their smoothness of manner, they also come out on the same side of an important division that emerges at the close of the opening chapter, when Emma and Mr Knightley, in the first of many differences, disagree over the way courtships should be conducted. Priding herself on having brought the Westons together, Emma holds out for the managed match, even if she only claims for herself (perhaps out of modesty) a role somewhere between that of 'the do-nothing and the do-all' (13). Mr Knightley, on the other hand, is against 'interference' on principle, not simply because it can lead to mischief but because it is demeaning in itself. Hence his remark, 'A straight-forward, open-hearted man, like Weston, and a rational unaffected woman, like Miss Taylor, may be safely left to manage their own concerns', and his advice that Mr Elton be helped to the best pieces of chicken or fish but be left to 'chuse his own wife' (14). Though lightly stated here (and later betrayed by Mr Knightley himself), the idea that individual choice is potent and worthy of trust gathers force as the narrative unfolds, even though most of the courtships we see offend against the principle of open and free exchange, and do so in a variety of ways – Emma's pairings are imposed, Frank Churchill's engagement is disguised, and Mr Elton rates social requirements over the person. The 'do-nothing' school turns out to be the equivalent in the sphere of courtship of deregulation in the economy. Mr Elton who is perfectly 'rational and unaffected' in his dealings with men (Knightley's phrase returns) practises a kind of sexual protectionism towards women, taxing his every word and gesture with gallantry. Deceit drives Frank Churchill to ever more elaborate feats of social engineering; and Emma, preparing for the ball at the Crown, detects a wilfulness behind his gallantry which causes her to reflect

---

[23] *Equivocal Beings*, pp. 191–203. Carol Kay, by focusing chiefly on sympathy and the 'impartial spectator', underestimates Wollstonecraft's debt to Smith; see 'Canon, Ideology', pp. 63–76.

on how her liking for him might not long survive intimacy (250). Even after the disclosure of his double act, he remains glibly evasive towards her, his composure saving him from the bared emotions that enable Emma, in the case of Mr Elton, to momentarily break through the wall of compliment and brush aside the 'zigzags of embarrassment' (132). Straightforwardness is the hallmark of the open courtship, and Mr Knightley's directness to Emma takes within its compass not only the occasional rudeness ('Nonsensical girl!'), but also heated criticism. Indeed it says much about the open style of courtship that Mr Knightley should retrospectively identify his fault-finding and 'fancying so many errors' as the cause of his falling in love.

It might be objected that in making her central couple so fully exemplify a relationship of the 'do-nothing' kind, Jane Austen was forced to rely on some sleight of hand. Emma and Knightley can well seem free of the tricks of conventional wooing when there is nothing between them so far as they are aware. A case against the 'do-nothing' paradigm could be made by observing that were it not for the author's construction of a plot that provoked each lover to be jealous of outside attention to the other, Austen's central couple might never have come together at all. Certainly, report that Frank and Emma are intended for each other, as are likewise George and Jane, serves to spur them on (118–19, 226). But such authorial dealings are on the plane of 'the invisible hand'. And the slow maturation of the lovers' feelings for each other, their unselfconsciousness, and the very unintentionality of their involvement, remain wonderfully fresh and must have been particularly salutary when regulated courting was the order of the day.

The give-and-take in the central relationship of *Emma* has been veiled by a tendency on the part of critics to put Mr Knightley on a pedestal, but he is in fact, as Mary Waldron has shown,[24] a hero with peccadilloes, and these contribute to the reciprocity that is such a key feature of his attachment to Emma. He errs most obviously when he explodes at the report that Harriet has chosen to turn down Robert Martin's proposal, refusing (as Emma points out) even to tolerate the idea that the young woman may have her own views on this matter. On this occasion his male partisanship is brought into the open, and there has been some possible hint of it before, when he half-jokingly equates matrimony with submission (38). But Emma's argumentative triumph is offset by her total misreading of Harriet so that a

---

[24] Waldron, *Fiction of her Time*, pp. 114–26.

balance between them is maintained; the one wrong in theory, as Waldron puts it, the other wrong in fact.[25] But Mr Knightley's error is a case really of his failing to preach what for the most part he practises. Emma proves to have more than enough strength of character to keep his prejudices in check, and in many instances she dominates over her mentor. It is she who first suggests that they dance, and who reminds him that they are not brother and sister as she takes his hand (331), she who sees in a flash that he 'must marry no one but herself!' (408), and she, remarkably, who is to remain mistress of Hartfield after the marriage. When Mr Knightley coldly informs Mrs Elton that only the mistress of Donwell will have the final say on arrangements there, he does not reckon on his abdication taking him to someone else's home (354–5).

Conventionally, women could expect the brief reign of their courtship to lead to a more subdued status as wives, but in *Emma* matrimony brings no lessening of power. Mrs Churchill rules the roost at Enscombe, Mrs Elton is 'queen of the evening' at the Crown and tries to boss all Highbury, and Emma after the collapse of her fantasies of control enjoys a control that is all the more complete. Women of power abound in the novels – Austen, long before the days of affirmative action, sees to it that they are far more plentiful than a sample of her society would allow. Conversely, her reason for leaving *The Watsons* unfinished may well have been that she hated to dwell on the hopeless situation of her spirited heroine. But rank is no guarantee of worthiness in the novels, rather the contrary. Though Lady Susan radiates a charm that jams all perception of truth (and has a queue of critics in tow),[26] she falls victim to her own deceit at last, and is worsted in courtship by the daughter she maltreats. Mrs Ferrars is nasty, Lady Middleton mean, Miss Osborne fickle, Lady Catherine de Bourgh conceited, Lady Bertram comatose, Lady Dalrymple dull, Lady Denham sordid, and all are snobbish. Though Austen goes out of her way to make such figures vivid, ensuring that they are favourites with her readers, she makes it clear that exalted position has done them little good. Emma is the exception to the rule in being admirable as well as magnetic. She owes her attraction, however, not simply to her gifts, but to the painful process of

---

[25] Ibid., p. 122.

[26] Roger Gard provides the fullest account of this *nouvelle*, but tends to endorse Lady Susan's view that her superior talents free her of obligation. There is no mistaking the irony, however, when Lady Susan counsels her friend to scorn all those 'whose Sensibilities are not of a nature to comprehend ours' (301). Gard convincingly argues that Austen's realistic handling of epistolary conventions limited her access to dramatic representation, making the epistolary novel an unsatisfactory form for her; see *Novels*, pp. 29–44.

self-discovery (by no means a 'humiliation') that does much to clarify the effects of her supremacy without damaging her social esteem. It is through Emma, moreover, that Austen takes furthest the analysis of high rank.

Harriet's story, which spans the entire novel (her engagement to Robert Martin is the last of the five to be made), repeatedly exposes Emma to an unfavourable light. From the start the very ground of the relationship is suspect. Emma, used to having her own way, and to taking approval for granted, chooses Harriet in the knowledge that she can count on her total compliance. Such companionship allows her to retreat into a fastness where her supremacy is never at risk; and Harriet increasingly stands between her and the world of sexual danger where men make advances. There are frequent hints at the vicarious life that Emma leads through her protégée. 'Oh! no, I could not endure William Coxe', she exclaims of the young man who has just popped into her mind as a possible replacement for Mr Elton (137). She is even caught indulging in lover's ruses (breaking her shoelace for example) to further her schemes, but always on Harriet's behalf. Particularly telltale is the timing of her idea that Frank Churchill is the obvious new suitor – she has recognized, only a page before, that she herself is 'quite enough in love' with him and would 'be sorry to be more' (265–6). The more Emma engages Harriet the more she keeps herself aloof, and her matchmaking is tied to her desire to reign alone. Austen's portrayal of this mechanism is subtle and profound, resistant to summary,[27] but a good pointer to its social significance is provided by a comic motif from *The Watsons*, where the caricatured Lord Osborne ('quite one of the great & Grand ones') insists on interposing a deputy between himself and the women who catch his eye. So Emma's namesake is asked to dance by Tom Musgrave who is also instructed to provide a description of her by daylight, and to do the talking on a visit to the Watsons' humble house. The explanation is that Osborne has grown 'unused to exert himself'.[28]

Though Emma's patronage of Harriet seems benign when compared to Mrs Elton's of Jane – the one as absorbed in raising her dependant's prestige, as the other is in making a meal of her protégée's penury – it is flawed, nonetheless, by her failure to distinguish between merit and rank. This failing is stressed when Emma ponders Harriet's report of her encounter with the Martins, while shopping at Fords, after news has broken of Mr Elton's engagement. Though her heart goes out to the disappointed family

27 The novel's treatment of this surrogacy is very much wider-ranging, for example, than the quasi-psychological account provided by Tony Tanner in his *Jane Austen* (1986), pp. 181–3.
28 *The Watsons*, see *Minor Works*, pp. 342, 333, 335, 338, 346.

who display such 'genuine delicacy' at the meeting, and whose worth has been evident all along, she reins this impulse back by telling herself that no end of virtue can outweigh 'the evils of the connection' (179). To this theme she returns, noting some internal distress at her ruthlessness, after one of the most poignant and neglected scenes of the novel, the visit – designed to last fourteen minutes – that she allows Harriet to make to Abbey-Mill Farm. The visit is by way of concession, for Emma has already outlawed the whole family to protect Harriet's status, and its shortness (Harriet has spent six weeks there the previous summer) and its formality (Harriet is brought and picked up by Emma in her carriage) are meant to give a clear signal that it is the last. The arrangement reveals an ugly underside to Emma's scheme for a radical make-over of Harriet, whom we see reduced from a person with a particular history and identity to a doll-like plaything, and the scene is no more kind to Emma for being half-filtered through her consciousness. At first the conversation at the Martins is as uneasy and flat as Emma could desire, but at the last minute all changes:

Mrs Martin's saying, all of a sudden, that she thought Miss Smith was grown, had brought on a more interesting subject, and a warmer manner. In that very room she had been measured last September, with her two friends. There were the pencilled marks and memorandums on the wainscot by the window. *He* had done it. They all seemed to remember the day, the hour, the party, the occasion – to feel the same consciousness, the same regrets – to be ready to return to the same good understanding; and they were just growing again like themselves, (Harriet, as Emma must suspect, as ready as the best of them to be cordial and happy,) when the carriage re-appeared, and all was over. (187)

The cruel precision of Emma's timing, like the stark abstraction of her plans, is seen to cut through a ganglion of feeling that is tender and complex in process. Indeed the scene not only deals in the bodily but exfoliates in an organic way. Harriet's growth over the course of the year – with which her regard for Robert has evidently kept pace ('*He* had done it') – leads on to a growing sense of unanimity that makes the group feel 'like themselves'. While the much notched window-jamb punches a perspective into the past, it frames a real and ever-continuous world that lies beyond the fitful grasp of 'pencilled marks and memorandums'. And it is *there* in the concrete fact of physical presence and shared experience that emotional affinity has its roots. Austen evokes the naturalness of such God-given process with a mastery that gives full weight to the charge of trifling with the feelings of others that Emma levels against herself: 'it was adventuring too far, assuming too much, making light of what ought to be serious, a trick of what ought to be simple' (137). Personal identity is taken seriously in *Emma*, and in one respect more so than in the other novels, for individuality is written particularly large in the actual mode of representation. Though reported speech is limited to fewer figures than is customary for Austen,[29] speech is quoted frequently, often at length, and diversified as never before, idiolect providing in many cases the chief instrument of characterization. It is no accident that we are given a monologue by Miss Bates before she is introduced (18), or that for pages of dialogue at a time no voice tags are required. Nowhere in fiction is Ben Jonson's maxim, 'speak that I may see thee', realized with greater comic panache or penetration.[30]

But if Emma's treatment of Harriet is bedevilled by her obsession with rank, that is only what is to be expected. Charging herself, finally, with having tried 'to arrange everybody's destiny' (413), Emma merely states what Harriet has all along considered to be her patron's rightful due. Awed on her first meeting to be invited to shake hands, Harriet looks upon Emma as infallible and omniscient ever after and is perfectly attuned to her mentor's belief that she is, in her own words, 'always right in any man's eyes'.[31] That high rank is specially conducive to illusion is of course a commonplace, but the idea was seminal to the Enlightenment, as might well be imagined of a movement rooted in protest against autocracy, whether secular or religious. In Jane Austen's time the critique of despotism found many fresh applications – to the Terror, to Napoleonic dirigism, even to the new phase of British colonial policy; and we know from her reading that Austen was well aware of these. It is a feature of such critique, furthermore, that it takes for granted that the political and psychological run into each other, as do also the national and domestic. David Hume makes this last elision when he remarks that the nastiness of despotism is known to all from 'observation in private life'.[32] In *Emma* Jane Austen refrains from supplying any topical pointers such as the geopolitical references that provide a submerged analogue to the action of *Mansfield Park*. She allows her drama to speak, rather, for itself, but in the knowledge that her comedy of illusion has the power to stir association in distant and less familiar fields.

Perhaps there is no better epigraph to the political aspect of *Emma* than the passage in which Adam Smith, in the course of a chapter on virtue, warns against the dangers of 'new-modelling'. It is the autocrat who becomes so 'wise in his own conceit' and 'so enamoured with the supposed beauty'

[29] MacDonagh makes this point, *Real and Imagined Worlds*, p. 129.
[30] Ben Jonson, *Discoveries*, ed. G. B. Harrison (1966), p. 78.
[31] For this and further instances, see pp. 84, 25, 38, 76, 404.
[32] *An Enquiry Concerning Human Understanding*, 5.1, fn. 8, pp. 121–2.

of his conceptions, that he falls into the habit of regarding those subject to his sway as so many pieces on a chessboard, forgetting that in human society every piece is alive and endowed with 'motion of its own'.[33] In *Emma* even Harriet, so ready to acquiesce, proves capable of making the very move that is most subversive to her mentor's plan in opting for Mr Knightley rather than Frank Churchill. Only with the collapse of their grand narrative, do Emma and she discover where their true feelings lie. Here again Austen verges, within her comedy of manners, on a topos much favoured by the Enlightenment: what might be termed the renewal that starts from the ruins of absolute rule. In his essay 'The Rise of the Arts and Sciences', David Hume maintained that despotism effectually puts a stop to 'all improvements' owing to its damping effects on the spirit of individual incentive and competition out of which new things grow;[34] but he argued, too, that autocracy was bound in the long run to fail in both the state and the domestic sphere, and for the same reason: 'human nature checks itself in its airy elevation'.[35]

Enlightenment paradigms run deep in *Emma*, which is perhaps why it, more than any other Austen novel, provides the blueprint for a plan widely used by writers of liberal fiction later in the century. Emma, as we have seen, progressively breaks through the cocoon of egotism that keeps her apart from Highbury until she is in more complete possession of the story, by the end, than any other character. In this respect she is the precursor of many heroines who are understood to receive their essential education from digesting all that is signified by the texts in which they figure. She is in company here with Esther Lyon in *Felix Holt* who compares her task of 'trying to make character clear before her' to the reading of a book, thus pacing George Eliot's reader who ideally learns what Esther does from the experience – 'to doubt the infallibility of her own standard', which is no less than Emma has done before her.[36] When Henry James, in his dialogue on *Daniel Deronda*, vividly describes Gwendolen Harleth's history as 'the universe forcing itself with a slow, inexorable pressure into a narrow, complacent, and yet after all extremely sensitive mind', he echoes Felix on what 'life thrusts into the mind', which includes, in his case, data as distressing as a 'splinter'.[37] George Eliot found many metaphors to illustrate

[33] *TMS*, VI.ii.2.17, 233–4.   [34] 'Of the Rise and Progress of the Arts and Sciences', *Essays* I, 179.
[35] 'Of the Balance of Power', *Essays* I, 355.
[36] *Felix Holt, The Radical*, ed. Fred C. Thomson (Oxford, 1980), p. 216.
[37] '*Daniel Deronda*: A Conversation', in F. R. Leavis, *The Great Tradition* (1948), p. 264; *Felix Holt*, p. 222.

the painful but liberating work of recognition that underlies the plots of her major fiction. No one forgets the candle on a tray, picking out concentric circles from random scratches, that is offered in *Middlemarch* as a parable of 'the egotism of any person now absent'.[38] But a fuller model for the heuristic process is developed in *Felix Holt* from Adam Smith's image of the animated chessboard, a figure better suited, after all, to the shifts of narrative. In context it is applied to Matthew Jermyn who presumes, over-confidently, that he can suppress the truth about the Transom family by manipulating his dependants, only to find that the most servile of his cat's-paws has a will of his own. So George Eliot asks her reader to 'fancy what a game at chess would be if all the chessmen had passions and intellects': 'You might be the longest-headed of deductive reasoners, and yet you might be beaten by your own pawns. You would be especially likely to be beaten, if you depended arrogantly on your mathematical imagination, and regarded your passionate pieces with contempt.'[39]

Though they undergo a similar process of recognition Esther and Emma have, of course, a very different text to read, and prove to be different kinds of reader too. Where Esther subdues herself to a higher truth and finds salvation through Felix, Emma remains as wilful and as economical with the truth as ever, and yet achieves a greater strength. There is a paradox here that goes back to the complexities of her character and it is never more fully displayed than at the moment of the last of her many discoveries, which is that Mr Knightley has no special feelings for Harriet after all. Emma's tender sympathies are evident in her reluctance to recognize that Mr Knightley is proposing to her rather than talking about his love for Harriet, but when the recognition does come she instantly decides to draw a veil over the whole matter of her friend's infatuation in case it should interfere with what she now most hopes for herself. So the last milestone in Emma's progress towards clarification turns out to be a boundary-mark, signalling the point at which she passes beyond 'heroism of sentiment' to the home territory of self-love, in particular of that unfashionable Stoic duty revived by the Scottish school, the care of self (431).[40] But Emma's refusal to let on about Harriet has other implications as well. It means, for one thing, that she emerges higher in the domestic knowledge stakes than Knightley does, and though her *suppressio veri* is small, and not 'material', it does allow her to snatch composure from the jaws of possible further shame. Indeed, Emma's sleight of hand not only underlines her renewed

---

[38] *Middlemarch*, ch. 27 (1965), p. 297.   [39] *Felix Holt*, ch. 29, p. 237.
[40] *TMS*, VI.ii.1.1, 219.

ability to seize and maintain control, but increases our sense of her stature, for it exposes a relative impercipience in Mr Knightley, who never thinks to inquire into why Emma kept backing away when he began his proposal. But the last word on Emma's handling of the last piece that falls into place in her mental recovery of Highbury is the sceptical observation of the narrator: 'Seldom, very seldom, does complete truth belong to any human disclosure.'[41]

---

[41] *Emma*, p. 431, and see above, pp. 11–12.

CHAPTER 8

Persuasion: *light on an old genre*

Though the *grande armée* was long defeated, and Napoleon on the first day of his voyage to St Helena when Jane Austen began writing on 8 August 1815, *Persuasion* is of all her novels the one most directly concerned with the effects of war. Patriotism has many moods, and the peacefulness of *Emma*, with its rural and indefinitely dated setting, is arguably as expressive of national feeling as the urgency of *Mansfield Park* with its explicit reminders of the ongoing campaign. But the plot of *Persuasion* points to a unique engagement with history, for it brings active service into the sphere of courtship for the first time. Its complicating presence there is already foreshadowed in *Mansfield Park* by the relationship between Fanny Price and her sailor brother William, whose limited time together is cut short by the summons to duty, and toned by the dread of parting. Wartime intimacies between naval men and women were inevitably broken in one way or another, and this is reflected in the multiple narratives of *Persuasion*, where events are kept to the period before Waterloo, the rupture between Commander Wentworth and Anne Elliot dating to some months after the naval action off St Domingo in 1806, and their renewed engagement and marriage to the early part of 1815, with the possibility of further action still pending. Captain Benwick returns after a long voyage to find his fiancée dead; Captain Harville and his fiancée marry without money in order to guard against such a fate, and Mrs Croft resolves the problem of absence by joining her husband on board whenever she can, after the trial of a lonely winter spent at Deal. The temporary peace with which the novel opens (and through which *Emma* was composed) allows Austen to bring her naval characters ashore, but the courtships they conduct there, whether in the past or the present, are shaped by their lives at sea. Though no character is killed in action, the pain of separation is dwelt on throughout, not only in Captain Benwick's loss but in the central fact of Anne's loss of hope after the miscarriage of her engagement. Love is viewed *sub specie mortis* as nowhere else in the novels. Sailors, as Admiral Croft bluntly sums the matter up, 'cannot afford to make long courtships in time of war' (92).

The extent to which Jane Austen draws on wartime experience in *Persuasion* is sharply brought home by a diary that her brother Charles kept for 1815 while cruising the Mediterranean in the *Phoenix*. Only the previous September his wife Fanny and daughter had died in childbirth on board the *Namur*,[1] but his new ship had to be joined a few weeks later, and the entries in his pocketbook show him racked by grief, and plagued by recurring nightmares of further misfortune to his surviving family. Finding solace in the fact that his case was not unique, Charles Austen records a story of bereavement that he witnessed on 18 April at Gibraltar, where a newly married wife had just disembarked in order to be reunited with her husband, a Captain Wills, only to discover that preparations for his funeral were under way:

his wife and his sister came from Falmouth in the same ship with the Seymours; Poor young creature she never saw him till he was a corpse. He was addicted to drinking it seems and of late had given away to it more than usual in consequence of an idea that he had formed that she would not come out to him, which it is to be hoped she will never know. This might be worked up into a sad story and when I first heard of it I said to myself other people too are afflicted and miserable as well as myself. But the violent shock was the worst part of it for poor Mrs W. who had only been acquainted with her husband for one month before marriage and only lived with him for three days afterwards – Dr Seymour thinks she will soon get over it.[2]

Charles Austen wrote regularly to his sisters throughout this period,[3] and the incident that he thought could be 'worked up into a sad story' would certainly have been handed on to Jane, who might at first glance have earmarked it for the satiric 'Plan of a Novel' that she was assembling, over the course of 1815, from various hints given her by friends. Her new novel was a sufficient departure from the old, however, to include material of an openly romantic kind; and the 'sad story' is in many respects Captain Benwick's to which Anne compares her seemingly irreversible loss, much as Charles Austen took the Wills' as a reflection of his own. The comparison is interesting, in any case, for what it shows up as distinct about Austen's emphasis. For one thing, the story is toned down, nothing matching the lurid temporal coincidence of death

---

[1] See Le Faye, *A Family Record*, p. 194; and Southam, *Jane Austen and the Navy*, p. 296.
[2] Charles Austen's pocketbook, entry for 18 Apr. 1815; Greenwich, AUS/102.
[3] Charles sent Jane three letters in February and March of 1815. See AUS/101; and Southam, *Jane Austen and the Navy*, p. 55.

and arrival, even if Louisa is later allowed to appear 'corpse-like' on the quay (110).

More telling, however, is the switch of gender in Benwick's history, especially in view of the Doctor's remark about Mrs Wills, reported by Charles, that 'she will soon get over it'. Captain Benwick who does, indeed, get over his grief for Fanny Harville to the extent of proposing to Louisa within a few months of her death, becomes the occasion for the famous exchange between Captain Harville and Anne Elliot on the subject of female constancy. Harville's sceptical smile and his claim that male feelings are the strongest are backed by an appeal to literature: 'all histories are against you, all stories, prose and verse . . . I do not think I ever opened a book in my life which had not something to say upon woman's inconstancy. Songs and proverbs, all talk of woman's fickleness' (234). Anne's reply that men, with the advantage of greater education, have had the pen in their hands, together with her counterclaim that women enjoy the dubious privilege of 'loving longest, when existence or when hope is gone' has the dramatic function of calling Wentworth's attention to her feelings, but it serves also as something of a manifesto for *Persuasion* itself. The picture that Harville paints of the sailor's lot in time of war is a representative one – anguished partings, tender reunions, the anxieties of absence are all insisted upon. Its truth is fully admitted by Anne, and it belongs, indeed, with those 'domestic virtues' that are said, in the novel's last sentence, to outweigh even the navy's great 'national importance'. But in a period that saw a premium placed upon male heroism, *Persuasion* focuses centrally on Anne, on a quiet and rather subdued woman who passes for the most part ignored, or even fades into 'nothingness' within her circle. What the novel effectively provides (with a patriotism modified by the end of hostilities) is a corrective to the values that have imperceptibly gained ground in wartime Britain. These values, borne of national militancy, and ingrained in the texture of everyday life, are viewed from a feminine standpoint, and set against a celebration of the strength of women.

The literature that comes under the spotlight in *Persuasion* belongs to the genre of the Regency verse romance. Scott and Byron are described as 'first-rate poets' in an age distinguished for its poetry, and Anne and Benwick discuss the merits of *Marmion* and *The Lady of the Lake*, as compared to those of the *Giaour* and *The Bride of Abydos*, while *The Corsair* is alluded to later (100–1, 167, 107–9). All these works were immensely popular and reveal, in their different ways, a strong bearing on the Napoleonic wars. Scott, who initiated the taste, and claimed to read *Orlando Furioso* every

year,[4] had revived the old tradition of the romantic epic, and followed
Ariosto in singing of love and of arms together. In his verse martial affairs
tower over romantic interests, however, and his heroines are a lot more
marginal than any summary of the plots in which they are involved can ever
convey. Byron, on the other hand, though adopting the same genre, writes
in conscious reaction against Scott, putting love at the centre of his stories,
and admitting only a strictly libertarian patriotism. Exotic though they are,
his Turkish tales remain finely tuned to the experience of the European
war, an attunement that makes them strangely consonant with *Persuasion*,
and his Levantine settings were by no means as remote to contemporaries
as might now appear. When Charles Austen wrote to his sisters from the
Phoenix, he was giving chase to buccaneers round the Greek archipelago,
and hobnobbing with Pashas. After Jane's death he equipped himself with
the works of Byron for a voyage;[5] but he was already a reader of Scott. In
fact, Jane had sent *Marmion* out to him in the Bermudas – together with
a rug – in 1809, and the gift of her own copy (we know that the poem
failed to please her at first)[6] suggests that she had identified the audience
at which she took it to be properly aimed. Opening as it does with an
elegy on Lord Nelson, *Marmion* puts in a puff for the navy, but this is
only a part of its clarion call for a general resurgence of national feeling:
the narrative climaxes in a long setpiece on the English victory at Flodden,
which served Scott as a trial run for *The Field of Waterloo*, a copy of which
Austen returned to Murray without comment.[7] We shall see that *Marmion*
offers another field of relevance, however. Its two highly contrasted women
characters, flanking the hero, look forward to Byron's similarly antitypical
heroines in *The Corsair* and so, too, to the contrast between Anne Elliot
and Louisa Musgrove in *Persuasion*. But Scott unceremoniously bundles
his ladies offstage whenever he can make a parade of his warriors – for who,
he asks, 'would listen to the tale / Of woman, prisoner, and nun, / Mid
bustle of a war begun?'[8]

---

[4] So Scott remarked to Edward Cheney, see Ian Jack, *English Literature, 1815–32* (1963), p. 381.
[5] Charles Austen, Private Journal, entry for 17 July 1826, AUS/118.
[6] 'Ought I to be very much pleased with Marmion? – as yet I am not', see To Cassandra, 20 June
 1808, *Letters*, p. 131. No further opinion is recorded though Jane Austen certainly got to know the
 poem well, for she adapted the couplet on the 'dull elf' in a letter, and her reading aloud of the
 first canto attracted praise. Sir Edward Denham's enthusiasm in *Sanditon* clearly implies criticism
 however (*Minor Works*, p. 351), and though James Austen had a high regard for Scott's novels, he
 appears lukewarm on the poetry: 'How Scott, in simple ballad rhymes, / Records the feuds of former
 times' (*Morning*, July 1814).
[7] To John Murray, 23 Nov. 1815, *Letters*, p. 297.
[8] Walter Scott, *Marmion*, 2nd edn (Edinburgh, 1808), v, xviii, p. 270.

To place *Persuasion* among the descendants of the romantic epic is not to say that it is like one. Wentworth does not desert Anne Elliot in the way that the Corsair abandons Medora to go out on a raid, or that Rogero, in Ariosto, dumps his Bradamant for a magic horse. It is Anne, after all, who breaks off the engagement, and it is Lady Russell who persuades her to do it. But if sexual agency is reversed, that is all the more reason to approach *Persuasion* as a rethinking of the Regency romance, or even it might be claimed – since Austen's copy of Ariosto survives[9] – of the genre as a whole. Scott seems to have contributed in two quite different ways to the new novel. On the one hand, *Persuasion* goes a long way to answering the complaint, made in his review of *Emma*, that Austen had sacrificed romance to prudence in her work, and had systematically undervalued the power and lasting effect of strong early attachments.[10] If Scott recalled Elinor Dashwood's self-reproachful rebuke of her sister, 'it is not meant – it is not fit – it is not possible',[11] he could hardly have overlooked Captain Harville's comment on Benwick, 'A man does not recover from such a devotion of the heart to such a woman! – He ought not – he does not' (183), or the famous dictum on Anne: 'She had been forced into prudence in her youth, she learned romance as she grew older – the natural sequel of an unnatural beginning' (30). But if *Persuasion* is in part a response to Scott's demand for more romance, it is also a retort to his poems, the heroines of which perfectly illustrate the way in which female strength is undercut by values honed to the waging of war.

That it is Anne who takes the decision that terminates her attachment to Wentworth for eight long years is in keeping with Austen's intention of replotting the war-romance from a domestic and female point of view, and thus in her brief moment of stock-taking at the novel's end, Anne insists not only that she was correct to be guided by the friend who proved to be her sole mentor, but that the freedom to make such a decision is a woman's right (246). No doubt Austen felt the need to clarify this point in her revised conclusion, since the sheer wrongness of Lady Russell's advice – and her importunacy in volunteering it – have the effect of concealing Wentworth's share of the blame. Only recently has the question of Wentworth's culpability been given due weight by a critic who shrewdly observes, 'We are

---

[9] Gilson, *Bibliography*, pp. 436–7.
[10] Walter Scott, *Quarterly Review*, 14 (Mar. 1816), collected in Littlewood, ed., *Critical Assessments*, I, 287–96, 296. The piece was unsigned, but it seems likely that Jane Austen knew the identity of the reviewer (whom she refers to as 'so clever a Man' in her reply to Murray; 1 Apr. 1816, *Letters*, p. 313). It is worth noting that the novel must have been fairly well advanced when the review appeared.
[11] *Sense and Sensibility*, p. 263.

surely not expected to suppose that Wentworth is justified in demanding that Anne choose between himself and the only other person in the world who cares a fig for her.'[12] The reader's natural bias towards the cause of love (which was apparently as active when the novel appeared as it is today),[13] also has the effect of obscuring the ways in which the breakdown of all connection between the lovers is war-related. The thread on which the fate of the whole relationship hangs is singled out when Wentworth accuses himself of having been too angry and too proud to write to Anne on his return to England in 1808 after his success in the *Laconia* (247), when nothing could have stood in the way of their reconciliation. The causes of his 'high and unjust resentment' are complex, but have much to do with the nature of Lady Russell's disapproval which seems to be founded in a dislike of the self-made man, and this prejudice is evidently augmented by 'the genius and ardour', not to mention the confidence, that are so much a feature of Wentworth's make-up (91, 29). A telling point in this connection is made by Southam in his *Jane Austen and the Navy* when he remarks that 'the traits which make Wentworth appear so "dangerous" to Lady Russell are the very qualities of character which won British Captains mastery of the seas'.[14] It is equally true of course that the qualities that repel Lady Russell are precisely those that are bewitching to Anne, who can only find the strength to refuse Wentworth by persuading herself that by freeing him she is acting in his interests. If Austen is fulfilling Scott's demand for passions that qualify as the 'tenderest, noblest and best', her repeated stress on Anne's 'self-denying' state at the time of her decision is nonetheless meant to sound a warning bell (28). In fact, patronage is the last thing that Wentworth wants, and it is hardly surprising that he should read the blend of self-renunciation and anxiety about material provision that sustain Anne's ultimatum as a 'forced' act of separation, and take himself off in a huff. His self-assurance, like his joke that he has always been lucky and *knows* that he 'should be so still', is part of the mind-set that equips him for a profession that is exposed to fatality and hazard at every turn. His belief that he has the capacity 'to foresee and to command his prosperous path' prepares him for his first ship, the seriously unseaworthy *Asp*, aboard which the lot of a pessimist would certainly not be a happy one (29). Though far from blind to risk, he shows that an attitude of self-reliance is of great value where risks

---

[12] Waldron, *Fiction of her Time*, p. 140.
[13] The reviewer in the *British Critic* (Mar. 1818) complained that the obvious moral of *Persuasion* was that 'young people should always marry according to their own inclinations and upon their own judgement'; see Littlewood, ed., *Critical Assessments*, 1, 314.
[14] Southam, *Jane Austen and the Navy*, p. 266.

exist, whether or not they are taken. Make-or-break is his attitude to the *Asp*: 'I knew that we should either go to the bottom together, or that she would be the making of me', and it pays off partly because of good luck and partly because of his cool estimate of danger (65–6). But this sangfroid is at odds with the compromises required of him on land, and his reluctance to adapt to the other domain (as Admiral Croft is slow to recognize posts in the landscape) vents itself in an anger that smoulders on, with epic force, for eight years.

Like the forward youth of Marvell's Horatian Ode, Captain Wentworth has 'through adventrous War / Urged his active Star', and his embodiment of up-to-date notions of male valour would have been immediately apparent to Austen's readers.[15] The male-authored Regency verse romance is full of praise of headstrong men, and insistent (to the point of prescription) on how susceptible women are to the magnetism of the warrior. Wentworth returns from the sea to drawing rooms well-versed in the sort of hero typified by the Hunter-King of the best-selling *The Lady of the Lake* (1810), whose exploits in the chase Scott describes (taking a leaf from Adam Ferguson) as 'mimicry of noble war', and whose character is distinguished by both the 'fiery vehemence of youth' and 'the will to do, the soul to dare', all qualities fatal to the defences of female modesty – 'Not his the form, nor his the eye, / That youthful maidens wont to fly.'[16] The 'little fever of admiration' that Wentworth inspires in the young women of the Uppercross neighbourhood – both the Hayter and the Musgrove daughters fall under his spell – has everything to do with his successful fulfilment of this stereotype, but the reader is left to understand that his full personality remains unengaged. The girls are more in love with him than he with them, nor is 'love' in any case the appropriate word, though the relationship with Louisa develops, nonetheless, to the point of social acceptance and beyond easy return (82). In fact, Wentworth plays along with the image of himself as the irresistible officer, falling in – innocently if irresponsibly – with expectations that are already in the air and given a distinct naval drift by an impatient Admiral Croft who demands that Frederick 'spread more canvas' and bring home one of the young ladies, no matter which (92). Wentworth, too, comes close to visualizing courtship in terms of the capture of a prize on land, as when he tells himself that he is 'ready to fall in love with all the speed that a clear head and quick taste could allow', and that he has a 'heart for

---

[15] 'An Horatian Ode', *The Poems and Letters of Andrew Marvell*, ed. H. M. Margoliouth (1971), I, 91.
[16] Walter Scott, *The Lady of the Lake* (Edinburgh, 1810), I, xx, xxi, p. 26. This proved the most popular of Scott's verse romances, see Jack, *English Literature*, p. 42.

either of the Miss Musgroves', or indeed for any 'pleasing young woman who came his way, excepting Anne Elliot' (61). It is testimony to the power of Austen's characterization that she manages to convey that Wentworth's taking on of this role is at once a kind of jocular defence, and a real betrayal of self, an insight clinched by Mrs Croft's response to his boast that when it comes to courtship he is not the man to be 'nice': 'He said it, she knew, to be contradicted. His bright, proud eye spoke the happy conviction that he was nice' (62).

The boiler-plated flirtation that Wentworth keeps up at Uppercross is thrown into slightly ugly relief by the unfurling saga of how he has displaced Charles Hayter in the heart of Henrietta Musgrove. Charles is described as a 'very amiable, pleasing young man', and, as one who has chosen the life of a 'scholar and a gentleman', he stands as a contemplative in relation to Wentworth by whom he is worsted as a suitor, despite the advanced stage of his relationship to Henrietta.[17] A string of military metaphors underlines his haplessness in this contest; Anne is pleased to note that Wentworth is aware of 'no triumph, no pitiful triumph' in stealing her young cousin's affections, and Charles after leaving her dangerously 'unguarded' is forced 'after a short struggle to quit the field', and then finds it necessary to 'withdraw' from that position also (73, 82, 89). In view of Louisa's extravagant opinion that only naval men know how to live, and that only they deserve 'to be respected and loved' (99), it is not surprising that Charles Hayter should rapidly lose favour with the Musgrove girls once Wentworth is on the scene, but the social void into which he temporarily falls is familiar because it is so much like the oblivion that has overtaken Anne. The long and eagerly awaited news that he has at last procured Dr Shirley's promise of a curacy at Uppercross scarcely provokes a response when he comes to tell it: 'Louisa could not listen at all to his account . . .: she was at the window, looking out for Captain Wentworth; and even Henrietta had at best only a divided attention to give' (78). Anne is the one to approve silently of the way Charles has got down to his books and refused an invitation to dine (proof to parents that he is 'studying himself to death'), and it is she, again, who observing with concern the potentially hurtful entanglement of the four, longs for the 'power of representing to them all what they were about' (82). *That* representation is the privilege of the reader, who sees that Wentworth and his admirers are kept in motion by forces that are irrational without being deep. The 'little fever' that grips the girls can readily be diagnosed as a hangover

---

[17] In the introduction to her edition of the novel, Linda Bree calls attention to the disparity between Charles Hayter's worth and low social status, see *Persuasion* (Ontario, 1998), p. 17.

of the war, but Austen is careful, at the same time, not to overstate the case for the 'inglorious arts of peace'. She avoids the pitfall into which Samuel Richardson piously lapsed when he exchanged Dryden's 'none but the brave' for his own lame 'none but the *good* deserves the fair', and plotted his last novel accordingly.[18] Charles Hayter's scolding of the child who climbs onto Anne's back is made to look ineffectual by the prompt action that Wentworth takes, and though Charles gets his deserts, it is only because Louisa loses no time in detaching her sister from the Captain.

AFFIRMING THE STRENGTH OF WOMEN

In the first volume of *Persuasion* Anne Elliot is one among many eligible women who have eyes only for Wentworth, even if in the course of the volume this number dwindles from five to two. In the second volume the situation is reversed. Frederick Wentworth finds to his alarm and mounting despondency that he has a plausible rival in the suave figure of William Elliot, heir to Kellynch Hall, and Anne's changing fortune is closely tied to her recovery of 'bloom', and to a gain of social stature. Through Wentworth's eyes we see her transformed, moreover, from a self-effacing drudge to a paragon of steadiness and resolution, even before his final admission that she has been in the right and shown exceptional endurance all along. So fulsome, indeed, is Wentworth's confession of wrong and so pronounced his period of 'penance' that his change of heart closely approximates the radical humbling attributed to Austen's heroines by critics of the Anti-Jacobin school (242–3). At a time when war had conferred a premium on the male virtues of courage and daring, Jane Austen reopened debate on sexual roles, and put a number of current stereotypes of female prowess on trial. The rival figures of Anne Elliot and Louisa Musgrove are at the centre of this contest.

What Captain Wentworth's relation to Louisa lacks in substance it makes up in style. Their affinity is self-consciously fashioned round a concept, and the concept in question, as active in what it excludes as in what it upholds, is 'firmness'. This is easily read, on Wentworth's side, as a rationale for his angry exemption of Anne from his newly declared openness to all-comers, for it is, ironically, in reaction to Anne that his quest for the 'character of decision and firmness' begins. The 'feebleness' that he sees so graphically displayed in her surrender to 'over-persuasion', now defines a broad sense of incompatibility that backs his silent oath that her power over him is 'gone

---

[18] *Sir Charles Grandison*, III, 367–8; Dryden's refrain is from *Alexander's Feast*, line 15.

for ever', while throwing into relief his own 'decided, confident temper' (61–2). Louisa's commitment to an ideal of strength is more complex in origin. Though she has always been the 'more lively' of the Musgrove sisters, it is clear that her desire to be decisive dates from the start of her relationship to Wentworth. Her scorn for easily persuaded women, fully voiced in her disdainful dismissal of Henrietta, so exactly echoes Wentworth's that she *appears* to act as if in possession of his story. Though she is not privy to the secret of the broken engagement, the Musgroves' theory that it was Lady Russell who induced Anne to turn down the proposal of Charles before he married Mary goes some way to explain Louisa's zeal in this cause. But the fullest explanation is that she is quick to learn or intuit Wentworth's views, and that she prides herself on being his star pupil. It is she who draws out the account of his experiences on the *Asp*, and his audacity in this all-or-nothing enterprise clearly leaves on her, of all his enraptured audience, the most lasting impression. 'What! – would I be turned back from doing a thing that I had determined to do?', she pledges on the walk to Winthrop (87), and resoluteness soon becomes, for her, an end in itself. When the visit to Lyme is mooted, Louisa proves to be 'the most eager of the eager', not because she is the keenest to go, but because she is 'now armed with the idea of merit in maintaining her own way' (94). 'Armed' is a suggestive word here, for there is a distinct male slant to the lessons that Louisa receives. Take, for example, the cue that Wentworth supplies when he speculates, in the course of the November walk, on where Admiral Croft will upset his carriage that day: 'my sister makes nothing of it – she would be as lieve be tossed out as not'. Louisa, with characteristic generosity, throws herself into this caricatured role, declaring that if she herself loved a man as Mrs Croft loves the Admiral she 'would rather be overturned by him, than driven safely by anybody else' (85). We see at the chapter's end, however, that Mrs Croft, who is equally at home on land and sea, has other plans – when at risk from a post she takes the reins.

Captain Wentworth's ideal of firmness in women is riddled with contra-diction. On the one hand, he upholds the virtues of daring and resolution that he so handsomely exemplifies himself; on the other hand, he insists on the essential passivity of the fair sex. The paradox is well brought home in the run-up to his parable-like speech on the nut when he lets slip that the worst thing about a yielding disposition is that 'you are never sure of a good impression being durable' (88) – from which it appears that impressibility is what he is really after. Ironically, it is Anne's ability to stand up to him, as well as her constancy in love that makes her the obvious referent, from the reader's point of view, of the symbolic nut that survives the autumn. It never occurs to Wentworth to question whether his two principal requirements from a suitor – a 'strong mind' and 'sweetness of manner' – are necessarily compatible, or to settle which of the two has the prior claim (62). And it is significant in this connection that in the argument about accommodating women on voyages he takes an extreme line ('I hate to hear of women on board'), thus exposing himself to his sister's rebuke that he talks as if 'women were all fine ladies, instead of rational creatures' (70). There seems to be some authorial prescription in Mrs Croft's seagoing which is far in excess, as presented, both of custom and of law,[19] and Wentworth's promised curtailment of such practice shows that he is indeed inclined, for all his talk of 'firmness', to expect women to keep in 'smooth water' for all their days (69). It is telling, too, that he falls back, in his defence, on 'gallantry', that hackneyed notion of courtship so caustically portrayed in *Emma* as a sort of insidious predation on the becalmed. In the words of Mr Elton's charade: long may lovely woman reign, and reign alone – until wedded to one of the 'lords of earth', or to a 'monarch of the seas'.[20]

Though the attitudes that Jane Austen displays in Wentworth's courtship of Louisa are not likely to lose their relevance, they emerge all the richer in implication when examined in relation to their period. Scott's popular verse romances, which so richly illustrate the impact of the Napoleonic wars on sexual politics, provide a good starting-point. *Marmion*, the poem Jane sent to Charles at sea, is particularly apropos in view of the two antithetical heroines who flank its eponymous hero: on the one hand, the bold Constance, who is seduced away from a nunnery by Marmion and becomes his lover while disguised as his page; and on the other hand, the gentle Clare, whom he determines to marry for her money, after slandering and killing the man she loves. At the poem's opening, the broken-hearted Clare is about to become a nun, 'And shroud, within Saint Hilda's gloom / Her blasted hopes and withered bloom';[21] but she is threatened with worse than loss of bloom, when she again falls into the hands of Marmion. Strength is granted her in this extremity, however, and it comes from her good male blood:

> Descended to a feeble girl
> From Red De Clare, stout Gloster's Earl:
> Of such a stem, a sapling weak,
> He ne'er shall bend, although he break.[22]

---

[19] See pp. 70–1. It appears from Brian Southam's definitive discussion of women on board that Mrs Croft's perennial passaging would not only have been strictly illegal, but very unusual as well, see *Jane Austen and the Navy*, pp. 276–9, 284–5.

[20] *Emma*, p. 73, and see the discussion above, pp. 208–11.

[21] *Marmion*, II, v, p. 82.   [22] Ibid., VI, iv, p. 322.

Clare's share in Red's true warrior worth is never put to the test, for her lover proves to be alive after all and comes to her aid. But when Marmion is finally treated to a heroic death scene on Flodden Field, Clare is conscripted as a nurse, and selflessly tends the man who has abused her at every turn. In this role she is upheld as a model of her sex:

> O, Woman! in our hours of ease,
> Uncertain, coy, and hard to please,
> And variable as the shade
> By the light quivering aspen made;
> When pain and anguish wring the brow;
> A ministering angel thou! – [23]

Austen makes her own feelings about this passage quite clear in *Sanditon* when she has Sir Edward Denham, an updated Lovelace, exclaim over it 'Delicious! Delicious!', and pronounce Scott immortal.[24] But if the *gentle* female has her strength underwritten by association with male valour and by the claims of patrilineal descent, and can do, in fact, very well without strength at all, what of the opposite type? Constance who knocks about as a page, and does much of Marmion's dirty work in order to strengthen her hold over him, is the fallen angel, and pays the ultimate penalty in being described as 'fierce, and unfeminine'; despite being more sinned against than sinning, she is damned by circumstances that have 'steeled her brow, and armed her eyes'.[25] In short, the female who wishes to be strong is offered no real choice at all. Value attaches to male virtues, particularly those of a martial or stoic kind, but any visible approach to the manly is subject to instant dispraise. When Scott wishes to present a super-heroine such as the Highland girl of *The Lady of the Lake*, he comes up with a strange solution to the problem of how to inject stature into his feminine subject. The Hunter-King in an erotic dream of Ellen finds 'the phantom's sex' suddenly changed and the girl transformed into the armed and menacing figure of her father, the giant Douglas.[26] Patriarchal protection is not the issue here; Ellen is given added value by her fleeting embodiment of the heroic, as when she is caught in animated speech: '"Minstrel," the maid replied, and high / Her father's soul glanced from her eye.'[27] This male-engendering of the heroine is not simply ascribable to Scott's conservative politics; it is rooted in the historical fact of conflict, and something very similar to it is to be found in Shelley's *The Revolt of Islam*, where the revolutionary warrior, Laone, is

[23] Ibid., VI, xxxi, p. 362.   [24] *Minor Works*, p. 397.
[25] *Marmion*, III, xvii, p. 149.   [26] *The Lady of the Lake*, I, xxxiv, pp. 42–3.
[27] Ibid., II, xiii, p. 61.

a kind of female image of the hero Laon, who is by way of self-portrait.[28] But Scott's blatant patriotism gives an unusual transparency to his tactics in the verse romances, and explains why their heroines are so clearly ancillary. His aim, as he ingenuously admits on returning to the present at the close of *Marmion*, is to supply 'A garland for the hero's crest, / And twined by her he loves the best'.[29]

It is at Lyme that Louisa's idea of female firmness is put to the test, and there is an unmistakably symbolic quality to the scene in which she jumps off the Cobb only to fall through Wentworth's hands. The jump which she refuses to be talked out of is given a thematic label by her cry, 'I am determined I will', and the scene enacts, almost choreographically, the quick undoing of the entangled threesome that has held centre stage. As a curtain-raiser to Louisa's leap and Wentworth's miscatch, the narrator brings in 'Lord Byron's "dark blue seas"' (109), which many readers would have placed as an allusion to *The Corsair*, a poem that Jane Austen had read in March 1814, and which had reached its sixth edition when Anne and Benwick hold their tête-à-tête eight months later.[30] The poem centres in the eclipse of a long-standing love by a rival whose charms suddenly prove short-lived, and it opens with a boisterous pirate song ('O'er the glad waters of the dark blue sea, / Our thoughts as boundless, and our souls as free') that foreshadows the bold heroine, Gulnare, who becomes a sort of honorary pirate herself after she has been rescued from the Pacha's seraglio by Conrad, the chief corsair, and has fallen in love with him.[31] Gulnare, in order to save Conrad from death and herself from reconfinement, murders her husband the Pacha, and in risking everything for her lover destroys their love, for Conrad, despite igniting Gulnare's rebellious spirit, is appalled – in the event – by its expression, and returns to his ever-devoted Medora. The turning-point in the relationship with Gulnare is reached when she sweeps aside his attempts to persuade her against the deed:

> But since the dagger suits thee less than brand,
> I'll try the firmness of a female hand.[32]

---

[28] See *The Revolt of Islam*, particularly V, lines 1882–90. Nigel Leask notes that Cythna is renamed after the hero just at the moment that she starts the revolt (from which Laon is debarred); see *British Romantic Writers and the East* (Cambridge, 1992), p. 132.

[29] *Marmion*, VI, 'L'Envoy', p. 377.

[30] The phrase also occurs in the second canto of *Childe Harold* (1812), but in *The Corsair* (1814), a poem that was still topical, it forms part of the opening line.

[31] *The Corsair*, I, 1–2; III, 510, *Lord Byron: The Complete Poetical Works*, ed. Jerome J. McGann, 6 vols. (1980–91), III, 150, 207.

[32] *The Corsair*, III, 380–1, *Works*, III, 202.

This couplet was all the more pivotal for appearing, in all contemporary editions, at the foot of a plate that showed Gulnare, dagger in hand, about to twist away from the shackled Conrad. The echo in it of Lady Macbeth's 'infirm of purpose! Give me the daggers' darkens the tone of Gulnare's bid for power, but Byron handles his headstrong heroine (whose name rhymes with 'dare')[33] with the utmost sympathy. He celebrates her rescue from the harem, and her maxim that love can only be experienced by the free,[34] showing that it is in defence of her freedom that she kills. Though as guilty as Cain, Gulnare is rational, whereas Conrad's reaction to the single incriminating spot of scarlet on her brow – more horrifying than anything he has met with in a lifetime of massacre and war – is bigoted: 'Blood he had viewed – could view unmoved – but then / It flowed in combat, or was shed by men!'[35] It is not Gulnare's moral licence so much as her freedom with gender that causes him to freeze and shudder in 'every creeping vein', and Byron with pointed sarcasm exposes his hero's double standard, even if perhaps, at the same time, his own.

A far cry from Scott's would-be homicidal Constance, upon whom the terrible judgement of being bricked into the nunnery wall seems to be visited almost as an act of poetic justice, Byron's transgressor emerges, after her desertion by Conrad, as a dignified, even tragic figure, and in the sequel to the tale achieves heroic stature in the male guise of Kaled, Lara's page, thereby erasing, in effect, the ignominy accorded to Marmion's 'unfeminine' page-companion. But what, then, did Jane Austen intend by her Byronic backdrop to Louisa's ill-starred leap? The answer seems to be twofold. For readers *un*familiar with *The Corsair* (posterity is mainly among them) the obvious inference is that Louisa comes a cropper to show up the consequences of an 'excessive romanticism'.[36] This is in line after all with Anne's warning to Benwick that in order to counter the effects of poetic despondency he should turn to prose to 'rouse and fortify the mind' (101). But for readers who knew the poem, the resemblance that arcs between Wentworth's amatory dilemma and the Corsair's would have been inescapable, however distant in feel the novel's domestic realism from the high adventure of the tale. The parallel is underlined by the distinctly Byronic cast that Austen gives her hero, who even shares a facial tic with the Corsair – a slight curl of the mouth that expresses scorn.[37] The scene on the Cobb unfolds a medley of Byronic motifs – leaps, strong arms, and

[33] *The Corsair*, II, 407–8; *Works*, III, 184.   [34] *The Corsair*, II, 502;. *Works*, III, 188.
[35] *The Corsair*, III, 428–9. *Works*, III, 204.   [36] John Halperin, *Life of Jane Austen* (1984), p. 303.
[37] See my article '*Persuasion*, Byron, and the Turkish Tale', *Review of English Studies*, 44 (1993), 65.

'lifeless' forms; and here the language, too, is given a Byronic twist, even down to the negatives and asyndeton that hallmark the early verse: 'There was no wound, no blood, no visible bruise; but her eyes were closed, she breathed not, her face was like death. – The horror of that moment to all who stood around!' (109). Though Austen was concerned to place the tales as emotionally indulgent (Anne and Benwick both see their histories mirrored in them, but the reflections prove unreliable), that was clearly not the end of the story.

While at work on *Persuasion*, Jane Austen copied out 'Napoleon's Farewell', the dramatic monologue penned by Byron shortly before the *Bellerophon* set sail for St Helena. Towards his hero Byron displays a measure of ambivalence, and the poem opens with the Emperor's admission that the 'gloom' of his Glory has 'o'ershadowed the earth', a view in keeping with his portrayal as a tyrant in *Childe Harold*, and in Pasley's much admired *Essay*.[38] From the perspective of the peace, Austen must have found much in Byron's tales that provided a welcome relief after the martial spirit of Scott's poems, particularly their partial eclipse of war by romance. Yet though erotic interest is central in them, political themes are always present – both western feudalism and oriental despotism come under fire, and private life is rendered throughout as acutely sensitive to the repercussions of social system.[39] The oppression of women is an especially salient concern. For Wollstonecraft – of whose work Byron was aware[40] – the harem repeatedly figures as a metaphor for the lot of women in English society, and the same transposal was made by figures as diverse as Richardson, Rousseau and Scott. Episodes such as the drowning of Leila in a sack from *The Giaour*, or the rescue of Gulnare from the burning seraglio in *The Corsair* are clearly intended, in context, to have a significance beyond the Turkish setting. But though Byron's concern with the emancipation of women is in earnest at this stage in his career – he was at the time courting the intellectual Anne Millbanke (who out-Harlowed Clarissa Harlowe)[41] – his view on what it comprises is almost diametrically opposed to that of Wollstonecraft. Where, for the author of the *Vindication*, exit from the harem entails a sexual fast, in the youthful Byron's scheme of things the harem gate opens onto the highway of grand passion. Where Wollstonecraft

[38] See Le Faye, *A Family Record*, p. 199. For *Childe Harold*, I, stanzas 15–16; *Works*, II, 16–7; and III, 312.
[39] Byron switches from Ottoman oppression in *The Giaour* to a European uprising of 'serfs' in *Lara*.
[40] Particularly through Christoph Meiners's *History of the Female Sex*, 4 vols. (1808), which Byron owned and referred to, see Caroline Franklin, *Byron's Heroines* (Oxford, 1992), pp. 102, 115–16.
[41] To Lady Melbourne, 5 Sept. 1813, *Byron's Letters and Journals*, ed. Leslie A. Marchand, 12 vols. (Cambridge, Mass., 1973–82), III, 108.

puts her reader under notice that she intends 'high treason against sentiment and high feelings',[42] and in particular dismisses lasting desire as a romantic shibboleth, the writer of the tales attaches a signal value to constancy. In sum, Byron attempts a consciously Romantic revision of Enlightenment feminism, in which love and freedom are paired. This involved him in rethinking the romance as practised by his chief contemporary model, Sir Walter Scott, who though he makes much of the warrior's power to attract, is tight-lipped about female desire itself, which ranks in his plots as a major source of transgression.

Byron's programme entailed experiment with new techniques: he had to find ways of suggesting the endurance of strong passion, to suggest its physical feel, and to convey the experience of loss. And for reasons that were not dissimilar Jane Austen faced related problems in *Persuasion*, and on them she brought greater resources to bear. Both writers found their own solutions to keeping alive scenes from far back in the past, and both refined on a representational impressionism that conveys a subjective immediacy.[43] It is in these directions that the main technical innovations of *Persuasion* lie, and Austen's success can be gauged from the praise of Maria Edgeworth, no admirer of *Emma*, who after singling out the novel's exceptionally vivid portrayal of 'the love and lover' exclaimed over the scene in which Wentworth at Uppercross comes to the aid of the climbed-upon Anne: 'don't you see Captain Wentworth, or rather don't you in her place feel him taking the boisterous child off her back as she kneels by the sick boy on the sofa'.[44] That second thought, 'or rather don't you in her place feel', goes to the heart of what is most distinctive about *Persuasion*, for it points not only to the way so much of the action is filtered through Anne, but also to the unusually physiological quality of that registration. Many of the intensest scenes pass with few words, and a notation of bodily signs doubles with – at times almost displacing – the summary of mental states. Where complexions in *Sense and Sensibility* tend to come, like eggs, in white or brown, the hues of *Persuasion* are ever-fluctuating, and at moments of crisis Anne is typically caught in a whirl of conflicting sensation.

Louisa and Gulnare are alike in aspiring to fulfil a masculine ideal of daring, only to be dropped by the male who has inspired their efforts.

---

[42] *Vindication*, p. 98; and see the whole of chapters 2 and 3, 'The Prevailing Opinion of a Sexual Character Discussed'. For an account of Wollstonecraft's asceticism in the *Vindication*, and of her changing attitudes towards sexuality over the course of her career, see Janet Todd's fine introduction to *Political Writings*, especially pp. xix–xxvi.

[43] For a fuller discussion see my article '*Persuasion*, Byron, and the Turkish Tale'.

[44] Southam, ed., *Critical Heritage*, [1], p. 17.

But where Austen shows how dangerously self-conscious Louisa is about Wentworth's regard, to the point of betraying a Tinkerbell-like dependence on him, Byron takes such male-centredness for granted. Like Louisa who becomes limp and hypersensitive after her accident – her brother bluffly likens her jerky movements to a dabchick's, Gulnare falls prey to spells of fear that leave her 'faint and meek', and her loss of nerve proves infectious:

> He clasped that hand – it trembled – and his own
> Had lost its firmness, and his voice its tone.[45]

Neither heroine lives up to the boast of being firm, but none of Byron's, in the absence of their lovers, ever do, for the reason that love, to quote one of his later heroines, is 'woman's whole existence'.[46] Medora after much languishing and fainting, dies of grief just before Conrad's return; and even in the male persona of Kaled, Gulnare expires after refusing to leave the spot where Lara was killed in battle. Anne Elliot, on the other hand, endures, regardless of all, and it is she who makes the claim that men in love are more self-centred than women, when she tells Harville that male constancy lasts for as long as 'the woman you love lives, and lives for you' (235).

In *Persuasion* it is surely as a corrective to this male bias that men are kept out of the picture as much as possible when it comes to demonstrating the strength of women. True 'firmness' is typically exemplified, throughout, at the expense of men, in competition with men, in unawareness of men, or simply in their absence. So Anne's breaking of the engagement runs counter to Wentworth's will; her calm and effective management of the accident at the Cobb is thrown into relief by his ineptitude there; and even the pungency and persistence of her feelings for him are independent of his presence – true to her sex, she can love 'when existence or when hope is gone'. Though Anne learns to exert herself and keep her feelings in check, her gentle manner is belied by the intensity with which she feels, and her power as a character has everything to do with inner intransigence – ultimately, with Austen's masterly dramatization of the conflict that this dictates. The headlong clash between feelings that remain unchanged and circumstances that appear wholly irrecoverable is realized through the jar of continuous and pluperfect tenses, kept up for a scene at a time, as in the aftermath to the couple's first remeeting (60–1).[47] Occasionally the

---

[45] *The Corsair*, III, 533, 539–40; *Works*, III, 208.   [46] See *Don Juan*, I, 1545–52, *Works*, V, 71.

[47] Though in a different context, the affective value of 'expanded verbs' in *Persuasion* is commented on by K. C. Phillipps in *Jane Austen's English* (1970), pp. 112–15.

pluperfect takes on a continuous form itself, underlining the monotony of domestic routines: 'Here Anne had often been staying' (36); 'She had never been staying there before, without . . .' (42). Sense, in the last instance, requires no more than a 'there she had always . . .', but this is to reckon without the affective value of the word 'never' which, after making a double bow in the opening sentence of the novel, haunts its first few chapters. 'Never' points, in this context, to a social ambience that excludes what is most real for Anne with utter finality. The world in which Sir Walter *never* takes up any book but the Baronetage, Lady Russell *never* wishes the past undone, or the hoped-for guest *never* arrives, is the world in which Anne is *never* considered by others, and her love of Wentworth *never* admitted (3, 29, 8, 12, 31). Beyond that world Austen shows another which corresponds to Anne's desires – a place of small, hand-fitted, cabin-like rooms, but from this warmer sphere evoked by the Crofts and by the household at Lyme, Anne is ejected by a subjunctive – 'these would have been all my friends' (98). Anne's passion may originate in feelings of dependence, but its survival is a triumph of self-containment. Finally, the perspective on self-reliance is widened when the novel unfolds (retrospectively and in breach of narrative convention) the portraits of two further resilient women – Mrs Smith and Nurse Rooke – who have learnt, not without hardship, to make a life of their own outside marriage.

In pursuing these directions, Austen aligns herself with many of the goals of Enlightenment feminism, and if her emphasis is in some respects strikingly unorthodox, there can be no doubt that this was the tradition out of which her perceptions grew. The insistence in *The Watsons* on the importance of the material basis of women's welfare puts paid to the canard that Austen was a Tory feminist – conservative writers were particularly reticent on this score, and Emma Watson's attack on her brother's remark that 'a woman should never be trusted with money' and her stout defence of her uncle's open legacy to her stepmother as 'most Liberal & enlightened' speaks for itself (351–2). We have seen, in any case, that these allegiances stretch far back in her career. The feminism of *Persuasion*, however, stands in such oblique relation to the classical discourse of the nineties, that it is perhaps best described as post-Enlightenment in its bearing.

Mary Wollstonecraft had argued in a famous passage from the *Vindication* that it was 'want of firmness' that stood in the way of women realizing themselves as 'rational creatures'.[48] Women are soft, she declares, for the same reason that the wealthy and great are supine – through being spared

---

[48] *Vindication*, pp. 125–6.

exertion and receiving the approbation of their fellows as their automatic due. They are the casualties of a social construction that has denied them the right to be challenged, and the remedy she proposes is a severe moratorium on the pleasures of the senses. Love and the cultivation of fine-feeling are included here, as they too are integral to a stereotype that has the overall effect of confining consciousness. Above all, in order to redress these culturally imposed limitations, women have to recuperate qualities that have traditionally been the preserve of men.

Jane Austen's continuity with Wollstonecraft in *Persuasion* is evident in the language Mrs Croft uses when she tries to convince her brother that women have a place on naval voyages; her brusque dismissal of 'idle refinement', and of the 'fine gentleman', and the distinction she draws between 'fine ladies' and 'rational creatures' breathe the air of the *Vindication* (69–71). When she goes on, moreover, to attribute all the 'imaginary complaints' she suffered at Deal to her lack of occupation during her period of forced separation from her husband there, her diagnosis finds a suitable subject in the valetudinarianism of the indolent Mary Musgrove, giving her views a truth within the text. Mrs Croft's robust presence and physical vigour (she walks until her feet blister), together with her readiness to take control – her adjustment to the Admiral's reins is 'no bad representation of the general guidance of their affairs' (92) – belong to the liberated woman of the 1790s (she is older than Frederick), and nowhere are Wollstonecraft's precepts more compellingly embodied. Anne's much quoted remarks on the relative confinement of women and the educational disadvantage of her sex are also of the Enlightenment, while her remark on the pen having been in men's hands goes back, as we have seen, to the old Steventon days of the family production of Susanna Centlivre's Whig and feminist play, *The Wonder*. But Jane Austen pursues her concern with women's independence into territory that had scarcely been touched by the Enlightenment – or darkened (as some might have it) by the enshrinement of reason and male achievement.

Nursing, as John Wiltshire has shown, is an important activity in *Persuasion*.[49] Anne is conscripted into the role of nurse at Uppercross when Mary's eldest son dislocates his collar-bone; later she takes control of the accident at Lyme, and prepares to nurse Louisa at the Harvilles'. That job falls, however, to Mrs Harville ('a very experienced nurse', 113), and then to Sarah, the retired nurserymaid of the Musgrove family, 'now living in her deserted nursery to mend stockings, and dress all the blains and bruises she could

---

[49] John Wiltshire, *Jane Austen and the Body* (Cambridge, 1992), pp. 165–70.

get near to her' (122). Finally we hear of Mrs Smith nursing herself through a period of grave illness with the help of Miss Rooke, a professional working at Bath. Jane Austen knew that nursing was regarded as an exclusively female pursuit, and was also conscious, as we have seen, that ministering angels were very much to the male chauvinist's taste. But she was aware, too, that it was a socially slighted and much under-appreciated vocation. And in *Persuasion* she turns to the stereotype of the nursing woman, determined not only to dignify it, and even to invest it on occasion with glamour, but to fashion it into an icon of female strength.

This preoccupation chimes in with the view expressed by Thomas Gisborne (whom Austen read with approval)[50] that both those who suffer illness and those who tend the ill constitute a sort of home-front engaged in a fight that calls for powers of endurance to rival those readily acclaimed in the military sphere. 'Fortitude', he writes, 'is not to be sought merely on the rampart, on the deck, on the field of battle. Its place is no less in the chamber of sickness and pain, in the retirements of anxiety, of grief, and of disappointment.'[51] Even the wording of this passage is echoed by Anne Elliot, as Stuart Tave has pointed out, when she wonders out loud, in the presence of Mrs Smith, on all the instances of 'heroism, fortitude, patience, and resignation' that the 'sick chamber' is witness to. Mrs Smith instantly qualifies Anne's idealism by remarking that it is the weakness of human nature rather than 'its strength that appears in a sick chamber', so adding a touch of sceptical materialism to Gisborne's Evangelical belief in the redemptive quality of experiential extremes (156). But Mrs Smith herself, confined to a 'noisy parlour, and a dark bed-room behind' and unable to move in her illness, is living proof that such capacity exists:

this was not a case of fortitude or of resignation only. – A submissive spirit might be patient, a strong understanding would supply resolution, but here was something more; here was that elasticity of mind, that disposition to be comforted, that power of turning readily from evil to good, and of finding employment which carried her out of herself, which was from Nature alone. It was the choicest gift of Heaven. (154)

There is no more pious moment in Austen's work, but the language, though raised, remains idiomatic – as natural as Mrs Smith's gift which is itself true to the old credo *nihil in intellectu nisi prius in sensu*. When Wentworth earlier makes his speech on the nut, and warns Louisa that life holds circumstances

---

50 To Cassandra, 30 Aug. 1805, *Letters*, p. 112.
51 Thomas Gisborne, *An Enquiry into the Duties of the Female Sex* (1797), p. 25. Quoted by Stuart Tave, *Some Words of Jane Austen* (1973), pp. 283–4.

that demand 'fortitude and strength of mind', the reader silently weighs Anne's ill-fated moment of persuasion against his own success in rising to the challenges of war. The fortitude of Mrs Smith mediates Anne's submission by demonstrating that patience and resolution can go hand in hand.

The active side of nursing is brought out, however, in the aftermath to the accident at Lyme, when Anne makes all the arrangements and takes Louisa under her charge. The moment at which she arrives at authority is also the moment Wentworth recovers his feelings for her:

'You will stay, I am sure; you will stay and nurse her;' cried he, turning to her and speaking with a glow, and yet a gentleness, which seemed almost restoring the past. – She coloured deeply; and he recollected himself, and moved away. (114)

By this stage, however, the role of nurse has undergone a change of uniform, for we are told, only a few pages before, of how Wentworth sped down to Plymouth (without proper leave) to break the news of Fanny Harville's death to Benwick on his first return to port, and of how he spent a week there comforting his friend (108). Earlier his tenderness towards Mrs Musgrove (not the readiest object of sympathy as she sighs over her lost son on the sofa), and his repeated sensitivity to Anne's physical condition, both at Uppercross and on the walk to Winthrop, have shown a caring nature under the mask of anger or irritation. So we see the navy in its 'domestic' guise conspicuously following the conventionally female pursuit of nursing, and sharing, too, in some of its hazards. It is while nursing Louisa that Benwick falls in love with her; and just before breaking the news of their engagement, Mary reports that she and Mrs Harville have come to 'love [Louisa] the better for having nursed her' – as it proves in his case (165, 167). So Benwick turns upside-down the chaste nursing of the dying Marmion by Clare in his beloved Scott, and turns back to front – inverting only the gender – the amorous nursing of Medoro by Angelica in *Orlando Furioso*, Scott's more robust source: 'Her wound to heal there was no herb or art.'[52] On shore, the navy show a healthy lack of self-consciousness about the constraints of gender. Harville, in the snug cabin that he constructs for his family at Lyme (the otherness of land to sailors is one strand of a rich non-satiric comedy in *Persuasion* altogether missed by Virginia Woolf),[53] brushes aside the strict boundaries allotted to age and sex by society such as we see it at Bath: 'He drew, he varnished, he carpented, he glued; he made toys for the children, he fashioned new netting-needles and pins with improvements;

[52] *Orlando Furioso*, trans. Sir John Harington, canto XIX, stanza 27, ed. R. Gottfried (1963), p. 173.
[53] In her famous essay Virginia Woolf complained that the comedy of this novel was comparatively dull and crude, 'Jane Austen', in *The Common Reader: First Series* (1962), pp. 180–1.

and if every thing else was done, sat down to his large fishing-net at one corner of the room' (99).

By way of answer to Wollstonecraft's doctrine of recuperation, Jane Austen finds sources of female strength that are *sui generis*, and while upholding women's active participation in the public world, celebrates men's domestic activities in the private one. Contrary to the austere rationalism of eighteenth-century feminists, she insists on the value of strong feeling, on the excitement of sexual attraction, and on the dignity of those who show the power to endure. To describe such a stance as post-Enlightened is at least to evade the charge, sometimes sweepingly made, that the Enlightenment itself was caught up in a 'dialectic', an inherent process of self-contradiction. The central thesis of this theory, which hails from Adorno and Horkheimer (out of Weber), has been stated succinctly: 'the permanent sign of enlightenment is domination over an objective external nature and a repressed internal nature'.[54] While the justice of this summation depends very much on what historiography selects from the eighteenth century as representative, there can be no denying that Wollstonecraft – as many of her admirers readily own – is among the figures who are most easily implicated in it.[55] In two persuasive and important early chapters of the *Vindication*, Wollstonecraft had attempted to account for sexual difference largely in terms of social construction,[56] and this vision, combined with an intact faith in revolutionary politics, inspired the hope that a radical *re*construction of sexual roles was possible on the lines of her rational plan. Such a confidence underlies her virtually total abrogation (at the level of polemic) of existing womanhood. Part of the strategy of the *Vindication*, indeed, is to insist on the towering distance between what is and what should be, so that in the same paragraph that singles out 'firmness' as a precondition 'allowing women to be rational creatures', Wollstonecraft speaks without qualification of the 'insignificancy' of the entire female sex.[57] Where the

---

[54] So Jürgen Habermas clinches the matter in his lecture, 'The Entwinement of Myth and Enlightenment: Max Horkheimer and Theodor Adorno', in *The Philosophical Discourse of Modernity* trans. Frederick Lawrence (Cambridge, 1987), p. 110.

[55] Janet Todd, for example, describes Wollstonecraft 'as undoubtedly caught in "the dialectic of enlightenment" to use the phrase of Adorno and Horkheimer', though the line of argument here is distinct from mine. See *Feminist Literary History* (Cambridge, 1988), pp. 110–11.

[56] *Vindication*, chs. 2 and 3, 'The Prevailing Opinion of a Sexual Character Discussed' and 'The Same Subject Continued'.

[57] *Vindication*, p. 126. A quite different picture emerges from the posthumously published *The Wrongs of Woman* (1798) where Wollstonecraft not only celebrates 'the culture of the heart', and attacks 'coldness of constitution, and want of passion', but also addresses such practical and ameliorative issues as legal equality and professions for women; see '*Mary*' *and* '*The Wrongs of Woman*', pp. 115, 153, 159, 148.

ideal exists in outright opposition to the real, those who live by it are indeed at risk from the nemesis eagerly foretold by the Frankfurt school: a return of the repressed.

It has been the thesis of this book that Jane Austen belonged to a partic-ular tradition within the Enlightenment, to what I have called its sceptical branch, and within this tradition the strictures of Adorno and Horkheimer can find little hold, chiefly because such criticism was already deeply ingrained in the Anglo-Scottish school which not only reacted against rationalism and related idealisms, but sought to find a logic in the real world, in the hope of changing it for the better. The forces of unreason are a central fact to the chief thinkers in this school, but the remedy proposed is not suppression, but rather a practised reckoning on the limitations of reason and of will. These dispositions are integral to Jane Austen's work, and integral, too, to the many fields of interest on which she drew. In her early encounter with the theory of the picturesque, she found a model of relation based on reconciliation with external nature rather than on dom-ination over it. Through her knowledge of the moral philosophers, she developed the sense that conscience was rooted in the complex workings of the psyche, and that judgement was refined by the modalities of social relation and had to be learnt, by degrees, like a skill. Her wide reading in the new liberal history reinforced her instinctive distrust of one-sided, mythological interpretation, and of precisely that sort of received ideology termed 'instrumental reason' by the Frankfurt school. This background placed Jane Austen at some distance from the majority of her fellow novel-ists, and more especially from those who took themselves seriously. She was disinclined to provide 'pictures of perfection', disinclined, too, to exhort or to lay down rules. But her lack of idealism not only enabled her to deliver a real world, but to restore to it a zest and bloom that rationalism had all but bleached away.

CHAPTER 9

Sanditon *and speculation*

Mr Parker, the arch-speculator whose dream it is to make Sanditon famous, is a figure of fun, but that can be said of almost all the characters (even Charlotte Heywood's understated good sense is at times comic) in a work more farcical and fantastic than anything Austen had conceived since *Volume the Third*. The speculator, to the eyes of the classical economist, is the chancer who overreaches in the hope of spectacular returns, the quack among entrepreneurs.[1] But during the war, and especially after Waterloo, property developers like Mr Parker were the order of the day, and often managed to get by, even if profits (as in the case of Regent Street) were very slow in coming.[2] How Sanditon's inauspicious beginnings are to pan out is far from clear. Tom Parker pins his hopes on the residency of his charismatic younger brother, but since the manuscript, known to Cassandra as 'The Brothers', ends before Sidney Parker ever speaks in person, the reader, too, is left guessing.

Critics in search of a controlling theme have mostly fixed on the contrast between the bustling enterprise of the town-planners and the quiet traditional life of the landed gentry as practised by the Heywoods at Willingden, and indeed by the Parkers themselves before they uproot to resettle on the exposed, sea side of their sheltering hill. Critics of the Anti-Jacobin school present this contrast in black and white, reading *Sanditon* as a last return to the Burkean vision of an organic community threatened by the selfishness and fragmentation that follow in the wake of 'improvement'.[3] If this is a solemn brief for a text so full of comic relish for the zany and the odd, at least the stress on social change rings true. Austen gives unexpected weight

---

[1] See Adam Smith's description of the type in *WN*, I.x.b.38, 130.
[2] Thirteen new spa resorts sprang up between 1800 and 1809, and another five were established by 1815 (*Sanditon* is set after Waterloo, though work on the resort has begun some years before); see Phyllis Hembury, *The English Spa, 1560–1815* (1990), pp. 310–11. Though the building of Regent Street was well under way by 1813, it was only after many setbacks that rent started coming in, and not before 1819 that huge debts began to be paid off regularly.
[3] See, for example, Butler, *War of Ideas*, pp. 286–9.

to the detailed apologies that Mr Parker advances for his schemes. Accused first by Mr Heywood and later by Lady Denham, his co-speculator, of attracting rich visitors to the resort who will have the effect of raising the prices of local produce, Mr Parker replies that such wealth can only act as a stimulus to the prosperity of the community as a whole (368, 392). Lady Denham, if a bit put out by the technicalities, is soothed by his assurance that the rich

'can only raise the price of consumeable Articles, by such an extraordinary Demand for them & such a diffusion of Money among us, as must do us more Good than harm. – Our Butchers & Bakers & Traders in general cannot get rich without bringing Prosperity to *us*. If *they* do not gain, our rents must be insecure – & in proportion to their profit must be ours eventually in the increased value of our Houses.' 'Oh! – well. – But I should not like to have Butcher's meat raised, though – & I shall keep it down as long as I can.' (392–3)

The theory that an increase in the money supply eventually works to the benefit of all was most famously stated by David Hume in his essay 'Of Money', which offers the premiss, 'Encrease the commodities, they become cheaper; encrease the money, they rise in their value.'[4] When Mr Parker predicts that 'the demand for every thing [will] excite the industry of the Poor and diffuse comfort & improvement among them of every sort' (368), he echoes Hume on the way an inflow of wealth 'keeps alive a spirit of industry in the nation', and exerts a transforming influence on society as a whole:

Accordingly we find, that, in every kingdom, into which money begins to flow in greater abundance than formerly, every thing takes a new face: labour and industry gain life; the merchant becomes more enterprising, the manufacturer more diligent and skilful, and even the farmer follows his plough with greater alacrity and attention . . . It is easy to trace the money in its progress through the whole commonwealth; where we shall find, that it must first quicken the diligence of every individual, before it encrease the price of labour.[5]

On this view, wages rise; and there lies the nub of Lady Denham's contention with Mr Parker, for her motive in contributing to his scheme is solely to maintain her set-up at Sanditon House where she employs an

---

4 Hume, 'Of Money', in *Essays Moral, Political and Literary*, I, 313, 316. The same case had more recently been argued by Malthus defending the Corn Laws in his pamphlet *An Inquiry into the Nature and Progress of Rent* (1815). There he specifically points out that 'an increase in the price of agricultural produce' will ultimately improve the value of property. But this part of his argument stems from the mainstream of political economy and was quite separable from his support of protectionism.

5 David Hume, 'Of Money', in *Essays*, I, 315, 313–14. A more complicated picture emerges, however, when Hume goes on to consider international trade.

army of servants on a budget she is determined to freeze, despite her great wealth (393). With this aim she hits on the curious expedient of keeping her housemaids relatively inactive in the hope that they will not ask for more (401), so that idleness is the end result of her economy. Her constant annoyance at Mr Parker's expenditure, and her objection that a doctor-in-residence will cause her 'Servants & the Poor to fancy themselves ill' reveal her to be no real Speculator at all, but rather (as Charlotte sees) one of the 'sordid' rich, determined to preserve her life of privilege at any cost (393, 402).

But what, then, of the 'notional older way' that Butler claims Austen to be defending in *Sanditon*? Where are the representatives of the 'inherited organic community reminiscent of the imaginative construct made by Burke'?[6] Decent and likeable the inheritors of Willingden certainly are, but the attitude Mr Heywood displays towards the new seaside resorts differs little from Lady Denham's: 'Bad things for a Country; – sure to raise the price of Provisions & make the Poor good for nothing' (368) – a response even less attractive for its hint that the poor will be spoilt by being better off. If anybody in the neighbourhood is committed to the cause of stewardship and community it is surely Mr Parker. We see him going out of his way to give his custom to those he has set up in business, to the extent of buying vegetables both from Lady Denham's gardener, Andrew, and from 'old Stringer & his son' who are struggling to establish themselves as grocers (381–2). We learn of the villagers of Sanditon almost exclusively through his speech, and his worries over their welfare are typified by the subscription he raises for the impoverished Mullinses, for which he tries to get the backing of Lady Denham who '*can* give, if she is properly attacked' (423–4).

Bifocal to the last, Jane Austen leaves us under no illusions about the superficiality and callowness that lie at the other side of Mr Parker's ingenuous good-nature. His reach-me-down equation of civilization with 'Blue Shoes, & nankin Boots' (383), and the pomp with which he conducts the 'prais[ing] and puff[ing]' part of his duties make him a prototype of PR in days when the commodity culture and service economy still had a long way to run. On the other hand, the home-bound Heywoods, even though they supply a perfect foil to the frenzied Parkers, are not at all easily taken for moral standard-bearers, as Roger Gard has shrewdly observed.[7] Their energies have gone into perpetuating what they have, and with fourteen children on their hands (a tally beyond 'reasonable Limits') they have grown 'older in Habits than in Age', while the twice-noted disrepair of their roads

---

[6] Butler, *War of Ideas*, p. 287.   [7] Gard, *Novels*, ch. 9, particularly p. 211.

(on which the Parkers overturn) together with their 'old' horse, suggest little interest in sociability (373–4). Their wisest decision is to encourage the children to get away whenever they can, and Charlotte's exhilaration on arriving at the coast is shared by the text itself which (unlike Mrs Parker) gives no fond backward glance at the Parkers' old estate, or at Willingden either. Installed in her room, Charlotte enjoys a feeling of release when she gazes over 'unfinished Buildings, waving Linen, & tops of Houses, to the Sea, dancing & sparkling in Sunshine and Freshness' (384). And though Mr Parker's instant longing 'to be on the Sands, the Cliffs, at his own House, & everywhere out of his House at once' (384) can only fall short of fulfilment (like much else about his project), his happiness is both genuine and infectious.

The hypochondria of the invalid part of the Parker family has often been cited as proof of Sanditon's decadence and of Austen's distaste for Regency culture *tout court*, but this is to muddle symptom and cause, for the Parker malaise long predates the recent move from their old country house where it showed as 'an early tendency', along with the taste for 'quack' medicine (412). Its psychological roots run deep in the economy of the landed gentry in fact.[8] With the connivance of his sisters, 'lusty' Arthur, the youngest son, has dealt with the problem of finding a profession by declaring himself delicate and choosing to 'sit down at 1 & 20, on the interest of his own little Fortune, without any idea of attempting to improve it, or of engaging in any occupation that may be of use to himself or others' (388). In this he is well matched with (and was perhaps intended for) the cosseted Miss Lambe, who, as a West Indian heiress, is 'as helpless & indolent, as Wealth & a Hot Climate are apt to make us' (409). Diana Parker, on the other hand, born with great energy of mind but suffering from 'want of employment' (412), finds a vent for her talents in activity that reads rather like a parody of her brother's speculation. She conjures up the ailments she sets out to annihilate, where Thomas is for ever talking up what he creates.

But the Parkers' quackery is, in any case, diametrically opposed to what might be described as the ideology of the coastal resort. And here they are foreshadowed by Austen's most famous valetudinarian, Mr Woodhouse, who keeps Emma from sight of the sea (where she plans to honeymoon) on the grounds that it spells death (101). Refusing at first to consider Sanditon for the same reason, the invalid Parkers, once settled there, huddle round

---

[8] Compare with this Adam Smith on the indolence to which the landed gentry are subject, and on the ills of primogeniture: *WN*, I.xi.p.8, III.ii.3–4.

a fire at the back of their quarters on a fine day, busily fending off the assaults of nature. Charlotte, on a visit, can hardly resist throwing open the window and putting out the fire, but makes do with praise of sea-breezes, all the more 'wholesome & invigorating' when taken with exercise (415). Such advice is a chief article of faith for Mr Parker who subscribes wholesale to the eighteenth-century medical dogma that was largely responsible for inspiring the seaside craze. The dogma has been well described as 'natural medicine', and its founder, a Dr Richard Russell of Brighton, later to be nicknamed 'l'inventeur de la mer' by Michelet, caught the ear of the public when he declared in 1752 that 'Nature cures many diseases by her own Power', in which process the sea had a central role.[9] Russell's work presents a curious blend of good sense (fresh air and food) and superstition – some of his cures read like a witches' brew (crab eyes and 'prepared woodlice'). But medicine underwent considerable progress in the second half of the century, and an aftercomer like Dr Robert White who queried some of the more doctrinaire aspects of the seaside cure (such as the universal benefits of icy water) also took pains to clear himself of all suspicion of snake-oil. Writing in 1796, White celebrates those 'applications which are known most to assist, and least to interrupt the effects of nature', and, while keeping this principle intact, consigns 'chimerical ideas' to a previous era dominated by 'the meanest quacks, and the most ignorant pretenders'.[10] A recent critic has argued that it is from an Augustan viewpoint that Jane Austen satirizes newfangled Romantic attitudes to the body in *Sanditon*,[11] but the quackery of the Parkers is made to seem backward-looking, and Charlotte's breezy dismissal of it is not so much moral as empirical. When Arthur complains that two cups of green tea have the effect of paralysing his right side, Charlotte dryly refers the matter to 'those who have studied right sides & Green Tea scientifically & thoroughly understand all the possibilities of their action on each other' (418).

Sanditon has been used, time and again, to cap the argument that Jane Austen was an eighteenth-century throwback who stood out against the taste for Romanticism in so far as she dared.[12] Where the argument

---

[9] Richard Russell, *A Dissertation on the Use of Sea Water*, 6th edn (1769), p. 32.

[10] Robert White, *Practical Surgery*, 2nd edn (1796), iv, vii; see also his *The Use and Abuse of Sea-Water* (1775). Praise of sea air goes back to Russell, but was given a whole chapter by Dr Anthony Relhan in the first Brighton guide, *A Short History of Brighthelmston* (1761). Jane Austen was herself a keen bather (and a great believer in the virtues of fresh air), see particularly her letter to Cassandra from Lyme, 14 Sept. 1804, *Letters*, p. 95.

[11] Wiltshire, *Jane Austen and the Body*, pp. 215–18.

[12] Butler remarks that the pressure on her, 'by now', to change her style could not be altogether resisted, *War of Ideas*, p. 290.

generally goes wrong is in assuming that Austen's chief debt to the past is to a tradition of rural nostalgia, rather than to the sceptical Enlightenment of her formative years, and the continuity of that vigorous movement passes unobserved in consequence. In fact the rise of the seaside resort through the latter half of the century and its great popularity in Regency times mark out an area of affinity between the Enlightenment and Romanticism, and in this space Jane Austen was evidently very much at home. Though Sir Edward Denham epitomizes almost every *un*enlightened brand of Romanticism with his vaunted amorality, his downgrading of sympathy and cavalier disregard for female rights, his praise of the sea nevertheless impresses Charlotte until she is put off by the number and inaccuracy of his literary citations. But his words on this topic (which would ordinarily show him to be a 'Man of Feeling') are of the kind inspired by Addison's much cited *Spectator* piece on the sublime ocean, a rhapsody which seems to have marked a decisive moment in the aesthetic recovery of the sea.[13] Natural religion, as voiced early on by Shaftesbury, fired up this cult which led by an easy transition to the habit of reverencing or at least admiring nature. Confidence in the healing properties of the sea was also originally founded on the premiss of providential design, and it too survived into an age of increasing secularism; with the result that the resort became an institution geared to pleasure-seeking, and a veritable Enlightenment icon. Circulating libraries, theatres, baths, assembly rooms, and specialist shops spoke to a public that believed that improvement and enjoyment went hand in hand, even if the bond was largely an imaginary one. Though there was much for Jane Austen to criticize in the triviality of seaside culture, the ethos of *Sanditon* seems especially secular – seldom elsewhere do twelve chapters pass with only the most cursory mention of the church or clergy.

Enlightened Romanticism found one of its most eloquent exponents in the painter John Constable, whose letters show him drawing simultaneously on belief in the immanence of the divine and on science as a principal means of unfolding the natural world. His famous skyscapes were preceded by a study of Luke Howard's (Linnaean) classification of clouds; and he saw his own desire to 'get at nature most surely' as analogous to that of the empiricist: 'Why', he asks, 'may not landscape painting be considered as a

---

[13] *Spectator*, no. 489, 20 Sept. 1712. See Alain Corbin, *The Lure of the Sea*, trans. Jocelyn Phelps (Oxford, 1994), ch. 2, 'The First Steps towards Admiration', especially pp. 43–50 and 122–4. See also John K. Walton, *The English Seaside Resort: A Social History, 1750–1914* (New York, 1983), ch. 2; and Sarah Howell, *The Seaside* (1974).

branch of natural philosophy, of which pictures are but the experiments?'[14] Seaside places provided him with the material for two of his most innovative series (the Weymouth pictures of 1816, and the Brighton ones of 1824), and unsurprisingly the sea and its peopled shoreline are almost invariably the focus of attention. Like Constable, Jane Austen seems to have disliked the more fashionable resorts, but to have overcome at the same time any limiting notion of the picturesque. For her, as for him, it was the sea that made the seaside,[15] and her natural description is at its tautest when dealing with it; yet such moments are replete with human interest also. In *Persuasion* the same paragraph that applies the words 'romantic' and 'wonderful' to the coast round Lyme presents the town itself, during its annual season, as 'animated with bathing machines and company' (95). And though post-Romantic eyes are inclined to disregard the yearly livening up of the old part of Sanditon (383), the intention here is unmistakably the same. Indeed, throughout her career Jane Austen linked the seaside with the sensuous and erotic. In *Pride and Prejudice* a fantasy of sea-bathing at Brighton topples into comedy when Lydia goes on to imagine row upon row of military tents 'stretched forth in beauteous uniformity of lines' (232). Fanny in *Mansfield Park* becomes unaccustomedly conscious of a dizzying light-headedness when, walking on Henry's arm at Portsmouth, she watches 'the ever-varying hues of the sea now at high water, dancing in its glee and dashing against the ramparts with so fine a sound' (409, 415). And in *Persuasion* Anne recovers her bloom at Lyme where she is held spellbound on the shore ('as all must linger and gaze on a first return to the sea, who ever deserve to look on it at all', 96), and where the varied directions of the breeze, light, and tide over the shallow bay are evoked with a precision and a suggestiveness worthy of Constable (102).

Sanditon is famous for the atmosphere of its setting, but the handling of its air and light is more strategic than has been recognized. Austen paints a single extensive landscape of beach, cliff, slopes and valleys, joined up, as never before, by devices such as the remarkably realized coach-journey from Willingden, Mr Parker's panoramic sketch of the coastline, and his account of the way storms ride in from the sea. The staple scene-setter, however, is the 'Sanditon Breeze', which begins satirically enough as part of Tom Parker's 'puff' and mingles mischievously with Sidney Parker's 'fashionable air'

---

[14] 'Painting is a science, and should be pursued as an inquiry into the laws of nature . . .' See C. R. Leslie, *Memoirs of the Life of John Constable*, 2nd edn (Oxford, 1980), p. 323.

[15] See To Cassandra, 14–15 Oct. 1813, *Letters*, p. 239.

(expected to be as beneficial in its effects), but which soon becomes real and fresh, taking on a life of its own when Charlotte is greeted by 'waving Linen' after breasting the 'health-breathing Hill' (383). Indeed the health-bringing Charlotte becomes a sort of personification of the breeze, relishing a two-hour walk even when it rises to the 'very fine wind' that keeps young Arthur muffled and indoors (406–7).

 A score of references to different kinds of breeze keeps the air in perpetual motion around Sanditon, and contributes to a pervasive sense of airiness and brightness in which the town itself plays a part with its new architecture ('light elegant') and favoured white colour (curtains, gowns, ribbons). In her first draft Jane Austen described the sea as dancing 'under a Sunshiny Breeze',[16] and the tonality and sensation at which she aimed was often also the goal of the new so-called 'white painters', though Constable especially springs to mind.[17] Unlike Turner for whom the 'objects of nature' (as Hazlitt had it)[18] tend to be less important than the medium through which they are seen, Constable uses the light and the breeze to reveal. Through their scanning and raking, they become analogous to the interpretative imagination – arguably itself a theme of his more impressionistic work, where dots, scrapes, and blobs, when looked at out of context, defy all reading. Similarly, *Sanditon* shows, over and over again, just what meagre data are sufficient to spark cognition, and does so, often, in visual terms. When Charlotte and Mrs Parker peer through a morning mist on their way down to Sanditon House they see a form, coming uphill, which they take at successive moments to be a gig, a phaeton, and a tandem – anything from one horse to four (425). Later through denser mist and the palings of the park, Charlotte glimpses 'something White and Womanish' that she instantly seizes on as Clara – in the company of Sir Edward. For the reader a scintilla of doubt remains (Charlotte's reliance on the ribbons seems suspect), but the couple are made the more riveting by it, and round their identity the plot was clearly to turn.

 Because the illness that interrupted the writing of *Sanditon* was already of long standing, much of the fragment was probably written with the inkling that it would be left incomplete. This would explain why Jane Austen played up the comedy at the expense of narrative requirements, and turned her last piece into something of a coda. The main theme of *Sanditon* is quixotry – the speculator, the seducer, and the quack are (as much as Shakespeare's

---

[16] See *Fragment of a Novel*, ed. R. W. Chapman (Oxford, 1925), note to page 56.
[17] Kenneth Clark, *The Romantic Rebellion* (1973), p. 248.
[18] 'On Imitation', *The Complete Works*, ed. P. P. Howe, 21 vols. (1930–4), IV, 76.

threesome) of imagination all compact; but the theme develops in a fresh way while incorporating many old motifs. Sir Edward's addiction to ego-bolstering literature rings a new change upon the female quixotry that had long been in vogue. And the mercenary motives that underlie his plan to abduct Clara leave his heroic pretences threadbare, making a mockery of his scorn for the novel that deals in 'ordinary Occurrences' or his demand for a display of 'Human Nature with Grandeur' (403). In *Sanditon*, however, books are not the only things to inspire the imagination – newspapers, let-ters, and gossip do as well. From Tom Parker's opening attempt to impose his mental map of the wrong Willingden on the Heywoods' farm (so trans-forming a labourer's cottage into a surgery) numerous Shandean distortions follow, culminating in Diana Parker's multiplication of Mrs Griffiths's party into a Creole family from Surrey and a seminary from Camberwell (the idea dies so hard that she considers the coincidence of a doubling of names). These farcical sideshows illustrate a central insight into the power of the once-made-up mind, as well as into the very mixed nature of its contents. But it is through the robustly sensible Charlotte – the most *un*quixotic of characters – that the workings of suggestibility are most fully examined. We see her, after her visit to the circulating library, unable to 'separate the idea of a complete Heroine from Clara Brereton', despite her accustomed distrust of the 'spirit of Romance', and eager, too, to try out one cliché after another on Clara's situation at Sanditon House. Although Jane Austen presents the process as almost involuntary – showing just how invasive popular fiction is – there is nothing deterministic about her view of social stereotypes. Charlotte is sufficiently well read to be conscious of the formulaic nature of the figments she juggles with, and – rather like the narrator of *Northanger Abbey* – tests them until, rejecting most, she arrives at a more distinct sense of the relationship between Clara and Lady Denham. The cancelled formu-las help her to consolidate old and new observations, and so to assemble, by hit and miss, a relatively convincing account (391–2).

Aware that she is impressionable, Charlotte is quick to notice the work of fantasy in others, and to pinpoint, in particular, the imaginative sources of the Parkers' invalidism which include the romance ingredient, 'love of the Wonderful' (412). But since a 'love of Distinction' is at work in them too – a diagnosis recalling the *Loiterer* essay on affectation – their hypochon-dria seems to qualify as a strain of Sensibility. Diana Parker is both the funniest and most complex of latter-day Quixotes, however; and, while her hectic activity rests on no grander motive than 'the glory of doing more than anybody else', the stream of incongruous military metaphor released by her presence simultaneously underlines her energy and her lack of an appropriate role (412–14). In her last letters Jane Austen twice apostrophizes the 'Imagination' that she saw embodied in her capricious and quirky niece Fanny Knight;[19] and this fascination is reflected not only in her good-humoured treatment of even the most bizarre characters in *Sanditon*, but in the way Charlotte's intelligence is visibly bound up with her hunches and with her openness to different voices and points of view. A Victorian critic went too far when he declared that each of Austen's characters 'plays in one person many people', but a quotation he makes from *Pride and Prejudice* applies well to all the main figures: 'people themselves alter so much, that there is something new to be observed in them for ever' (43).[20] If Charlotte fails to get things right at first, it is because her reading of the world is dialectical, and depends, as all reading must, on stimulus as well as perception. The 'ever' of fiction is notional but the unfinished state of Charlotte's story (and the strange absence of any word about where it was to go) brings home the unusually open present tense of Jane Austen's fiction, showing how speculation – for characters and readers – prepares the ground for discovery and gives lustre to the real.

The most lasting accusation levelled against Austen by critics of the Anti-Jacobin school is that the war of ideas involved her in 'a campaign against subjectivity' that kept her exploration of consciousness continually in check.[21] The charge relies for its historical and formal credibility on comparison with first-person narratives that are by no means synonymous with 'Jacobin' fiction. It is in any case unfair, seeing that Jane Austen took the lead among third-person narrators in finding new ways to express the self. In company with Ann Radcliffe she refined the technique of free indirect speech, shifting it to a point where the line between character and narrator vanishes, and she also pioneered other modes of disclosure such as talking-to-the-self, and thinking-out-loud that look forward to the interior monologue.[22] She was attracted, too, by traditions (such as empiricist psychology, and the picturesque) that opened new vistas onto the socially uncovenanted self, while retaining a suspicion of those (like Evangelicalism) that underplayed the force of the instinctual. As a novelist she was forever pushing on the bounds of expression, and her attempts in *Persuasion* and *Sanditon* to convey the feel of physical sensation, prior to its mental tagging, place her among the founding figures of Impressionism.

---

[19] To Fanny Knight, 20 Feb. and 13 Mar. 1817, *Letters*, pp. 328–9, 333–4.
[20] Richard Simpson, in Southam, ed., *Critical Heritage*, [I], p. 250.
[21] Butler, *War of Ideas*, pp. 294, 296.
[22] For an example of each see *Sense and Sensibility*, pp. 165, 70.

Marilyn Butler was surely never on weaker ground than when she complained that Austen chose 'to omit the sensuous, the irrational, the involuntary' because she disapproved of such things.[23] In fact, Austen had less to fear on this score than her alleged opponents, for the two-tier system of morality that she shared with the sceptical Enlightenment took the whole self on board, salvaging social benefits from a range of human energies that had been sunk under the label of vice. She could afford to be less anxious about human conduct than those moralists who felt that the entire social fabric depended (according to creed) on revelation, reason, or benevolence. One of the less advertised features of her novels – particularly marked in the later ones – is the way recognition is tied to self-assertive acts. Whether it is Fanny Price discovering that she can act *in propria persona*, Emma suspending 'heroism of sentiment' to secure Knightley for herself, or Anne Elliot taking command at the Cobb, expressed desires make for clarity. Nor indeed could there be a more attractive or social brief for the realization of will than what Henry Tilney describes as the 'contract' of marriage.

Jane Austen was a mistress of 'the sensuous, the irrational, and involuntary': she represents them in her novels with unprecedented insight and skill. Not being content to rest there, however, she does so on her own mediative terms. In common with her Scottish mentors, she understood that a social tempering of the self was intrinsic to normal development, and that there was no moral refinement without self-command. Like them, too, she held that 'principles' were an indispensable guide to conduct, but that they were likely to be ineffectual in the absence of an acquired sensitivity to others.[24] While she coaxed her readers into a clear-eyed recognition of human voracity, stripping away what Adam Smith had called the veil of deceit, she shared his conviction that nature had not 'abandoned us entirely to the delusions of self-love'.[25] Her courtship plots allow her to highlight an unstable, formative phase of early adulthood (in *Sense and Sensibility* she speaks of the critical 'four years'),[26] and to focus on the convergence of the private and public, the instinctual and conventional in a way that keeps the theme of sociability in constant view. Indeed, her comedies have a double aspect that answers to the sceptical Enlightenment's two-tiered system in the human sciences. They revolve on an axis that has rival traditions at its poles, traditions that were united (like the warring ideas of Shaftesbury and Mandeville) by reference to a received nature that was mixed. On the

[23] Butler, *War of Ideas*, p. 295.   [24] See particularly *TMS*, III.3.22; III.5.1; also *EPM*, appendix 3.
[25] *TMS*, III.4.7, 159.   [26] *Sense and Sensibility*, p. 140.

one hand, courtship in her novels is the hunt for a partner, a competitive struggle in which status, reputation, and assets of all kinds play a decisive role. On the other hand, her plots celebrate personal choice, and her main characters uphold the 'natural' virtues when, disarmed of the wrong pride and of some illusion, they bond with each other and arrive at a clearer sense of their world. That Jane Austen stuck to her kind of comedy is no surprise for she knew how important it was in enabling her to combine faith in improvement with a severe realism. But she realized, too, that the way to finding a better self began with forgetting the self, and that there was no quicker route to that than laughter.

Select bibliography

Place of publication is London unless otherwise stated

UNPUBLISHED SOURCES

Austen, Charles, Diaries and Private Journals, National Maritime Museum, Greenwich, AUS/101–29.

Austen, Francis, 'Remarks on the Island of St Helena', National Maritime Museum, Greenwich, AUS/6, ff. 39–58.

Austen, Francis, Letters, National Maritime Museum, AUS/8.

Austen, Francis and Charles, Admiralty Papers, Public Record Office, ADM 37–53, passim.

East India Company's Court Books and Minutes, India Office.

Austen, James
  in the Austen-Leigh Archive in the Hampshire Record Office (HRO), 23M93/60/3/1–2:
    'Journal of a Tour through Hampshire to Salisbury'.
    Poems collected and transcribed by his son, including 'The Œconomy of Rural Life'.
  in the Chawton archive:
    Poems collected and transcribed by his son (distinct from the HRO collection, which it overlaps, though there are at times slight differences between versions).

Hancock, Tysoe Saul, Letterbook, British Library Add. MS 29,236.

Hastings, Warren, Hastings Papers, British Library Add. MS 29,125–76.

Knatchbull, Lady (née Fanny Knight), Diaries and Letters of Lady Knatchbull, Kent Archives Office, U951 F24/1–69; C102–9.

PRIMARY SOURCES

Abernethy, John, *Physiological Lectures* (1817).

Annual Register (1785–).

Anti-Jacobin (1797–).

Anti-Jacobin Review and Magazine (1798–).

Austen, Caroline, *Reminiscences of Caroline Austen*, introd. Deirdre Le Faye (Overton, Hants., 1986).

Austen, Henry, *Lectures upon Some Important Passages in the Book of Genesis* (1820). *A Sermon in Aid of the Fund Raising for the Vaudois* (1826).

Austen, James, ed., *The Loiterer* (Oxford, 1790), facs. edn ed. Li-Ping Geng, 2 vols. (Ann Arbor, 2000).

The Complete Poems, ed. with introd. David Selwyn (Chawton, 2003).

Austen, Jane, *Fragment of a Novel*, ed. R. W. Chapman (Oxford, 1925).

The Novels of Jane Austen, ed. R. W. Chapman, 3rd edn, 5 vols. (Oxford 1933).

Minor Works, vol. VI of *The Works of Jane Austen*, ed. R. W. Chapman (Oxford, 1954).

Catharine and Other Writings, ed. Margaret Anne Doody and Douglas Murray (Oxford, 1993).

Jane Austen's Letters, ed. Deirdre Le Faye (Oxford, 1995).

Collected Poems and Verse of the Austen Family, ed. David Selwyn (Manchester, 1996).

Austen Papers, 1704–1856, ed. R. A. Austen-Leigh (1942).

Austen-Leigh, James Edward, *Memoir of Jane Austen*, ed. R. W. Chapman (Oxford, 1963).

Austen-Leigh, Mary-Augusta, *Personal Aspects of Jane Austen* (1920).

Bage, Robert, *Hermsprong; or, Man as He is Not* (1796), facs. edn, introd. Stuart Tave (1982).

Baretti, Joseph, *A Journey from London to Genoa*, 2 vols. (1770).

Barham, Joseph, *Considerations on the Abolition of Negro Slavery* (1823).

Bickerstaffe, Isaac, *The Sultan; or, A Peep into the Seraglio* in *Supplement* to *Bell's British Theatre* (n.d.).

Blair, Hugh, *Lectures on Rhetoric and Belles Lettres*, 3 vols. (1806).

Boswell, James, *The Life of Samuel Johnson*, ed. Roger Ingpen, 2 vols. (1925).

Buchanan, Claudius, *Eight Sermons* (1810). *Christian Researches in Asia* (1811; New York edn, 1812).

Burke, Edmund, *The Works of the Right Honourable Edmund Burke*, 8 vols. (1803).

Burney, Fanny, *Camilla*, ed. Edward A. and Lillian D. Bloom (Oxford, 1983). *Evelina*, ed. Frank D. MacKinnon (Oxford, 1930).

Butler, Joseph, *Fifteen Sermons* (1726; Edinburgh, n.d.).

Byron, George Gordon, *Byron's Letters and Journals*, ed. Leslie A. Marchand, 12 vols. (Cambridge, Mass., 1973–82).

The Complete Poetical Works, ed. Jerome J. McGann, 6 vols. (Oxford, 1980–91).

Centlivre, Susanna, *The Wonder: A Woman Keeps a Secret* (1714), 3rd edn (1736).

Chesterfield, Lord, *Letters Written by the Earl of Chesterfield to his Son*, 4 vols. (1775).

Clarkson, Thomas, *A Portraiture of Quakerism*, 3 vols. (1807). *History of the Abolition of the Slave Trade*, 2 vols. (1808).

Coleridge, Samuel Taylor, *Conciones ad Populum* in *Collected Works of Samuel Taylor Coleridge*, I, ed. Lewis Paton and Peter Mann (1971). *Coleridge: Poems*, ed. John Beer (1974).

Cowper, William, *Poems of William Cowper*, 2 vols. (1813–14).

Crabbe, George, *Complete Poetical Works*, ed. Norma Dalrymple-Champneys and Arthur Pollard, 3 vols. (Oxford, 1988).

Darwin, Erasmus, *Zoonomia; or, the Laws of Organic Life*, 3rd edn, 2 vols. (1801).

Edgeworth, Maria, *Belinda*, ed. Kathryn J. Kirkpatrick (Oxford, 1994).
The Novels of Maria Edgeworth (1893).

Edinburgh Review (1802–).

Eliot, George, *Felix Holt, The Radical*, ed. Fred C. Thomson (Oxford, 1980).

Ferguson, Adam, *An Essay on the History of Civil Society* (1767), ed. Duncan Forbes (Edinburgh, 1966).

Fielding, Henry, *Tom Thumb, and The Tragedy of Tragedies*, ed. L. J. Morrissey (Edinburgh, 1970).

Genlis, Madame de, *Adelaide and Theodore, or Letters on Education*, 2 vols. (Dublin, 1785).

Gilpin, William, *Observations on the River Wye* (1782), 5th edn (1800).
Observations on Cumberland and Westmoreland (1786), facs. edn (Poole, 1996).
Observations Relative Chiefly to Picturesque Beauty (1789).
Remarks on Forest Scenery (1791), facs. edn (Richmond, 1973).
Three Essays (1792).

Gisborne, Thomas, *An Enquiry into the Duties of the Female Sex* (1797).
The Testimony of Natural Theology to Christianity (1818).

Godwin, William, *Thoughts Occasioned by the Perusal of Dr Parr's Spital Sermon* (1801).
Enquiry concerning Political Justice, ed. F. E. L. Priestley, 3 vols. (Toronto, 1946).
Caleb Williams, ed. David McCracken (Oxford, 1986).
Collected Novels and Memoirs of William Godwin, ed. Mark Philp, 8 vols. (1992).
St Leon, ed. Pamela Clemit (Oxford, 1994).

Goldsmith, Oliver, *An History of the Earth and Animated Nature*, 8 vols. (1774).
History of England, 4 vols. (1779).

Hamilton, Elizabeth, *Memoirs of Modern Philosophers*, 2nd edn, 3 vols. (1800).
The Cottagers of Glenburnie (Edinburgh, 1808).

Hartley, David, *Observations on Man*, 2 vols. (1749).

Hazlitt, William, *Winterslow* (1902 edn).
The Complete Works, ed. P. P. Howe, 21 vols. (1930–4).

Henry, Robert, *The History of Great Britain*, 6 vols. (1771–93).

Holcroft, Thomas, *The Adventures of Hugh Trevor*, ed. Seamus Deane (Oxford, 1973).

Hume, David, *Essays and Treatises on Several Subjects* (1777).
The History of England, introd. William B. Todd, 6 vols. (1778, repr. Indianapolis, 1983).
Essays Moral, Political, and Literary, ed. T. H. Green and T. H. Grose, 2 vols. (1898).
The Letters of David Hume, ed. J. Y. T. Greig, 2 vols. (Oxford, 1932).
Hume's Dialogues Concerning Natural Religion, ed. Norman Kemp Smith (Oxford, 1935).
David Hume: Philosophical Historian, ed. David Norton and Richard Popkin (Indianapolis, 1965).

A Treatise of Human Nature, ed. L. A. Selby-Bigge (Oxford, 1968).
David Hume: Political Essays, ed. Knud Haakonssen (Cambridge, 1994).
An Enquiry Concerning the Principles of Morals, ed. Tom L. Beauchamp (Oxford, 1998).
An Enquiry Concerning Human Understanding, ed. Tom L. Beauchamp (Oxford, 1999).
Hunter, John, *Observations on Certain Parts of the Animal Œconomy* (1786), ed. Richard Owen (1835).
A Treatise on the Blood, Inflammation, and Gun-Shot Wounds, 2 vols. (1812).
Hutcheson, Francis, *An Inquiry into the Original of Our Ideas of Beauty and Virtue* (1725), 2nd edn (1726).
A System of Moral Philosophy, 2 vols. (1755).
Inchbald, Elizabeth, *Lovers' Vows* (1798).
Jenner, Edward, *An Inquiry into the Causes and Effects of the Cow Pox* (1800).
Johnson, Samuel, *Yale Edition of the Works of Samuel Johnson*, iv, *The Rambler*, ed. W. J. Bate and Albrecht Strauss, 16 vols. (New Haven, 1969).
The Letters of Samuel Johnson, ed. Bruce Redford, 3 vols. (Oxford, 1992).
[Johnson, Samuel], *Johnson and Boswell in Scotland: A Journey to the Hebrides*, ed. Pat Rogers (New Haven, 1993).
Keats, John, *The Letters of John Keats*, ed. H. E. Rollins, 2 vols. (1958).
Knight, Richard Payne, *The Landscape: A Didactic Poem, addressed to Uvedale Price* (1794), 2nd edn (1795).
The Progress of Civil Society: A Didactic Poem in Six Books (1796).
An Analytical Inquiry into the Principles of Taste (1805), 4th edn (1808).
Lambert, Anne Thérèse, *The Works of the Marchioness de Lambert* (1749).
Lennox, Charlotte, *The Female Quixote*, ed. Margaret Dalziel (Oxford, 1970).
Locke, John, *The Reasonableness of Christianity* (1695).
Macartney, George, 'A Journal of an Embassy', in *Some Account of the Public Life, and a Selection from the Unpublished Writings of the Earl of Macartney*, ed. John Barrow, 2 vols. (1807).
Macaulay, Thomas Babington, Baron, *Critical and Historical Essays*, 3 vols. (1891).
Mackenzie, Henry, *The Mirror*, 3 vols. (Edinburgh, 1779–80).
Malthus, Thomas, *Essay on Population* (1798), ed. James Bonar (facs. edn 1926).
An Inquiry into the Nature and Progress of Rent (1815).
Mandeville, Bernard, *The Fable of the Bees*, ed. F. B. Kaye, 2 vols. (Oxford, 1924).
Mathison, Gilbert, *Notices Respecting Jamaica* (1811).
Meiners, Christoph, *History of the Female Sex*, 4 vols. (1808).
Montesquieu, Charles, *The Spirit of the Laws*, trans. T. Nugent, 2 vols. (1750).
More, Hannah, *Cœlebs in Search of a Wife*, introd. Mary Waldron (Bristol, 1995).
Paine, Thomas, *Rights of Man, Common Sense, and Other Political Writings*, ed. Mark Philp (Oxford, 1995).
Pasley, Charles, *Essay on the Military Policy and Institutions of the British Empire*, 2nd edn (1811).
Percival, Thomas, *A Father's Instructions: Tales, Fables, and Reflections* (1775), 2nd edn (1776).
Observations on the State of Population in Manchester (n.d.).

Poetry of the Anti-Jacobin, 4th edn (1801).

Pope, Alexander, *Poetical Works*, ed. Herbert Davis (Oxford, 1974).

Price, Uvedale, *A Letter to H. Repton* (1795), 2nd edn (Hereford, 1798).

    An Essay on the Picturesque: A New Edition, 2 vols. (1796).

    Essays on the Picturesque (1810)

Priestley, Joseph, *Disquisitions Relating to Matter and Spirit* (1777).

Quarterly Review (1809–).

Radcliffe, Ann, *A Journey made in the Summer of 1794* (1795).

    The Italian, ed. Frederick Garber (Oxford, 1981).

    The Romance of the Forest, ed. Chloe Chard (Oxford, 1986).

    The Mysteries of Udolpho, ed. Frederick Garber (Oxford, 1991).

Repton, Humphrey, *Fragments on the Theory and Practice of Landscape Gardening* (1816).

Reynolds, Joshua, *Discourses on Art*, ed. Robert R. Wark (Huntington, 1959).

Richardson, Samuel, *The Novels of Samuel Richardson*, Shakespeare Head Edition, 18 vols. (Oxford, 1930).

Roberts, William, *Memoirs of the Life and Correspondence of Mrs Hannah More*, 4 vols. (1834).

Robertson, William, *The Works of William Robertson, to which is prefixed An Account of his Life and Writings, by Dugald Stewart*, 10 vols. (1821).

Russell, Richard, *A Dissertation on the Use of Sea Water*, 6th edn (1769).

Scott, Sir Walter, *Marmion*, 2nd edn (Edinburgh, 1808).

    The Lady of the Lake (Edinburgh, 1810).

    The Field of Waterloo (Edinburgh, 1815).

    Waverley, ed. Claire Lamont (Oxford, 1986).

Shaftesbury, Anthony Ashley Cooper, Earl of, *Characteristicks*, ed. P. Ayres, 2 vols. (Oxford, 1999).

Sharp, Samuel, *Letters from Italy* (1766).

Shelley, Percy Bysshe, *Poetical Works of Shelley*, ed. Thomas Hutchinson (Oxford, 1960).

Sheridan, Richard, *The Dramatic Works of Richard Brinsley Sheridan*, ed. Cecil Price, 2 vols. (Oxford, 1973).

Sherlock, Thomas, *Discourses*, 4 vols. (Oxford, 1812).

Smith, Adam, *The Works of Adam Smith, with an Account of his Life and Writings by Dugald Stewart*, 5 vols. (1812).

    Lectures on Justice, Police, Revenue and Arms, ed. Edwin Cannan (Oxford, 1896).

    An Inquiry into the Nature and Causes of the Wealth of Nations, ed. R. H. Campbell and A. S. Skinner, 2 vols. (Oxford, 1976).

    The Theory of Moral Sentiments, ed. D. D. Raphael and A. L. MacFie (Oxford, 1979).

    Essays on Philosophical Subjects, ed. W. P. D. Wightman and J. C. Bryce (Oxford, 1980).

Smith, Charlotte, *Desmond*, ed. Antje Blank and Janet Todd (1997).

Smith, Sydney, *The Works of the Rev. Sydney Smith*, 4 vols. (1839).

Smollett, Tobias, *Travels through France and Italy*, ed. Frank Felsenstein (Oxford, 1981).

Southey, Robert, *Letters from England* (1807), ed. Jack Simmons (1951).

    Life of Wesley, 2 vols. (1820).

    The Poetical Works of Robert Southey, 10 vols. (1845).

    The Life and Correspondence of Robert Southey, ed. C. C. Southey, 6 vols. (1850).

Sterne, Laurence, *The Life and Opinions of Tristram Shandy, Gentleman, & A Sentimental Journey through France and Italy*, 2 vols. (1900).

Thompson, Benjamin [Count Rumford], *Essays, Political, Economical, and Philosophical*, 4 vols. (1796).

Thomson, James, *The Seasons* and *The Castle of Indolence*, ed. James Sambrook (Oxford, 1972).

Varma, Devendra P., ed., *The Northanger Novels*, 7 vols. (1968).

Villiers, George, Duke of Buckingham, *The Chances; A Comedy with Alterations*, altered by David Garrick (1773).

    The Rehearsal, ed. D. E. L. Crane (Durham, 1976).

Voltaire, *The History of Charles XII King of Sweden*, trans. from the French, 6th edn (1735).

    Works of M. de Voltaire, 38 vols. (1761).

    Oeuvres complètes, 52 vols. (Paris, 1877–85).

West, Jane, *A Gossip's Story* (1798).

[Whately, Richard], '*Northanger Abbey* and *Persuasion*' (unsigned review), *Quarterly Review*, 24 (Jan. 1821), collected in Littlewood, ed., *Critical Assessments*, I, 318–19.

White, Gilbert, *The Natural History and Antiquities of Selborne*, ed. Richard Mabey (Harmondsworth, 1977).

White, Robert, *The Use and Abuse of Sea-Water* (1775).

    Practical Surgery, 2nd edn (1796).

Wilberforce, Robert Isaac and Samuel, *The Life of William Wilberforce*, 5 vols. (1838).

Wilberforce, William, *A Practical View*, 16th edn (1827).

    The Correspondence of William Wilberforce, ed. R. I. and S. Wilberforce, 2 vols. (1840).

Wollstonecraft, Mary, '*Mary*' and '*The Wrongs of Woman*', ed. Gary Kelly (Oxford, 1980).

    Mary Wollstonecraft: Political Writings (A Vindication of the Rights of Men; A Vindication of the Rights of Woman; An Historical and Moral View of the French Revolution), ed. Janet Todd (1993).

Wordsworth, William, *William Wordsworth*, ed. Stephen Gill (Oxford, 1984).

SECONDARY SOURCES

Aarsleff, Hans, *The Study of Language in England, 1780–1860* (Minneapolis, 1983).

Andrews, Malcolm, *The Search for the Picturesque: Landscape Aesthetics and Tourism in Britain, 1760–1800* (Aldershot, 1989).

Anstey, Roger, *The Atlantic Slave Trade and British Abolition, 1760–1810* (1975).

Armstrong, Isobel, Introduction to *Pride and Prejudice*, ed. James Kinsley (Oxford, 1990).

Armstrong, Nancy, *Desire and Domestic Fiction* (Oxford, 1987).

Badt, Kurt, *John Constable's Clouds* (1950).

Barrell, John, *The Political Theory of Painting from Reynolds to Hazlitt* (New Haven, 1986).

Barry, Norman P., *On Classical Liberalism and Libertarianism* (New York, 1987).

Barton, Margaret, and Sitwell, Osbert, *Brighton* (1935).

Beer, Gillian, *Open Fields: Science in Cultural Encounter* (Oxford, 1996).

Blanning, T. C. W., *The Culture of Power and the Power of Culture: Old Regime Europe, 1660–1789* (Oxford, 2002).

Bradbrook, Frank W., *Jane Austen and her Predecessors* (Cambridge, 1966).

Bree, Linda, Introduction to *Persuasion* (Ontario, 1998).

Brewer, John, *The Pleasures of the Imagination: English Culture in the Eighteenth Century* (1997).

Brewer, John, and Porter, Roy, eds., *Consumption and the World of Goods* (1993).

Brissenden, R. F., *Virtue in Distress: Studies in the Novel of Sentiment from Richardson to Sade* (1974).

Bromwich, David, *Hazlitt: the Mind of the Critic* (Oxford, 1983).

Brooke, Christopher, *Jane Austen: Illusion and Reality* (Cambridge, 1999).

Brown, Ford K., *Fathers of the Victorians* (Cambridge, 1961).

Bryant, Arthur, *Years of Victory, 1802–1812* (1945).

Butler, Marilyn, *Jane Austen and the War of Ideas* (Oxford, 1975; repr. with new introd. 1987).

    Romantics, Rebels and Reactionaries (Oxford, 1981).

    'History, Politics, and Religion', in J. David Grey, ed., *The Jane Austen Handbook* (1986).

Butler, Marilyn, ed., *Burke, Paine, Godwin, and the Revolution Controversy* (Cambridge, 1984).

Byrne, Paula, *Jane Austen and the Theatre* (2002).

Campbell, R. H., and Skinner, Andrew S., eds., *The Origins and Nature of the Scottish Enlightenment* (Edinburgh, 1982).

Campbell, T. D., *Adam Smith's Science of Morals* (1971).

Canton, W., *History of the British Bible Society*, 2 vols. (1904).

Carnall, Geoffrey, *Robert Southey and His Age* (Oxford, 1960).

Cassirer, Ernst, *The Philosophy of the Enlightenment*, trans. Fritz C. A. Koelln and James P. Pettegrove (Princeton, NJ, 1951).

Castle, Terry, Introduction to *Northanger Abbey, Lady Susan, The Watsons and Sanditon* (Oxford, 1990).

Chapman, R. W., 'Jane Austen's "Warren"', *TLS*, 7 May 1931, 367.

Chitnis, Anand C., *The Scottish Enlightenment and Early Victorian English Society* (1986).

Christie, I. R., *Stress and Stability in Late Eighteenth-Century Britain: Reflections on the British Avoidance of Revolution* (Oxford, 1984).

Claeys, Gregory, *Thomas Paine: Social and Political Thought* (Boston, 1989).

Clark, J. C. D., *The Language of Liberty, 1660–1832* (Cambridge, 1994).

Clark, Kenneth, *The Romantic Rebellion* (1973).

Cobban, Alfred, *Rousseau, and the Modern State* (1964).

Collins, Irene, *Jane Austen and the Clergy* (1994).

　Jane Austen: The Parson's Daughter (1998).

Copeland, Edward, and McMaster, Juliet, eds., *The Cambridge Companion to Jane Austen* (Cambridge, 1997).

Copley, Stephen, and Garside, Peter, eds., *The Politics of the Picturesque* (Cambridge, 1994).

Corbin, Alain, *The Lure of the Sea*, trans. Jocelyn Phelps (Oxford, 1994).

Cronin, Richard, and McMillan, Dorothy, 'Harriet's Smith's Reading', *Notes and Queries*, 49 (2002), 449–50.

Cunningham, Andrew and Jardine, Nicholas, eds., *Romanticism and the Sciences* (Cambridge, 1990).

Daston, Lorraine J., *Classical Probability in the Enlightenment* (Princeton, NJ, 1988).

Davies, Hugh Sykes, *Wordsworth and the Worth of Words*, ed. John Kerrigan and Jonathan Wordsworth (Cambridge, 1986).

Dawkins, Richard, *The Selfish Gene* (Oxford, 1976).

　The Blind Watchmaker (1986).

Deane, Seamus, *The French Revolution and Enlightenment in England* (1988).

Dennett, Daniel, *Darwin's Dangerous Idea* (Harmondsworth, 1995).

Devlin, D. D., *Jane Austen and Education* (1975).

Doody, Margaret Anne, *Frances Burney: The Life in the Works* (New Brunswick, 1988).

　Introduction to *Catharine and Other Writings* (Oxford, 1993).

Drescher, Seymour, *Econocide: British Slavery in the Era of Abolition* (Pittsburgh, 1977).

Duckworth, Alistair M., *The Improvement of the Estate: A Study of Jane Austen's Novels* (Baltimore, 1971).

Emsley, Clive, *British Society and the French Wars, 1793–1815* (1979).

Everett, Nigel, *The Tory View of Landscape* (New Haven, 1994).

Farrer, Reginald, 'Jane Austen', *Quarterly Review* (July 1917), in B. C. Southam, ed., *Jane Austen: the Critical Heritage* (1987).

Feiling, Keith, *Warren Hastings* (1954).

Fergus, Jan, *Jane Austen and the Didactic Novel* (1983).

Fitzgibbons, Athol, *Adam Smith's System of Liberty, Wealth, and Virtue* (Oxford, 1995).

Fleishman, Avrom, *A Reading of Mansfield Park* (Baltimore, 1967).

Forbes, Duncan, *Hume's Philosophical Politics* (Cambridge, 1975).

Fox, Christopher, Porter, Roy, and Wokler, Robert, eds., *Inventing Human Science: Eighteenth-Century Domains* (Berkeley, CA, 1990).

Franklin, Caroline, *Byron's Heroines* (Oxford, 1992).

Frye, Northrop, *A Natural Perspective* (1965).

Fulford, Tim, *Landscape, Liberty, and Authority* (Cambridge, 1996).

Furneaux, Robin, *William Wilberforce* (1974).

Galperin, William, 'The Picturesque, the Real, and the Consumption of Jane Austen', *Wordsworth Circle*, 28 (1997), 19–27.

Gard, Roger, *Jane Austen's Novels: The Art of Clarity* (1992).

Garner, Lesley, 'A Literary Landscape: Chawton House', *Gardens Illustrated* (March 2001), 74–80.

Gay, Penny, *Jane Austen and the Theatre* (Cambridge, 2002).

Geng, Li-Ping, 'The *Loiterer* and Jane Austen's Literary Identity', *Eighteenth-Century Fiction*, 13 (2001), 579–92.

Gibbon, Frank, 'The Antiguan Connection: Some New Light on *Mansfield Park*', *Cambridge Quarterly*, 12 (1982), 298–305.

Gilson, David, *A Bibliography of Jane Austen* (Winchester, 1997).

Greene, D. J., 'Jane Austen and the Peerage', *PMLA*, 68 (1953), 1017–31.

Grey, J. David, ed., *The Jane Austen Handbook* (1986).

Jane Austen's Beginnings (Ann Arbor, 1989).

Gribbin, John, *Science: A History, 1543–2001* (2002).

Griswold, Charles L., *Adam Smith and the Virtues of Enlightenment* (Cambridge, 1999).

Habermas, Jürgen, 'The Entwinement of Myth and Enlightenment: Max Horkheimer and Theodor Adorno', in his *The Philosophical Discourse of Modernity*, trans. Frederick Lawrence (Cambridge, 1987).

The Structural Transformation of the Public Sphere: An Inquiry into a Category of Bourgeois Society, trans. Thomas Burger (Cambridge, 1989).

Halperin, John, ed., *Jane Austen: Bicentenary Essays* (Cambridge, 1975).

Hampson, Norman, *The Enlightenment* (Harmondsworth, 1968).

Hardy, Barbara, *A Reading of Jane Austen* (1979).

Harlow, Vincent, 'The New Imperial System, 1783–1815', in *Cambridge History of the British Empire*, II (Cambridge, 1940).

Harris, Jocelyn, *Jane Austen's Art of Memory* (Cambridge, 1989).

Hembury, Phyllis, *The English Spa, 1560–1815* (1990).

Hicks, Philip, *Neoclassical History and English Culture: From Clarendon to Hume* (1996).

Hill, Bridget, *Women, Work and Sexual Politics in Eighteenth-Century England* (1994).

Hilton, Boyd, *The Age of Atonement: The Influence of Evangelicalism on Social and Economic Thought, 1785–1865* (Oxford, 1988).

Holmstrom, K. G., *Monodrama, Attitudes, Tableau Vivant, 1770–1815* (Stockholm, 1967).

Honan, Park, *Jane Austen: Her Life* (1987).

Hont, Istvan, and Ignatieff, Michael, eds., *Wealth and Virtue: The Shaping of Political Economy in the Scottish Enlightenment* (Cambridge, 1983).

Hough, Graham, *Selected Essays* (Cambridge, 1978).

Howell, Sarah, *The Seaside* (1974).

Hubback, J. H. and E. C., *Jane Austen's Sailor Brothers* (1905; facs. edn, Stroud, 1986).

Jarvis, William, *Jane Austen and Religion* (Stonesfield, 1996).

Johnson, Claudia L., 'The "operations of time, and the changes of the human mind": Jane Austen and Dr Johnson Again', *Modern Language Quarterly*, 44 (1983), 23–38.

Jane Austen: Women, Politics, and the Novel (Chicago, 1988).

'A "Sweet Face as White as Death": Jane Austen and the Politics of Female Sensibility', *Novel*, 22 (1989), 159–74.

Equivocal Beings: Politics, Gender, and Sentimentality in the 1790s (Chicago, 1995).

Jones, Peter, ed., *Philosophy and Science in the Scottish Enlightenment* (Edinburgh, 1988).

Kaplan, Deborah, *Jane Austen among Women* (1992).

Kay, Carol, 'Canon, Ideology, and Gender: Mary Wollstonecraft's Critique of Adam Smith', *New Political Science*, 15 (1986), 63–76.

Kelly, Gary, *The English Jacobin Novel, 1780–1805* (Oxford, 1976).

English Fiction of the Romantic Period, 1789–1830 (1989).

Kirkham, Margaret, *Jane Austen: Feminism and Fiction* (1983, rev. edn 1996).

Knox-Shaw, Peter, '*Persuasion*, Byron, and the Turkish Tale', *Review of English Studies*, 44 (1993) 47–69.

'Fanny Price Refuses to Kowtow', *Review of English Studies*, 47 (1996), 212–17.

'*Sense and Sensibility*, Godwin, and the Empiricists', *Cambridge Quarterly*, 27 (1998), 188–95.

'*Northanger Abbey* and the Liberal Historians', *Essays in Criticism*, 49 (1999), 319–43.

'What Jane Austen Meant by "Raffish"', *Persuasions*, 22 (2000), 105–8.

'Jane Austen's Nocturnal and Anne Finch', *English Language Notes*, 39 (March 2002), 41–54.

'*Persuasion*, James Austen, and James Thomson', *Notes and Queries*, 247 (December 2002), 451–3.

Lane, Maggie, *Jane Austen's England* (1986).

Lawson, Philip, *The East India Company* (1993).

Leask, Nigel, *British Romantic Writers and the East* (Cambridge, 1992).

Le Faye, Deirdre, *Jane Austen: A Family Record* (1989).

Jane Austen's 'Outlandish Cousin': The Life and Letters of Eliza de Feuillide (2002).

Levine, Joseph M., *The Battle of the Books: History and Literature in the Augustan Age* (Ithaca, NY, 1992).

Littlewood, Ian, ed., *Jane Austen: Critical Assessments*, 4 vols. (Mountfield, 1998).

Litz, A. Walton, '*The Loiterer*: A Reflection of Jane Austen's Early Environment', *Review of English Studies*, 12 (1961), 251–61.

Jane Austen: A Study of her Artistic Development (1965).

MacDonagh, Oliver, *Jane Austen: Real and Imagined Worlds* (1991).

McKeon, Michael, *The Origins of the English Novel, 1600–1740* (Baltimore, 1987).

McKillop, Alan Dugald, *The Background of Thomson's Seasons* (Minneapolis, 1942).

McMaster, Juliet, ed., *Jane Austen's Achievement* (1976).

McMaster, Juliet, and Stovel, Bruce, *Jane Austen's Business* (1996).

Manuel, Frank E., *The Prophets of Paris* (New York, 1972).

Marshall, Peter H., *William Godwin* (New Haven, 1984).

Marshall, Peter, and Williams, Glyndyr, *The Great Map of Mankind: British Perceptions of the World in the Age of Enlightenment* (1982).

Moler, Kenneth, 'The Bennet Girls and Adam Smith on Vanity and Pride', *Philological Quarterly*, 46 (1967), 567–9.

    Jane Austen's Art of Allusion (Lincoln, 1977).

Monaghan, David, *Jane Austen: Structure and Social Vision* (1980).

Mossner, Ernest Campbell, *The Life of David Hume* (Oxford, 1954).

Mullan, John, *Sentiment and Sociability: The Language of Feeling in the Eighteenth Century* (Oxford, 1988).

Neill, Edward, 'The Secret of *Northanger Abbey*', *Essays in Criticism*, 47 (1997), 13–32.

Nokes, David, *Jane Austen: A Life* (1997).

Norman, E. R., *Church and Society in England, 1770–1970* (Oxford, 1976).

Norton, David Fate, *David Hume: Common-Sense Moralist, Sceptical Metaphysician* (Princeton, NJ, 1982).

Norton, David Fate, ed., *The Cambridge Companion to Hume* (Cambridge, 1993).

Noxon, James, *Hume's Philosophical Development* (Oxford, 1973).

Otteson, James R., *Adam Smith's Marketplace of Life* (Cambridge, 2002).

Outram, Dorinda, *The Enlightenment* (Cambridge, 1995).

Park, You-me, and Rajan, Rajeswari Sunder, eds., *The Postcolonial Jane Austen* (2000).

Peyrefitte, Alain, *The Collision of Two Civilisations: The British Expedition to China 1792–4*, trans. John Rothschild (French edn 1989; 1993)

Phillipps, K. C., *Jane Austen's English* (1970).

Phillipson, Nicholas, and Skinner, Quentin, eds., *Political Discourse in Early Modern Britain* (Cambridge, 1993).

Pocock, J. G. A., *Culture and Politics from Puritanism to the Enlightenment* (Berkeley, CA, 1980).

    Virtue, Commerce and History: Essays on Political Thought and History, Chiefly in the Eighteenth Century (Cambridge, 1985).

    Barbarism and Religion. I: *The Enlightenments of Edward Gibbon, 1737–1764*; II: *Narratives of Civil Government* (Cambridge, 1999).

Poovey, Mary, *The Proper Lady and the Woman Writer: Ideology as Style in the Works of Mary Wollstonecraft, Mary Shelley, and Jane Austen* (Chicago, 1984).

Porter, Roy, *Enlightenment: Britain and the Creation of the Modern World* (2000).

Porter, Roy, and Mikuláš, Teich, eds., *The Enlightenment in National Context* (Cambridge, 1981).

Raphael, D. D., 'The Impartial Spectator', in Andrew S. Skinner and Thomas Wilson, eds., *Essays on Adam Smith* (Oxford, 1975).

Rivers, Isabel, *Reason, Grace and Sentiment: A Study of the Language of Religion and Ethics in England, 1660–1780*. II: *Shaftesbury to Hume* (Cambridge, 2000).

Roberts, Andrew, *Napoleon and Wellington* (2001).

Roberts, Warren, *Jane Austen and the French Revolution* (1979).

Rogers, Pat, *Johnson* (Oxford, 1993).

    Introduction to *Persuasion* (1994).

Roll, Eric, *A History of Economic Thought* (1987).

Roper, Derek, *Reviewing Before the 'Edinburgh', 1788–1802* (Cranbury, NJ, 1978).

Ross, Ian Simpson, *The Life of Adam Smith* (Oxford, 1995).

Ryle, Gilbert, 'Jane Austen and the Moralists', in B. C. Southam, ed., *Critical Essays on Jane Austen*.

Said, Edward W., *Culture and Imperialism* (1993).

Sales, Roger, *Jane Austen and Representations of Regency England* (1994).

Schama, Simon, *Citizens: A Chronicle of the French Revolution* (1989).

Sellers, Susan, ed., *Feminist Criticism: Theory and Practice* (Hemel Hempstead, 1991).

Simpson, Richard, 'Jane Austen', *North British Review*, Apr. 1870, in B. C. Southam, ed., *Jane Austen: the Critical Heritage* (1968).

Singer, Charles, *A Short History of Scientific Ideas* (Oxford, 1982).

Skelton-Foord, Christopher, 'To Buy or to Borrow? Circulating Libraries and Novel Reading in Britain, 1778–1828', *Library Review*, 47 (1998), 348–54.

Skinner, Andrew S., and Wilson, Thomas, eds., *Essays on Adam Smith* (Oxford, 1975).

Southam, B. C., 'The Silence of the Bertrams: Slavery and the Chronology of *Mansfield Park*', *TLS* (17 Feb. 1995), 13–14.

Jane Austen and the Navy (2000).

Southam, B. C., ed., *Critical Essays on Jane Austen* (1968).

Jane Austen: the Critical Heritage. I: 1812–1870 (1968); II: *1870–1940* (1987).

Jane Austen: Northanger Abbey and Persuasion: A Casebook (1976).

Specter, Michael, 'Rethinking the Brain', in Matt Ridley, ed., *The Best American Science Writing 2002* (New York, 2002).

Spence, Jon, *Becoming Jane Austen* (2003).

Spence, Jonathan, *The Chan's Great Continent: China in Western Minds* (1998).

Stephen, Leslie, *History of English Thought in the Eighteenth Century*, 2 vols. (1876, 1962 edn).

Stewart, John B., *Opinion and Reform in Hume's Political Philosophy* (Princeton, NJ, 1992).

Stewart, M. A., ed., *Studies in the Philosophy of the Scottish Enlightenment* (Oxford, 1990).

Sutherland, Kathryn, 'Fictional Economies: Adam Smith, Walter Scott and the Nineteenth-Century Novel', *ELH*, 54 (1987), 97–127.

Sykes, Norman, *Church and State in England in the Eighteenth Century* (Cambridge, 1934).

Tallis, Raymond, *In Defence of Realism* (1988).

Tanner, Tony, *Jane Austen* (1986).

Tave, Stuart, *Some Words of Jane Austen* (1973).

Thomas, Hugh, *The Slave Trade* (1997).

Thomas, Keith, *Man and the Natural World: Changing Attitudes in England, 1500–1800* (Harmondsworth, 1983).

Thompson, James, *Between Self and World: The Novels of Jane Austen* (1988).

Till, Nicholas, *Mozart and the Enlightenment* (1992).

Todd, Janet, *Sensibility: An Introduction* (1986).
    Feminist Literary History (Cambridge, 1988).
    The Sign of Angellica: Women, Writing and Fiction, 1660–1800 (1989).
    'Jane Austen, Politics and Sensibility', in Susan Sellers, ed., *Feminist Criticism: Theory and Practice.*
Todd, Janet, ed., *Jane Austen: New Perspectives* (1983).
Todd, William B., ed., *Hume and the Enlightenment* (Edinburgh, 1974).
Tomalin, Claire, *The Life and Death of Mary Wollstonecraft* (1974).
    Jane Austen: A Life (1997).
Trevor-Roper, Hugh, *Catholics, Anglicans, and Puritans* (1988).
Trott, Nicola, 'The Coleridge Circle and the "Answer to Godwin"', *Review of English Studies*, 41 (1990), 212–29.
Tucker, George Holbert, *A Goodly Heritage: A History of Jane Austen's Family* (Manchester, 1983).
    Jane Austen: The Woman (1994).
Tuite, Clara, *Romantic Austen: Sexual Politics and the Literary Canon* (Cambridge, 2002).
Uglow, Jenny, *The Lunar Men* (2002).
Venturi, F., *Utopia and Reform in the Enlightenment* (Cambridge, 1971).
Virgin, Peter, *Sydney Smith* (1994).
Waldron, Mary, *Jane Austen and the Fiction of her Time* (Cambridge, 1999).
Walton, John K., *The English Seaside Resort: A Social History, 1750–1914* (New York, 1983).
Watson, J. Steven, *The Reign of George III, 1760–1815* (Oxford, 1960).
Wiesenfarth, Joseph, *The Errand of Form* (New York, 1967).
Willey, Basil, *The Eighteenth-Century Background* (1940).
Williams, Michael, *Jane Austen: Six Novels and their Methods* (1986).
Williams, Raymond, *The Country and the City* (1973).
Wiltshire, John, *Jane Austen and the Body* (Cambridge, 1992).
Wind, Edgar, *Hume and the Heroic Portrait: Studies in Eighteenth-Century Imagery*, ed. Jaynie Anderson (Oxford, 1986).
Woolf, Virginia, 'Jane Austen', in *The Common Reader: First Series* (1962).
Yolton, John W., *Thinking Matter: Materialism in Eighteenth-Century Britain* (Minneapolis, 1983).
Yolton, John W., Price, John V., and Stephens, John, eds., *The Dictionary of Eighteenth-Century Philosophers*, 2 vols. (Bristol, 1999).

Index